WISH YOU WERE HERE

A PEOPLE'S HISTORY OF PINK FLOYD

First published in Great Britain 2023
by Spenwood Books Ltd
2 College Street, Higham Ferrers, NN10 8DZ.

Copyright © Richard Houghton 2023

The right of Richard Houghton to be identified
as author of this work has been asserted in
accordance with Sections 77 & 78 of the Copyright,
Design and Patents Act 1988.

All rights reserved. No part of this book may be reproduced in any form or by any electronic or mechanical means, including information storage or retrieval systems, without permission in writing from the publisher, except by a reviewer who may quote brief passages.

A CIP record for this book is available from the British Library.

ISBN 978-1-915858-11-5 (hardback)
ISBN 978-1-915858-18-4 (paperback)

Hardback printed in the Czech Republic via Akcent Media Limited

Design by Bruce Graham, The Night Owl.

Front cover design: Neil Paterson
Rear cover images: XXXX
All other image copyrights: As captioned

WISH YOU WERE HERE

A PEOPLE'S HISTORY OF PINK FLOYD

Richard Houghton

Spenwood Books

ABOUT THE AUTHOR

Richard Houghton lives in Manchester, UK with his wife Kate and his pomapoo Sid. He is the author of more than 20 music books and has compiled authorised 'fan histories' of a number of acts including Jethro Tull, Simple Minds, Orchestral Manoeuvres in the Dark, the Stranglers, Fairport Convention, Shaun Ryder and The Wedding Present. He can be reached at iwasatthatgig@gmail.com.

ACKNOWLEDGEMENTS

Although this book contains a significant amount of new material, and has been fully revised since it was originally published in 2017 as *Pink Floyd – I Was There*, and I'd like to thank (again) the following for their help in producing the first edition of the book: James Hicks; Planet Rock; John Scott Cree for permission to quote from his ebook, *A Superfluous Man*; John Dolan at the Cork *Evening Echo*, for his permission to reproduce Jack Lyon's piece on Pink Floyd's appearance at the Arcadia in Cork, and Irish Jack Lyons for the same; Col Turner for permission to reproduce excerpts from his blog; Matt Johns from brain-damage.co.uk for featuring my appeal; yeeshkul.com; and Liam Creedon at pinkfloydz.com.

I'd like to thank once again the many editors of local newspapers around the UK who kindly featured my original letter appealing for Pink Floyd fans to come forward with their stories and my contributors, who have been so kind as to share with me their memories and stories of seeing Pink Floyd and both Roger and David solo.

And I'd also like to thank the following for their help in producing the 2023 edition of this book: Ron Geesin, whose book, *The Flaming Cow: The Making of Atom Heart Mother*, is available from The History Press; Elliot Tayman, whose 1977 *Animals* review originally appeared in Issue 40 of *Brain Damage* magazine; Bruce Pegg, for permission to quote from his book, *Goin' Down De Mont – A People's History of Rock and Pop Concerts at Leicester's De Montfort Hall*; David Gordon, for some great images; Jerry Ewing at *Prog* magazine, who kindly published my updated appeal for a few more Floyd fans to share their memories with me; Thom Lukas, whose website is at thomlukas.com; Mick Morgan and Marci Connelly, for beating the drum; Claire Lucie Sonck and her father Gaston, for permission to publish the photographs on page 211. I'd especially like to thank Bruce Graham for the book design, Neil Paterson for the cover and Bruce Koziarski for the web design.

Finally, I'd like to thank Kate Sullivan for her continued forbearance. And the coffees. Shine on.

Richard Houghton
Manchester, UK
July 2023

WISH YOU WERE HERE

SPECIAL THANKS

Phil Davies, James Hise, Raymond Dollard, Peter Lush, Bones, Gareth Jones, Michael Perryment, Christopher McHugo, David Hillier, Brian Paone, Gordon Phinn, Martyn Ward, Alain De Repentigny, Mario Lefebvre, Mark, Gemma & Russ, David Millington, Alexey Sharonov, Philip Simmons, Michael Morgan, Benjamin Dobie, Jeffrey Mccollough, John Riccardi, Mark Beaton, Olivia & Pete Marsh, Garth Armstrong, Len Saunders, Graham Day, Thomas Snider, David Coney, Stephen Lane, Glen Thurston, Myriam Vallée, Peter Reynolds, John Coney, Michel Tournay, Lisette Auger, Rob Pascoe, Michael Allen, Simon Phillips, Mike Watts, Luca Piovesan, Matthew Scaife, Gary Goodson, Ira Knopf, Dan Walker, Nick Walpole, David Gaylor, Bruce Dixon, Dominik Macak, Romain Fouray, Stephen Gardiner, Kevin Crisp, Sziládi József, Christian Martin, Anders Misfeldt, Paul J Love, Ian Clementson, Alan Burton, Charles Whalley, Tommy Pitsch, Christopher Leith, Barry Stanley, Richard Lowe, Peter Smith, Robert Moist, Jimmy Partridge, David Godfrey, James Heine, Henry Doyle, Martin Sandford, John Johnstone, Jamie Pipe, Andrew Webber, Dave Long, Michael Coldwell, Gregg Widel, Todd Nelson, Rob Thrasher, Alain Guinot, Darren Hayward, Tim Marshall, Peter Marshall, Aspi Tantra, Rosie Tantra, Selina Tantra, Brian Smith, Barry Fox, Randall Hill, Todd Bennett, Jason Pyke, Howard Miatt, Tommy Bush, Gavin Costar, George Robinson, Mark Earnest, Mark Reed, Johnny Rivera, Mel Giles, Mary Kellam, Richard Kelley, Michael Connelly, Michael Yeomans, Lindsay Fulcher, Andrea Borsotti, Ian Tandy, Michael Corner, Richard Lyon, Joseph l Sanchez, Steven McGinley, Robin Atkinson, David Hughes, Ronald Shepcar, Paul Dawson, Philip Parsons, Elliot Tayman, Richard Banks, Margaret Bills, Petee Chios & Leigh, Susan Stewart, William Martin.

SHARE YOUR GIG MEMORIES

If you saw Pink Floyd live, or any other classic rock band, and would like to share your memories for inclusion in a future *People's History*, please get in touch at iwasatthatgig@gmail.com.

Shine on.

INTRODUCTION

When I was getting into music in my teenage years, I was very aware of Pink Floyd. Growing up in a small East Midlands town in the early Seventies, the cover of *The Dark Side of the Moon* cover was everywhere, displayed in the windows of LNA Records, Clark's Records and Woolworth's on our local high street, along with Led Zep's *Physical Graffiti* and Deep Purple's *Mark I & II*. The Floyd album was, of course, a cultural phenomenon, eventually selling over 45 million copies around the world and a sign that Pink Floyd were a huge band. But I have a confession to make – I've never seen Pink Floyd live.

I had the chance. In 1977, when I was 16, the *Animals* album was being toured and friends from school were arranging to write off to the Empire Pool box office and buy tickets. I remember being asked whether I wanted to go. Getting to London for the Wembley show would have been an hour on the train from Wellingborough to St Pancras, and easily doable after school (I was in the sixth form at the time, in the first year of 'A' levels). But I already had a ticket to see Black Sabbath that same week, and money was tight. So shelling out for two lots of train fares in the space of a few days was beyond my budget. And I wasn't particularly a fan, not because of a dislike of their music – I had bought *Animals* the week it came out – but because I had a distorted image of what a Pink Floyd crowd would be like. My Floyd-loving school mates were long-hairs who smoked dope. And one of them was a Trotskyite and an Arsenal supporter to boot. A room full of dope smoking long-hairs with radical political views and dubious football allegiances wasn't going to be my scene. (Black Sabbath fans may have worn filthy denim but they were of course all clean-living types who drank beer and wouldn't dream of taking drugs.)

Reading these accounts of their live performances, I wish I'd caught that train to London and seen Pink Floyd at Wembley, despite my teenage misgivings. Or, failing that, tried to catch up with them on one of their later tours. This is your chance to experience again or – if you're like me – experience for the first time what it was like to see Pink Floyd live.

The Pink Floyd story has been told many times but this book tries to tell it anew through the words of people who have seen or met Pink Floyd. It's a fan's eye account of one of the biggest bands in the world. It doesn't claim to be historically accurate, and there are many gaps in the story that someone wanting a complete history of Pink Floyd will find lacking. Try Mark Blake's *Pigs Might Fly: The Inside Story of Pink Floyd* or Nick Mason's excellent *Inside Out: A Personal History of Pink Floyd* for fuller accounts of the band's history. But everyone who has contributed to this book has helped me to tell the Pink Floyd story and all are able to make the same claim: 'I was there'.

Richard Houghton
Manchester, UK
August 2023

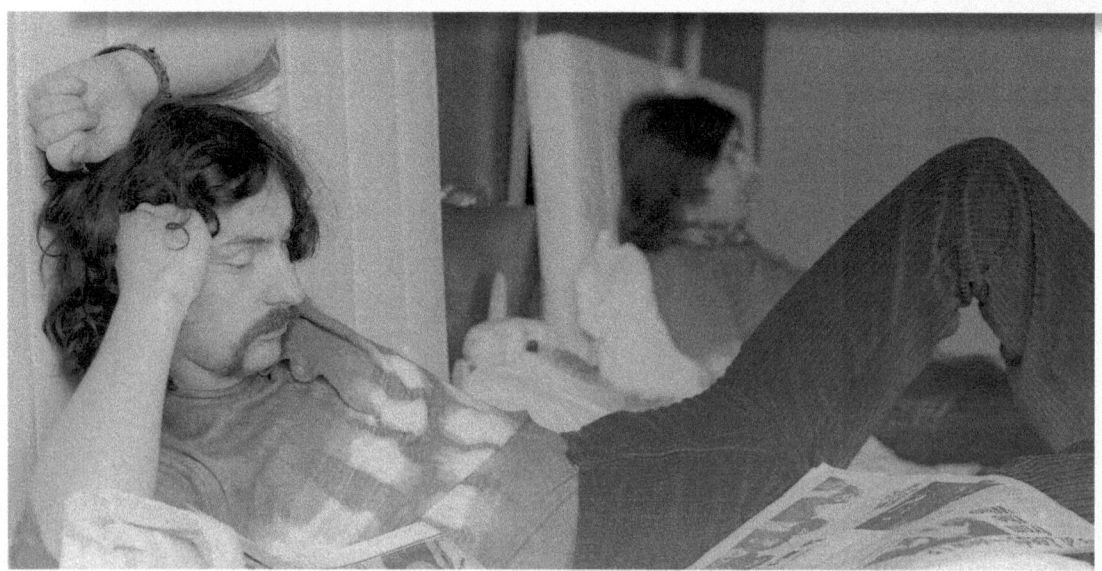

Photos: Thom Lukas

BEGINNINGS

Pink Floyd emerge from Cambridge in England in the Sixties, a time of optimism and free thinking. The original settled line up of the group, after a number of personnel changes, is Syd Barrett, Roger Waters, Nick Mason and Richard Wright. They perform nine times in various locations in 1965 before moving to London where, as part of the emerging underground scene, they take part in a number of 'happenings'.

PETTY CURY
1960s, CAMBRIDGE, UK

I WAS THERE: NIGEL LESMOIR-GORDON

I was 13 when I first heard 'Heartbreak Hotel', and 13 when I met Storm Thorgerson in Petty Cury in Cambridge. There was an immediate understanding that we were coming from the same place, with the same outlook, and the group expanded to include David Henderson, David Gale, Nick Sedgwick and Andrew Rawlinson. Jenny was a major part of the group but I didn't really get together with her until I was about 17. A lot of our early girlfriends were not readers of books, although Jenny was. They were intelligent but they didn't share our enthusiasm for poetry and avant-garde writing like William Burroughs and Samuel Beckett.

David and Roger were actually about the same age as me and Storm Thorgerson and David Gale and Nick Sedgwick in what you'd loosely call 'the Cambridge' set. We were beatnik anarchists in those days, and trying not to be forced back into the world that we inherited from our parents. They'd all been through the Second World War and what they really wanted to do was put the world back together again. But unfortunately for them we read Jack Keroauc and we heard Elvis and we decided that we would live our lives differently. And when LSD came on the scene, that was another thing we thought would change the world.

I thought that what was happening in Cambridge was happening everywhere in the UK. It took me a while to realise that it was only Cambridge, Oxford, London, Liverpool and Manchester where there were little clusters of free thinking avant-gardistes. I thought it was happening everywhere but it wasn't. I had a few rude awakenings then, and going down Oxford Street in my Granny Takes a Trip jacket turned a few heads.

First of all, we discovered grass and we all loved to get stoned, Syd included.

Syd was younger. He was at the County with Storm, so he was on the fringe of our group. But very soon he was assimilated into the group because he was an outstanding person. He looked beautiful, he wrote poetry, painted and he occasionally played the guitar. We used to go round to his mother's house on Sunday afternoons for jam sessions.

Roger was there. Roger and Syd both lost their fathers when they were young, and they bonded initially through that. We used to hang out and smoke pot in Syd's mother's basement and all sorts of people turned up with guitars.

In one of the books about Pink Floyd, Libby Gausden says, 'Syd worshipped Nigel.' Dougie Fields said Jenny and I were the most beautiful couple he'd ever seen, and that Syd always wanted to meet us. Jenny was, in my opinion, the prettiest girl in Cambridge, and I guess I was one of the best-looking guys in Cambridge. And I was writing poetry and I was doing poetry readings with Pete Brown, Mike Horovitz, Spike Hawkins, Ted Milton - the London beat poets. I used to get them down to Cambridge, and I think perhaps what impressed Syd I was that I was an active living poet with a beautiful girlfriend. I don't know if it's true. I wasn't aware of it at the time.

MARQUEE CLUB
13 MARCH 1966, LONDON, UK

I WAS THERE: JENNY SPIRES

Just over a year since I first met Syd Barrett, he invited me to a gig at the Marquee in London where they were playing. It was one of a series called 'The Spontaneous Underground'. I hadn't seen the band play for ages, but they were back together and had recently played at a private party near Cambridge. Now, I really saw a difference in them from when I'd seen them back in the days of '(I'm a) King Bee' and Bo Diddley, when they were mainly a covers band. Syd was playing more guitar solos and they seemed much more jazzy, less bluesy. They were doing some of their own material as well.

I WAS THERE: NIGEL LESMOIR-GORDON

They were called The Tea Set to start with. I got them their first gig in London, at the Marquee Club. Steve Stollman from ESP Records in America started these Sunday afternoon sessions – music, poetry and I said to Steve, 'I know a band you might like to have play.' And he said, 'Yeah, sure, why not? Get them down here.' So I rang them and said, 'I've got you a gig Sunday afternoon at the Marquee, but please don't call yourselves The Tea Set.' So they actually came as Pink Floyd.

SYD BARRETT'S FIRST TRIP
SUMMER 1966, CAMBRIDGE, UK

I WAS THERE: NIGEL LESMOIR-GORDON

Syd Barrett's First Trip is a film I shot in 1966, filmed in the chalk pits at Cambridge, in the Gog Magog Hills. I was at film school and had an 8mm camera. I used to film everything. We went down there and me, Jenny and Syd got talking and we decided that I would shoot this stuff of him. And that's me on the balcony of 101 (Cromwell Road) without my shirt on. Jenny shot this. That film is as it came out of the camera. It's not edited. It's just what I shot. And I think it's rather charming.

CHELSEA COLLEGE
28 SEPTEMBER 1966, LONDON, UK

I WAS THERE: ROGER KINSEY

I could have been the last person to book them as The Tea Set before they changed their name to Pink Floyd. In my last year at Chelsea College, from September 1966 to June 1967, I was Sports and Societies Secretary as well as Publicity Officer for the College's Student Union. As such, I had to organise the Freshers Week events during late September, before the academic year began. I have the original copy of the Freshers Week schedule, which I produced, and on it in my hand writing is the name of the group I booked to entertain the freshers in the College Bar on the Wednesday night of 28 September 1966. The group I booked was The Tea Set.

I have vivid and clear memories of seeing the group perform in our very small bar area, with Syd Barrett with his face all made up, and the liquid light show and the incredible 'way out' sounds, the like of which no one had heard before. I paid them the princely sum of £15 cash for their appearance.

WISH YOU WERE HERE

ALL SAINTS CHURCH HALL
30 SEPTEMBER 1966, POWIS GARDENS, LONDON, UK

I WAS THERE: JENNY SPIRES

In the summer of 1966, I moved to London. Syd had a different girlfriend now, Lindsay Corner, who was also from Cambridge. They were living together in a house near Cambridge Circus. I saw quite a lot of them at the time, as Syd was still inviting me to gigs to see the band play. I didn't go to any of the London Free School shows at the time, but this is where they first got to grips with their amazing light shows. However, I was at some of the rehearsals for these shows at Cromwell Road, when they were experimenting with syncing the sound together with the ink slides of Pete Wynne-Willson.

I WAS THERE: MARTIN O'SHEA

I was living in London in the summer of 1966 and one evening, when visiting my brother who lived in Talbot Road, Notting Hill, his partner said there was an interesting group playing just down the road. We walked down to the nearby All Saints church hall where we found this group of three musicians, preparing to play. The audience was some six to eight people. They were just interested spectators – it was not a 'performance'. There was a liquid light projection being set up by a fourth person. The group were not on a stage but just standing by us, on the same level. They were half looking across to each other and half looking towards the light projection. The keyboard player looked up at me and, smiling, said 'oh, hi Martin'. I realised that it was Rick Wright, who I had met a few years previously in somebody's house in South Ruislip, along with three or four other people, to discuss a 'Ban The Bomb' demo which was coming up at a nearby US airbase. We got on at this small meeting, because not only did we have the same striving for peace but we were both studying architecture and, being the same age, could compare our college experiences.

Soon after that, there was indeed the demo. I quickly got arrested for sitting down in the road outside the airbase and spent the night locked up. I never learnt if Rick actually got to the demo let alone got arrested. As this had happened in, I think, 1962, and so much had happened to both of us since those early days, I was most surprised that Rick actually remembered my name and enquired as to my well-being.

I thoroughly enjoyed the rehearsal and shortly after that the band, now titled Pink Floyd, started playing at the UFO Club in Tottenham Court Road. I went there from the beginning and had some great Friday nights and Saturday mornings. Not only was the

Pink Floyd there from the start but they were followed by Soft Machine, Arthur Brown, Procol Harum, Tomorrow and other crazy bands. They were the great days of Pink Floyd and they are memories, albeit coloured by quantities of LSD, I shall always remember.

I WAS THERE: NIGEL LESMOIR-GORDON

101 Cromwell Road was where we all moved to. A lot of us went to London, some to art college, some to film school. I went to the London School of Film Technique. I was washing up in Churchill College and John Dunbar, who married Marianne Faithfull, came to say hello to me and he said, 'You should go to my dad's film school.' So I went there. I knew Bill Barlow, who was the main letting person at 101 Cromwell Road because I lived in one of his houses in Cambridge and I got a room there. I missed Jenny a lot and I asked her to come and live with me and she said, 'I can't do that. My parents would be too upset.' So I said, 'All right, I'll marry you.' Syd for a while lived upstairs with Duggie Fields in the top flat. Christopher Case, Bill Barlow, John Tate and I were the main inhabitants of the first floor flat, and that's when the LSD arrived.

The LSD we had came from the Sandoz laboratory in Switzerland where Albert Hofmann stumbled across it, and he despatched some to Timothy Leary, and Leary had a friend in London called John Eason, and the acid we took came from the Sandoz laboratory so it was very pure. Completely pure. The LSD took us all by storm, and we loved it. We had some scary trips as well of course. I went to one of the Free School gigs. I can't remember much about it. I wonder why?

THE ROUNDHOUSE
15 OCTOBER 1966, CHALK FARM, LONDON, UK

I WAS THERE: JENNY SPIRES

One of the gigs I went to in October 1966 was at the Roundhouse in Camden for the launch of the underground newspaper, *IT (The International Times)*. The Roundhouse was a cavernous train depot which Arnold Wesker, the playwright, had launched as a centre for arts and culture in London. The *IT* party was a large gathering of poets, musicians, writers, actors, dancers, artists and models, all with a common purpose, dressed in fancy dress and the latest hip vintage of the London scene, and people who were very much on the underground in London. This movement was later to be called Counter Culture. Both the Floyd and Soft Machine played. Soft Machine was another band we became closely connected to at this time. Pink Floyd now had a new set of music. Syd had been writing some wonderful songs and pretty much everything they did was their own. The gig was lit by their synced and pulsating light show… It was a very exciting evening. Around this time, I watched Syd write 'Chapter 24'. He literally sat on the floor, the *I Ching* in front of him, and wrote it. We were all reading the *I Ching* at this time. He later gave me his copy.

CORN EXCHANGE
12 NOVEMBER 1966, BEDFORD, UK

I WAS THERE: MICHAEL WHITE

I went to two Pink Floyd concerts in Bedford in 1966 and 1967. The first was at Bedford Corn Exchange and, being a guitarist myself, my first impression was noticing the band were kitted out with all new Selmer amplifiers. I remember Syd was playing a Telecaster, Roger was playing a Fender Precision Bass. Via the musical press, ie. *Melody Maker*, I heard about Pink Floyd and was intrigued to read about their style – psychedelic music. During the first half of their set they performed blues-type music, which seemed to go down well with the audience. For the second part of their set they launched into their psychedelic-type music, at which point the audience drifted away, leaving me and only a handful of others to see the music through, which we really enjoyed.

The second time I saw them was in a bingo hall in Bedford in October 1967. I am not sure how much input Syd Barrett had into this performance as he was leaning at the back of the stage, enjoying the light show.

ALL SAINTS CHURCH HALL
29 NOVEMBER 1966, LONDON, UK

I WAS THERE: IRISH JACK LYONS

By the end of 1966, Mod had faded. Halfway through the year, I'd been barred from the Mod fulcrum, the Goldhawk Social Club in Shepherd's Bush, on a complete misunderstanding with the club secretary Ted Woolgar. The demise of Mod spread throughout like a bad germ and most of the leading faces didn't want to be seen attached to a lifestyle now in its death throes. Despite all this, somehow I was still dressing up like a well-plumed peacock – yes, Mod head to toe – but there weren't many places to cater for my delicate Mod tastes. Hair was getting longer and people were scruffier. Change was in the wind. Pop art, no longer the preserve of the avant-garde few, was now the property of the masses and we had entered the gates of hell to be met by the chorus 'Swinging London' and dreadful hipster trousers with garish white belts. I suppose the writing was really on the wall when I saw the poster of Lord Kitchener pointing an accusing finger at me and when I saw The Beatles costumed in military jackets. Yes, Mod was well and truly over.

By this time, I had moved into a draughty attic at 109 Holland Road. I told people I lived in Holland Park because it sounded better. I still maintained my job as a legal filing clerk for Baron and Warren at 8 Kensington Square (another posh address). I can't remember where, but I saw a handmade poster someone had stuck on a wall announcing a band I had never heard of called The Pink Floyd, playing at the church hall in Powis Gardens in Notting Hill. (I found out later the church hall was All Saints Hall.) Notting Hill was only two stops on the Tube from Shepherd's Bush, and being a loner (that has been the bane of my life), I dragged myself along. I was heartened by the sight of a smattering of no more than six or seven Mods but nearly everyone else was part of this new fashion, with long hair, beads and bell-bottomed trousers. The atmosphere was quite friendly and very posh. For me, music has to be performed in its right setting. When The Who ran their Tuesday residency at the Marquee from November 1964 to April 1965, the small intimate venue was perfect. It was like a Pop Art revue with cool jazz overtones.

As soon as Pink Floyd started up at All Saints Hall, with the crude strobe lighting effects and their sound, for me it was perfect. They used picture slides which bounced around the stage and blossomed into a myriad cosmic fragments. The cavernous echo of the church hall was just right. What I noticed about the Floyd was that half the time they were an ordinary R&B band and then just when you thought you had them pigeon-holed, they would play something like Bo Diddley's 'Roadrunner' and halfway through that they'd go off into a tangent and you'd hear the swirling psychedelic tones of 'Interstellar Overdrive'. They would also play a lengthy version of 'Arnold Layne' – this was before it was properly recorded and released. It was impossible to keep one eye on Syd Barrett and the other on Rick Wright as he pruned a garden of the most unbelievable sounds on his keyboards. I used to make a point of standing as close as possible to the organ just to hear it and float off into another galaxy. A lot of keyboardists would normally use a Hammond or a Vox Continental, but Wright played a Farfisa and the sound was hypnotic. I met a few people that night, told them I was a Mod filing clerk in a musty office, and went back to 109 Holland Road feeling I had discovered something special.

WEDNESDAY, 28TH SEPTEMBER

3pm
College House opens.
Tea available for those who arrive early.

8pm
Bar Social. — *The Tea-Set*

Clockwise from top left: Roger Kinsey booked the band that was still calling itself The Tea Set; Jenny Spires was a friend of Syd Barrett and attended several early Pink Floyd shows; Martin O'Shea wanted to ban the bomb and popularise the mandolin. Both projects remain ongoing; Jenny Spires with Syd Barrett

Jack Lyons/"Irish Jack" London 1965

The Bitta Sweet 1966–1968
Brian Fieldhouse — Al Atkins — Albert Hinton — Bruno Stapenhill — Lawrence Farley

Clockwise from top left: Michael White (pictured, right) and his band Acceleration wonder how fast a Rolls-Royce can do 0 to 60; Irish Jack Lyons witnessed the fading of Mod and the flowering of psychedelia; Bitta Sweet, the band that Ken Ford managed and West Bromwich's contribution to the world of psychedelia; Mike Fox might have witnessed Pink Floyd's first show at the Roundhouse

ROUNDHOUSE
3 DECEMBER 1966, CHALK FARM, LONDON, UK

I WAS THERE: MIKE FOX

I was a teenager living with my parents in London in the Sixties and saw what might have been Pink Floyd's first London show, at the Roundhouse. I don't remember if they were headlining or what other bands were playing, but I had gone specifically to see a new band Pink Floyd that I had learnt about from *Melody Maker*. By the time I got into the venue they had already started playing; it was a Bo Diddley number, 'Road Runner'. Their set was a mix of R&B numbers and original material. I recall being very impressed with Syd Barrett's guitar style in their instrumental numbers such as 'Astronome Domine'.

I later saw them at UFO in Tottenham Court Road, possibly twice. UFO was a small basement club that operated on a Friday night and they were now playing all original material, which I enjoyed very much. As a guitarist myself, I was again impressed with Syd's improvisational style. Their performance was enhanced by an impressive light show.

THE MARQUEE
22 DECEMBER 1966, LONDON, UK

I WAS THERE: STEPHEN COMBES

It was at the Marquee on Wardour Steet. I really can't remember whether this was as part of the Spontaneous Underground club and therefore on Sunday afternoon. It could equally have been one weekday evening. Either way, it was dark outside and very dark inside, illuminated only by the light show. This was the first time I had seen the effects which could be created by holding a naked flame to warm liquid dyes held between two glass plates. This was projected on to the backdrop to the stage by a spotlight situated right behind me. It was very interesting when the whole thing caught fire! The music was very progressive and kind of new to me, as I was more interested at that time in early American blues and its Sixties interpretation. I went to this show with a couple of friends that I'd travelled from Manchester with for a few days. During the same trip, we also caught The Cream (before they dropped the 'The') at the Roundhouse, known then as Centre 42. There were other acts but I can't remember them. I don't think we had more than a couple of hours sleep the whole trip, but it was memorable.

Pink Floyd play the first of a series of shows at UFO at the Blarney Club in Tottenham Court Road, London a reported eleven times, with their first appearance being on 23 December 1966 and their last on 28 July 1967.

UFO
23 DECEMBER 1966, LONDON, UK

I WAS THERE: JENNY SPIRES

Shortly after The Roundhouse, the Underground club UFO was opened by John 'Hoppy' Hopkins and Joe Boyd. The Floyd became the resident band there. They played their own music, mostly songs composed by Syd, which consisted of long extended pieces of 'free improvisation', with slide guitar and feedback. The band had totally gelled and simply jammed together through the middle eight. This, with the alliteration of Syd's words, became their calling card. It was intoxicating, enthralling and an incredibly creative period for them. Very soon, their unique sound meant they became the most popular band on the underground. It was actually just a very small band of people then with one sensibility, moral philosophy and aesthetic. It paralleled that of flower power in the States, and out of it grew the hippie movement here, which, unfortunately, started to become much more commercial when the clubbers on the London scene turned their gaze on the new 'in crowd' and joined in with floaty kaftans and bells. It was a creative, heady and innovative time to be young in London…

I WAS THERE: COL TURNER

Sometimes you can be in the right place at the right time. I guess that's what happened to me back in 1966 and 1967, and those events had an enormous impact and influence on my life. It was in London in late 1966 and I was just an ordinary guy going through the growing up phase. I would have been 20 at the time. The fad back then was to be either a Mod or a Rocker. I had chosen the former and hung with a crowd who were well dressed, short-haired, and into bands like Herman's Hermits, Gerry and the Pacemakers and, of course, The Beatles. Then one night something happened that was to change my life and the lives of many others. Someone in our crowd had heard that a unique thing was happening at a club in Tottenham Court Road in London. The club was called the

WISH YOU WERE HERE

Blarney Club and, as we were to discover later, they leased the club out, usually on a Friday, to a group of people who were going to try some experimental 'happenings'. The club was called UFO. So off we went, not quite knowing what to expect.

As we approached the club, we saw a long-haired guy dressed in only his underpants and wearing strings of tiny bells. As if this wasn't strange by itself, he was spinning around and around in the middle of the road. We were later to discover that he and many others had taken a cocktail of LSD – which was legal then – and speed.

I remember thinking at the time, should we go in? The people milling around were totally different to the people I usually associated with, but certainly they were very friendly. Nothing ventured, nothing gained. So down a steep flight of steps we went and paid our admittance fee of ten shillings (50p). Into the double doors on the left we went, and into a new world.

It's hard to describe the scene but I will try to paint the picture. The noise from the crowd was deafening, the smell of incense overpowering and – the heat! It was a cold night but the heat being generated by sweaty bodies was awesome. Just about everyone was wearing tiny bells and either sitting staring into space (stoned) or prancing around (also stoned) or just plain stoned!

There was a band playing, although I can't remember who, and while we certainly didn't fit in with these people we decided to stay. I was to become one of the 'Beautiful People' and saw many, many bands that came out of England in the Sixties. I saw Floyd at almost the start and have followed them and let them shape my life since, seeing them more than 30 times in total.

So there we were, a group of out-of-place people sharing a unique experience. Several bands came and went and, again, I don't remember who they were, but suffice it to say that they all probably went on to bigger and better things, as UFO was the birthplace of many other great bands. It was the early hours when in walked another group of long-haired musicians, all carrying their own equipment. Across the floor they walked, stepping up onto the stage. There were no curtains or wings, just a plain old stage about three feet high.

Twang, they started to tune up, playing some very weird chords. 'This could be good,' someone said. 'Hello, we're The Pink Floyd,' said one of them (probably Syd, and note the 'The') and away they went. Now I wish I could tell you that they blew me away, but I can't say that, because although they were different, the music – which from memory was all original – had a very jazzy feel to it and I have never been a great lover of jazz. I remember thinking that it was a strange combination of rock and jazz they were attempting. However, as they went along, I realised that this band had something. I can't remember what songs they played that night, with one exception. They launched into a piece that must have lasted at least 40 minutes that I'm betting was an early version of 'Interstellar Overdrive'. I think everyone around had the same thought: brilliant in parts, but mainly boring. They were using a very rudimentary light show which consisted of a slide projector with printer's ink placed between two slides. As the ink heated up it 'popped' between the slides, projecting bubbles of colour on the band and the back of the stage. I was lucky enough to help a friend to do this one night. Sadly, it was run by the club and not Floyd, so I can't brag about being part of Pink Floyd, however small a part.

The crowd, which was probably a few hundred in the early days, but which later was to become many hundreds as the fame of UFO and Floyd spread, were appreciative at the end of each number and many danced a strange dance or twirled their heads as the music was playing. Now I could be wrong but I think Floyd were the last band to play that night. They were given the honour of being the UFO house band and usually were top of the bill and last to play. At other places, such as Middle Earth, they did not always get top billing and therefore appeared early. All the 'in' clubs in the Sixties put on at least three bands, and sometimes as many as seven.

I reckon that Floyd's session that night lasted for about two hours, which was very long by other band's standards. One hour in those days was considered good – two hours was unheard of! They left the stage with little fuss, once again carrying their own gear, I think they may have had just one roadie, but I do remember them packing up their own stuff. So that was it, I had seen my first Pink Floyd gig. What did I think of it overall? Unique, jazzy, boring – and brilliant!

I had to see them again. I saw them many times after this night. It wasn't love at first sight but they had certainly teased me into coming back for more. Floyd, who had started out as an underground band, were now getting some attention. They still played UFO and Middle Earth, plus a few other London underground clubs (about 14 UFOs and nine Middle Earths, according to the official records) between December 1966 and mid-1969. I had the good fortune to be at most, if not all, of these gigs, plus others in Hyde Park and Alexander Palace. But now the dreaded fame was starting to overtake them. Before 'Arnold Layne' and 'See Emily Play' were released, we had been able to see and hear Floyd in a somewhat elitist environment, although the clubs where they played were not restricted. If you didn't fit in, you really didn't want to come back. I soon learned that my then short hair was 'not acceptable', and let it grow as quickly as it could.

The early concerts were a sight to behold, with Floyd playing a new number or two at just about every gig. They were exciting times as Floyd were experimenting like crazy. I probably heard at least a dozen different versions of 'Interstellar Overdrive', each night a little different and always lasting between 30 and 40 minutes. Syd would often go off in his own direction, leaving the rest of the guys wondering when he would come back and play something they could identify, so they could join back in! They often lounged around at the back of the stage – which was very small with nowhere to hide – waiting for Syd. It was pretty obvious even then that they were Syd's band. They were also not consistent, in that in most songs on most nights they played like nothing you had ever heard and yet other times they would produce crap. Of course, everyone was behind them because they were 'our band' or 'the underground band'. So when 'Arnold' and 'Emily' came along, everyone in the underground was pissed off. Floyd were getting attention from people outside of our group. That wasn't on; we had a contract with Floyd and they with us, they were 'our band'. Of course, that wasn't written down anywhere. It was just accepted. Although I never spoke to any of the guys, it was common knowledge that Floyd were apprehensive about their oncoming fame. In my opinion, that's very evident in a lot of their later songs, eg. 'Welcome to the Machine'. It's very easy to look back now and see how silly we were being, but that's how we all felt in those days. I must have seen them do poor old 'Arnold' and 'Emily' countless times but I don't remember how they played them. I do remember a lot of new people were starting to invade the clubs. The boys had hit the big time and the audience was rapidly changing. It got to the stage where the threat of violence to us poor hippies was becoming very real. Then someone had the bright idea to get the Hell's Angels in to protect the hippies. Bizarre as it sounds, it worked!

So now the audiences consisted of hippies, Hell's Angels, an assortment of what we would now call teeny boppers, and the odd thug. Many of these newcomers took up the hippy lifestyle and so it's very true to say that Pink Floyd were true founders of the hippy movement. Floyd were changing too. The gear was getting upgraded and roadies were now on the job. But the music – what can I say? They were getting it together. Okay, I know Syd was on the skids by now, but the music was still some of the best they ever played. It had now got to the stage where UFO had outgrown the cellar at the Blarney Club and had to be moved to the Roundhouse just to fit in the crowds for Floyd. I'm very confused as to what club went where and when, but Middle Earth also relocated from the cellar in Covent Garden to the Roundhouse.

I WAS THERE: NIGEL LESMOIR-GORDON

We used to go down the UFO Club every Saturday. The Floyd were the house band. And that's when Peter Wynne-Willson started doing light shows between two plates of glass with ox gore and paint, squeezing them together and putting them under the lamp. Syd was all right then. He was still playing very well. Then I began to hear reports that he was behaving oddly.

UFO

30 DECEMBER 1966, LONDON, UK

I WAS THERE: JENNY SPIRES

Around this time, I met the film-maker Peter Whitehead. We immediately became friends when he offered me a lift from 'Granny Takes a Trip', where I had been modelling some clothes, to Earlham Street, where I was now staying with Syd and Lindsay, Peter Wynne-Willson and Susie Gawler-Wright. (Pete and Susie did the lights for the Floyd.)

Peter Whitehead told me he had been shooting a film about the London scene. I knew his films, *Charlie is my Darling* and *Wholly Communion*, and agreed when he offered to show me the footage of this latest film, *Tonite Let's All Make Love in London*. He said he hadn't got a soundtrack yet. I suggested he use Syd's band, as they were the latest up-and-coming band in London, so he came down to UFO to see them play.

Peter knew Syd from Cambridge and they became friends. They met at Juliette Mitchell's when they were both doing painting, before Syd went to Camberwell. After Cambridge, where he read Physics and Crystallography, Peter went to the Slade School of Fine Art to study painting and then switched to film making. Syd and he hadn't seen each other for a couple of years, since Peter had had an exhibition of his paintings at The Lamb in Milton. Syd and Anthony Stern had one there the following week, and now Anthony had also become Peter's assistant, learning to make films. Small world. He worked with Peter in the States when he was making his film *The Fall* before he left for San Francisco to make his own film *San Francisco*, a la Peter Whitehead and using a tape recording given him by Pete Jenner in '68.

I WAS THERE: IRISH JACK LYONS

Sometime later, someone told me that 'that' band I had been telling them about was playing every week at an all-night venue in Tottenham Court Road. They said it was an Irish dance hall called the Blarney Club but 'beatniks with long hair' ran it on a Friday night! I ventured along (as usual, very much on my own). Again, I met friendly people with cultured English accents and a million miles from Mod. The club was run by 'Hoppy' (John Hopkins) and an American, Joe Boyd, advertising itself as UFO. I presumed this meant Unidentified Flying Objects, though some said it meant Underground Freak Out. Within a short space of time, I had become a regular, watching Pink Floyd every week and sometimes The Soft Machine (who were called after a book of the same name by William S Burroughs). UFO, it turned out, was the place to be and the place to be seen.

WISH YOU WERE HERE

Although still dressing as a Mod, my musical tastes and sense of snobbery was in good shape. I'd elected to go along to see a guy playing piano at the London School of Economics. I found a comfortable table and sat with a coffee watching the remarkable skills of Ron Geesin, who mesmerised his audience playing long complicated key structures to the point where nobody was quite sure what was going on. I had a chat with him after and, at the end of the conversation, he smiled and said in a strong Scottish accent, 'Yes, low self esteem, man.' I thought he was talking about himself, telling me he wasn't a very confident player. He sensed my confusion and added, 'London School of Economics, LSE, Low Self Esteem!'

I saw very many people perform at UFO, from Mike McGear (Paul McCartney's brother) to the Liverpool Scene, Scaffold, Adrian Henri, Keith West's Tomorrow, Soft Machine, Zoot Money's Dantalion's Chariot, Fairport Convention, Sun Trolley, Third Ear Band and The Crazy World of Arthur Brown. Like many people, I'm sure I saw more than that. The record that was endlessly played every week, sometimes two or three times a night, was a dance-y single called 'Granny Takes A Trip' by The Purple Gang. As soon as I heard the name of the band, for some reason I assumed they were a San Francisco outfit. The psychedelic atmosphere and floating bubbles in UFO's probably suggested to me that this band with the amazing song were American. Imagine my shock many years later when discovering that The Purple Gang were a jug band from Stockport in the industrial north of England. The song had got its name from the clothes shop 'Granny Takes A Trip' in the King's Road and naturally, because of its connotations to acid by 'granny taking a trip', was duly banned by the BBC. The strange thing about it is that the record became the UFO's anthem and yet it had nothing to do with psychedelia. It just sounded like a psychedelic record. I used to watch people freak dancing to the record. Later, the dance moves became known as 'idiot' dancing, which was well espoused by the character William 'Jesus' Jellett at the Bath Rock Festival and many other festivals after that.

A couple of minutes' walk further up the street from UFO was a small bar which featured psychedelic sounds and strobes upstairs. It was a popular hangout for punters and artists, because UFO didn't start until the cinema above it closed at 10pm. It was situated on the corner of Tottenham Court Road and Windmill Street and may have been called the Rising Sun. I befriended Mick Farren, who had a band called The Social Deviants and wrote articles for the new underground newspaper, *International Times*. This was primarily based on the New York hippy newspaper, *The Village Voice*, and cost one shilling (5p) to buy. I'd usually buy myself a half glass of Watney's Brown Ale and slip upstairs to hear the music. It could be anything going on. Beat poets, backed by a guy in the corner cross-legged with a sitar – anything. One night upstairs I saw this low-sized woman with long black hair reaching to her hips with a microphone in her hand and screaming her head off. I got fed up after ten minutes and returned downstairs for another drink at the bar. Later, a small group of people were stood behind me and I glanced back over my shoulder to discover that one of them was the woman who'd been hysterical upstairs. I looked at her and she returned a vague Japanese smile. One of the group called her 'Yoko'.

Mick Farren told me about his friend Hoppy and a group of like-minded activists who had started up this new revolutionary newspaper. I knew Hoppy from the admission table at UFOs and was curious about the publication. A couple of weeks later, I paid an uninvited visit to the bowels of 102 Southampton Row and was greeted by Barry Miles and four or five curiously amused editorial staff. They were looking at my Mod gear and lent a keen ear when I told them I was from Shepherd's Bush, that I had been christened 'Irish Jack' by Kit Lambert, The Who's manager, and was a friend of Pete Townshend. *The* Pete Townshend.

I paid another few visits. They were posh, friendly people who spoke with intelligence about anarchy, communism and legalising marijuana. I was fascinated by their dialogue and the way nobody objected when I would make my own cup of coffee and just sit there literally listening in to everything. But what didn't sit well with me was their continual reference to the police as 'pigs'. To my Shepherd's Bush upbringing a copper was a copper – some were good, others were not.

BIRDCAGE CLUB
21 JANUARY 1967, EASTNEY, PORTSMOUTH, UK

I WAS THERE: HORREY HAMILTON

They had quite a repertoire of songs and a projector with cellophane going around with different psychedelic images on it. It was about six bob (30p) to get in. The Birdcage was owned by a guy called Ricky Farr, whose father was the boxer, Paul Farr. It was quite a Moddy club. In them days there was always the Mods and Rockers. The Birdcage was always a very Mod club. Jimmy James and the Vagabonds, The Action, Geno Washington and the likes of Rod Stewart, who was with a group called the Steampacket, all played there. The Who used to come down quite a bit. I remember Ricky Farr saying that the Pink Floyd were coming down. Although they were on the circuit, I don't think that they were fantastically well known.

WISH YOU WERE HERE

UFO
27 JANUARY 1967, LONDON, UK

I WAS THERE: MARTIN O'SHEA

It was a Friday night through Saturday morning. I would get on my way there from my shared flat near Baker Street Tube about 11pm, after dropping some acid. The club was in the basement, below some sort of theatre or cinema which was always closed by the time I got there. Down steps to the right, someone at the lower door taking the entrance money. How much was it now? I cannot remember; maybe ten shillings (50p). Into the club room, which was pretty dark, with some projections going on and maybe a film in one corner. Most people there seemed to be smoking and a familiar odour filled the air, as well as incense.

The first week or two it was Pink Floyd for the bulk of the night, with maybe a small group or single artist between times. The Floyd, with liquid projections and the sound just like the liquid, running, swirling and merging, the line of the guitar, the structural build-up of keyboard and dancing bass, a truly new and searching music, sent my consciousness to areas known only in sleep or those rare and magic moments.

On a further visit, there was this crazy William Burroughs bunch, and yes, a William Burroughs' film in black and white, of cybernetics and not just of eyesight but of the very thought process. The Burroughs' bunch are called Soft Machine and their music takes the score and bends it and stretches it. The score lines merge into one and tear apart, taking you through levels never dreamed of in good old rock and roll.

Then next week, Pink Floyd and then Soft Machine, these two bands equally tax and pay into the imagination, sounds that will follow me beyond my memory. Like a doped-up fool, I stand with my head right by these great speakers and I hear the sounds, like the roaring of a multicoloured sea; not realising then that this sea will come back to me again and again, and even now, some 50 years later, that roaring remains, a reminder of the night's good vibrations.

There is, in this unique and one and only club, a sense of new level music and the crowd who go there are part of this discovery. There are projections here and there, bits of movies on that corner, a poet reads some beat up poem, some people dance like there's no tomorrow, actors ridicule the establishment and the smoke shows through light projections. The reek is a giveaway. We are reminded that certain things are not allowed and the last thing anyone wants is for the place to be closed down. For those who cannot do without some smoky relief, there is always a toilet cubicle. I have no memories of alcohol use, maybe a glass of orange at the 'bar' (which is little more than a table), maybe a Coke or just a large glass of water to keep the moisture up. Dancing and interpreting to these crazy sounds is addictive; one moment you are swirling in some oriental grace and then the next, pounding like a rock machine.

Other nights it may be Arthur Brown on fire, with flames painted on his face and a crazy head gear topped by a paraffin torch flaming into the club's atmosphere, singing 'Fire' like a medieval torment, or maybe the Procol Harum with their mystic order, translating beloved Bach into a Californian purple haze.

Oh those great nights at UFO – the energy, the rediscovery of bits of yourself, of bits of humanity, that had for so long been buried in money and matter, in ego and impressing. And the stroll home at 5.30 or so in the morning, with maybe a coffee in some lonely Soho bar, maybe a chat with the pigeons at Marble Arch, or just a wander as the sun creeps up through the chimneys and smoke rings.

SOUND TECHNIQUES RECORDING STUDIO
12 JANUARY 1967, LONDON, UK

I WAS THERE: JENNY SPIRES

On seeing the Floyd, Peter Whitehead thought they were great. He had heard them in Cambridge, but they were just a cover band then. Now, he spoke to Pete Jenner and booked Sound Techniques Recording Studio, a he had used several times before. I think most people agree this is some of the best footage there is of this early Floyd, doing 'Interstellar Overdrive'. You can clearly see Syd's Binson Echorec sitting on top of Rick's organ. Peter moved in, among and around in between them filming. He also filmed one of Nick's songs, 'Nick's Boogie'. I was sitting on the stairs behind them all watching. The film won an award and was shown at the New York Film Festival that year, introducing the Floyd to the States. Syd was just so natural, he was relaxed and they were all locked into that sound. They were on their way in January 1967.

Syd was absolutely thrilled to do this for Peter, but just before we filmed them, I was in Cambridge for Christmas and Syd rang me to say he was coming to collect me because he wanted to play me an acoustic version of his new song 'Arnold Layne', which they were then to record as a single when we got back to London.

But Syd was beginning to look tired. Not long after recording 'Arnold Layne', the band signed a contract with EMI and the increase in their work schedule was immense. They travelled up and down the country playing in so many very different places and venues, to audiences in the provinces who were expecting rock or soul or something similar they could dance to. The year before this Syd had a recurrence of glandular fever. He first had it in 1964 and it took him a while to recover. Now he was overworking, writing all the music for the band and playing gigs every night up and down the country. It was a hard slog for them all, but Syd seemed most notably affected.

In keeping with the times, he had also been experimenting with LSD and smoking hash, but it wasn't helping with the busy schedule. He never took any other kind of drugs at this time, except pot. He was against amphetamine and there was not Mandrax available yet. The rest of the band preferred a pint but their lifestyle, with irregular meals and late nights, was taking its' toll on them all and especially on Syd's energy. In time, he started to look more and more tired, and was devoid of energy.

COLLEGE OF ART & TECHNOLOGY
10 FEBRUARY 1967, LEICESTER, UK

I WAS THERE: JOHN ANSTEE

They had a cine projector with clouds projecting onto the background. It was unlike anything we'd seen before. I didn't know their music. They were just a new group turned up. And we just went down to see who they were. It was next to nothing to get in to see them, probably two or three shillings (10p or 15p). It wasn't really my cup of tea. I loved Bob Dylan.

FALMER HOUSE COURTYARD
11 FEBRUARY 1967, BRIGHTON, UK

I WAS THERE: RICHARD EVANS

I saw them at Sussex Uni in 1967 with Syd on vocals. They were supported by Soft Machine, who were equally as good. Many people ended up in the moat, which was full of dry ice. It was a truly memorable evening 50 years ago. My problem is I can't remember what happened yesterday!

ADELPHI BALLROOM
20 FEBRUARY 1967, WEST BROMWICH, UK

I WAS THERE: KEN FORD, AGE 19

I was at the Adelphi gig with the young band I managed called Bitta Sweet. I was also a trainee electrician. I was particularly interested in the special light show as we were experimenting with flashing lights. I think it was a midweek gig, as not too many were there. Tables were taken out of the bar to form a platform for the projection equipment and leads were run out to the tables. I can remember coloured paints and oil were put onto glass slides and somehow placed in front of the projector, and then heat from a blow torch was applied to make the bubbles 'boil' on the stage back drop. On a key change, the slides were flicked to make the image quickly change. If there was any normal stage lighting, it was either switched off or greatly dimmed. They played 'Arnold Layne' and they may have played 'See Emily Play'.

Al Atkins, our singer, remembers that white sheets were draped over the amps and speakers to allow the bubbles to be seen everywhere. Al and Bruno Stapenhill went on to form the first Judas Priest band, with Bruno coming up with the name from a Bob Dylan song.

I WAS THERE: ALBIE HINTON

I remember clearly when they played at the Adelphi Ballroom. Our band, Bitta Sweet, went to see them after reading about them and their London gigs in the *News of the World*. They reported that girls were taking their tops of during a gig at London's UFO Club. It was good publicity but we had no such luck in West Bromwich. Still, I thoroughly enjoyed the show. However, the majority of the crowd seemed to be overawed by them and the crowd just didn't seem to get it. Personally, I thought they were way ahead of their time and that West Bromwich just wasn't ready for it, I was particularly impressed with Syd Barrett and Roger Waters. This gig inspired us to build our own flashing light rig. The Move tried to jump on the psychedelic bandwagon with their spiral light show, but it didn't quite come off. Of course, they went on to be successful in their own right.

RICKY TICK CLUB, THAMES HOTEL
25 FEBRUARY 1967, WINDSOR, UK

I WAS THERE: JOHN MANSFIELD

When I came out of the army in December 1958, I went to a jazz club in Windsor at the Star and Garter pub. There were only about ten people there and nearly all of them were male. I said to the band leader who was running the club that it was like a gay club. 'You want to get some girls in here.' I went round to the local Wimpy bar and international club. I persuaded all the foreign girls to go there, and when word got around that all the girls were at the Star and Garter in Windsor, all the boys started going there. It became very popular. And then the bandleader said 'why don't you run the club? And I'll just run the band.'

At that time there was only a few groups to book, so I booked them all because there was nobody else to book. The Ricky Tick was a badge I placed on each different venue for that particular evening. I booked shows in Windsor, Slough, Guildford, Maidenhead and Reading. I used to use the call box at Windsor railway station. People would phone up and I'd answer it. If the phone rang and I was waiting in line, I used to push to the front and push people out of the way and say 'that's for me'. We were getting enthusiastic audiences. The venues were always packed out. People would come because it was the Ricky Tick Club. We had Pink Floyd. They played at the Thames Hotel in Windsor and at the Ricky Tick in Hounslow, which was in a ballroom above a car showroom. We had Pink Floyd about ten times. They were playing psychedelic music – with lights

ASSEMBLY HALL
2 MARCH 1967, WORTHING, UK

I WAS THERE: JOHN FEEST

When I saw Pink Floyd at Worthing Assembly Hall, they were supported by a local band called The Switch. I was unimpressed by Pink Floyd. They looked scruffy and had no presentation to their act. Obviously, they improved over the years. 'See Emily Play' is a great song and so evocative of the era.

WINTER GARDENS
7 MARCH 1967, MALVERN, UK

I WAS THERE: IAN SMITH, AGE 19

I remember the evening well. I was on a blind date that night with a very cute girl called Yvonne. There was a dance every Tuesday night at the Winter Gardens back then and I was lucky enough to see most of the top groups of that era. On the night in question, the place was nowhere near full, presumably because not many people had heard of the Floyd. There was no sophisticated light show and certainly no Algie (the flying pig). The band just had their instruments and amplifiers and performed in front of a pink curtain that was draped behind them. When they started to play, I wasn't quite sure what I was hearing. There was no doubting their musicianship of course, but I was used to my music being a little less 'heavy'. My preference lay with groups like The Searchers, The Hollies, Small Faces etc. so I have to say I wasn't all that impressed with the early Floyd stuff and we left the dance a bit bewildered, little realising what a phenomenon they would go on to become. That was then but now I am a huge fan as is my daughter, who I introduced to the Floyd several years ago.

'ARNOLD LAYNE' RELEASED
10 MARCH 1967

Pink Floyd's first single reaches No.20 in the UK singles chart.

AGINCOURT BALLROOM
12 MARCH 1967, CAMBERLEY, UK

I WAS THERE: JOHN SCOTT CREE

In January 1967, I had a teeth job in hospital. The school boy in the next bed was certain from his reading of music papers that a band called Pink Floyd were going to be big. Soon after, in March 1967, I went to see Pink Floyd play at the Agincourt. They were supported by Sky, the re-named Condors from way back, who were still playing good covers (Otis Redding by now) but, in the middle of their set, they blew it for me by playing Cliff and the Shadows' 'In The Country'. I don't know what Pink Floyd must have made of it all. It penetrated their between sets recreation. It was a strange evening. There was a disparate crowd of less than 40 of us, of whom perhaps a dozen were from Sandhurst, the training school for army officers over the road. They were very jolly with their blazers and ties and well-dressed lady friends, and danced holding hands in a big circle to some of Sky's numbers. Pink Floyd seemed to go down less well with them, and the crowd was reduced in size by their absence from the second set.

Pink Floyd were incredibly loud. Their drummer had a double bass drum kit which he played with timpani beaters. He was still inaudible. I'd thought The Who were loud, but this took the biscuit. The excitement was augmented by their novel light show. One extended number would feature flashing coloured lights placed around the stage. The next would feature blobs of colour exploding over the almost static, fur-coated, bespectacled Syd Barrett, shaking his bowed, fuzzy-haired head from side to side over his guitar. The lighting effect was created by two people at the back of the hall. I watched them insert slides containing what looked like splodges of oil paint into a projector, and then heat them with a Bunsen burner. They had two such projectors, which enabled them to rotate them with the stage lighting. It was an amazing evening which seemed in some way historic. I asked the cloakroom staff for the poster – they seemed glad it was all over. I remember only 'Candy and a Currant Bun' from the evening, but, when it was released, I bought 'Arnold Layne'. I sold the poster for £10 when times were hard.

CLIFTON HALL
23 MARCH 1967, ROTHERHAM, UK

I WAS THERE: MARTYN SHARPE, AGE 19

I was a junior reporter on the *Rotherham Advertiser*. I wasn't a Pink Floyd fan as such, but one of the perks of the job – which included free entry to watch my beloved Rotherham United and tickets for all the cinemas in town; there were at least five then and there are none now! – was getting into gigs for nothing. My memory of the show is very hazy. I recall a light show of sorts. If you can visualise a lava lamp magnified onto one of the walls inside the hall, that'd be about the size of it. But the music passed me by. Joni Mitchell, Joan Baez, Joe Cocker were more my taste then, and still are today... The gig was hugely memorable and still resonates even now because it was the night I first met my wife. I was standing on the balcony scanning the assembled girls dancing below – it was the usual tactic at the time – and saw Janice bopping around with a friend. We left the gig together, and I drove her home in my white Austin Healey Sprite. On the way, I delivered a dreadful chat up line which still haunts me even today: 'Bet you've never been home in a sports car before...'. I know it sounds dreadful, and it's not improved with the passage of time, but Janice must have spotted some redeeming feature. Three years later we got married, and we're still happily together. I've not played a Pink Floyd album since that night... perhaps I should. They can at least take the credit for bringing us together!

TOP SPOT BALLROOM
31 MARCH 1967, ROSS-ON-WYE, UK

I WAS THERE: ROGER ARNOLD

It was a totally new and exciting experience for me. It was only half full. I leaned over the balcony, watching the wives or girlfriends melting candle wax over a projector to make a light show behind the band. It was mind-blowing stuff. The set was stopped about two thirds of the way through due to Harvey, the owner, shutting them down as they exceeded noise levels. It was a sad blow as it was great music. We managed to see them again several times in later years. And this was a long time ago!

I WAS THERE: TIM CHANCE, AGE 15

Door prices were 12/6p (63p) for top bands but on that night, it was probably 16/- shillings (80p). However, I didn't pay anything as I worked there that night. I collected used glasses from around the balcony every Friday and Saturday evenings. I loved bands and all music as well as collecting autographs. The club was jammed full when the band came on stage. They had those Sixties liquid wheel projectors all over the walls and ceilings. They started with a piece of music I have never heard since. It was psychedelic, endless meandering keyboards, having no tune and then they followed with another endless piece just the same. There was no 'See Emily Play'. In fact there was not one commercial single. I was gutted.

There was a sound monitoring device in the Top Spot, controlled by the chap who activated all the spot and mood lights. There was an upside down traffic light that shone towards the stage. You would see green when a band started and then, if the volume went higher than a pre-determined level, you were given an amber light. If you did not turn it down or even went louder, you had a red light. I cannot recall what the rules were exactly but if you had perhaps two or three red lights, then Harvey Fear, the Top Spot's owner, would switch off the band's power. I doubt if the Floyd played more than 15 minutes before all their power was cut and Harvey kicked them off stage. They were gone before I could get their autographs.

BIRDCAGE CLUB
1 APRIL 1967, EASTNEY, PORTSMOUTH, UK

I WAS THERE: MICK PERRYMENT, AGE 16

I saw the Floyd at the Birdcage. I was hoping my 16-year-old self would have written more in his diary. After all, I had written down the complete set list for The Who and the clothes they wore when they played at the Cage in February of that year, plus I got drumsticks and Pete's plectrum. But all I wrote was 'saw the Pink Floyd at the Cage and they were too brilliant for words!'. So that was it. I remember Roger Waters doing the strange vocals on 'Astronomy Domine' and the projected dripping oil in the background, which was revolutionary at the time.

I was also at the Hendrix show in November. My diary says, 'At 8.50 we saw Pink Floyd, Nice, Jimi Hendrix, Move, Amen Corner, The Outer Limits, Eire Apparent at the Guildhall. Jimi and Floyd fantastic. Fabulous fantastic show.' I used 'fantastic' a lot in 1967.

FLORAL HALL
7 APRIL 1967, BELFAST, UK

I WAS THERE: MICHAEL MCFAUL

I saw the band on three occasions they came to Belfast. I'm not aware of any other visits they made here. The first was at the Floral Hall, a memorable venue as it was the only licensed ballroom near Belfast at the time. It is located high up on Cave Hill beside Belfast Zoo and now derelict. The admission fee on the night was eight shillings and sixpence – equivalent to about 42p in today's money. I also saw Manfred Mann, Dave Dee, The Wild Angels and others there back in the Sixties. The Floyd gig attracted a fairly small crowd as they were only just making a name for themselves then. They did the light show with some great outer space visuals alongside 'Astronomy Domine'. It would probably would seem very tame by today's standards. Syd Barrett was very loud but he seemed to hold it together throughout.

The second time I saw them was in 1968 at Queen's University. Barrett had gone, and from memory it was a fairly routine affair without the light show.

 PAVILION
10 APRIL 1967, BATH, UK

I WAS THERE: BILL FORD

I'm pretty sure they had a light show but recall nothing spectacular about their playing, which I think was pretty average. In the context of the time I went to see them as I would go to see any other 'pop' band – they had had at least one hit single, 'Arnold Layne', by then – and I judged them accordingly. I liked their record and its sound, which was rather different for the times, but remember my friend thinking both them live and their single rubbish. Four or five months later, I saw Tomorrow at the same venue. Now they were a real eye-opener. I was in a pop band at the time and the guitarist and I immediately left to form our own 'progressive' band, with some success.

I WAS THERE: PHILIP PARSONS

Bath was a delight in those days and thanks to the promoter, Freddie Bannister, we had top bands at the Pavilion every Monday. By today's standards, it was ridiculously cheap – The Who (my favourites), Beatles and Stones at pocket money prices. For most of the Sixties, there was an almost continuous run of great artists. The one time it did not happen was when the Pavilion flooded. At short notice, and to the amazement of all, the gig was transferred to the world-famous Pump Rooms, part of the Roman Baths complex. The British Birds played, their guitarist a smiling Ronnie Wood, where there was normally a sedan chair and string quartet. It never happened again. The acoustics of the Pavilion were not ideal (it was normally a roller skating rink), but its large capacity meant that the more famous bands could be attracted. I usually attended with a group of music-mad friends, mostly from the local senior schools, and there was a lot of excitement that Pink Floyd were coming to play. One of my friend's mothers was a cleaner at the Pavilion and she used to get a lot of the groups' autographs for us, but sadly not the Pink Floyd.

In those early months and throughout 1967 we were, to a certain extent, deluding ourselves. We thought that we were part of the cultural change that was to become

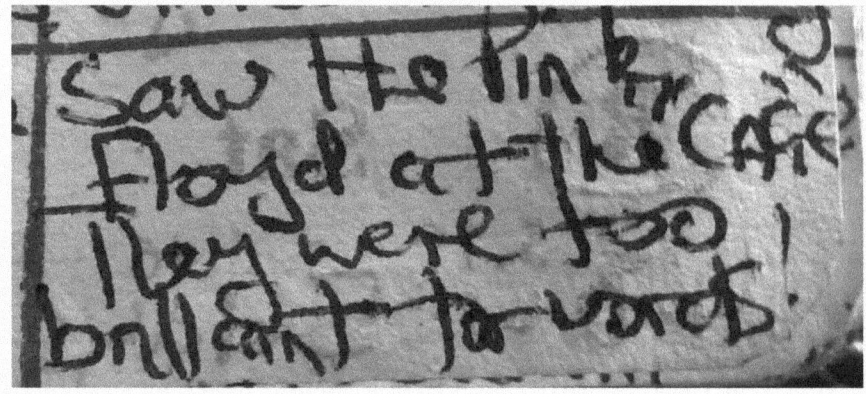

Clockwise from top left: John Feest was unimpressed by Pink Floyd; Roger Arnold only saw two thirds of the Floyd's show at the Top Spot Ballroom; Mick Perryment told his diary Pink Floyd were 'too brilliant for words'; Tim Chance with his band Salubrious Union and his pre-CBS 1962 Fender bass

Mon April 3rd
Fantastic new Group
The Loot
(Baby come closer)
Adm 5/-

Mon April 10th
The Unique Sounds of
The Pink Floyd
(Arnold Lane)
Adm 5/-

Mon April 17th
It's
Dave Dee, Dozy, Beaky, Mick & Tich
Adm 5/6

Mon April 24th
Bannister Promotions are pleased to announce that their legal representatives have negotiated a definite appearance of
The Who
Adm 5/6

7.30 — 10.30

Clockwise from top left: Michael McFaul remembers Syd Barrett being very loud; Kelvin Scudamore thought the *Evening Chronicle* review harsh; Bath poster; Bill Ford with his band Birth; Philip Parsons remembers an unforgettable live experience the 'summer of peace and love'. To us, it was always the music that was the most important, and there was a local club in Bath that had picked up on the psychedelic influence, with the recently released 'Arnold Layne' and The Smoke's 'My Friend Jack' being particularly popular. We were very fortunate that a friend had a brother who lived in the States and we were getting to hear albums (particularly The Doors) before they were available in the UK. The Floyd have always been perfectionists, and were so even in those days. I don't think everybody in the audience was ready for the treat or had the faintest idea what was about to happen. But there was a growing number that got it. There was an incredible buzz around them, as they had such a unique sound, particularly on their lengthier numbers. It was just not that accessible for the three minute single aficionados. But, ironically, the single was the reason that most were there at the Pav. It is Rick Wright's soaring organ that I can still hear (a Farfisa, I think). It was like changing gear. Syd did not leave a lasting impression. Back then, I could fixate on a single note and I was obsessed by the technology of reproducing music. I still am. The subject, Arnold Layne, was also the topic of much discussion. Even at the Knebworth concert, with all the generator problems, they still managed to deliver an unforgettable live experience. This all started for me on that Monday night in April 1967.

In 1967, I was 'very friendly' with a young lady who lived near Victoria Park in Bath. At Christmas of that year she received an LP from her cousin. With it was a hand-written message (I think on the sleeve), 'I have just left my old band, Jokers Wild, and I am joining a new band, this is their latest album.' The album was *The Piper at the Gates of Dawn*. The note was from David Gilmour. I was already a Floyd fan, but little did we realise what this would mean to the world of music; our world. I have seen the Floyd many times and their music remains important to me to this day. I was extremely fortunate to spend most of the weekend on stage at the 1970 Bath Festival, as I was part of the stage team and can be seen in some of the stage photos.

I WAS THERE: KELVIN SCUDAMORE

The Bath and Wilts *Evening Chronicle* reviewed this show the next day and was taken more by the light show than the music, saying 'three electricians should have taken a bow at the Pavilion, Bath last night. Instead four people took the applause – four people who had apparently haphazardly thumped out music.' The reviewer described the show as 'interesting', quoted Roger Waters and concluded with a quote from Nick Mason: 'If psychedelic is producing LSD feelings, then we are not. But if psychedelic is light and sound then we are.' The review then read, 'The rest of the group are Syd Barrett, lead guitarist, and Rick Wright, organist. The electricians are Peter Wynne-Wilson, Peter Joliffe and Les Braden.'

My own memory of the gig is more in black and white. Black and white shadows with the group making screeching noises. All I knew of the band was 'See Emily Play', so to expect all the music to be melodic was a disappointment. This was only the third or fourth band I had seen, so I didn't know too much about the 'scene' but I did think at the time that I wouldn't bother to see them again. In subsequent years, I have spoken to friends who were there (some of them musicians) and their comments were"t favourable. They were 'out of tune' at best. I suppose this was a moment in time.

I WAS THERE: MALCOLM SUTTON

I was at two gigs of Pink Floyd when they played at the Pavilion in Bath in 1967, when they released 'Arnold Layne' and then 'See Emily Play'. I was blown away by the visuals they used as a backdrop to their music. It was amazing, and I remember actually looking at the machine that was making these wonderful effects. It was a disc in front of a projector which seemed to heat up coloured liquids that were revolving and running into one another to create the patterns on the stage. I had never experienced anything like it before.

K4 DISCOTHEQUE, WEST PIER
15 APRIL 1967, BRIGHTON, UK

I WAS THERE: MARY GREEN

I was so lucky as I was living in Chalk Farm, London in the early Sixties and saw Pink Floyd at the Roundhouse. I think it must have been one of their earliest gigs. It is never to be forgotten as I had never heard anything remotely like it, and I was smitten from then on. I then moved down to Brighton and they played at the very first or second Brighton Festival. They played at the end of the West Pier where there was a small hall. It was a really still night and the music floated over the sea. It was magical. At that festival, they dyed the sea as well! Those were the days. They also played in a little club, I think in Bognor Regis, that was so small that they just walked through the audience to get to the stage. Apart from seeing them a few times up in London, they also played at the Brighton Dome. I can't remember dates or where else I saw them – it was the Sixties after all!

WISH YOU WERE HERE

ALEXANDRA PALACE
29 APRIL 1967, LONDON, UK

I WAS THERE: IRISH JACK LYONS

For the *14 Hour Technicolour Dream* at Alexandra Palace – which was meant to be a fund raiser after the newspaper had been raided – I had a hip-looking kaftan made up by my Italian tailor and miracle-man-with-a-scissors in Lillie Road, Fulham. I'd spent a lot of time studying the keyboard work of Rick from Pink Floyd, and since I couldn't play keyboards and couldn't tell a C minor from a dominant seventh, I thought the next best thing was to fashion a kaftan that would fall off my shoulders like Rick's did. The only thing was Rick Wright's kaftan fell from his shoulders with a certain majesty and grace whilst mine looked positively hideous.

I'd turned up at various Floyd gigs and made myself familiar to the band. I engaged in conversation with them and, despite their initial wariness, I managed to prise from them that they were from Cambridge, had studied architecture at Regent Street Poly and had parents who had left wing leanings. Yes, very hip. Except that wasn't completely true. Roger Waters explained with Herculean patience one night that only he and Syd were actually from Cambridge... 'not the other two'. I got the impression that Nick Mason and Rick Wright were quite happy to string me along with the completely false impression that they were all from Cambridge. Miraculously, one night after their performance at the Marquee and whilst in the Ship bar a few doors up from the club, I found myself alone with the man with the amazing eyes and the soft posh Cambridge accent.-.Syd Barrett. He had a habit of forgetting your name and just as you were about to impatiently remind him that you were on your third time of reminding, he would watch your lips move and almost simultaneously say, 'Yes, Jack, isn't it?'. Whatever we were talking about, I couldn't believe I had him on my own away from the madding crowd and at some stage in the conversation he stunned me by saying, 'I'm Roger, actually.' I was used to having the piss taken out of me by self-important artists so I ignored his sarcasm and continued our conversation feeling rather wounded. About a week later, I was talking to Roger Waters and mentioned Syd taking the piss. Roger looked at me with an incredulous expression on his face and said, 'Jack, his name's actually Roger. Syd's his nickname.'

On Saturday 29th April, I ventured up to Alexandra Palace in my 'hip' kaftan... and underneath dressed as a complete Mod. The soon-to-be-fabled *14 Hour Technicolour Dream* was already underway. There was so much going on it was impossible to take in everything. Alex Harvey, Crazy World of Arthur Brown, Social Deviants, Savoy

Brown Blues Band, The Purple Gang, Tomorrow, Soft Machine and many more bands performed. I was transfixed by a lesser-known outfit called Sam Gopal and the Indian style music, and with Sam Gopal himself on hypnotic tabla. Rumours abounded that Pink Floyd were delayed travelling back from Europe and may not even show up. Everybody seemed to be tripping. The night wore on and there was still no sign of Pink Floyd. What a wonderful world we lived in back then, with no computers and no mobile phones. Everybody just had to enjoy what was going on and hope for the best.

As dawn broke, Alexandra Palace was imbued by a strange ambience as shafts of light poured through the rose window and splayed across the floor in wide arcs. No mechanical aid or artificially applied phenomena could match such a streak of nature. Not even Rick's Azimuth Co-ordinator could have produced such natural brilliance. The pleasure area appeared to look completely different almost as if the floor had shifted somehow to the left (I had been tripping much earlier) and, now wiping the sleep from my eyes, I saw the members of Pink Floyd with their manager Peter Jenner setting things up around the stage.

I pushed my way to the front and claimed my usual spot, halfway between Rick on keyboards and Syd on guitar who, incidentally, looked like he didn't know where he was. It was all a bit of an anti-climax. Pink Floyd were the buzz name at the time and a great many people had waited all night for their arrival, but the band looked wrecked and travel weary and did not put in an inspiring performance. As the clock moved to 7am and the *Dream* limped to some kind of finale, I noticed two of my roadie friends from the Ship bar in Wardour Street, climbing the huge scaffolding surrounding the famous Ally Pally Willis organ.

They both sat perilously at the top, somehow armed with a stray microphone which they had commandeered and managed to make live on a lead extension, and began to 'propogate the faith' from their lofty perch... 'We need a bloody revolution in this country… we need freedom of expression…we need free education, free hash…' – a huge cheer from below – 'and we need someone like Pete Townshend to talk to Harold Wilson…'. I hadn't tripped well. I was itchy, tired and hadn't been to sleep for 24 hours. It was time to go home.

I WAS THERE: JENNY SPIRES

I saw Syd at the *14 Hour Technicolor Dream* and he looked physically shattered and something else; he was disaffected. He didn't seem to be enjoying it. To be fair, they had done a gig in Holland and then rushed back to play at the happening the same night, so it was inevitable that they would be tired. But the now familiar haunting and breathtaking strains of what later was to become *Piper at the Gates of Dawn* streamed across the valley from the heights of Alexandra Palace on that beautiful morning. Syd was living in the spotlight 'over the top' and was expected to be live and perform for everyone. The onus for the band was almost all on him then.

I WAS THERE: COL TURNER

I was lucky enough to be at the most acclaimed event to come out of the London hippy scene in the Sixties, the legendary *14 Hour Technicolour Dream* held at the Alexandra Palace (Ally Pally to the locals). The organisers of UFO had apparently decided that they would open UFO up to all and sundry in one big and massive happening. They had hired out a huge London venue and surprises were promised. The word was out that this was an event not to be missed. Rumours were flying thick and fast about who was to perform. Names such as The Beatles, The Who and Pink Floyd were being bandied about, but no one really knew who would be there, except the organisers. The event was due to commence at 8pm and go through to 10am the next day. I remember arriving quite late, probably around 11pm. The reports say that 10,000 people attended this happening but if they did, many must have gone home by the time we arrived. The impression I got, and still have, is that there were not that many people. There were certainly more people than at a normal UFO, and the place was enormous in comparison to the cramped cellar in Tottenham Court Road but – 10,000? I somehow think not.

The main stage area was set along the far wall from where we came in, and about halfway into the hall a second stage was set up. This was to the left, although to get to the main stage you had to skirt around the middle stage. It was a bit chaotic in that nobody seemed to know what band was to perform and on which stage they would be. This meant that we were moving from stage to stage to try to suss out who was the best to watch. I think the acoustic-type acts (including a very strange assortment of poets) were given the middle stage, with the louder rock acts on the main stage. The problem was a lot of these bands were on at the same time and were drowning each other out! Now, I will let you into a secret about that 'happening'. I believe LSD was now illegal (or it was soon after, as people were starting to get a bit paranoid about getting busted). As far as I know, the first designer drug ever to hit the market surfaced that day. From memory, it was called STP and was an offshoot of LSD. It was supposed to give you a three day trip. What has never been reported before is that it was distributed free to all who attended and wanted it. Don't ask me the details because I can't remember where it came from, but you can be assured that most of those who were there were stoned off their heads on this new acid. Also given out freely were banana skin joints, which was the fad at the time thanks to Donovan's song, 'Mellow Yellow'. (Don't try it, it doesn't work!)

Now if you have ever studied this period of time, you will know that this was the event where John Lennon first saw Yoko Ono. I didn't see Lennon but vaguely remember seeing Yoko, although I didn't pay that much attention as she was just one of the many strange and wonderful people there that night.

In all, 41 groups are supposed to have played, sang danced or recited poetry, including Yoko Ono, Binder Edwards and Vaughn, Ron Geesin, Barry Fantoni, Alexander

A PEOPLE'S HISTORY OF PINK FLOYD

Trocchi, Christopher Logue, Michael Horovitz and the 26 Kingly Street group, The Utterly Incredible Too Long Ago To Remember Sometimes Shouting at People, Alexis Korner, Champion Jack Dupree, Graham Bond, Ginger Johnson, Savoy Brown, 117, The Pretty Things, The Flies, The Purple Gang, Crazy World Of Arthur Brown, The Soft Machine and of course Pink Floyd. I have also been advised that The Creation and John's Children also performed. There are some I certainly remember but others – sorry, the mind is blank.

Arthur Brown of 'The Crazy World Of Arthur Brown' fame was as popular as Pink Floyd at that time, and deservedly so in my opinion. Every time that Arthur played, he would make the most amazing stage entrances. He would appear through trapdoors, swing in on ropes or suddenly appear in a cloud of smoke from out of nowhere. This night he decided to appear as one of his alter egos, the 'God of Hell Fire', and promptly appeared to set light to his hair! This man was utterly fantastic. He never let his audiences down and had one of the greatest voices ever. However, after Arthur's set things began to slow down and I have to admit I was getting a bit fidgety. I mean you can only take so much poetry!

I was now hanging out to see Floyd, who were star billing and not due to come on to the main stage until the early hours. We filled in the time as best we could. A lot more people were drifting off and there were a lot of empty spaces. I was hoping this was going to be worth the wait. Many of us were starting to get tired as dawn came around. Bodies were lying in huddles as people crashed out. Then the dawn arrived in a triumphant pink hue, the light came cascading in from the huge windows and, amidst this awesome display of nature, Pink Floyd took the stage. They were wearing outfits with flared trousers and satin shirts that I had not seen them wear before. People began to awake and hold hands as the first notes of, I think, 'Astronomy Domine' reverberated through the massive hall. Sadly I can't remember what else they played but my best guess would be 'Arnold Layne', 'Nick's Boogie', 'Interstellar Overdrive' (which I'm certain was the final number) and probably some other stuff from *Piper* (which was still to be released at that time), although no doubt not in that order.

I do remember the atmosphere was electric. Floyd played as gods, probably sensing that this was a very special time. There was an extraordinary connection between the band and the audience. It was as if the guys had suddenly realised that they had become great musicians but wanted to hang on to the lives they were used to, but knew at this point that there was no turning back.

Then the magic happened. Syd's mirror-disc telecaster caught the dawn's pink light. Syd noticed this and, with drug-filled eyes blazing, he made his guitar talk louder and louder, higher and higher as he reflected the light into the eyes of his audience and christened those of us lucky enough to be there as followers of Pink Floyd for life.

MOULIN ROUGE
3 MAY 1967, AINSDALE, SOUTHPORT, UK

I WAS THERE: PATRICIA WILLIAMSON-LEE

I was a student at what was then Southport Technical College when the Leavers' Ball was held at the then Moulin Rouge in Ainsdale. (It is now a Toby Carvery.) At that time, I had not heard of Pink Floyd but they had been booked as the main act. I hadn't experienced that type of music before, being more into Motown and soul. I clearly remember the psychedelic lighting all around. At the time I didn't appreciate just how famous they were to become. My brother-in-law was, and still is, a great fan of Pink Floyd and when I told him about this gig he didn't believe me!

KITSON COLLEGE
6 MAY 1967, LEEDS, UK

I WAS THERE: TONY GAVINS

Can anybody really remember those early Pink Floyd gigs, I wonder? I didn't get to the Queens Hall shows, but I was at the Kitson College one and the Leeds Town Hall and Leeds University shows. My memories of Kitson more concern the audience. The band were already on stage when we arrived, so we must have spent a little too long in the Cobourg Tavern, just over the road from the gig. As we wandered in, there appeared to be as many walking out as walking in. This is because the crowd was split between 'townies' who were hoping for a couple of hours of 'Arnold Layne'-type stuff and weren't getting it, and students who were into 'Astronomy Domine' and 'Interstellar Overdrive'. The students were wearing floppy hats and tie dye t-shirts and the townies their best suits (really!). The psychedelic projections appeared to be provided both by students from the local art college and guys with the band, although I'm not sure if that was the case. The atmosphere was like nothing we had experienced before.

This was a time when pop music was polarising. Townies were going for straight good time pop, such as Tamla Motown, and students for so-called progressive/underground music. I heard a few of those leaving complaining that the music was making them feel physically sick. It was probably the unique nature of the sounds the Floyd were creating with the very pronounced bass. We all looked so cool in 1967, with our flowing locks and colourful, hippy-dippy clothing. I recently went to see a good tribute band, Think Floyd. We all looked like we'd come from a plumbers' convention. Not at all cool.

QUEEN ELIZABETH HALL
12 MAY 1967, LONDON, UK

I WAS THERE: JENNY SPIRES

Syd was so happy. He had written a couple of good singles, 'Arnold Layne', and now, 'See Emily Play', aka 'Games For May': Syd's 'Emily' was his *Alice in Wonderland*. He had also written most of the songs for their shows now: 'Astronomy Domine', 'Chapter 24', 'The Gnome', 'Matilda Mother' and, with Rog, 'Pow R. Toc H.'. The whole resounded throughout at *Games for May* on at the Queen Elizabeth Hall. It was a triumph. Syd had his new fuzz box, a Tone Bender, and in this orbit the band came over as psychedelic, yet something quite avant-garde too. On stage they hammered and sawed wood into sound effects and an Acme whistle was blown. It was more like a happening really. Just about everyone was there, as bubbles were blown and someone else handed out daffodils, while all was bathed in Pete Wynne Willson's beautiful light show.

ST GEORGE'S BALLROOM
13 MAY 1967, HINCKLEY, UK

I WAS THERE: GRAHAM AUCOTT

We saw Pink Floyd in the mid Sixties at the St George's Ballroom. Once was enough, as we didn't understand this psychedelic music. I remember the ballroom had all its walls covered in exploding paint slides operated by roadies with a box of matches. So much for health and safety!

I WAS THERE: JOHN LEEKEY, AGE 16

I saw Pink Floyd at St George's Ballroom. They used to be groups on every week – The Troggs, The Who, Jeff Beck with Rod Stewart, Cream, The Move. But when Pink Floyd were on, just before 'See Emily Play' was out, no one had heard of them apart from 'Arnold Layne' so although me and my friend went we did not appreciate them. It was like nothing we had heard before. We went there every week to dance and drink and have a good time. With Pink Floyd you listened to the music. I stood at the back of the room with the Pink Floyd road crew and they had Bunsen burners making all the psychedelic features across all the room. It was so much ahead of its time and we told all our friends: 'We have just seen one of the groups that will change the face of music.'

 CLUB A' GO GO
19 MAY 1967, NEWCASTLE-UPON-TYNE, UK

I WAS THERE: TERRY FERGUSON, AGE 17

I paid five shillings (25p) to get in. In those days, they used a paint slide projector for background effects with lots of cables on the floor. There was no health and safety.

I WAS THERE: MARTYN WARD

I went with my girlfriend (now wife) to see Pink Floyd at the Club A' Go Go. The main purpose of going was to see if I could contact Syd Barrett, an old school pal who I had not seen for several years. Roger, as I knew him, and I were great pals at Morley Memorial School in Cambridge, where a Mrs Waters taught. We had moved on to Cambridgeshire High School for Boys in 1957. As we progressed up the school, our interests developed and changed, so we had less and less in common and hence less contact.

   The gig was post 'Arnold Layne', and was memorable for being the first psychedelic light show I (and perhaps Newcastle!) had ever seen. The club was pretty small, so there cannot have been a huge crowd there. In truth, the only number I can recall is the inevitable 'Interstellar Overdrive'. When the band left the stage, I greeted Syd who wondered what I was doing in Newcastle. (I was a student there.) We had a brief chat, but Syd's glazed eyes told a scary story and he was keen to depart. That, sadly, was the last contact I had. I was so saddened by Syd's subsequent decline and demise, but I have many happy memories of a cheery, funny, talented childhood friend.

FLORAL HALL
20 MAY 1967, SOUTHPORT, UK

I WAS THERE: BILL BEAVER, AGE 19

In the late spring of 1967, I was somehow led to make the 15-mile trek from Leyland to Southport to see an up-and-coming group, who had just had their first hit with a song about some deviant whose raison d'être was stealing clothes from washing lines. I was aware from the press and TV that Pink Floyd were part of the so-called psychedelic scene and I liked their single 'Arnold Layne'. My own favourite artists at the time were The Beatles, who in February had trailered the psychedelia of *Sgt. Pepper* with the acid-soaked 'Strawberry Fields'. I also liked The Kinks and The Bee Gees, as well as Tamla and soul acts such as The Four Tops and Otis Redding. I was suffering from some kind of musical and sartorial schizophrenia; I couldn't decide if I wanted to be a Mod or something else (the 'something else' being whatever The Beatles were). I went with a group of some five friends, but I can't remember where or how I heard about the concert, or even how I got there – or back!

I have a clearer recollection of what happened outside the venue than the concert itself. As we walked along the wide pavement outside the Floral Hall, two or three of our group became slightly separated from us. They were approached by a gang of young Liverpudlians, one of whom asked, 'Can you lend us thrippence (3d, equivalent to about 1p) for the bus?' When this request was refused, a knife was produced, which had the desired effect of extorting rather more than 'thrippence'. So much for the Summer of Love!

The venue itself was a typical Fifties/Sixties ballroom, which until the beat boom of the early Sixties had hosted rather more sedate gatherings, with bands catering for ballroom dance devotees with an endless supply of quicksteps, fox trots and waltzes. Pink Floyd seemed oddly out of place. The audience, which probably numbered about a couple of hundred, was largely composed of Mods – short hair, sharp suits with ridiculously long vents and brogues – and the support was a Tamla/soul disco. The sound quality was good by Sixties standards. As for the Floyd, I'm sorry to say that I wasn't familiar with the line-up. In fact, they came over as fairly faceless characters. They played with their heads down making little, if any, eye contact with the audience, seemingly totally absorbed in their music. Or quite possibly, they wished they were somewhere else, rather than playing their hit in a provincial dance hall to a crowd of uninterested Mods.

The only time I remember anyone speaking was when (I assume) Syd Barrett mumbled, almost grudgingly, 'This one's called 'Arnold Layne'.' What really fascinated

Clockwise from top left: Mary Green doesn't remember much about the Sixties; Graham Aucott and many others in the provinces didn't get psychedelic music; Martyn Ward (seated, fourth left, and pictured left) didn't need to look cool in the Sixties – he had street cred from going to Morley Memorial School, Cambridge with the boy he knew as Roger but known to the world as Syd (circled in red)

BARBEQUE 67

**TULIP BULB AUCTION HALL
SPALDING, LINCS.**

Non-stop Dancing 4 p.m. (in afternoon) to 12 p.m. (at night)
SPRING BANK HOLIDAY MONDAY, MAY 29th
To the top six —
**JIMI HENDRIX EXPERIENCE   CREAM
GENO WASHINGTON AND THE RAM JAM
BAND   MOVE
   PINK (PSYCHEDELIC) FLOYD
ZOOT MONEY AND HIS BIG ROLL BAND**
All supported by **SOUNDS FORCE FIVE**
Licensed Bar applied for. Hot Dogs. Covered accommodation.
Ultra Violet Lighting Knockout Atmosphere.
Discotheque from 4 p.m. Admission £1 (pay at the door).
Or Tickets in advance from Clarke's (Music Services), 16 Broad
Street, Spalding; Fords of Spalding Ltd., Priory House, 3 The
Crescent, Spalding.   LG26-5L

Clockwise from top left: Marilyn Leader didn't tell her parents she was going to a pop festival 60 miles away with two boys she had only just met; Margaret Hersom hasn't been a fan since realising she couldn't dance to the Floyd; it was all happening in Spalding me was the strange back drop – oil on slides and projected onto screens. It was primitive indeed by today's standards, but certainly innovative in 1967. The only other chart groups I'd seen live up until then were Manfred Mann, The Troggs and Pinkerton's Assorted Colours (the latter two miming their latest hits at the local Top Rank) and none of them had any backdrops as such.

As for what the group played, I have to come clean and admit that I recognised only 'Arnold Layne'. Due to my short concentration span at the time (and now), 'three-minute classic pop singles' appealed to me and 'Arnold Layne' fell neatly into this category. The rest of the material played on the night did not, being largely meandering free-form instrumentals. These didn't endear the group to the audience, most of whom wanted their disco back. I seem to remember that they played two sets with the disco in between. The final heresy I have to report is that Pink Floyd were actually subjected to muted, but none-the-less audible, slow handclapping by the no-nonsense Lancastrian audience, or at least some of them. I didn't join in – I was still mesmerised by the slides.

I WAS THERE: TOMMY FLUDE

I was in a band from Liverpool called Solomon's Mines. We were playing the Cavern one night when our manager said to us, 'We're on in Southport in a couple of weeks.' We said 'who with?' and he said, 'Well, either John Mayall, or this band from London.' I was a very keen John Mayall fan at the time and I was most disappointed when he then said it was going to be the band from London, whose name he couldn't remember. On the night, it was quite a big hall and there were a lot of people in there, 1,000 or so. When we'd finished our set, we took our gear off the stage and took it out to the side door to load the van up. Then we went back in for a couple of beers and watched the guys from London. I remember going in and thinking that the music wasn't very impressive. We didn't know any of the songs, and it was monotonous and non-melodic, and quite heavy in its drumming and bass. But they had this screen behind them, with a backdrop of jellies and bubbles and psychedelia going on in all these different colours, and we stopped for ten minutes and thought 'what's happening here?'. We were intrigued by the projection.

I WAS THERE: JACK JONES

We were Mods and we went to the Floral Hall every Saturday night as there was always a gig on. It wasn't Motown, but the people appreciated a good band anyway. I didn't go out and buy the records but I did like listening to their music. I remember watching one of the roadies doing the light show, which was a projector with slides of oil and coloured water. He blew on them with a hairdryer and the images were projected onto a screen.

I had seen them at the Moulin Rouge in Ainsdale just a couple of weeks before, when they played the art college ball. We were a crowd of people that went to all the gigs at the Floral Hall. It had top bands on every week in that era, everyone apart from The Beatles and the Rolling Stones. I was at a party a few years ago and bumped into a bloke who used to be the assistant manager at the Floral Hall. He told me, 'I got into trouble for paying £265 for Fleetwood Mac. But I got into even more trouble the following year when I booked Pink Floyd and it cost £450 quid!'

GROSMONT WOOD FARM
25 MAY 1967, CARDIFF, UK

I WAS THERE: JACQUELINE YOUNG

I saw and spoke to Pink Floyd in May 1967 at a barn dance in Grosmont, South Wales. Syd Barrett was lovely. He wrote a poem for me after reading a poem my mum had written in my autograph book. He was scruffy and a bit smelly in a fur gilet thing he was wearing, but he had a lot of patience with a young fan. I got their autographs which were lost when I moved house. They were playing with Fleetwood Mac, and Mick Fleetwood was incredibly tall! I saw Pink Floyd a few times after that. They even sneaked me in through the fire escape once when I didn't have a ticket!

TULIP BULB AUCTION HALL
29 MAY 1967, SPALDING, UK

I WAS THERE: MIKE WATTS

Barbecue '67 at the Tulip Bulb Auction Hall is often referred to now as Britain's first rock festival, but back then it was just an opportunity to catch a lot of great bands in one place on a Whitsun bank holiday for £1. My friends Dave, Keith, Steve and I drove up to Spalding from South London in Dave's rather grand 1950s Austin Princess. We arrived in the afternoon just as Floyd were starting their set. They'd just scored a chart hit with 'Arnold Layne', but were very much at the bottom end of the bill. They were playing to a sparse crowd on a low stage at the back of a tulip bulb warehouse with their liquid light-show projected onto a white sheet behind them. My abiding memory is of Syd Barrett sitting cross-legged on the deck for much of the performance. I'd seen them a month before at the *14 Hour Technicolour Dream* when they memorably played as dawn broke over Alexandra Palace and theirs seemed the most fitting music of the event. They had a much harder job to make an impact in Spalding but, to be fair, they were having to contend with barbequed burgers, baking hot weather and fellow headliners Cream, Geno Washington and Jimi Hendrix!

I WAS THERE: MARILYN LEADER, AGE 15

I was in my last year at school in Leicestershire. My friends and I used to do some washing up at the university halls after school and at the end of each week we would walk down the main road to go and collect our wages. We were walking down the main road one day when this car pulled up and these two boys started talking to us. They were from London. I never did work out what they were doing going towards Leicester. They said, 'What are you doing this afternoon?' and asked us if we would like to go to a pop festival in Lincolnshire. We said 'we don't know'. They said Jimi Hendrix was playing so we readily agreed to go with them. They mentioned other groups as well, but they didn't mention Pink Floyd. We came from very respectable homes so we told our parents that we were going into Leicester and then babysitting in the evening so we would be home late. They would never have let us go otherwise. We didn't really have much idea where we were going or who else was on the bill part from Hendrix.

We arrived at a large barn in Spalding and joined a lot of people trying to get in through a sliding door. My friend got in but I hadn't when the door closed. I went round the back looking for a way to get in and found the stage door. By this time, we knew that, amongst others, Jimi Hendrix, Pink Floyd, Cream and Zoot Money were due to perform. I chose the least well-known name, Zoot Money, told the doorman I was his wife and he let me in. It was already very crowded but I found my friend and we got a place to stand somewhere quite near the front. Although I was quite young, I had already seen a lot of live bands but Pink Floyd were quite magical. I loved the way they looked, especially Syd Barrett. And it was the first light show I'd ever seen, with lots of pink and green.

Afterwards, we found out where Jimi Hendrix was staying and went to try and get his autograph but he wouldn't come out of the hotel. Mitch Mitchell and Noel Redding did though. The former wrote his name on my arm using moles as dots for the Is. I kept my arm covered in a plastic bag for weeks. Then we had to find a way of getting home so we started hitch-hiking. It was usually very easy to get a lift if you were female. Some Mods in a Mini stopped for us. It was quite a squash with six of us in there and quite a distance back to Leicester, on mostly rural roads. My parents were not at all pleased when I arrived home in what must have been the early hours of the morning. They didn't believe my babysitting story.

In the Seventies, a friend's sister married Nick Mason and we went to several parties at his house in Highgate but I didn't meet him – because the parties were always when he was away!

 COLLEGE OF ART
9 JUNE 1967, HULL, UK

I WAS THERE: SUE ADAMSON, AGE 17

Three friends and I attended the Pink Floyd gig at the Hull College of Art. Unfortunately, we only stayed until maybe the end of the second number, as it was so loud it was too painful on the ears! We were accustomed to loud PA systems as my boyfriend at the time played regularly in a local band. The acoustics in the college probably didn't help, as I recall it was an odd-shaped room with large pillars here and there, which would probably have bounced the sound all over the place. It certainly didn't stop me from enjoying their music in subsequent years.

I WAS THERE: MARGARET HERSOM (NEE JOHNSON)

I was at the Pink Floyd gig at Hull College of Art in 1967 and wasn't impressed. My friends and I loved to dance (it was a 'going down' dance, after all) and after a few minutes of Pink Floyd realised they weren't a group to dance to. After what seemed like 15 minutes of one number, a lot of people had drifted off. I've never been a fan after that initial experience.

I WAS THERE: DON MAGUIRE

I was 17, 18 at the time. I was at a football end of the season get together and someone said 'the Floyd are on at the art college tonight', which was only a small venue. We dived in a couple of taxis about nine or ten o'clock to go there. What sticks in my mind is that it was six shillings (30p) to get in, and I think we got away with only paying five shillings (25p) because the guys on the door were all ex local rugby players and they used to take a little bribe. We got in and it wasn't that full. The thing that struck me was the light show. I'd never seen anything like it. It was all pink and pale blue and sepia. It was unbelievable. 'Arnold Layne' had been a hit by this stage. The art college was on Anlaby Road and about half a mile away there's a little lane that goes off under the flyover and it's called Arnold Lane. And I remember a guy turning round to me and saying, 'It's fantastic how they managed to write a song about Hull.'

TOWN HALL
14 JUNE 1967, FARNBOROUGH, UK

I WAS THERE: IAN MILLER-HALL, AGE 19

I went with my 17-year-old brother and some mates. Syd Barrett and co were an eye-opener with their magic lantern show et al. Syd mentioned their new single, 'See Emily Play'. There were 17 people in the audience and we were bemused by some of the music they played.

This gig is unverified.

'SEE EMILY PLAY' RELEASED
16 JUNE 1967

'See Emily Play' is Pink Floyd's second single. It reaches No. 6 in the UK charts. The band appear on BBC Television's Top of the Pops three times to promote the single. The second appearance, on 13 July 1967, finds Syd unenthusiastic and complaining that 'John Lennon doesn't do Top of the Pops'.

LOCARNO BALLROOM
23 JUNE 1967, DERBY, UK

I WAS THERE: TEZ MARTIN

We supported Pink Floyd at the Rolls-Royce Apprentices Ball at the Locarno. Our band was called Thorndike Mordecai Imagination and I was the bass player. Syd Barrett was with them then. They were just making a name for themselves. People knew the name and were aware of their first couple of singles. On the night we didn't take much notice of them.

We played all the current R&B things, like most local bands, and a couple of original songs. The Locarno had a revolving stage. We went on first, then the stage revolved, we went round to the back and they came round to the front. You got set up around the back and then, when the previous act finished, the stage rotated and you were straight on, so it kept the continuity.

They had a very, very primitive light show at the time, basically a big white sheet draped over the amplifiers and a projector that projected the weird colours and the stroboscopic type effects onto the sheet. The dance floor cleared when they went on because obviously you couldn't dance to the music that they were doing then, although they did loads of gigs that year.

Because it was so unusual, everybody was stood around the perimeter of the dance floor and most people were making comments along the lines of 'these are shit'. It was just too weird at the time. The audience wasn't like the type of audience they would have had at the UFO Club. That was a pretty innovative sort of thing that they had going on down in London. You hadn't got an audience like that in the north. It was just a bit too strange for everybody.

We shared a dressing room with them but we didn't interact with them much at all. Looking back, we supported the Graham Bond Organisation at the Rialto in Derby and they had Jack Bruce and Ginger Baker with them, who later went on to form Cream with Eric Clapton. But we didn't take any notice of them either!

PAVILION
3 JULY 1967, BATH, UK

I WAS THERE: PETER CLINICK

I saw Pink Floyd at the Bath Pavilion. I am not sure which date, but the one thing that stuck in my memory is of the light show (the liquid wheel, etc) and the fact that for some reason they played with their backs to the audience for almost all the gig. All except Nick Mason, who obviously didn't.

STOWMARKET CARNIVAL
15 JULY 1967, STOWMARKET, UK

I WAS THERE: NIGEL BRAY, AGE 14

My late father, Ivan, was a member of the Round Table association and on the Carnival Committee. He was contacted on the afternoon of the carnival, presumably by the group's manager, saying that their motor home/caravan was delayed and they needed somewhere to freshen up and use as a base camp before moving to the concert site and dressing rooms later that evening. My father agreed to allow them to use our house for this purpose but without first warning my mother that they were on their way. She had no idea who they were, of course, or what was going on.

Looking back, the events of that day were quite amusing and I often wonder if the surviving members of the band recall them. Picture if you will number 30 Chilton Avenue, Stowmarket – a typical double bay-fronted 1930s semi, with a narrow drive by the side of the house leading to a rather run down garage with double wooden doors with frosted glass panels at the very top. I arrived home on my pushbike to find the kitchen window and one of the garage doors open. Standing outside the kitchen window was a very tall man with long hair, where my mother was handing him a glass of water through the open window and instructing him to 'stay there!'. This, of course, was Roger Waters. As I got nearer to the garage, I realised there were three other men and two young women in there. I remember the girls looked like Susan George in Afghan coats – hippies, I guess.

Inside the garage, my mother had assembled deck chairs, card tables, towels, soap and water, and a few nibbles and drinks in a makeshift changing room. Apparently, she preferred that they didn't come in the house because they 'looked unkempt'. She informed me that she was going to have a word with my father for inviting these scruffy young people to use our home as their headquarters.

Still not fully appreciating quite who I was in the presence of, I made the acquaintance of Roger Waters, Syd Barrett, Rick Wright and Nick Mason. It was great – and so different! They gave me a signed promotional A3 sized photograph of the band (in top hats, I think) posing with mannequins. This was rolled up into a cardboard cylinder and kept safe for many years. Sadly, when my parents passed away a search of their house revealed nothing. How I wish I still had it, and autographed by all four great musicians.

The only other thing I remember my dad mentioning, apart from the mix up with their caravan that left them with nowhere to freshen up, was that – via their manager, I imagine – they requested half of the £150 fee up front. These ridiculously small sums really do put things in perspective when you consider the worldwide popularity which was to eventually follow.

It was somewhat lost on me at the time, but it's kind of surreal thinking about it all now. The small provincial market town of Stowmarket in Suffolk didn't know quite what had hit it that evening: a culture shock and introduction into psychedelia and the beginnings of a new wave of almost life-changing music!

I WAS THERE: VALERIE CLEMENTS, AGE 15

My friend Lynda and I were both 15 and went to the concert. Before it started, we decided to try and obtain their autographs and managed to seek them out. No one had got any paper to write on, so they signed their autographs on our arms. I don't think we washed them off for quite a while! I also remember the band getting changed in Ivan and Jean Bray's garage, who were friends of my parents, as they lived near the cricket meadow.

I WAS THERE: MIKE HAYDON

I was a member of the Stowmarket Round Table who employed Pink Floyd to give an evening performance on the Cricket Meadow in Stowmarket. We hired them because they were cheap, never realising that about one week later their first record would be successfully issued. Music 'festivals' were rare then, certainly for Stowmarket. They gave an inspiring performance of a new style of music for us and were supported by a number of camp followers and, I'd estimate, 1,000 locals. The event was the finale to the Town Carnival Day and we in Round Table submitted a float in the carnival in the afternoon, with many of us dressed as pink ladies, supposedly for publicity for the event in the evening. Why as 'ladies' I cannot recall, and certainly none of us have taken to crossdressing since. It was a charity function but I don't recall it being a great financial success. I don't imagine Pink Floyd will recall it either. The decibels did really upset the locals. We got more press from that than from bringing this inspirational talent to the town!

I WAS THERE: ERIC ALLARD, AGE 17

They came to the sleepy little town of Stowmarket and played at the town's annual carnival. It was round about the time that 'See Emily Play' was in the charts. There were three bands booked on the bill to support them, including my band which was called Our Generation. I think they'd been booked a few months beforehand. The story goes that they did it for a cheaper fee than they would have charged because it was booked before their career had started to take off big time. So we probably got them for a bargain price. They certainly got paid a lot more than we did.

Clockwise from top left: Sue Adamson walked out of the Hull Art College gig because Floyd were too loud; Tez Martin (third left) rocks the Roy Orbison look; John Fletcher saw David Gilmour's pre-Floyd band, Joker's Wild, and thought they were indeed a joke; confirming the British male's tendency to don a frock at the earliest opportunity, Mike Haydon was one of those who dragged up as the 'Pink Ladies' to advertise Pink Floyd in Stowmarket; Peter Clinick recalls the Floyd having their backs to the audience in an early version of 'the Poznan'

Clockwise from top left: Desiree Shelley decided not to tell her parents she was off to get stoned and have free love at Stowmarket Carnival; Eric Allard's band Our Generation on the Stowmarket carnival float; For hippy Lindsay Fulcher, Floyd coming to Stowmarket was like a visit by aliens; Valerie Clements decided to go on the slide in the Swinging Sixties; Stowmarket Carnival advert

We were quite actively involved because I don't think Stowmarket had really heard of Pink Floyd in those days. It was called 'underground' music then. I'd heard of them but not really listened to them. It was a completely different experience for myself because we were playing more soul music, which was very much in vogue in the mid-Sixties. We took our band on a carnival float and mimed to some of our own stuff to promote the concert. Some people thought *we* were Pink Floyd!

It was a football and cricket meadow. I can't remember the running order. We may well have been the first band up. We played on a lorry trailer with bales of hay. We had about two feet of space to stand in and I remember it was quite cramped. I think they played in the stand on the main stage, but we were on a side trailer because, logistically, they had to swap bands around and they were already set up with all their gear. We did our set and then the two other bands played and then Pink Floyd closed the show. It was very different music to what we had been listening to. Being a guitar player I very much appreciated it but I'm not sure that everybody else understood it.

They were a great band. The only regret I have is that I don't think anybody took any photos of them. It was certainly an experience. After that I got hooked and bought some of the early albums. I hadn't really listened to them before. It opened my eyes. I'm still playing. I play for my own amusement. I did a little tribute to Floyd on Facebook, a version of 'See Emily Play', to mark the 50th anniversary of the carnival. I just did the guitar parts. With a bit of loud guitar and a few other bits and pieces you can get somewhere near it.

I WAS THERE: LINDSAY FULCHER, AGE 15

As country cousin hippies, we turned up to see Pink Floyd that summer's evening in our paisley or African print kaftans and flares (this was pre-loons) and floaty dresses, wearing flowers in our hair and with cowbells on thongs, carrying lighted joss sticks. As I look back now it was all a bit of a patchouli haze! I was 15 and rather nervous of taking drugs but I was already drinking – probably cider! Pink Floyd, including Syd, arrived like beautiful ethereal aliens from another planet. It was exciting for us as we had heard of Pink Floyd but it wasn't at all crowded and we could walk up to the stage if we had dared. It was all very relaxed and not really big deal at all. They were just starting out, otherwise what would they have been doing in Stowmarket?

They only had about six speakers, piled on either side of the stage and their 'light show' consisted of rainbow-coloured bubbles projected onto a not very large screen above them. But their music was magical and quite unlike anything else we'd ever heard. 'See Emily Play' had been released only a few weeks before and was at number three in the Top 40. The concert ended at 11.30pm!

The next time I saw Pink Floyd was at Earl's Court in May 1973, when a large-scale model plane flew over the audience and crashed into a sun disc above the stage with a spectacular explosion. By then they had added quite a few more speakers that stood like high towers at either side of the stage. It was quite a transformation from Stowmarket and that six speaker set up.

I WAS THERE: WILLIAM MARTIN

I could not believe the advert in the *East Anglian Daily Times* that Pink Floyd were playing at Stowmarket Carnival. I had already bought the singles 'Arnold Layne' and 'See Emily Play', so off I went. The stage was at the side of the field and not too far away was the funfair. The stage consisted of two lorry trailers surrounded by scaffold poles covered in tarpaulins. I was at the front next to the stage and so close to the group. There was a large crowd in front of the stage but many people just walked by, not knowing who they were. I can remember one or two lighting towers to project colour slides onto the group. I can also remember the roadies, etc., with very long hair and wearing tight, brightly coloured loon pants. I expect they played some of the LP, *The Piper at the Gates Of Dawn*, which was coming out in August.

Looking back now I was lucky to see them in 1967 and it was indeed a magical concert. I went on to see them another six times, including both their Knebworth appearances, Wembley and *Live 8*. And twice at Earl's Court, the last time being 15th October 1994, which was the last concert of their last ever tour.

I WAS THERE: DESIREE SHELLEY

I was just a young teenager and wasn't allowed to go by my parents, so it was a time of deceits and lies! It was also a magical time for us emerging hippies, where life was full of flowers and free love. I contacted my friend who I went to the event with and we had such a laugh. We were actually stoned most of the time so I can't remember much at all (but don't tell the kids or grandchildren!). My friend also reminded me that we went to London to see them in Hyde Park, which had been erased from my memory completely. Life was so much easier then. Yes, we were rebels and disobeyed the parents, but it was all harmless fun. Kids today have far too much stress in their unexciting lives.

50 years later I am a qualified medical herbalist having worked throughout my life as a nurse. I trained at Addenbrookes in Cambridge where I worked with Rosie Barrett, Syd's sister. Today I am a champion for using cannabis for medical care. CBD oil is accepted medically to be an effective pain killer and a treatment for cancer and many other health benefits. So life comes full circle. Here's looking forward to the next revolution!

VENUE UNKNOWN
SUMMER 1967, ST TROPEZ, FRANCE

I WAS THERE: JOHN FLETCHER
I first saw Dave Gilmour in summer 1967 at a small club in southern France, near St Tropez, where I was staying with the Gilmours, being a university flatmate of Pete, Dave's brother. He was playing with most of Jokers Wild, his Cambridge group, and I was frankly underwhelmed. There was no hint of the superstardom to come and they were like any average band, unlike the obvious talent I had witnessed many times before in relatively unknown bands like The Animals, The Big Three, The Yardbirds, Mayall with Clapton and so on. However, Dave obviously gelled in Floyd after 1968. Pete and I were again with the Gilmours that summer in New York and Dave visited our Bristol flat around the time he was joining Pink Floyd. We all loved their music and played what I called the *Emily Lane* LP over and over. Pete brought it back from New York.

I WAS THERE: BARRY GAWTHROP
My local school band was Jokers Wild, who had David Gilmour on guitar, who later joined Pink Floyd. Locals did not understand their music unless you were on the same drugs. At the time, the local band that could pack venues was The Soul Committee, a seven piece-brass section. Dick Parry was in the group and went on to work with Pink Floyd.

REDCAR JAZZ CLUB, COATHAM HOTEL
16 JULY 1967, REDCAR, UK

I WAS THERE: BRIAN SMITH
I booked them for Redcar Jazz Club – over 50 years ago now! The contract was made on 12th April 1967 by our London agent, Jim Godbolt Agency Ltd, and signed on their behalf by AE King. The terms were to appear for one evening performance for a maximum of one hour, split into two separate sessions, with all the group's gear to be set up by 6.30pm. They would take to the stage at 8pm. The contract included many additional clauses which we imposed on all our booked groups. Our support act that night was the Silverstone Set (who would also do two sessions, the first starting at

7.30pm). The contracted salary for Pink Floyd was £200 guaranteed or 60 per cent of the evening's gate, whichever was the higher. The actual attendance figure was 691 (consisting of members and guests) giving a cash return of £252 – making a small profit for the club after other band costs were taken into consideration. Our official capacity was 1,000, which included seated at tables and standing.

A rather unusual happening occurred just prior to Pink Floyd taking the stage. The roadies were setting up the group's light show from a position towards the back of the ballroom on a specially prepared table which had on it the single lamp to be used and several powerful slide projectors. Some commotion was occurring and one of the roadies caught my attention and pointed out that there was a problem with the light show equipment and it was not working correctly. I was unavailable to help in any way so brought in my wife, Jean, to assist. She was at the time was doing other duties in the club. She promptly got sat down at the table and got the equipment working to everybody's satisfaction. Her recollection of what she did 'was to play around with some liquids on the slide projector and get the correct focus on the stage backcloth, manipulating the lamp etc. until a positive reaction was given to me from the front stage occupants.' Her efforts worked and she got the 'show on the road'. The psychedelic effect of the light and colour, said to be essential to the group's music, thankfully happened. I heard it said later in the evening by the roadies that this equipment had been giving problems in the recent weeks.

I WAS THERE: NEV HENDERSON

I was guitarist in a local group, The Delmonts, that played Sixties music and particularly Beach Boys numbers. I was also on the committee of the Redcar Jazz Club. On Pink Floyd's visit to the club, and after the support act had finished their first set, my main recollection was of all these Marshall speaker cabinets being piled on top of each other on the stage. There seemed to be loads of them. Then the road crew proceeded to drape white sheets over them. I was now totally confused. When they started to play, I thought that I had never heard such a loud band ever. There was a sense of bewilderment with this loud cacophony of sound. However the audience loved them and showed their appreciation.

The reason for the white sheets then became clear. All these colourful liquid-like shapes began running all over the sheets, stop for a moment and then begin running again. This procedure continued throughout the show, but I was still puzzled. Then I saw a person with a projector at the rear of the hall, a blow torch in one hand and a hairdryer in the other. A substance was squeezed from a tube (possibly oil paint) and heated with the blow torch to make it run. This was then cooled with the hairdryer to make it stop. This action was projected onto the stage sheeting, creating this great psychedelic effect. The performance itself was enjoyable, yet deafening, with their early hit singles, 'Arnold Layne' and 'See Emily Play', and the manic energy of Syd Barrett commanding the evening. I remember thinking afterwards that the only words I heard during the performance were 'there are no other words' from 'See Emily Play'. However they must have had some effect on me, since I now own several of their CDs and listen to their music.

TWO RED SHOES
20 JULY 1967, ELGIN, UK

I WAS THERE: MIKE GORDON
When they played Albert Bonici's Two Red Shoes in Elgin, I couldn't afford to go to the show but I watched some of the rear of the backdrop screen through an open back stage door. It was so different from other groups at that time.

BALLERINA BALLROOM
21 JULY 1967, NAIRN, UK

I WAS THERE: PAULINE ISAACS
The first Floyd gig I attended was in 1967 in a wee dance hall called the Ballerina Ballroom in the small Moray town of Nairn, near to Inverness. Following the release of 'Arnold Layne' and 'See Emily Play', we expected to see some more of the standard three minute pop song material but what we saw and heard was something completely different. The Ballerina Ballroom was only a small place and there were probably only about 200 to 300 youngsters present. Being 1967, the band members wore flowery shirts and kaftans, as did most of the audience. Their music was unlike anything I had ever heard before and we soon realised that we couldn't dance to the music. Each track played on for about 20 minutes and we just stood and swayed to these long music tracks. The backdrop was also something the likes of which we hadn't experienced before, a psychedelic light show which looked like ink blobs on wax. It was so new and quite revolutionary.

I WAS THERE: CHRIS KEARNEY

My dad, Dennis Kearney, saw Pink Floyd when they played the Ballerina Ballroom in Nairn back in 1967, when he was 19 years old. He's remained a big fan of Pink Floyd ever since seeing them that night. He recalls that you couldn't actually see the band as they were behind a screen, with all the patterns and sounds being projected. He also remembers meeting them after they played and doesn't recall getting a full conversation out of them. He shook hands with them. When he shook Syd Barrett's hand and tried speaking to him, Syd opened his mouth and a fake tongue fell out.

I WAS THERE: ROB MULLEN

I was on a weekend break in Nairn. There was a concert on the Saturday night at the local Town Hall and Pink Floyd was the only band playing! I remember 'Pow. R. Toc. H' and 'Interstellar Overdrive'.

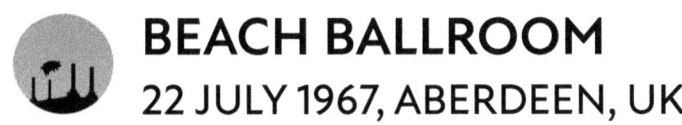

BEACH BALLROOM
22 JULY 1967, ABERDEEN, UK

I WAS THERE: IAIN WOLSTENHOLME

I saw Pink Floyd in Aberdeen in 1967. Having spoken with chums who were also there, we think that cost of admission must have been less than ten shillings (50p) as they were a bit new, despite having charted with their first two 45s, 'Arnold Layne' and 'See Emily Play'' which, if I remember correctly, they omitted from their set. It seems that, even at this early stage, they could not trust Syd Barrett to perform his self-penned numbers reliably so they just ignored them. It also might explain why they used backing tapes when 'live' on stage. It was the first time we had experienced this and it was done in such an obvious way. We just could not understand at the time, yards away from the band, how the music kept going while a couple of members wandered about clearly not actually playing anything as the music continued. The only ones rooted to the spot were the rhythm section members of Waters and Mason.

That is what it looked like to us anyway, and we had only had a couple of drinks, and certainly nothing mind-altering in those early days of burgeoning psychedelia. We might have been mesmerised by the light show, but neither that nor the overall performance were that great. I suppose we expected to hear the hits played by chart groups in those early days of rock 'n' beat! Pink Floyd in the shape of Roger Waters liked to think they had progressed beyond soul music and were in some way superior. I remember him kind of doing down the early soul movement in an interview.

Initially, I bought 'Apples and Oranges'/'Paint Box', 'It Would Be So Nice'/'Julia Dream' and 'Point Me at the Sky'/'Careful With That Axe, Eugene' – three non-album and, as it turned out, non-charting singles. Syd's early music was very inventive and clearly influenced the other band members' writing at the time, and it is sad he burned out so soon.

Zoot Money's Dantalian's Chariot appeared a couple of weeks after at the same venue. We spoke to Zoot Money's light show operatives and told them their show was better than the Floyd's and they were rather pleased, but probably knew already that they were ahead of that fashionable game. For a brief moment, their light shone brighter and crazier than that of Pink Floyd.

I WAS THERE: ARTHUR WYLLIE

I saw Pink Floyd when they appeared at the Beach Ballroom while 'See Emily Play' was in the charts. This was my first experience of seeing a top group there and it was the probably the worst that I have ever seen. They were so bad that I did not even recognise 'See Emily Play'. The only act that could rival them for being so bad was The Casuals. They could not even play their instruments.

COSMOPOLITAN BALLROOM
23 JULY 1967, CARLISLE, UK

I WAS THERE: PETER WILSON

The main act of the night was the pop band The Fortunes. The place was full as usual. It appeared that there was no place on the main stage for the Floyd so they were in the area that led to the foyer and cloakrooms with an access to the upper bars. The Floyd set up. Cue the music and fire up the oil lamps and the lighting bouncing along the curving wall. This was a first experience of the Cosmo for me although I had previous as a college boy in London.

The sad thing that haunts me to this day is that people were passing by the Floyd to go either to the bars or cloakrooms. Did they take it in it? Did they appreciate that It was different, a new era, or were they worried that they might lose their place at the front of stage when The Fortunes performed? When people ask me about the music scene of the Sixties, it's a tale I tell about the night The Fortunes took the Floyd to the wall.

I WAS THERE: TERRY MAXTED, AGE 22

I believe I was a member of the support band for the Pink Floyd gig, although it is notoriously difficult to remember anything from the 1960s with certainty! The band was The Cordettes (not very cool sounding, but it was inherited). We also supported The Who at the Market Hall about a year earlier. I seem to remember being a bit disappointed by both the Floyd and their light show, which consisted mostly of projected oil slides. Many bands at the time had good nights and not so good nights, possibly due to equipment not being as reliable as it is now. There was a story that Pink Floyd had tried to borrow a Hammond Organ from local musician Brian Atkinson and that he had refused the request, implying that they were at least having keyboard problems so may have had other issues to deal with.

TOP OF THE POPS STUDIO
27 JULY 1967, LONDON, UK

I WAS THERE: JENNY SPIRES

The next big schedule was 'See Emily Play' and the *Top of the Pops* performances. The final one was to become the final and absolute non-event for Syd. By this time, I was watching from the side lines because Syd had been all but whisked away and into the music business. He had become hot property and was to take his roll call in *Top of the Pops*. He was no longer able, it seemed, just to hang out and had no time to stop. 101 Cromwell Road, where he was living then, was a notorious place where we all used to hang out the year before, playing music and talking. Occasionally, the band rehearsed there too in the very early days when Rog Waters also lived there.

The Floyd now needed yet another single, and their album *Piper at the Gates of Dawn* was on the horizon, most of which Syd had conceived. Then, they had an American tour booked, followed by one with Hendrix in the UK.

THE PIPER AT THE GATES OF DAWN RELEASED
5 AUGUST 1967

Pink Floyd's first album, largely written by Syd Barrett, reached No.6 in the UK album charts.

THE REDCAR JAZZ CLUB

COATHAM HOTEL   7 p.m.   THIS SUNDAY

THE

PINK FLOYD

PLUS

THE SILVERSTONE SET

Members 7/-   Guests 8/6

JULY 23rd THE MOODY BLUES

WINDSOR BALLROOM   FRIDAY, 21st JULY   8 p.m. to 1 a.m.

THE ALAN BOWN SET
THE REAL McCOY
THE SKYLINERS

TICKETS 10/-   Licensed bar.

Modern Dancing Enterprises

SATURDAY, 15th JULY

ASSEMBLY ROOMS ELGIN	VICTORIA BALLROOM FORRES
THE T-SET	NEWTON'S THEORY Plus—THE GO-GO GIRLS
8-8.30 p.m.—3/- After 8.30 p.m.—5/6	8.45-11.45 Admission 6/- Bus returns to Kinloss and Findhorn

TWO RED SHOES BALLROOM
Columbia Recording Stars...
Latest release—"See Emily Play"
Into the Charts—
Melody Maker/New Musical Express
First week—Position 27—Watch it climb!

THE PINK FLOYD
This is the group that brings its own lighting to set the scene oscillating and vibrating with Way Out Sets
Also starring—THE COPYCATS
Need we say more! Only note the date—
THURSDAY, 20th JULY
Note the place—ELGIN
9 p.m. - 1 a.m.   Admission 8/6
Buses from Buckie, Forres, etc.

KEITH—LONGMORE HALL
FRIDAY, 21st JULY
A double attraction—The fab sets
THE SLATER STREET FEW
—Plus—**THE RISING SUN**
9 p.m. - 1.30 a.m.   Admission 6/-
Buses from Elgin, Buckie via coast, Huntly, Aberlour, Craigellachie and Dufftown, 8.30 p.m.

FRIDAY, 28th JULY—
THE POWERHOUSE—Plus—**THE REBEL SOUNDS**

Tel: ELGIN 7058 and 7803

LATE TRAINS FROM REDCAR (Sunday)
Last two trains to Middlesbrough and Thornaby: 10-45 p.m. and 11-8 p.m.
Last two trains to Saltburn: 11-3 p.m. and 11-33 p.m.

CLUB DANCES
When late transport is arranged by the Club it is essential that bus tickets be purchased before 10 p.m. as the Bus Company has to be informed the number of buses by this time.

It is a condition of a late licence bar that ticket holders only are allowed in a dance after 10-30 p.m.

No Pass Outs after 10 p.m.

CAR PARKING
Cars may be parked without lights on the Seaward side of the Promenade.
Park Back in Head out, this way of parking is only permitted when the Red Lamps are in position, they are removed at 10-45 p.m.
NO PARKING behind Coatham Hotel.

AFTER THE SHOW . . .

COSTA BRAVA
ESPRESSO GRILL
171 HIGH STREET
(Opposite Bus Station)
Tel.: Redcar 4303

Music   Espresso Coffee

GOOD MEALS SERVED ALL DAY AT REASONABLE PRICES

REDCAR JAZZ CLUB

COATHAM HOTEL
WINDSOR BALLROOM

FORTHCOMING ATTRACTIONS

Sundays at 7-30 p.m.
(Doors open 7-0 p.m.)

Clockwise from top left: Redcar Jazz Club ad (Brian Smith); ad for the Two Shoes in Elgin; Redcar Jazz Club (Brian Smith); Arthur Wyllie didn't recognise 'See Emily Play'

Clockwise from top left: Peter Wilson thinks anyone in Carlisle who wasn't interested in seeing the Floyd support The Fortunes was unfortunate; Peter Ashwell rocks the Carnaby Street look; Alan Wolsey in his pre-psychedelic gear; Blackpool was the first of several Floyd shows Simon Phillips saw; Peter Raines was not impressed by the cacophony of noise

HATCH END
AUGUST 1967, LONDON, UK

I WAS THERE: SALLY GLEN

When I was growing up, as a youngster, Richard Wright and his family lived in a house opposite my family. This was at one end of Hatch End. A few years later, my family moved to the other, more affluent area of Hatch End. Shortly afterwards, Richard and his family also moved... Again, almost opposite us in the same road. His mum and my mum were best friends and I can remember visiting their house many times. I was a dog lover even then and as they had two golden retrievers, Copper and Shandy, I would often pop over to see them. Richard was there sometimes. He was very fond of those dogs. I can remember sitting in their back garden shortly before their first album, *The Piper at the Gates of Dawn*, was released and they were discussing album covers. As an artist, I submitted a sample cover for *Piper*. It wasn't chosen, but I was chuffed to bits that they even looked at it. It was Richard who got me my copy of *Piper* when it was released. It was in mono! As I remember him, Richard was quite a shy soul, and it didn't surprise me that he hid behind his keyboards. He was softly spoken and gentle. I was truly saddened when he died. For me, he was Pink Floyd.

PATMOS
AUGUST 1967, GREECE

I WAS THERE: NIGEL LESMOIR-GORDON

I lost touch with Syd but I remained friends with Roger and David. Roger came round once to 101 and said, 'I've got this car, guys. Do you want to come down to Greece in it? I want to go to the island of Patmos.' So Rick, me, Jenny, Russell Page, David Gale, Roger and Judy got in this car, a pink Chrysler Plymouth Powerglide, and we went down there. I didn't have a driving licence so I never got to drive it, but Rick and Roger took it in turns. We woke up one morning on the autobahn in Germany and I said, 'Why are we parked on the side of the road, Rick?' He said, 'This car will only go backwards.' We managed to get it towed off the autobahn and taken into a garage and the engineer said 'this car is kaput. It is finished. It's not going anywhere.' we caught a train. And I remember Russell had only got five quid. He'd come to Greece with five quid. Of course, five quid went quite a long way then. We were getting a free ride in a car, you see. Roger Waters was never really into drugs, or mind-expanding substances as I prefer to call them. Roger had a terrible trip on Patmos when we went there, a terrible time. He was cast into hell. He didn't really get off on LSD.

ARCADIA
17 SEPTEMBER 1967, CORK, IRELAND

I WAS THERE: JACK LYONS

Having spent seven years in London working as a clerk filing legal papers I was back in Cork – and jagging. At home one night in Gillabbey Street, an ad in the *Echo* jumped off the page at me: 'Pink Floyd at the Arcadia, Sunday, September 17.' I had to read it several times to believe it. I had known Syd Barrett and the other members of the Floyd since their residency days at the old Marquee Club in London – as well as the Free School in Powis Square when they played for practically nothing. So when I heard they were coming to the Arcadia in my own native Cork, I volunteered myself into Eason's in Patrick Street, bought 50 blank badges and went home to colour each one with what can be best described as badly drawn psychedelic-inspired art.

I didn't stop there; I then made up a couple of equally badly drawn psychedelic posters and called in to Martin Bennett, Gents Outfitters, on North Main Street, persuading the purveyor of 'crombies and cardigans' that if he allowed me to Sellotape the two posters on his window, his premises would be thronged in no time with customers looking for psychedelic clobber. The two posters bore the legend 'Pow-R, Toch-H and Interstellar Overdrive'. Mr Bennett wanted to know what the strange message meant but I was at a loss to explain. I just thought the wording was hip.

I think I, and several members of my family, must have passed by the shop a dozen times that day, glowing in wonderment at my handiwork let loose upon an unsuspecting public. No other form of postering was used in those days, apart from Dave, the boy who pushed the Arcadia barrow around town to let people know what was going on at the Arc.

Then Johnny Chisholm pushed our Echo through the letterbox and there was the big four inch by five inch ad with the words 'PINK FLOYD' emblazoned across the frame. Eight shillings admission (40 new pence) and patrons were strongly advised that admission was limited. Local Cork band Four-Plus-Two were to provide the support. When my badges were completed, I took them down to the manager and owner, Peter

WISH YOU WERE HERE

Prendergast. Genial entrepreneur that he was, he was amazed anyone would go to so much bother. He gave me two free tickets and handed me a fiver for my work.

I walked back into town in a daze to meet my girlfriend Maura outside the Saxone, feeling like Brian Epstein. On Sunday teatime before the gig, I took her up Wellington Road to the Glenvera Bed and Breakfast to meet the band. Maura – now my wife – got as far as the hallway, took one look at Syd Barrett's high hair-do and refused to enter their room. I carried on.

They remembered me from a few months earlier and we sat down and grooved. I was half expecting a tab of acid but couldn't believe it when Syd handed me a bottle of Club Orange, saying in his posh Cambridge accent: 'Sorry, Jack – afraid that's all we've got.' Meanwhile, down at the Arcadia, the Floyd's roadie was glued to a stool in Handlebars pub. My brother, Pat, had dropped down early to take a look at the gear and seeing that there was no one to empty the van he set the gear up. Pat was a roadie for a local band called The Martells and they had just the night before done a successful gig for Sullivan Quay past pupils.

The gig was great. The two preceding nights, the band had played Belfast and Ballymena, and the Cork gig was the only one they ever did in the Republic of Ireland. It must have been some 225-mile drive in a day! I was familiar with nearly every song on their debut studio album, *The Piper at the Gates of Dawn*, which had been released the previous month. The album, hailed as one of the best ever psychedelic rock albums, took its name from the title of a chapter in Kenneth Grahame's *The Wind in the Willows* and was the only one made under founder member Barrett's leadership – he left the band a few months later. The album included classics such as 'Astronomy Domine' and 'Interstellar Overdrive', but the only songs Maura recognised at the gig were 'Arnold Layne' and 'See Emily Play'.

After the concert, we didn't stay too long chatting as my wife had to be at work next morning at the Lee Boot and I had to be on bus duty at Capwell. That night has come to attain almost biblical proportions in Cork, since thousands have claimed to be there, but there weren't more than 200 lost souls in the Arcadia!

Many years later, I was walking down Oliver Plunkett Street and noticed an old hippy Volkswagen van parked and laden with the usual eco and clean energy stickers, and there on the windscreen was one of my badly drawn Pink Floyd psychedelic badges. 'Interstellar Overdrive' it said, in my handwriting. I hung around for an hour to see who owned the van but nobody showed up. Nowadays, I spend my free time accumulating diner sores on restaurant seats, swapping yarns with my peers about the good old days, and every now and then someone brings up the subject of the 50 badges and the Pink Floyd's drunken roadie.

PAVILION
21 SEPTEMBER 1967, WORTHING, UK

I WAS THERE: SUZANNE DUMBLETON (NEE GODDIN)

Myself and my school friends regularly attended pop concerts at the Assembly Hall or the Pavilion in Worthing on Thursday nights. We were about 15 years old at the time and saw many great groups who then were up-and-coming. To name a few, The Who (four times!), Cream, the Small Faces, Manfred Mann, the Move, the Spencer Davis Group, Geno Washington and many more.

When we went to the Assembly Hall to see Pink Floyd, they played 'See Emily Play' and 'Arnold Layne', which were the only songs anyone had heard of and we were surprised by them. The spooky psychedelic lighting and sound was like nothing we had heard before. The smoke machine added to the slightly druggy feel of the evening. I felt uncomfortable by the music, because most groups apart from the Move were very normal poppy groups. Their music was a world away from the Pink Floyd of later years. I never became a Pink Floyd fan. We continued to go to these concerts until we left school and got jobs. And after a while, the groups were not as good for some reason. I fondly remember those years when we could afford to see great groups for anything between ten and eleven shillings (50p to 55p). I know it was cheap for a great evening. No alcohol only coffee. Happy times.

5TH DIMENSION
27 SEPTEMBER 1967, LEICESTER, UK

I WAS THERE: JOHN BISHOP

I went with a friend, as we both lived quite close to the venue. There was only a handful there on the night. I went on to buy the first album, *The Piper at the Gates of Dawn*.

I WAS THERE: DAVE STEWART

I was lucky to see the Floyd at this ground-breaking Leicester club, of which I was member number seven of 150. Saturday night gigs were invariably all-nighters with a free bacon roll in the morning. We also saw them at Notts County Football Club. Also on the bill on this day/night gig (on 10 May 1969) were The Move, Long John Baldry and Georgie Fame. The pink pig was also there.

I WAS THERE; TONY WESTON

I was in a band called Hal C Blake. We were one of the resident house bands who played on Sunday nights at the 5th Dimension, alternating every two weeks with Ten Years After the following week. The 5th Dimension was over a bus garage and there was only one way in, up a huge flight of stairs. I wanted a Marshal 100 watt PA system and the wait at local music shop Moore and Stanworths was six months. I tracked down Jim Marshall, called him and said I wanted a PA. He said 'go to Moore and Stanworth'. I explained the wait, said I was picking up some stuff for my dad and would be down later in the week and asked if there was any chance of getting one. He hummed and aahed. I told him I would pay him cash and pay the shop price. The line went quiet and he said, 'When can you be here? I'll have one ready!'

A couple of days later, I had a van load and ended up in Slough at the Marshall factory with our roadie. I rang the factory doorbell and Jim Marshall answered it and introduced himself. It was a really small factory, but full of guys building the amps. Jim was a really great guy. We had a joke together and I handed over the cash. Our roadie helped me load the PA onto the back of the van. The speakers were stood upright, inside the back doors and visible through the rear windows.

It was the early afternoon when I drove back up the M1 home to Leicester. About four miles south of Leicester Forest East Services, a newish Ford Zodiac was tailing me. In those days, the M1 was not that busy. As we came to the exit, the Zodiac started flashing its headlights. I slowed and it overtook us. Inside the car were four guys with longish hair, waving at me to pull over. Instead, I sped up and overtook them. I signalled and turned on the exit ramp. They passed me again and were hanging out the windows waving, so we pulled over. We got out of the van and these guys got out of their car.

It was Syd Barrett and Roger Waters and two other band members. They were playing at the 5th Dimension that night and did we know the way? I knew they were at the club that night, and as we had no gig, we were heading there ourselves. I joked about the flight of stairs and us being the house band. They followed us to the club, on Humberstone Road. They saw the stairs but weren't bothered as they had roadies, so we all agreed to meet before the first set.

In the break, we hung out and partook of the goodies available. A great night was had by all. The place had a couple of hundred attendees and went well. They had an array of lights that were really home-made, in boxes. But their light show was not bad and we even copied some of the cabinets for our show. We never played a gig together and we never met again. That was how group life was back then. We all travelled the motorways, met up and moved on.

I WAS THERE: RAY DRAYCOTT, AGE 19

The 5th Dimension was a small club above the Provincial garage on Uppingham Road. There were only twelve of us in the audience and – honestly? – I thought they were boring. There was no singing, just music with a crude light show as a backdrop. I went to see them because I bought 'Arnold Layne'. I was so disappointed. The club closed a couple of years later and then the garage burnt down. The Pink Floyd I saw was a million miles away from the group we now know.

SAVILLE THEATRE
1 OCTOBER 1967, LONDON, UK

I WAS THERE: KEN TOOKE

In 1967 I met Pink Floyd at the stage door of the Saville Theatre in New Compton Street, London. I asked Syd Barret about 'Arnold Layne' and 'See Emily Play'. He said that one of them he wrote on a train. He signed an autograph for me and just signed it 'Syd'. I also got him to sign as Roger.

VICTORIA ROOMS, UNIVERSITY OF BRISTOL
7 OCTOBER 1967, BRISTOL, UK

I WAS THERE: MIKE DAVIES

All new and upcoming groups, once signed to a record label, had to do the dance hall and theatre rounds in order to get more well known out in the country. This happened to the Floyd and they did one such date at a hall in Bristol. Unfortunately for them, me and a few hundred Mods turned up to see for ourselves this new happening group, who we mistakenly thought would give us something to dance to! We were amazed at what we were hearing and soon wanted them gone from the stage, so dancing to soul music would restart. To help us achieve this, a whole load of booing started, with the old-style pennies being thrown at the group. After threatening to leave the stage if this continued – which it did – they eventually did walk off at which point we went back to dancing to the latest soul sounds on record.

THE PAVILION
13 OCTOBER 1967, WEYMOUTH, UK

I WAS THERE: BRIAN INKPEN

When Pink Floyd played Weymouth in October, 1967, I was the drummer in one of the supporting acts, Denise Scott and the Soundsmen. Also on the bill was Freddie Mack and the Mack Sound. The gig was promoted by the Steering Wheel Club in Weymouth and another member of the band still has a copy of the poster, which describes it as 'the Explosive Sound of Pink Floyd'. But it was far from that.

They rigged up a big white sheet at the rear of the stage and during their act, which I seem to remember was basically all instrumentals, psychedelic images were portrayed on the white sheet. We were playing pop covers and Freddie Mack was playing soul music, so Pink Floyd were a complete contrast. It was something that nobody had seen in our area and I watched with some disbelief as the promoter clearly had no idea what he had booked. It was certainly different, and very much different to the music they became famous for.

I WAS THERE: MICHAEL BILES, AGE 19

I attended with friends from the college. It was a student dance, organised by South Dorset Technical College. I do not recall the line up or the songs on the playlist, except for 'See Emily Play'. I do recall seeing some of the crew placing coloured water onto slides and then fixing in front of a projector to create patterns around the ballroom. It was a successful student event. The students' union had not had such a high profile group in previous concerts. Weymouth did not host many top name groups at any venue, apart from The Hollies summer show in 1964 which ran for six weeks and the Rolling Stones performing in a local cinema.

I WAS THERE: DAVE HICKS

My then girlfriend (now my wife) Ena and I saw Pink Floyd at the Weymouth Pavilion. They had a large white sheet as a backdrop, and a roadie poured paint onto glass slides and projected the images onto it to create colourful images. Many members of the audience, who were used to listening to the Stones and The Who, etc. were not familiar with Pink Floyd's music and stood around looking confused.

I WAS THERE: BRIAN LANE

The show was in the Ocean Room. They used a slide projector to melt slides to show psychedelic images on a screen as they played songs like 'See Emily Play' and 'Arnold Layne'. But they are very vague memories as it was a long time ago!

I WAS THERE: JULIE LONG, AGE 15

They were doing the rounds of seaside ballrooms as they were just starting out. My mother worked at the Pavilion Ballroom on the coffee bar. As the special effects were being set up, they came and had coffee. I grabbed the opportunity of getting their photographs on a black and white promotional photo. Sadly, it's been lost in one of several house moves over the years.

They struck me as very polite and well-educated young men. I was especially impressed by Syd. He had an almost other worldly aura about him. I just had an instinct that this was going to be the start of something big. At that time, the Floyd had a very small following outside of London. The songs and fairy tale lyrics were lost on people from small towns who were used to what I call 'bubblegum pop music' but somehow I fell for it, being a bit of a dreamer myself. I've been hooked on the Floyd ever since. I followed their career avidly and have never failed to be amazed at the music they have produced over the years. All praise to Mr Gilmour! They have been the soundtrack to my life ever since meeting them on that heady warm evening in the summer of love all those years ago. My husband passed away eight years ago. He was also a fan and I had 'Wish You Were Here' played at his funeral.

I WAS THERE: IDRIS MARIN, AGE 17

It was the South Dorset Technical College summer ball. They had 'See Emily Play' in the charts and that was the only record that they played that I knew. I was a Mod and to be honest I was disappointed. And so were a lot of my friends. I'm not sure what we were expecting. But we were all into soul music and it didn't cut the mustard for me.

I remember the light show. I think it was the first time I ever saw one. There was a guy about ten or 15 metres back from the stage and he had a metal frame like a bar stool about ten feet off the deck with a slide projector and a blowlamp. Between the slides were various coloured oils and he was dropping them into the slide projector and putting the blowlamp on them and they were just bubbling all around and making psychedelic images that were projected up onto the stage.

CESAR'S CLUB
14 OCTOBER 1967, BEDFORD, UK

I WAS THERE: PETER ASHWELL

The Pink Floyd's gig at the Cesar's Club in London Road, Bedford on that date in October was very exciting for us and an opportunity to don all our favourite gear, defying the gloomy weather. The show had been advertised in the local *Bedfordshire Times* newspaper that our parents would have bought and our excitement about the Pink Floyd had been building throughout that year of 1967 as they had been gigging, appearing on BBC1's *Top of the Pops* and had a spot on BBC2's *Look of the Week* during that year. The advertising was a bit low key, but this only served to fuel the feeling of exclusivity for the event.

By playing a smaller venue that was more well known for bingo seemed radical, a bit daring and even dangerous or subversive in a way. This gig, supported by The Tecknique, was just before the Pink Floyd embarked on a tour of North America. So for us, the size of the audience was not a surprise and proved to be far too great for this smaller Bedford venue. We were therefore lucky to get in at all. This was in the days of just queuing up and getting your ticket at the door minutes before a performance.

But having managed to get into this low ceilinged, standing room only, hot and sweaty throbbing place after at least one song ('Arnold Layne', 'Scarecrow') had been played at the start of the set, the excitement was electric ('Astronomy Domine', 'Paint Box') and the volume ear-splitting. In fact, the volume proved to be so loud that as the music got heavier ('Set the Controls for the Heart of the Sun', 'Interstellar Overdrive'), we made the decision, together with some others, to go outside where the volume became more bearable and we were able to enjoy and appreciate the sound much better.

After maybe two or three extended songs later, we were joined outside by a gang of middle-aged and older ladies. They had come for their evening session of bingo and the management had to stop the band playing to let the bingo start and probably avoid these ladies rioting and swinging there handbags to gain entry. After all, for them, serious money was at stake!

But for us, it was a night – or rather an early evening – of unforgettable alternative, innovative, psychedelic rock. I sensed at the time that musically things would never be the same again, but then we got the exceptional onslaught delivered by Jimi Hendrix.

DUNELM HOUSE, UNIVERSITY OF DURHAM
28 OCTOBER 1967, DURHAM, UK

I WAS THERE: PETER RAINES, AGE 19

I entered Durham University in October 1967 as a naive northern 19-year-old boy. I had heard Pink Floyd's hit 'See Emily Play' during the summer, so coming into the uni's coffee bar one day I thought 'what's on the B-side?'. It was a song called 'Scarecrow' and I put it on. It was a little two-minute ditty, but with sounds and lyrics that were mesmerising. Shortly after, I discovered they were playing at the uni's Dunelm House. It was intended to be a dance rather than a concert so I joined up with probably 400 other students and went along. What happened in the next 30 minutes was extraordinary.

The heaving dance hall was reduced to 15 people up against the stage. Roger could have spat in my face I was that close! What we listened to for the next hour or so was like 'Interstellar Overdrive' times ten on any drug you like. It was a cacophony of noise – not music – without the slightest hint of melody. Now I've seen the archive clips of them playing at the UFO Club and people dancing to 'Interstellar Overdrive'. You could not have danced a single step that night.

There was, however, something tangible going on but I had not realised the state of health that Syd was in. They had just had a tour of the United States cancelled because of Syd and this was the first gig afterwards. You have to admire how they came through that period of so-called psychedelia, late Sixties experimentation and folk whimsy to become the number one progressive band of the Seventies. But, please, never another night like that night in Durham.

November 1967 sees Pink Floyd embark on their first North American tour. The tour starts later than planned due to visa problems. Seven shows are completed along with TV appearances on The Pat Boone TV Show, American Bandstand *and the Los Angeles show,* Boss City TV Show. *As the tour goes on, Syd's mental state causes serious concern. On both* American Bandstand *and* The Pat Boone Show, *he confounds his hosts by not responding to questions and staring off into space. He refuses to move his lips to mime to 'See Emily Play' on Boone's show.*

I WAS THERE: JENNY SPIRES

I didn't see much of Syd until after the American tour when I noticed he had changed so much. He just looked ill, dark and confused. On seeing him my only thought was, 'Who is supposed to be looking after him?' 'What has happened to him?' Has he actually been spiked with something? I had heard so many stories about his behaviour in America that it was hard to know what to believe, but his eyes were now black, dull, deadened. In conclusion: we were all living 'over the top', staying up late and going out a lot.

Beginning on 14 November 1967, Pink Floyd embark on a 31-show tour in 16 UK cities, a package headlined by Jimi Hendrix. Hendrix is allotted 40 minutes, and Pink Floyd 15 to 20 minutes. Syd was not enjoying the tour. Arriving in a new town, he would go for a walk, only returning to the venue a few minutes before Floyd were due onstage. He'd play the show, go off again and come back hours later, in time for the second. One night, he doesn't turn up at all. Davy O'List of The Nice, who are also on the bill, stands in for him.

GUILDHALL
22 NOVEMBER 1967, PORTSMOUTH, UK

I WAS THERE: JOSIE CHANDLER (NEE CLARK), AGE 15

I was there with my friend Carole. We could only go if my dad picked us up afterwards. I lived in Portchester and Carole in Paulsgrove, so we would have missed the last buses. We sat quite near the front and I remember Pink Floyd going behind the big speaker quite a lot and smoking what we imagined were joints.

I WAS THERE: MICK SHERIDAN

I went to see Hendrix mainly. Pink Floyd was a bonus. I had the poster for that show, and someone didn't believe me that there were that many bands on that night and I lent it to them and never got it back. I paid ten shillings (50p) to see them that night. I couldn't afford 12/6 (63p). My mate paid seven shillings (35p). I went with my friend Richard Calder. We left school, we had something to eat and then we went in. We didn't know there were that many bands on. The first band were called The Outer Limits. I remember they played 'Reach Out, I'll Be There', the Four Tops number. There was someone called Eire Apparent, who played three numbers, one of which was 'My Back Pages' by The Byrds, then Amen Corner, then The Nice and then Pink Floyd. Their special effects were a bed sheet behind them, a big white sheet that the lights went onto. It was almost comical. There were so many bands on they didn't get a chance to play their full effects. They played about three numbers. Then it was The Move and then Hendrix. Pink Floyd went down okay, but everyone had come to see Hendrix.

COVENTRY THEATRE
19 NOVEMBER 1967, COVENTRY, UK

I WAS THERE: DAVE JONES

I saw 'The' Pink Floyd, as they were then billed, at the Coventry Theatre in 1967. I remember thinking at the time that their performance was appreciated by some members of the audience, but others were somewhat bemused!

SOPHIA GARDENS
23 NOVEMBER 1967, CARDIFF, UK

I WAS THERE: CHRIS BROWN, AGE 17

We saw them at what was a small venue. It's not there anymore. I doubt if there were more than 250 people in there. As for the show, I don't remember much about it but 'See Emily Play' was being played a lot on the radio so that would have been one of the reasons we went. I think in those days you could only buy the tickets from the venue itself. I went with my mate Glyn Hayes. We are still going to see bands together now.

COLSTON HALL
24 NOVEMBER 1967, BRISTOL, UK

I WAS THERE: MARTYN COLE, AGE 15-16

I was a Mod. I was into The Who, the Stones and The Beatles. Pink Floyd were definitely something different. I went to the concert because we could see four or five current chart names all on the same bill. So it was that a school friend and myself got tickets to see a 'roadshow' at the Colston Hall in Bristol. The artists played an afternoon matinee and an evening show. We went to the matinee. The bands playing included Jimi Hendrix, Pink Floyd, The Nice (with Keith Emerson in the line-up), The Move and Eire Apparent. One of the other bands there was the original Amen Corner with Andy Fairweather-Low. Hendrix had had a couple of hits, including 'Purple Haze'. The

Move were second billed, as they were the up and coming group at the time. I recall Hendrix setting fire to the amps and his guitar with lighter fuel and The Nice playing 'America' whilst throwing Bowie knives across the stage into wooden targets. Pink Floyd played 'See Emily Play' and The Move played 'Fire Brigade'. Pink Floyd were a bit more than pop music, a bit alternative. The fact that we sat in the stalls quite stationary, and that nobody got up and leapt about but just listened to the music, was neither here nor there.

I've revisited their music in the past ten to fifteen years. Everything's loaded in the car and I've got a CD player in the garage. If I get to go up the garage for the day and just pottering about, I often put their CDs on and listen to them. They are my 'go to' band if I've got a few hours to spare.

OPERA HOUSE
25 NOVEMBER 1967, BLACKPOOL, UK

I WAS THERE: SIMON PHILLIPS, AGE 15

I heard 'Arnold Layne' on the radio and, around the same time, they appeared on TV twice within a week. I missed the first but everyone at school was talking about it. I tuned in over the next few nights and, sure enough, they were on again (possibly the shows were *Scene Special* and *Look of the Week*.). I duly bought 'Emily' and *Piper* although I missed their *Top of the Pops* appearances as we were on a family trip to Italy at the time.

When the Hendrix/Move/Floyd tour was announced, they were coming to Blackpool, 15 miles from where I lived. Tickets were four shillings and sixpence (23p). My parents were okay with me going so long as it was to the early show – thankfully, as it turned out, from the Hendrix point of view. We got to the Opera House around sixish. The stage was a mess of all sorts of amplifiers, loads of them in two rows. We were in the centre stalls, about twelve to 18 rows back from the stage. When the show started, the place was about half full and the compere invited those in the circle to come down into the stalls a) for warmth, and b) to make the place look fuller. Imagine – this was Hendrix and the Floyd playing for pennies!

The various support bands went through their five-to-ten minute slots. Just before Pink Floyd came on, a huge white sheet was draped across the rows of amplifiers. The compere, who might have been Pete Drummond, introduced them as 'fresh from wooing the hippie emporiums on America's West Coast'. They played about 15 to 20 minutes and definitely did 'Set the Controls' and 'Interstellar Overdrive'. I remember writing down 'Stethoscope' as being the other song but it was more likely to have been 'Pow R Toch H'. I was still a bit unsure about the album's song titles and often got those two mixed up. All set lists that I've seen for this date have the early and late shows the wrong way round.

They wore exactly the same clothes as they do in the photographs of them cutting a cake and drinking champagne, except that Syd wore the hat that Nick has on in the photographs. We (or, at any rate, I) had no idea of Syd's struggles at the time and I can say that, at that show, he seemed in good form and he and Rick led the band through a dazzling 'Interstellar Overdrive'. The light show was of the liquid oil type played onto the band and the white sheet behind them. They also had a strobe low down at the front which projected their silhouettes high up onto the backdrop of the stage and the stage curtains in the Hendrix footage weren't closed at all other than for Hendrix. The sound was loud but clear and each instrument could be distinguished. The combination of light and sound was exactly what I hoped it would be from the reviews I'd read of their London shows. I was mesmerised but all too soon it was over. Afterwards, The Move did about 20 minutes at deafening volume, and then Hendrix did about 50 minutes.

After the show, we had about an hour to kill before our bus home. We slipped into a pub for one pint (very nervously as we were so young) and then walked along the promenade. We saw a very dirty and dusty Ford Transit parked up outside a club. It was covered in graffiti, amongst which were references to Pink Floyd, so we looked in the cab and, bugger me, Rick Wright was sitting behind the wheel in his stage gear. We tapped on the window and said we'd been to the show. We all got his autograph and asked where Syd was. He pointed into the club (no way we could blag our way in there!). We chatted for a couple of minutes and went for our bus. And that was it really. I was so shocked when, just a few weeks later, it was announced that Syd was out of the band.

PALACE THEATRE
26 NOVEMBER 1967, MANCHESTER, UK

I WAS THERE: STEVE BERNING

They were third on the bill on the Hendrix tour, with The Move, Amen Corner, The Nice, Outer Limits and Eire Apparent. They did a set of no more than 20 minutes. Having spent the intervening period believing that I had seen Syd Barrett, the seeds of doubt were cast the more I read about his unreliability and, to me, the 'clincher' was that on several gigs on this tour he was replaced by Davy O'List of The Nice. However, I wrote to one of the music monthlies (*Mojo* or *Uncut*) and they confirmed that Syd had appeared at this gig.

I WAS THERE: JOHN HALLIWELL

I went with my girlfriend Sue, now my wife. Our claim to fame is that Floyd's psychedelic van slowed to a stop and we were asked the way to the Palace Theatre! It's hard to believe that this was only six years before the mighty *Dark Side*. The tribute band Manc Floyd come to our local theatre, the Met in Bury, every year and they are as good as it's going to get.

THE DOME
2 DECEMBER 1967, BRIGHTON, UK

I WAS THERE: JOHN FINCH

I remember them playing two songs supporting Jimi Hendrix at Brighton Dome. One was 'Set the Controls for the Heart of the Sun'. It was a great evening and Hendrix had to pull out all the stops to headline such great bands.

THEATRE ROYAL
3 DECEMBER 1967, NOTTINGHAM, UK

I WAS THERE: PAUL MAYFIELD

It was the first Hendrix tour. I think I paid ten shillings (50p) and went with four friends. We knew a little bit about Pink Floyd because they'd released 'Arnold Layne' as a single. They couldn't play it on the radio because there'd been some offence taken at the words. To this day I'm not quite sure what it was. 'See Emily Play' was a fantastic song and to me probably their most memorable. In December 1967 they were breaking new ground. Like many bands of the Sixties it was all new to us and the light show was pretty fantastic also. The level of sound was so incredible. There was no health and safety restriction over the level of sound. In the old Theatre Royal in Nottingham the big old amplifiers and the speakers were wrapped right around the whole of the stage and the ceiling and the sound was such that you almost felt yourself pinned back in the seat. I think they did 'Interstellar Overdrive' but I can't be sure.

GREEN'S PLAYHOUSE
5 DECEMBER 1967, GLASGOW, UK

I WAS THERE: GORDON PHINN, AGE 15

For those of us who lived through it, already glued to our transistor radios and Dansette record players, 1967 was an endless explosion of revelations. Every month, and sometimes week, amazing music charged our imaginations. Spring's double A-side of 'Penny Lane'/'Strawberry Fields Forever' might be regarded as an opening salvo. We'd been primed with *Revolver* and many ace singles in '66 – The Yardbirds, The Spencer Davis Group, The Animals, The Kinks, The Byrds, Dylan, the Stones and Simon and Garfunkel. The pop song was advancing by leaps and bounds, continually breaking down barriers the industry thought permanent. The summer brought *Sgt. Pepper's, Piper at the Gates of Dawn* and *Are You Experienced*, a triumvirate of glorious catastrophe for the conventional.

My good friend Angus McRuary and I owned all three albums between us and our mutual listening sessions were exercises in awe punctured by the usual teenage gossip. And it was Angus who insisted, despite mine and my mother's reluctance, that we buy tickets for the December visit to Glasgow's Greens Playhouse of the now infamous Hendrix Package Tour, featuring so many '67 breakout bands it now seems pure boomer fantasy to even list them. I had turned 15 a month before and the only rock concert I'd attended was 1965's *Kinks Live At The Kelvin Hall*, whose Beatles-like hysteria can be easily accessed. as the gig was recorded and is still available on CD. With severely limited live concert experience, one is easily impressed. And yet the revolutionary barrage of glorious rock that we heard that night, the first show of two, was, and is in memory, undeniable.

Pink Floyd appeared as a trio, or maybe Syd was hiding in the back somewhere, but I sure didn't see him, and their sound, as an organ trio, was somewhat reduced, though still redolent of that mysterioso vibe they came to perfect in the '69 to '72 era. 'Set the Controls for the Heart of the Sun' was strangeiosity personified even in its early versions. The release on the *Early Years* box set of their Stockholm '67 performance gives an accurate sense of their live sound, albeit with a psychedelic guitar that was absent in Glasgow.

ROYAL COLLEGE OF ART
6 DECEMBER 1967, KENSINGTON, UK

I WAS THERE: NIGEL LESMOIR-GORDON

And there came a time when Peter Jenner, who was the Floyd's manager then, had a cottage in the Black Mountains. And Syd, me, Gay, Lindsay, Jenny and Stash de Rola went down there and stayed for a week. And Lindsay Corner came as well. That's the first inkling I had that Syd was slightly off his trolley. Because the first thing he did was shit on the doorstep, which seemed inappropriate. And then he spent one night standing on a wine bottle, pressing his hand onto a wooden beam. I don't know how many hours he did it for. We thought it was just eccentricity. We had no experience of mental illness. We wouldn't recognise a mentally ill person if they were shoved under our noses, unless they were raving. We thought Syd was just an eccentric poet, so we took all this quite lightly.

Stash used to wear a black velvet suit. His jacket was all gold and braid, and he wore these amazing high heeled shoes with buckles - court shoes. Someone said, 'Stash, we need some logs for the fire.' And he said, 'Don't worry, I'll get them.' He went out and he was gone a while. When he came back he was covered in mud and carrying cans of oil. So we said, 'We asked you for logs, Stash, not cans of oil. And you're covered in mud.' And he said 'let all mud be velvet!'.

At the Royal College of Art gig, we noticed that Syd was not playing. He was not contributing to the band. The guitar was round his neck and his arms were down by his side, and this was after the trip to Wales. It was the first sign that things were adrift.

CHISLEHURST CAVES
8 DECEMBER 1967, CHISLEHURST, UK

I WAS THERE: LINDA GOULDSBROUGH, AGE 15

All I can remember is sand on the floor, buckets and rags for the loo, the big smell of weed and psychedelic lights. They were a brilliant group but it was a long time ago…

PAVILION BALLROOM
14 DECEMBER 1967, BOURNEMOUTH, UK

I WAS THERE: ALAN WOLSEY

In those days one could not afford 15 shillings (75p) in the space of one month so I had to miss the Weymouth Pavilion show, but saved up for 'the big one' in Bournemouth. I was sat second row back on the right side of the centre aisle. They were playing right there in front of me… Roger on bass and cymbal. They played weird stuff in those days! Although it was more than 50 years ago it seems like it was only yesterday. Their repertoire in those days was limited, so their set could only include 'Arnold Layne' and 'See Emily Play' at around three minutes each and 'Set the Controls for the Heart of the Sun', 'Take Up Thy Stethoscope and Walk' and 'Scarecrow.' They may have done another track off the album but I can't remember. In the words of the late DJ Tommy Vance – 'what a band!'.

With Syd struggling, the band recruit David Gilmour to help out. Between 12 and 20 January 1968, Pink Floyd perform four shows with Syd Barrett and David Gilmour both on guitar.

I WAS THERE: NIGEL LESMOIR-GORDON

I rang David and said they wanted a guitarist because Syd was freaked out. There was an argument about who made that phone call, and David said, 'It was definitely Nigel.'

Syd lived for a bit at 101. He lived at Earlham Street and then he moved away and I lost touch with him. The last time I saw him in Cambridge, he was riding his bike. This was in the Seventies. I waved. He got off his bike and he walked up to me and he said 'one day you won't need that beard'. And he walked back to his bike and cycled away. Jenny used to see him in supermarkets shopping but he didn't acknowledge her.

MIDDLE EARTH, ROUNDHOUSE
JANUARY 1968, LONDON, UK

I WAS THERE: COL TURNER

The debate as to when the Summer of Love actually occurred in the UK has raged for years. Some say 1967 while others claim 1968. It could be claimed that there were in fact two 'Summers of Love', being '67 and '68, although they melded together and seemed as one. This is when Flower Power and hippies were at their peak. At the centre of this movement in the UK and a driving force behind it were two bands. One of course was The Beatles. The other was Pink Floyd.

The Beatles had already been on the world's stage for some time but Floyd had not really yet broken through outside of Europe. Those summers were an amazing time to be alive. It was as if the whole world was bathed in sunlight. Even the winter of 1967-68 felt warm. The atmosphere was electric. People respected people. The London clubs were packed, as countless bands, many now world famous, played for what seemed like 24 hours a day. In those times it was the custom to 'give 'em a flower' as we passed out flowers to any passing stranger. Free love? You bet, although I won't go into detail!

My hair by now had grown long and I was associating with the 'inner core' of the underground movement. I was living in several hippie pads around London, mainly in Shepherd's Bush. It was while I was staying there that I sometimes spotted the Floyd's not-too-flashy van parked in the street. The Floyd were living 'down the road' in Notting Hill Gate so it may have been a roadie's house or perhaps one of the boys had a lady friend. Who knows?

I had helped out on a few light shows at Middle Earth and was one of the unofficial unpaid DJs. However, one night a paid DJ turned up and we had a bit of a debate as to what records should be played. I lost, he won. His name: John Peel, who later went on to record the BBC shows with Floyd. I got to know him casually but, to be honest, John and I never really hit it off.

In the early days of Floyd, I must confess to not even knowing the individual members' names. That came sometime after I started to follow them. I just remember four guys who each had a personality. Both UFO and Middle Earth had by now located to the Roundhouse at Chalk Farm. I can't quite recall the arrangement but suspect that UFO was on the Friday, with Middle Earth being on Saturday. This meant that many, many bands were passing through these clubs.

Trying to keep track of who was in which band and when became an almost impossible task. What I am going to tell you next is not in any history book about Pink Floyd, but all the same I am going to record this as I remember it. It would have been early 1968, most probably around January. I think it would have been at Middle Earth. This particular night I remember Floyd coming on in the early hours, as was the custom by now. After they had been playing for a while someone remarked along the lines of, 'Hey, Floyd are a five piece tonight.' I checked the stage and sure enough there were five guys playing. I can't remember who was on which instruments but think it's a safe bet that Nick was the drummer, Rick the organist and Roger on bass… But who was playing lead? And what was the fifth member playing?

I have a very vague idea that it was another lead guitar but wouldn't swear to it. So just who were members four and five? It was around this time that Syd was being prepared for his departure and Dave was in the wings waiting to join officially. The records show that in January 1968 Pink Floyd played five gigs as a five piece with Syd and Dave sharing the same stage.

All of the gigs recorded in the history books were 'out of town' but Floyd were comfortable with the Middle Earth and UFO crowds and I suspect it would have been their way of saying thank you and farewell to Syd and 'please give a big welcome' to Dave. This event has not been recorded before and I'm not prepared to swear on a stack of bibles that it was Syd and Dave but that's how I remember it. It's a story I have told my friends for years, and it's a vague memory because at the time it was insignificant, but I'm convinced it's true.

Whether this gig took place is disputed by other Floyd historians.

I WAS THERE: JENNY SPIRES

David taking over was seamless, and out of necessity initially, and in the end proved to be the making of the Floyd, Syd's too. But, earlier in the year, the band had signed a contract with EMI. This was the music business and it included an 'advance'. The band had no money, so they had to fulfil the contract and work. With Syd not performing, they had to leave him behind. 'C'est la vie,' Syd would be the first to say. It's what he had said to me three years earlier when they had been served a writ for £5 at Stanhope Gardens, for playing too loud. 'We just have to pay it,' Syd wrote. 'We can't stop now... C'est la vie.'

In those days, the Floyd seemed to struggle for their sound but David, we knew, was a brilliant guitarist. He was in a local band, Joker's Wild, who were great to dance to and covered a lot of music in the hit parade then. They played every week at a club we went to, Les Jeux Interdit, and Dave could sing. He did a great 'In the Midnight Hour' which had been a hit record. Now, it only took for him to find his beautiful tone in Pink Floyd.

PAVILION BALLROOM, HASTINGS PIER
20 JANUARY 1968, HASTINGS, UK

I WAS THERE: KEN TOOKE

I saw Syd's final gig with Pink Floyd at Hastings Pier (sadly destroyed by fire years later). They had plenty of room at the ballroom and I don't know what they played but sadly they didn't play the hits. After the gig, the others had left and I spoke to Nick Mason and asked who the new guy was. It was David Gilmour.

I WAS THERE: COL TURNER

A new dawn was breaking as Dave replaced Syd. The music became a lot slicker with Dave in the band. The experimentation on stage was becoming less and the songs more polished. With all due respect to Roger, it was not apparent to me that he was now the leader. Ok he used to do the count-ins ('one, two', etc.) and most of the song introductions, but if I was asked who led Pink Floyd when Syd went, I would have said nobody. They performed as a unit. Roger was to only to become the dominant one much later on.

I remember a very special 'happening' one night. I was sitting on the steps that led down to UFO (at the Blarney Club) one night staring at my thumbs (if you don't know what that means I'm not about to tell you!). Floyd were pounding away in the club when out of the doors came this whacking great balloon. Now if you can imagine a condom about four feet in circumference and about half a mile long, you may have some idea of the size of this mother. It was inflated from within the club and a crowd of people pulled it out and along Tottenham Court Road. Don't ask me why – it just was! I've often wondered if that's where the idea of the inflatable pig came from all those years later. Did that 'happening' stick in Roger's mind?

With David Gilmour in the line-up, Pink Floyd continue gigging, interspersing UK shows with performances and TV appearances in Contintental Europe.

INSTITUTE OF SCIENCE & TECHNOLOGY
9 MARCH 1968, MANCHESTER, UK

I WAS THERE: CHRIS MCHUGO

I first did not see them when they failed to turn up to (I think) The Twisted Wheel in Manchester in June or July 1967. I was at the end of my first year of university. By 1968/69, I was Social Secretary at UMIST. We booked Floyd but they had a contract rider for a 16 square foot tower in front of the stage for the light show. I think *Saucerful of Secrets* had only just been released but *Piper* was well known. The audience sat on the floor.

In May 1969, the band came to Manchester Poly and performed with Ron Geesin. Some of that show was recorded and made it onto *Ummagumma*. I was at the Bath Blues Festival in Shepton Mallet in 1970, when Floyd played *Atom Heart Mother* very early in the morning, at about 2am if I remember correctly.

In 1973, a tape of *Dark Side* became an integral part of the soundtrack of an overland journey with a VW micro bus from London to Katmandu and back. Then, somehow, I was also a security guard at Wembley Arena with a circular projection screen for the *Wish You Were Here* tour... and I saw *The Wall* at the O2 in 2010!

MAYFAIR SUITE, BELFRY HOTEL
25 MAY 1968, SUTTON COLDFIELD, UK

I WAS THERE: PETER SMITH

When 'Arnold Layne' was in the charts I saw them, supported by Marmalade, at a club in Bournemouth. I also saw them at the Belfry in Sutton Coldfield. My then wife-to-be and I sat stage left by a French window, looking out onto the gardens of what is now a huge golf course and conference centre. Roger Waters split his trousers halfway through their set and had to change behind the stage, meanwhile begging a light for his fag from us. A truly different night. They were supported by local band Raymond Froggat. I also saw them with mates several times at the Carlton Club in Erdington, Birmingham which was later to be called Mothers. They were brilliant every time.

UNIVERSITY COLLEGE LONDON
14 JUNE 1968, LONDON, UK

I WAS THERE: DAVID GODFREY

I first saw Pink Floyd and their legendary oil projector at a basement club in Tottenham Court Road called the Blarney Club, or UFO. This was mid to late 1967 and there were 30 to 40 people present. The music was awesome. The following year they were booked to play the Midsummer Ball at University College, London. The room was crowded but within five or ten minutes the room emptied leaving a grand total of four people (me included) listening to their music! Those who left missed the incredible innovation of 'Set the Controls for the Heart of the Sun' and the instrumental 'A Saucerful of Secrets' amongst other great tracks, including Syd Barrett's 'Jugband Blues'. It was an amazing evening enjoyed by so few and missed by so many... I was a fan then and still a fan today, with treasured early albums including *Piper at the Gates of Dawn* and the double album *Ummagumma* on vinyl...

WISH YOU WERE HERE

THE COCKPIT, HYDE PARK
29 JUNE 1968, LONDON, UK

I WAS THERE: COL TURNER

It seems as if just about everybody was dropping LSD (acid) and I suppose I look back on those times with rose-coloured glasses. At many of the earlier happenings, Lennon, McCartney, Jagger and other celebs could be seen hanging around like any other person. You wouldn't dream of asking for an autograph as that was very uncool. I did have the pleasure of meeting Brian Jones (of the Rolling Stones) one night and I got into an amazing rave with him about nothing in particular. But all this was changing. London was the focal point for all the world, or so it seemed. Carnaby Street was now the hub of this universe and the British Invasion was in full swing. Then came the day that the whole movement crystallised into one amazing and beautiful happening. The date – 29 June 1968. Blackhill Enterprises, which consisted of the individual members of Floyd plus Pete Jenner and Andrew King, decided to put on the first free concert in London's Hyde Park. A free Floyd gig – I wasn't going to miss this even if I was struck by lightning! So off we went.

The concert was due to begin after lunch, and it was a Saturday. The records show the supports as being Roy Harper and Jethro Tull. I don't remember much about the supports, although I did get to see Tull a few times and they were always brilliant, so I guess that day was no different. As we arrived (early for once) I couldn't believe my eyes. There were people everywhere. I had been used to seeing Floyd from about six feet away from the stage. Now I was relegated to about 60 feet back!

People were seated on the grass, some having the good sense to bring something to sit on. The smell of hash and incense wafted on the summer breeze. The clothes people were wearing were just lovely, with every shade of psychedelic colour. Many wore tiny bells that tinkled as they moved. Flower Children could be seen everywhere, blowing bubbles with tiny bubble makers. The Beatles' 'All You Need Is Love' blasted over the PA just as we arrived, and seemed to be repeated about every 20 minutes. Then the moment arrived.

Pink Floyd took the stage and it was still daylight. I think this was the first time I had seen them during the daylight hours. The crowd had now grown to many thousands and I was glad we had arrived early, because those at the back would have had a very restricted view. However, they would have still heard what in my opinion was probably Pink Floyd's finest concert. Having seen many Floyd concerts it is hard to pick a favourite, but this day was extra memorable for the atmosphere alone. I can't remember the exact sequence of what they played that day, and I think that 'Arnold' and 'Emily' had been dropped by now. I do recall that most of *Piper* featured for the first set. I think this was David Gilmour's first big London gig since joining Floyd about four or five months before. Perhaps he had something to prove that day. ('I'm as good as Syd'?)

The sun was setting as Floyd came back for the second set in the twilight. The light show was a bit weak at first because a few rays of sun were still poking through. But this gave the band a strange glow that only added to the atmosphere. I have a feeling that the second set consisted of *Saucerful* but I can't be 100 per cent sure of exactly what was played and in what order. 'Interstellar Overdrive' may have been the final number, if previous gigs I had seen were anything to go by.

This day was the day the underground reached its pinnacle. Floyd had proved to all present that they were going to be around for a long time to come.

I WAS THERE: MIKE GODWIN

I saw the Floyd with Syd six times. Subsequently, I saw them at a Hyde Park free concert where they debuted *Saucerful* and at one or two other concerts – one in the back room of a pub, another at Plumpton racecourse; *Atom Heart Mother* twice, *Echoes* – and then a very long gap until they appeared unannounced at the Barbican tribute concert to Syd. I also saw Nick Mason's Saucerful of Secrets last year, but that was essentially a tribute band rather than a Floyd gig. I had stopped following them immediately before they broke through with performances of *Return of the Son of Nothing*, the provisional title for *Dark Side of the Moon*. I can't really explain why I gave up then.

A SAUCERFUL OF SECRETS RELEASED
28 JUNE 1968 (UK)

Recorded both before and after Syd Barrett's departure from the group, A Saucerful of Secrets *is the only non-compilation Pink Floyd album on which all five band members appear. It reaches No.9 in the UK album charts and No.158 in the US* Billboard *200. Nick Mason has declared it his favourite Floyd album.*

Pink Floyd embark on their second North American tour in July and August 1968, playing 19 shows in total.

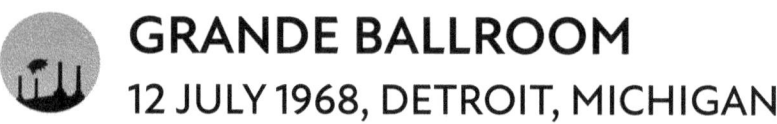

GRANDE BALLROOM
12 JULY 1968, DETROIT, MICHIGAN

I WAS THERE: DAVID EPPES

I saw Floyd in 1968 at the Grande Ballroom, even before they were at the top. We drove from Cleveland to Detroit thinking 'who in the hell is Pink Floyd?'. We smoked a doobie or two on the way and when we got there it was the usual crowd lined up and checked by security. There was a support band but I don't remember who they were. By that time, everybody was getting smoked up and wound up. And then Floyd came on. They played a song or two and then 'Astronomy Domine' came on and everybody stopped in their tracks and sat down. The set list was six songs in total – 'Interstellar Overdrive', 'A Saucerful of Secrets', 'Set the Controls for the Heart of the Sun', 'Astronomy Domine' and 'Flaming'. Since then, I have been a Floyd freak. They are the best band ever!

The remainder of 1968 is spent gigging around the UK and Europe.

QUEENS HALL
27 SEPTEMBER 1968, DUNOON, UK

I WAS THERE: JAMES BADDOCK

I saw Pink Floyd three times in 1968 (although the last one might have been in 1969 – it was a long time ago!). The first time was at Dunoon Town Hall. We travelled up from Irvine in Ayrshire and took the ferry across the Firth of Clyde from Greenock. The weather was not good, shall we say, and the ferry was rolling fairly noticeably, even with stabilisers, but we got to the gig with only one of us being affected by seasickness. It was the local Saturday night dance, so I suspect that the locals expected them to play 'See Emily Play' so that they could dance to it and it was very noticeable during the warm up band's set that there were two elements to the audience – the locals, who were treating it as a dance (which, to be fair, was what the support band was doing – playing the current hits), and the Floyd fans, who were sitting around the edge of the dance floor, willing the support band to get off the stage.

Unfortunately, Pink Floyd hadn't arrived yet – apparently, they'd been delayed en route and had been forced to catch the ferry after ours, by which time the weather had deteriorated still further. When they did arrive, they simply walked across the dance floor, with David Gilmour looking distinctly green around the gills. However, they were on stage within a quarter of an hour, and kicked off the set with 'Astronomy Domine', followed by 'Let There Be More Light'. By then, the locals had all but disappeared, and the Floyd fans were gathered in front of the stage. There was no light show, not even a glitter ball, just the Floyd.

The remainder of the set was 'Interstellar Overdrive', 'Corporal Clegg', 'Set the Controls for the Heart of the Sun' and 'A Saucerful of Secrets'. David Gilmour seemed to have recovered somewhat by the time they started, but I suspect there were no more than about 40 or 50 of us in the audience, and with the house lights pretty much on all the time, there wasn't a huge amount of atmosphere, to be honest. But, give them credit, they turned up and played.

REGENT STREET POLYTECHNIC
23 NOVEMBER 1968, LONDON, UK

I WAS THERE: NIGEL MOLDEN

I arrived at the Regent Street Polytechnic in Central London in September 1967 to study for a Sociology degree. The Department of Commerce and Social Studies was situated in the Main Extension Building in Little Titchfield Street in the centre of W1. The building was also the site of the Department of Architecture. It was well known that three of the students had formed a band whilst studying and had now left to pursue a career in music. The three students were Roger Waters, Rick Wright and Nick Mason, and the group was already known as Pink Floyd. Although that year has become known by the astonishing misnomer of the *Summer of Love*, it was an extraordinarily vibrant and creative time not only in music but also in the theatre, film and fashion. There was also a growing social and political awareness and the Polytechnic was in the middle of it.

The band, with Syd Barrett, had already played at the Poly Rag Ball on 4 March 1967, appearing in the gymnasium in the Main Extension Building which was billed as The Large Hall. It was a particularly significant date as it was less than a week before the release of their first single on EMI. Indeed, the Students Union itself was little more than a year old and the event was one of the first that established the college as a top venue for groups and artists who were to become household names such as Cream, Jimi Hendrix and Fleetwood Mac.

There was no doubt in my mind during my first week at the college that I would put myself forward to join the Dance – later Ents – Committee. With the start of this academic year, bands were being booked to appear every second week. I have a distinct memory of a discussion about a particular date that had become troublesome as a result of an act withdrawing. The booking agency could only offer two possible substitutes – Honeybus or Pink Floyd! Some members of the committee said that we had booked Pink Floyd quite recently; others, including myself, pointed out that they had two hit records and were really making a name for themselves on the underground scene. And so the band was booked for a second appearance almost by accident. The appearance took place on Saturday 23rd November 1968, again in the gymnasium.

It was a packed house which meant something in the region of a thousand people. I seem to recall that their fee was £150. By this time, Syd Barrett was no longer in the group and had been replaced by David Gilmour. Their appearance was a great success and showed, beyond any doubt, that the band was on its way to much greater recognition. The event remains memorable for me as I made the introduction with words to the effect of, 'Welcome back to the Polytechnic…'. The stage was a very low wooden podium and, whilst waiting for them to be ready to start, for a reason that is hard to determine, I crouched down to make myself less conspicuous. Nick Mason mistook me for a member of the audience and, in the vernacular, told me to get off. He was no more understanding when I said that I was making the introduction. It seemed that *love and peace* had not yet taken hold. But no matter, it was the intensity of those early performances that drove them forward.

UNIVERSITY OF KEELE
27 NOVEMBER 1968, STAFFORD, UK

I WAS THERE: SIMON PHILLIPS

This was my second Floyd show. I was 16 and living in a small town in Lancashire, so it wasn't as though the Floyd were regularly appearing nearby (although I've since realised that I missed another gig in Blackpool, 15 miles away – bugger!) My friend's sister was at Keele University and told us the Floyd were playing there in the November. OK, how to get there? Looked at the map it was about 80 miles and neither of us drove. Even worse, we had school the next day so how do we get back that night? We looked into hitchhiking but our parents vetoed that. Amazingly, my dad offered to run us there and back. We asked him what he'd do while we were watching – he made it clear that he wouldn't be sitting in the car so we got him a ticket too.

The student union was a typical small hall with a balcony running round three sides and about ten feet deep, so you could get several rows of people standing there. We got a position upper left right against the barrier so the stage was about 45 degrees down and to our left – a great view. There was a lot of equipment on the stage – from memory it was all the stuff on the back of *Ummagumma*. About 15 minutes before they were due on, three guys with really long hair came on and started checking over the equipment. We assumed that these 'scruffs' were the roadies but, after ten minutes, they settled down to the instruments and started to play. At the time, it was probably the longest hair I'd seen but, looking at photos from that period, it doesn't seem that long at all. I really enjoyed this show. The excitement of actually seeing them for the first time, at Blackpool, had gone and I was able to relax (well, a little!) and enjoy the show.

It was a mix of Syd-era ('Flaming', etc) and post-Syd ('Eugene', 'Saucerful'). Roger introduced most of the songs. They weren't particularly loud so, again, we could hear each song clearly. I recognised 'Careful With That Axe, Eugene' a few weeks later when I bought the 'Point Me At The Sky' single. There was no light show other than whatever stage lights were already in the hall. We got out to the car and my friend and I scribbled down as many song titles as we could remember. My dad had enjoyed the show – he thought they were 'interesting' (he was probably about 50 at the time). It wasn't his last Floyd show!

DUNCAN OF JORDANSTONE COLLEGE
12 DECEMBER 1968, DUNDEE, UK

I WAS THERE: FRANCIS BOAG

It was quite a small art college with maybe 800 students, before it became part of the university in Dundee. The Christmas Revels, as they were called, was a big fancy dress ball where the hall was decorated for three weeks. There would be maybe half a dozen bands and a big party that lasted until well into the early hours of the morning. The year I did it the theme was Heironymus Bosch. The hall was all decorated in Bosch stuff from his painting, *The Garden of Earthly Delights*, and the stage was a big monster's mouth. The band were quite impressed with that. They thought it was a great place to play and a great atmosphere.

They'd done 'Arnold Layne' and things like that and so were well out of our usual price range. We had to push the boat out and twist a few arms to get a band as big as that. I think the fee was £450, which was a lot of money for 1968. It almost bankrupted us.

There were five or six bands on – a mixture of Highland cèilidh bands and Latin bands. And the genesis of what became the Average White Band a few years later were there and met up for the first time that night, in two separate bands, because they were from Dundee. Alan Gorrie had left the art school by that time and gone down to London and was playing in the Scotch of St James, and there was the local in-house art school band, Combustion. It was quite a line up for an arts school.

One of the main attractions was the light show. You saw Pink Floyd on TV and, okay, it was black and white TV, but you'd see them playing the Marquee or wherever and it seemed that the light show was quite a selling point. We booked them through an agency and just assumed they'd be bringing their light show. But they didn't bring it with them so we made one up ourselves. One of the students did it behind them and projected it over the hall. Nobody knew it wasn't their light show. I saw the V&A exhibition recently and that showed you the projector they were using, and they were using pretty much the same stuff at the time – projectors with 3-In-One oil and inks and stuff.

I don't know if the roadies came up and did their stuff in the afternoon. My memory is that we talked to the band about the light show and what we were going to do. Looking back now, although it seemed quite a visionary thing with the light show and psychedelia and all that, it was a pretty simple set up; a projector, and the heat on the projector made the oil go all over the place and the coloured things on the slides. I don't think anyone in the audience knew it wasn't their light show and the band seemed quite happy with it.

They went down really well. They didn't play an assortment of hit songs. It was free-flowing. In the hall, everyone was dancing and jumping about all over the place. People hadn't heard much like that really. It was quite unstructured but they were enjoying doing what they wanted to do, rather than having people shouting 'play 'Arnold Layne' or 'See Emily Play''.

They played long guitar solos and drum solos, big long numbers which were improvised and free-flowing. This was just the thing for all the art students, who were all drunk. We didn't know Pink Floyd were going to go on to such magnificent heights, of course. They were just a pretty good band for a wee art school in Dundee. It was a long night. There weren't a lot of drugs. There was one guy who maybe smoked marijuana every now and again. For everybody else it was just beer. There was plenty of that!

I WAS THERE: DUNCAN FENWICK, AGE 18

Although not an art student, I had worked with a Dundee construction company that summer and made a few lifelong friends of architecture/town planning students who were also working the building sites during the summer recess. They were also students at where the gig took place. I was waiting to go to physiotherapy school in London in April 1969.

A PEOPLE'S HISTORY OF PINK FLOYD

The favourite watering hole of the art college crowd was The Tavern, better known as the Tav in Dundee's Hawkhill, situated behind the art college. Most who attended the gig would have met up here first and had a few pints before going to the gig itself. The pub is legendary amongst Dundee students of the late Sixties and Seventies. I think it was knocked down in the Eighties for redevelopment.

The gig itself was fancy dress and there were a few colourful and imaginative costumes (as you would imagine, being an art college crowd) on display that night. The one that stands out for me was that of Manus McGinty, now a Scottish artist, who went as a six foot tall penis. He made it himself from paper mache and from inside the construction he had the inside bladder of an old lace-up football filled with liquid (milk or something similar) with a rubber tube attached which exited via the top of the penis. When he squeezed the football bladder, milk or whatever, would 'ejaculate' from the top of his six foot penis.

I was kitted up as a woman, dressed up in a full length green satin ball gown and cosmetically 'made up' by a girl called (I think) Alison, the girlfriend of architecture student Mike Rodgers, both of whom also attended the gig. Other art college student friends who attended were Nigel Cram, Donny Coutts and Ron Jupp.

Of the gig itself, from memory, lots of us would have been drunk by the time Pink Floyd took to the stage. The actual venue was in the college gymnasium which had a stage at one end. I remember leaning on the stage front which was covered in drawing paper coloured by purple crayon, looking up at David Gilmour and standing in front of his amps. As I was watching the band, some guy propositioned me and touched me up, so either my fancy dress was very convincing (I also had long curly hair with a ribbon in) or he was extremely drunk – probably the latter. I managed to fend him off by giving him a slug of dark rum which I had in a half bottle concealed in my 'cleavage'. Memory is hazy but I think the band were quite aloof and just got on with their performance. There was a light show projected behind them which would have been fairly standard for that era. I seem to remember a Dundee band having the same sort of show at that time. I think they played 'Arnold Layne', 'See Emily Play', 'Set the Controls for the Heart of the Sun' and 'Astronomy Domine' amongst others. For a small, out of the way town like Dundee, it was extremely exotic and surreal to have, what was becoming a major band with their own unique sound play in the town.

I got home early in the morning around 6am and was back out to work on the building site by eight. I was still drunk and although I had managed to discard my ballgown, I forgot my face was made up, had a ribbon in my hair and completely purple hands and forearms from leaning on the front of the stage. I got a pretty raucous reaction from my fellow non-student, building site buddies and a rather disgusted,

Clockwise from top left: Chris McHugo (first & second photos) has had quite the Floyd journey; James Baddock remembers a colourful set from a seasick Pink Floyd – David Gilmour was green about the gills; Nigel Molden booked Pink Floyd for a fee of £150; David Godfrey recalls first seeing Pink Floyd at the Blarney aka UFO;

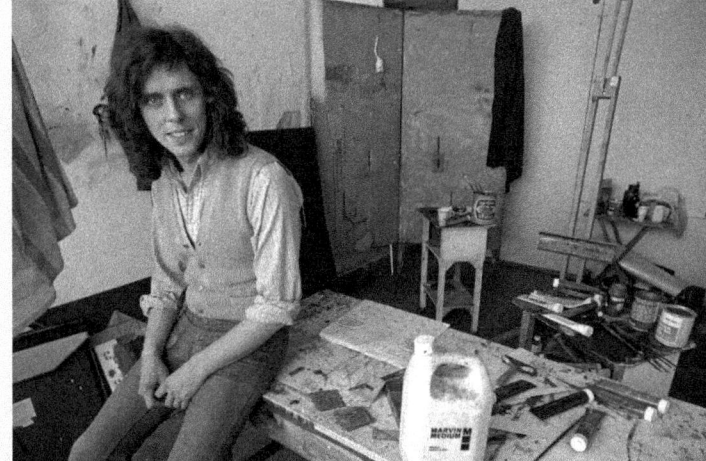

Clockwise from top left: Duncan Fenwick recalls one of the gig-goers dressing in fancy dress as a six-foot penis, as you do; Francis Boag wearing his trend-setting t-shirt; Joe Smernicki doesn't recall the Floyd going down well at the Christmas Revels, unlike the ale; Ron McHoul enjoys the Summer of Love with a young Swedish friend; Jan Nowak supported Pink Floyd at Dundee Art College disappointed reaction from my father who was delivering building materials to the site in his lorry. I don't think he ever forgave me for shaming him in front of his work-mates. I was 18 years old and didn't give a fuck.

Quite spookily, Pink Floyd have been an ongoing thread in my life. Having seen them in Dundee for the first time in 1968 I then saw their free concert in Hyde Park in 1970. In the late seventies a work colleague introduced me to a former manager of the Floyd, I only remember his first name, Roger and he lived in a flat overlooking the roundabout at the top of Muswell Hill. In 1992 I met an American woman whilst holidaying in Australia and became friends with her. She introduced me to a sound engineer back in Los Angeles called Rick Hart, who was soundman for the Floyd on their Wall Tour in the late Seventies or early Eighties. He did the Earl's Court gigs as far as I know. Then, having returned to live in Scotland in 2006, I met up and become friends with a guy called George Franchitti, through our membership of the same golf club. George's youngest son Marino, a racing driver, is married to Holly Mason, Nick Mason's daughter. Small world, isn't it?

I WAS THERE: RON MCHOUL

The theme of the Revels was based on the painter Hieronymus Bosch, hence the title 'Bosching Machine'. I can't remember too much about the Revels that year – it could have been the drink then or my poor memory with the passage of time now!

I WAS THERE: JAN NOWAK

The annual Revels was the student event of the year – great music, loads of booze (and other illegal substances) and everyone out to have a good time. It really was the Swinging Sixties! My band was also on the bill. We played in the bar for the whole evening except for when Pink Floyd did their set. In the midst of all the drunken hedonism, even the bar was closed to allow everyone to see Pink Floyd in action.

In those days most bands were able to carry their gear in a Ford Transit van or even a couple of cars and this certainly applied to us. We all had our own instruments and an amplifier to deal with plus the drummer's gear and a small PA set up. As we were setting up our playing area in the bar, I can clearly remember the guys who had organised the event being astonished that Pink Floyd had arrived in a massive lorry and had taken six tons of gear on to the main stage. We all found this to be incredible. Although it is now normal for bands to arrive with mega amounts of gear and support staff, it certainly wasn't then.

I had never witnessed anything like their set before, being more used to mainstream blues and rock bands, but their presentation was incredible. Their music was complemented by a psychedelic light show which made the whole thing even more surreal. Pink Floyd had a great, big sound that varied from being melodic, even wistful, to hard and solid and totally outwith the realms of other experimental music at that time. It was definitely more unique than *Sgt. Pepper* in its construction. I suppose the effect could best be described as experiential. It wasn't just something that you listened to. The combination of the bohemian environment, music and lighting made the event truly unforgettable. When we resumed our position in the bar afterwards, our sound came over as thin and crap by comparison. But who cares? We were on the same bill.

I managed to retain one of the posters from the event but, sadly, lost this many years ago. But I did manage to obtain a ticket from the event from one of my friends who was also a student at the art college at the time and my band is listed for the event. Unfortunately, the spelling of my surname is incorrect – but that's show business! The gig took the inspirational name of Bosching Machine after a picture of the artist Hieronymus Bosch was placed in the window of a washing machine in the Perth Road laundrette much favoured by art college students. Also, the dress code of the evening required all of the punters to come attired in a style appropriate to being 'A Friend of Batman'.

I WAS THERE: WALTER SIMMS

My memories of the 1968 revels are that they were entitled The Bosching Machine. Students were supposed to dress as Hieronymus Bosch-type characters in fancy dress. I recall being with Joe Smernicki and others that day at the end of our first term. Whether we were still pretty green and overawed at the end of what was our first term, we did not enter into the spirit of it and dress up. We did however get 'tanked up' from lunch time in the pub – or pubs – until the appointed hour arrived. I certainly hadn't heard of Pink Floyd so it was a mystery to me and my memories do no credit to them whatsoever!

Worse for wear, I remember going into the big hall to watch and listen and found the place light on an audience. I left to go to the smaller hall, where another band had everyone leaping about. I went back again to see Pink Floyd but not much had changed and I went right up to the stage and hung around for a bit, but the booze had killed all my listening buds. I left to go back to the dancing, presumably because most of the girls were there too. It was a poor introduction to the band but, then again, I was a Pentangle/Fairport/John Martyn fan by then.

A fellow lady student met them in connection with some other activity organised by the Revels committee. She told me a story which involved one or two of the band helping to remove paint which she got covered by!

I WAS THERE: JOE SMERNICKI

I was a first year art student when Pink Floyd played at the annual Christmas Revels. A whole wing of the college was given over to the Revels, with Floyd playing the main hall. Several other bands and various entertainments would have been on over the night and through until three o'clock in the morning. One of the bands would most likely have been a college group called Sleepy People. Almost certainly around would have been a couple of the founder members of the Average White Band, who were students there at that time.

Re Pink Floyd's performance on the night, I have to say it wasn't overwhelmingly, positively received. The band had been known at the time to lay on impressive light shows but chose not to on that night, with only the college lighting effects, courtesy of a slide projector, coloured inks and washing up liquid! Music-wise, the night wasn't hugely memorable. It was exciting perhaps, but I have no memory of virtuoso performances. One regret I have from the evening is that one of the band threw a drumstick to the audience which was caught by a friend, Nick, next to me. He immediately threw it back. Oh dear! We had no idea of future memorabilia markets.

NEW MARQUEE
13 DECEMBER 1968, LEEDS, UK

I WAS THERE: PAUL HATFIELD

It was a small venue based at Marc Altman's Dance School. I saw loads of Floyd types here, notably The Nice. I seem to remember the show was based around *The Piper at the Gates of Dawn*. I saw them at Leeds University too, where they were a bit more expansive, but I always felt they struggled to get a decent sound. They were still good though, and produced an atmospheric night.

CAVENDISH BALLROOM
29 JANUARY 1969, TOLLCROSS, EDINBURGH, UK

I WAS THERE: ANDREW MCCRACKEN

In our final year at Edinburgh University, three of us bought the Desired Effect mobile discotheque, which had been set up a year before. We had a gig in January 1969 with several bands including Pink Floyd. When we arrived, we discovered that we were setting up on the same stage as the band, and playing when they were having a break. When we switched on at the end of their set, our equipment barely filled the hall. It was somewhat embarrassing, as we were on full volume and the sound was dreadful. Happily, one of the Pink Floyd roadies connected us up to their amps and saved the day (or night).

UNIVERSITY OF ST ANDREWS
16 FEBRUARY 1969, ST ANDREWS, UK

I WAS THERE: SHEILA BENTLEY

I went to that concert and only recently came across the ticket when I was going through some old papers. The ticket is very small, only about nine centimetres by six centimetres, but the design is brilliant. The reverse, which shows my ticket was number 311. I have no idea how many were sold altogether. I was in my first year at the university and probably went with friends from my hall of residence, though I can't remember exactly who. We were very impressed with the light show, which moved round the walls but I'm afraid that's about all I can remember. The music was loud and the songs were a bit too long and shapeless for me – I didn't stay till the end!

I WAS THERE: PHILIP HULME-JONES

I was a student from 1966 to 1970. The concert was in the Younger Hall, not the Students Union. I was sitting on the balcony with my girlfriend – later, and still, my wife. The hall seemed to be full. There may have been one or two empty seats on the fringes, but it was pretty much a sell-out. When previous bands visited the Younger Hall – eg. The Searchers, The Merseybeats, Unit Four plus Two – people danced while they played, and this was the first band I heard there when the audience just sat down and listened. The St Andrews crowd was quite reserved, and I don't recall it being particularly noisy. There was a large gong on the stage, and David Gilmour wore an outdoor coat with the collar turned up throughout.

We were curious. We wanted to see stars who were famous at a national level, which we didn't see many of, and for some people there was an awareness that Pink Floyd was a bit different to, say, the Liverpool groups. But St Andrews in the Sixties was a conservative place. It was a long time ago and St Andrews in 1969 was a very different place – different to St Andrews in 2017, let alone London, Manchester or Newcastle.

There would have been guys in that audience wearing collar, tie and jacket, people who regularly attended the folk club in the Star Hotel, and even people who attended concerts by the Scottish National Orchestra when they came to St Andrews.

The women made more of an effort than the men to dress with the times – a few would have been trying to cultivate the flower power look. A lot of people in St Andrews thought of Pink Floyd as just another pop group at that time ('See Emily Play') and it was a bit exciting to see people who were famous. No doubt a few people who followed the music scene more closely than I did thought of it as music growing up. We had parents who saw almost any popular music as rebellious. My father's favourite music was *The Black and White Minstrel Show*, although he did concede that 'Elvis Presley has a good voice'.

I WAS THERE: DANNY RAFFERTY

I would have been in my second year at university. I was doing English, History and Moral Philosophy. Those of us who were brought up in the Sixties still depended on the very erratic signal from Radio Luxembourg for our pop music and I think that's where I'd come across Pink Floyd, although there were some television programmes. Earlier on, there was *Six Five Special* and *Ready Steady Go!*, which became *Top of the Pops*, which was very popular when I was a young student.

Like a lot of people my age I liked British blues – The Yardbirds, Fleetwood Mac, Chicken Shack, the less poppy side of popular music. So many things were really opening up at that time. The American West Coast groups had become popular – The Doors, Love. And there was a lot of what today we would call World Music too, Indian film music and that kind of stuff, and I was always into the traditional Scottish and Irish traditional music. And I was very much into jazz. Pink Floyd were just that little bit different. I'd never had a record of theirs. I'd heard of them as being quite an avant-garde pop group but I didn't really know their music all that well. People used to hear about them and just exchange records and listen to each other's records. When I heard there was a concert being held in St Andrews, there was no way I was going to miss it. It was right on my doorstep.

I dragged a friend along. I don't think anybody there that night knew anything about Pink Floyd. St Andrews is a bit off the beaten track. There weren't many really big groups because, being a small university, it didn't really attract major groups. The Younger Hall is a big auditorium where the graduation ceremonies take place. There was no heating. It was a Sunday night in the middle of February and the place was freezing.

The audience was pretty quiet and pretty passive. Everybody was sitting down on chairs. I'd say the place was only about half full. I don't think the audience was really familiar with their music or knew what to expect. They were presenting their music to an audience that wasn't fully familiar with their repertoire. They didn't have a light show that night and I don't remember any pyrotechnics. It was a bare stage.

I don't remember that much interaction between the group and the audience. The band might have complained about the temperature of the place a couple of times. But the music was absolutely fabulous and they didn't short change the audience even though the circumstances were less than fully advantageous. They could easily have just gone through the motions, played a couple of numbers and said, 'That's it.' But my memory is that they played a very full set. They played a very long and extended version of 'Set the Controls for the Heart of the Sun'.

If you look at pictures of them from that time, Roger Waters had a big army greatcoat on and I remember him wearing that greatcoat on the night. Military cast-off clothing was quite popular then. It was cheap for one thing, and quite practical for another. He was wearing that, almost a full-length kind of coat. That was the sensible thing to wear that night because it was so bloody cold.

I WAS THERE: MIKE ROBBIE, AGE 20

I was a local to St Andrews and went with some friends. I don't remember much of the concert (we were all a wee bit wasted on the night) so I'm afraid don't really remember much about it. However, something must have stuck as I went on to buy most of their records and am now in the process of collecting some picture discs. I did see them again at Earls Court in 1994 and I went to see *Their Mortal Remains* at the V&A in London.

I WAS THERE: KEVIN THURLOW, AGE 19

I was into them and that sort of music, but I don't remember much about the gig. Things like colour wheels and visual effects at gigs were pretty new then. And then there was the psychedelic stuff, etc., which explains a lot about why I don't remember. It was the Sixties after all…

KEE CLUB
15 MARCH 1969, BRIDGEND, UK

I WAS THERE: HOWARD JOHN

I was doing the posters for the Kee Club in 1969 and got free entry to see them. I'd seen them before with Syd at Sophia Gardens for the infamous 23 November 1967

Hendrix gig, with The Move, Eire Apparent, Amen Corner et al. I also caught them at the Aberavon Lido later, in December 1969, a much heavier event with hordes of police patrolling the aisles in search of the evil pot, as well as a few festival sets.

My main memory of the Kee Club event was sitting right by the tiny stage with Dave Gilmour's Strat regularly parting my hair. The place was rammed and the low ceilings and stone walls created a thick sweaty atmosphere that was liberally infused with exotic smokes. It was in the run-up to the release of *Ummagumma*, so if my fuzzy memories are right, we got a few tracks from that album like 'Set the Controls' mixed with old favourites like 'Interstellar Overdrive', but I might be mixing it up with later gigs.

Bridgend had been an unlikely destination on the circuit for years, with major acts playing at the YMCA, a large enough hall to attract John Mayall and other bands that were part of the Blues Crusade. But the YM got a bit too straight for some of us, so when the Kee Club was first mooted, we urged Clive Mayall (no relation) to get it together. It became a regular weekend hangout for the head set. No bar, just soft drinks and the opportunity to get our hands on new publications like *IT* and *Oz*.

Despite its minimal facilities the Kee Club was, for a short period, a mecca for the hippy sector with bands like Love Sculpture, Pink Fairies, The Nice and an early version of Yes. Perhaps because it was so small, it was a perfectly intimate venue for individual acts like Roy Harper who, apart from his own gigs at the club, once turned up as a late replacement for Tyrannosaurus Rex, only to find that the stage PA had packed in so he had to do the whole set from a cramped deejay pulpit at the other end of the hall. Predictably, it was one of the best gigs I'd been at, and I saw a lot of Mr Harper at various festivals and clubs. We made regular pilgrimages to Les Cousins in Soho.

It all ended for the Kee when the owner decided it wasn't profitable and instructed staff not to clear up one night. Mysteriously, the litter ended up stacked around the pillars and spontaneously ignited, which was the end of a wonderful but all too short era when Bridgend became a go-to gig venue for some of the biggest names in late Sixties prog rock and agit folk.

I WAS THERE: ROBERT WOOD

I saw Floyd at the Kee Club in Bridgend, South Wales. It was a small basement venue that held about 80 or 90 people. I remember it as being hot, sweaty and loud. It was a huge PA for the time and my ears took 48 hours to recover. The highlight was 'Set the Controls for the Heart of the Sun.'

I WAS THERE: HUW EDWARDS, AGE 17

I had just bought the first Floyd album, *The Piper at the Gates of Dawn*, and started down the road. You can imagine my delight when I heard they were playing at the tiny Kee

Club (formerly Zachary Rack) in my home town of Bridgend. We walked into our local, The Wyndham (now a Wetherspoons) and in the corner of the bar the band were drinking Worthington E! The concert was amazing... A packed shoebox, standing room only... They did numbers from *Piper* and the upcoming *Saucerful of Secrets*. I particularly remember an amazing rendition of 'Astronomy Domine'. They performed two numbers destined to be live classics and which appeared on *UmmaGumma*, 'Set The Controls for the Heart of the Sun' and 'Careful With That Axe, Eugene'. It was hot, I was 17, it was loud. The music was sublime.

March 1969 was the start of a long-term love affair with the Floyd. I saw them live a number of times after that, the highlight being Crystal Palace. My one regret was the 1969 Shepton Mallet Festival, the forerunner to Glastonbury. Due to the weather and other delays, the Floyd didn't come on until the early hours, after Led Zeppelin and Johnny Winter. They debuted *Atom Heart Mother* with full orchestra... I slept right through it.

I WAS THERE: SIMONE MORTON

I know I was at the Pink Floyd gig because I kept the ticket for a while, but I don't actually recall anything of that night…

I WAS THERE; STEVE TILEY

I was working during the day but I used to be the DJ at the Kee Club in the evenings. We mostly played American West Coast stuff like the Grateful Dead, Quicksilver Messenger Service and Jefferson Airplane but we'd play a bit of Floyd and Edgar Broughton. People used to come from everywhere, because it was the only club for miles around where the emerging British underground bands could play. Yes played there, and they played there before they were called Yes, when they were called Mabel Greer's Toyshop. Edgar Broughton played there, and The Pretty Things around the time of SF Sorrow.

I was there every night, because I was the DJ. I used to do the lights as well. It was hands-on and run on a shoestring. When Pink Floyd played, it was absolutely packed to the gills. You couldn't move in there. They started off and then a mate of mine called Paul, from Cardiff, went up on the stage, stopped the band and got everybody to sit down. Because everybody was clamouring to see them, and because it was only a smallish place, you were knackered if tall people were standing up in front of you. Everybody sat down after a couple of minutes and they continued playing.

It was a small stage and they were packed quite tightly on the stage. I think Roger Waters even had to lean over a little bit because the ceiling was so low. Syd Barrett had gone by then and Dave Gilmour had joined. The only albums they had out were *The Piper at the Gates of Dawn* and *A Saucerful of Secrets*. In the underground community, they were really big. It was about the time when they were starting to get noticed, and people were thinking 'this is something special here'. They were booked by the guy who owned the club.

We had a little cubbyhole above the stage. I used to climb the ladder on the side of the stage and go in there. Most of the lights were wired up to switches that looked like doorbells, so you'd press the button for on and off. And we made the strobe lights from record decks. We cut circles out of the deck, put coloured gels on them, put a bulb behind them and then mounted them on the side of the wall and just turned the record player on so that, when the deck was spinning, you had a mini-strobe light at 78 rpm. It was a great little place.

I WAS THERE: NORMAN WHITEHALL (AKA DOUGALL DEEJAY)

I was deejaying with a colleague – John Gough – in the late 1960s, in Bristol. We had one of the first mobile discos in the country. I was the equipment man and poser, John had the records. He knew everything that was going on in the music scene and we presented a great show on the road around the Bristol area. He was raving about a new band and said we needed to go and see them in Bridgend. A few days later, we hitch-hiked from Bristol over to Bridgend; there was no money in discos in the pioneering days!

We found what was a basement club and, as we queued with an excited crowd, we were told it was a 'members only' club. Sure enough, as we tried to enter the doorman confirmed this. Despondent after our hike to get there, we were wandering around Bridgend at a loss, when we noticed a bunch of long-haired guys emerging from a small newsagent's shop eating liquorice and various other stuff. John immediately recognised them as Pink Floyd! We went over to them, introduced ourselves, explaining our dilemma and how we had hiked all the way from Bristol to see them. Roger Waters said, 'No problem, just follow us.'

As we all approached the club entrance, the doorman again tried to stop us. Roger just turned and said 'they're with us'. Sorted! Minutes later, we were ensconced in their tiny dressing room where their roadie/driver was busy taking an amplifier to bits on the floor. We spent the whole evening there, apart from when we were watching their set. They readily shared their stash of special (!) smokes with us, which they had hidden in the broken ceiling. The whole gig was magical and we returned home on cloud nine, not realising just what a piece of musical history we had witnessed.

A year or two later, we saw them again at the Colston Hall in Bristol and managed to blag our way backstage. Surprisingly, the band recognised us immediately and we had some more quality time chatting with the guys, who were already on the verge of the stratosphere musically. At the Colston Hall gig they had a quad speaker set up, with WEM speakers in each of the four corners of the venue. At one point, they stopped performing and all sat down on the stage to drink tea, while there was a sound effect playing of doors opening in different places and chains being dragged and people walking right across everyone. It was an amazing sound experience for that era.

EMPRESS BALLROOM
21 MARCH 1969, BLACKPOOL, UK

I WAS THERE: FRANK YATES

It was Blackpool College's end-of-term bash. The logo was a tripper with an erect Blackpool Tower protruding between his legs – you can guess the rest! Floyd were known for 'Arnold Layne' and 'See Emily Play', and the masses were expecting more of that. They got none of it. They got 'Astronomy Domine', 'A Saucerful of Secrets' et al. The audience didn't like it and made their displeasure known. There was jeering and booing, and there were reports of coins being thrown. Floyd did what they became famous for and simply turned the stage lights down, and then turned their back on the audience and played on. There were only three of us high in the balcony, and we enjoyed it. I'm not sure those getting drunk on the dance floor did!

The Azimuth Co-ordinator was a panning control system for quadraphonic sound. Pink Floyd are the first band to use it in their live shows, with Rick Wright moving the sound from speaker to speaker around the auditorium. The first machine is stolen following a concert at the Queen Elizabeth Hall in London. A second is built for the band's Royal Festival Hall show in April 1969.

ROYAL FESTIVAL HALL
14 APRIL 1969, LONDON, UK

I WAS THERE: RAYMOND DAY

I think it was billed as the *Azimuth Co-ordinator* tour, the first surround sound thing they did. I caught them at the Royal Festival Hall, although I had already seen them in Bromley a couple of years earlier with Syd. I went with Chris Jones and the support were East of Eden (a fine band – I've got their album *Mercator Projected*) and Hippopotomi. Floyd were good, and I remember it was the first time I'd seen a light show. We knew all the Floyd songs because *The Piper at the Gates of Dawn* was basically their set. I saw a bloke there I knew and he was wearing a pink suit!

I WAS THERE: SIMON PHILLIPS, AGE 17

I'd always been quite jealous of the people living in London who had been able to see the Floyd on a regular basis so, when the Royal Festival Hall show was announced, my friend and I decided we'd try and get to it. We wrote off for tickets (no internet!) and had an anxious wait for a couple of weeks until an envelope finally arrived with the tickets. My friend was already going to be in London but I was faced with the return trip from Lancashire to London on my own. This may not sound like a big deal but I'd only ever been to London once, years earlier on a family holiday, so having only just turned 17 it was quite daunting. We didn't know London particularly well – we looked at a map to find the location of the hall and agreed to meet in the middle of Waterloo Bridge at a particular time. (It sounds like a wartime romance!) The train journey down was uneventful and we duly met up and went to the hall. First impressions from the outside were that it was 'a bit of a shithole'; that whole South Bank area of London was, and is, a Sixties concrete jungle.

Inside, we bought a programme which promised lots of new songs. Our seats were just over halfway back from the stage and almost dead centre, which as it turned out was a great position for the quad effects. The first thing we noticed was the birds. The 'tweet tweet tweet' went on and on for about an hour before the show started. We assumed that the birds must be nesting in the pipes of the enormous church organ that dominated the back wall of the hall and were worried that they'd spoil the show – they were so loud. Don't forget we'd never heard 'Grantchester Meadows' or 'Cirrus Minor' at this point. Anyway, Dave and Roger ambled on and started to play and the birds gradually seemed to settle down – ha!

The Man section of the show seemed a little shambolic and disjointed – they gave the appearance of making it up as they went along. This was particularly so around the hammering and sawing wood and during the tea break. The audaciousness of doing that, actually stopping the show and sitting down on the stage to drink a cup of tea – how very English! It was an unbelievable moment when Rick suddenly stood up and started playing a trombone – WTF did that come from?

The Azimuth Co-ordinator was amazing. Back then, I didn't even have a home stereo so to hear the sound coming from all round the hall was indescribable. The two sections that I particularly remember were the very loud sound of a train coming straight through the hall from front to back, and the footsteps walking in circles around the perimeter of the hall. Rick also sent music to different parts of the hall.

The second set, *The Journey*, was better, although still a little disappointing if I'm honest. It was much more coherent and more musical than the first set, as everything was run together as a suite. They made great use of the quad system and I recall at least one 'merman' wandering around the auditorium, climbing onto the backs of seats. My disappointment was due to a lot of the songs being old numbers which had been renamed (and sounded a lot more exciting) in the programme. I remember writing their more familiar names in the programme on the journey home. It was quite something to see Rick as a tiny figure playing the church organ at the end of 'A Saucerful of Secrets' – the sound was rich and 'thick'. They did 'Interstellar Overdrive' as an encore, which I was chuffed about. It was a very interesting, very enjoyable show and I remember feeling that I'd actually been present at one of the London 'happenings' that I'd read about in the music press.

What amazes me now is that, after the show, I managed to get back across London to Euston station and catch the last train back to Lancashire. I have absolutely no recollection of what I'd have done if I'd missed it, although they had what was called the Milk Train which ran at about 4am in the morning – I don't know if it took passengers or not. On the train, I could see half a dozen other people dotted around looking through programmes from the show. I couldn't believe it when many years later I came across a recording of it – what a shame they didn't record it themselves (ditto *Games For May*).

TECHNICAL COLLEGE
26 APRIL 1969, BROMLEY, LONDON, UK

MY WIFE WAS THERE: CHRIS SAMPSON

My daughters enjoy my wife's story about lying on the floor, gazing at the ceiling, during a Pink Floyd gig at Ravensbourne college of art (formerly Bromley Technical College). My own abiding memory is of *A Saucerful of Secrets* played on the mighty Colston Hall pipe organ in Bristol around that time. My wife was studying at Stockwell College and the students from there would attend art school dances at neighbouring Ravensbourne. Floyd were on and, whatever the reason for finding herself horizontal on the dance floor, it provided a good perspective on the light show.

WISH YOU WERE HERE

MOTHERS
27 APRIL 1969, BIRMINGHAM, UK

A performance which provides material later released as part of Ummagumma *is recorded.*

I WAS THERE: PAUL 'PIG' JENNINGS

I saw them at Mothers when they recorded the *Ummagumma* album and I saw them down at the Ally Pally for the *14 Hour Technicolor Dream*. There was a load of bands on, and it was an all-nighter. They were just so different. I also saw them at Knebworth – although I went for the support acts! But they were good. I remember the aeroplane coming over the back and crashing into the stage.

Three albums were recorded at Mothers. One was by a blues band and that was absolutely bloody dire. I don't know why they released it. We didn't know beforehand that Floyd were going to record the gig and that it was going to be filmed, because that would've probably doubled the audience with people saying 'I want to be in the film' kind of thing. But I turned up and I could see an amount of recording gear, including the cameras. I think it was recorded mainly off the desk. There could've been other gear as well, because there was gear all over the place, but then Floyd always had a load of gear with the electronics, the keyboards and this and that. I remember the drummer, Nick Mason, having a great big gong at the back. They always had a lot of gear because they were quite experimental.

I WAS THERE: BOB MANSFIELD

My earliest memory of the band was actually back in 1968 and '69 when they played at Mothers Club in Erdington, Birmingham. I was a roadie for a local Coventry band playing similar music – prog rock – who actually knew Pink Floyd and often when they played Mothers – a local club above a furniture warehouse in Erdington High Street, Birmingham – they would go backstage, which was an open room behind the stage, and play pool with the band. Our drummer was particularly friendly with Nick Mason as they had a similar style and sound on drums. Mothers hosted some of the most (now) famous bands virtually every night of the week and we were present when part of *Ummagumma* was recorded live. Our manager was friends with DJ John Peel who had a regular Friday night spot, eventually leading to our band playing on one of his nights.

MANCHESTER COLLEGE OF COMMERCE
2 MAY 1969, MANCHESTER, UK

Another live performance, parts of which feature on Ummagumma, *is recorded.*

PARLIAMENT HILL FIELDS
9 MAY 1969, HAMPSTEAD, LONDON, UK

I WAS THERE: CHRIS SAMPSON

I would hitchhike to London from Cardiff at the weekend and there was always a free concert somewhere. Pink Floyd played the Camden Fringe Free Festival at Parliament Hill Fields, so it was horizontal listening on the grass, which provided a very spacey soundtrack to the stars and the lights of planes passing in the night sky. It was a tremendous atmosphere. The show lasted until the early hours, and afterwards we walked to the nearest Tube station and dossed down, watching the eerie automatic postal trains come through before the first service at 5am.

I WAS THERE: DEN BOUNDY

I saw Pink Floyd twice, firstly at the Fairfield Halls in Croydon, South East London. I was really impressed with the huge banks of speakers they had on stage, the massive J Arthur Rank-type gong, and the fantastic light show they played to. The second time I saw them was at a free concert on Parliament Hill Fields. It was about 2am. The music sounded quite eerie echoing around in the still night air and we were in complete blackness apart from the stage. They were preceded by the Crazy World of Arthur Brown, whose record 'Fire' was climbing the charts at the time. Arthur's helmet of flames really stood out in the darkness.

LOCARNO BALLROOM
15 MAY 1969, COVENTRY, UK

I WAS THERE: TONY GREEN, AGE 15

It was the College of Art's May Ball, entitled 'It's A Drag', and was the first major concert

I attended. I had left school in July 1968 and was working in a factory for the princely sum of £4 per week. Also working on the same section at this particular factory was a young man named Paul Padun. Coventry was a hotbed of progressive music in the Sixties and Seventies, partly due to Lanchester Polytechnic and also the recently opened Warwick University. Paul managed a band in his spare time called Asgard who played at various venues in Coventry, including the International Centre within the old cathedral ruins. Asgard were a three-piece band who played Pink Floyd and Nice-inspired music. They eventually broke up and Paul moved to London in the early Seventies and worked as a roadie for a while for Pink Floyd as a lighting technician. He sadly died young in 1980.

I think the concert admission ticket price was around ten shillings (50p). My fellow concert-goers were school friends a couple of years older than me. A couple of the lads were about to be enrolled into art college. There were two support acts, a band from the Birmingham area called the Wellington Kitch Jump Band, and Spooky Tooth, who were signed to the Island record label and who released a couple of albums and a single entitled, 'Better by You, Better Than Me'.

The concert was well attended. Obviously, Pink Floyd were the top of the bill, or 'headliners' as they say these days. I can remember 'A Saucerful of Secrets' being played and, at one stage of the concert, Nick Mason lying beneath the cymbals and bashing them from underneath! There were special buses organised from Broadgate in the city centre to take people home to various areas around the city. I remember turning up for work the next day feeling extremely tired and my ears still ringing from the previous evening.

TOWN HALL
16 MAY 1969, LEEDS, UK

I WAS THERE: TONY GAVINS

It was the unveiling of the Azimuth Co-ordinator, which was a method of distributing the sound between different speakers dotted in all corners of the hall. I remember that I had not heard much of the music played that night before. Nor since. I still have my programme from the gig somewhere. Another memorable feature of the show was a group of performers dressed as alien creatures who wandered from the back of the hall up the aisles of seats, scaring the punters to death with their long tentacles. I think a few of them nearly got chinned as at first it didn't appear to be a part of the show, but more like a few clowns taking the piss.

A pal of mine had a fine hi-fi system and he shoved a pair of cans over my ears, left me in a darkened room, put 'Careful With That Axe, Eugene' on full volume and left me to listen. The album, *Ummagumma*, had just come out and this was my first listen. When the first scream came, I nearly evacuated the contents of my bowels.

I WAS THERE: LES LAMB, AGE 15

I first heard 'See Emily Play' when it played on the car radio as I was travelling back from Butlins in North Wales with my parents. I was immediately hooked. I was still at school and in those days to hear anything other than pop music you had to listen to the pirate ships. Radio 270 moored off the Yorkshire coast was my favourite but they were not to last much longer in that Summer of Love of '67. I was into Hendrix, the Doors and the other West Coast US bands as well as the Stones and other blues/progressive bands. I did not own a record player (I taped what I could off the radio) so my scope was a bit restricted. However, I was interested in the Floyd and I managed to hear snippets from their first album, which I thought was okay – in parts. I started work in 1968 and at least had a bit of cash to spend. I lived in Leeds and me and my mates, although into progressive/underground music, hadn't at the time been introduced to the poly/uni disco scene, so we spent our money on Ben Sherman's, pinstripe turn up Oxford baggies and patent shoes. Any clubbing was done at the local Mecca, which played two or three decent rock songs a night if you were lucky!

Come the spring of 1969, I bought a couple of tickets to see the Floyd at Leeds Town Hall. My best mate John worked at the DSS and I worked as an insurance clerk. We both had freshly grown long hair – well, it was over our ears – and we waited in anticipation for the big night. We decided to go for a quick drink after work and then straight to the concert. We were both wearing our working suits and matching shirt-and-tie sets, which were the fashion at the time. I also had a silk hanky in my top pocket! We turned the corner and saw the queue. It was like a mini-Woodstock. I had never seen so much long hair and so many tie-dye shirts, velvet loon pants and Afghan coats at any one time, before or since. We looked at one another and then whipped off our ties and took our jackets off to try and look at least a bit civilised.

We had front row seats and discussed what songs they would play. We were expecting 'Emily' and the other popular songs from the *Piper* album. What came next completely blew us away. The sound system from nearly 50 years ago was unreal. They played a set from the forthcoming *More* soundtrack. By the end, we were absolutely gob smacked. I still have the programme from that concert. Anyway, I managed to buy a record player. The first album I bought was *A Saucerful of Secrets*.

Clockwise from top left: Andrew McCracken was grateful to the Floyd's road crew; Cavendish Ballroom ad (Andrew McCracken); Danny Rafferty (right) with his gig-going friend Andy Harwich; Sheila Bentley in paisley in St Andrews; Huw Edwards first saw Floyd at the Kee Club

Clockwise from top left: Norman Whitehall got to hang out in the Floyd's dressing room; Tony Green recalls Nick Mason laying down and playing his cymbals from underneath; Bob Mansfield at a time when men grew their hair longer than women did; Les Lamb removed his tie when he realised the dress code at a Floyd show

I WAS THERE: GARY SHEPHERD, AGE 16

I went with a friend. We were sat in the orchestra stalls directly behind Nick Mason. We arrived late and had to be guided down the steep steps of the orchestra stalls by an usherette with a torch. Apart from the concert being awesome, my particular memories include Nick Mason giving me his water bottle as he went off stage for the instrumental interval, John Peel sitting cross-legged on the floor in the middle of the main walkway down to the stage, the screams from the crowd as the 'creatures' came out under darkness during 'Careful With That Axe, Eugene' and (I think) Roger Waters turning a lever on a big black box and making the sound move direction around the hall. Hell, I had only just got stereo!

I met Nick Mason several time at Goodwood (I was a Goodwood Road Racing Club member until recently). Not as friends, but just to nod to and say, 'Hi... nice car.' I was too nervous to do anything else. I did, however, get a personalised 50th birthday greeting from Roger Waters. Both he and Nick lived near where we lived in Hampshire.

Back in the day I went to see a lot of bands – The Who, Free, Led Zep and the Stones – and a host of obscure groups like the Incredible String Band and Tyrannosaurus Rex. My only big regret is never seeing Jimi Hendrix live as he was – and still is – my biggest musical icon. Now his tour with Pink Floyd as a support... that would have been awesome. I now live in New Zealand with my wife and a whole host of animals and wonderful scenery, but Floyd still blasts out of my speakers across the valley. A truly awesome band.

ROUNDHOUSE
25 MAY 1969, CHALK FARM ROAD, LONDON, UK

I WAS THERE: GUðBJÖRG ÖGMUNDSDÓTTIR

The first time I saw Pink Floyd play was at a benefit concert for Fairport Convention, who had been in a car accident which killed their drummer and a friend of theirs. Pink Floyd headed the bill which included the groups Eclection, Blossom Toes, Family and The Pretty Things. By the time Pink Floyd hit the stage, it was late and there was an 11 o'clock curfew on the concert. Sadly, I don't remember the three songs they managed to play but after about 20 minutes on stage, playing great music with all kinds of instruments which included an enormous gong, the electricity was turned off. That really pissed off me and the rest of the audience, so things got a bit rowdy, but I escaped the Roundhouse unhurt. I remember this concert fondly.

ULSTER HALL
10 JUNE 1969, BELFAST, UK

I WAS THERE: MICHAEL MCFAUL

The third time I saw them was in June 1969 at the Ulster Hall. I was downstairs in the back row with my girlfriend and a guy appeared part way into the gig dressed in a diving suit and helmet. He sat beside us, unnerving my girlfriend, and towards the end he got up and started prowling round the audience. I was never sure how this fitted in with the concert or indeed whether it was part of the show or just some guy doing something weird. This was around the time they launched *Ummagumma* and had the big gong on stage, which Waters enjoyed hammering. They also had the Azimuth Co-ordinator, which I suppose was an early version of surround sound. A great gig. One treasured possession I have is the original sheet music for 'Arnold Layne', the song that turned me on to Pink Floyd in late 1966.

MORE RELEASED
13 JUNE 1969

Floyd's third album reaches No.9 in the UK album charts.

COLSTON HALL
14 JUNE 1969, BRISTOL, UK

I WAS THERE: JOHN FLETCHER

We saw them in Colston Hall around 1969 when they had the new quadraphonic surround sound and it was awesome. I was lucky because of my connection to the band to sit right behind the guys controlling the sound.

DOME
16 JUNE 1969, BRIGHTON, UK

I WAS THERE: KEN TOOKE
It was 1969 when I next saw Pink Floyd, at Brighton Dome. I saw them twice at Brighton Dome. On this occasion, I got backstage via the stage and David Gilmour signed my autograph book on my Pink Floyd page. This was opposite my autographs of Fairport Convention and he said, 'I see you've got young Martin Lamble, deceased.' (Lamble was the Fairport's original drummer, killed in May 1969 in a post-gig road accident.) I asked Pink Floyd what musicians they admired and they mentioned the US group HP Lovecraft.

PHILHARMONIC HALL
21 JUNE 1969, LIVERPOOL, UK

I WAS THERE: SIMON PHILLIPS
We bought tickets for this as soon as we'd seen the London show. They were good seats, in the stalls and about 20 rows back. I went with the same friend I'd been with in London but my brother wanted to come too. With him being younger (not yet 15), my parents thought it a bit risky so up stepped Dad again and he drove us to the show and back (now his second gig… and still not his last). It was tighter than the London show, more rehearsed, particularly the first set, and they didn't seem to make as much use of the Azimuth Co-ordinator as previously, or maybe it was just less effective, being a much smaller hall.

FREE TRADE HALL
22 JUNE 1969, MANCHESTER, UK

I WAS THERE: GRAHAM GUNNS
I'd been an avid fan after hearing them in 1967 and buying 'Arnold Layne' and 'See Emily Play'. In 1969, me and my mate John, aged 17, decided to go and see them. It was called *The Man* concert and we didn't know what to expect. It was an eye-opener

with all the lighting and sound effects. One strange effect was an amplified man breathing hard, walking around the theatre, up the stairways across the gallery and back down the opposite stairs – very eerie! I had the programme, a thin A4 thing with *THE MAN* on the front, up until recently. Memories of lost times.

I WAS THERE: PETER ROYLE

Not living anywhere near London, I never got to any of the really early gigs at the Roundhouse or the UFO Club. I first saw them at the Free Trade Hall in Manchester in 1969. That was amazing. I seem to remember that in the middle of one piece, maybe 'A Saucerful of Secrets' or 'Careful With That Axe, Eugene', a big hairy gorilla (suit, I presume!) emerged from a side door carrying a burning torch and proceeded to wander climb all around the sides of the hall. Or was that just the result of what I'd been smoking on the way there?

I do remember they introduced a new song, which they said was called 'Daybreak', so I was quite surprised to find it appearing on *Ummagumma*, called 'Grantchester Meadows'. They actually had someone playing trombone for 'Jugband Blues'. I was there a few years later, too, when they made breakfast on stage, for 'Alan's Psychedelic Breakfast'. That was when they had half an orchestra and choir on stage for *Atom Heart Mother* – a grossly underrated album.

QUEEN'S COLLEGE
24 JUNE 1969, OXFORD, UK

I WAS THERE: PETER DE MONCEY-CONEGLIANO

Don't ask me how I, a working-class grammar school boy, went to Oxford. I must have been really clever when I was 17. Anyway, it was the happiest time of my life, with complete freedom and no responsibility, and when the only worry I had was what party to go to that evening and what outfit to wear to it. And here I was, in the last term of that extravaganza, and my very own college had booked the Pink Floyd for its Commem Ball! They played in a marquee in the front quad. You could stand or dance right in front of them amongst all the hearty Oxford types in their dinner jackets with their crates of champagne. Dave Gilmour had already replaced Syd Barrett, but they played a lot of early stuff plus the new direction they were heading with *Ummagumma* and *More*, their latest albums. I had not seen them live before, but I had been a fan since *Piper at the Gates of Dawn* had come out in the summer of '67, and I had played it to death at my birthday party in college in February 1968 to create a genuinely psychedelic atmosphere.

ROYAL ALBERT HALL
26 JUNE 1969, LONDON, UK

I WAS THERE: PAUL DAWSON

The first concert of theirs I saw was the legendary Albert Hall gig in June '69. I just went along to see what they were like and it was (and remains) the greatest rock concert I have ever seen. It was entitled *The Final Lunacy*. The quadraphonic sound system (cutely named the Azimuth Co-ordinator) was most impressive. I loved the blend of free form music with the songs and the *musique concrete* as they made a table on stage and sat down to a cup of tea. An air raid siren marked the end of the first half and Rick played the pipe organ with a choir accompaniment in *Saucerful* to terminate the main show. 'Set the Controls' was the encore. I was hooked, and saw them as often as possible after that. A few months later, they played the Albert Hall again, but it was much less memorable. No pipe organ for *Saucerful*, although it was the only concert of theirs at which I saw them perform 'Heart Beat, Pig Meat'.

In 2014, I happened to be standing next to Roger at the JFK baggage carousel. He was on his own. He and I had been first off the plane, so it was pretty empty and there was quite a wait for the baggage to arrive. I was tempted to go over and tell him that the June '69 gig was the greatest rock concert I have ever attended, but it struck me that this was tantamount to saying he'd been going downhill for 45 years, so I let it pass.

PRESIDENT'S BALL, TOP RANK SUITE
30 JUNE 1969, CARDIFF, UK

I WAS THERE: CATHERINE COULSON (NÉE JOHNSON), AGE 14

It was June 1969 at the Top Rank Suite, Cardiff. They'd been booked as part of the celebrations to honour Charles' investiture as Prince of Wales! I went with my boyfriend, Graham, who was an accomplished musician and played lead guitar in his own band. We were in the crowd waiting for Pink Floyd to perform when Graham was approached by a member of staff and asked whether he was in the band. Back then, he had long hair and a beard, so really looked the part. Graham answered 'yes' and was told he was needed backstage as they were 'on' in ten minutes. We stayed in the dressing room with them both before and after their performance. I tried on Nick Mason's white-fringed leather jacket, suggested he use his scarf as a hatband (!) and got their autographs on my wrist, of which

I made a Sellotape copy, sadly long since disappeared…

My lasting musical memory of that gig is Roger's scream in 'Careful With That Axe, Eugene'.

DENNE HILL
1969, HORSHAM, SUSSEX, UK

I WAS THERE: ROB DOLTON

As a young child in the late Sixties, my dad used to take us to the top of Denne Hill in Horsham and we would hear loud music from below, coming from a place I now know was Chesworth Farm. In my teens, I was told Pink Floyd used to rehearse there but I've never followed it up to see how true it was. I do know one of the band had a house in the Causeway in Horsham, so it's possible.

SAM CUTLER STAGE SHOW, RAINSBROOK
13 SEPTEMBER 1969, RUGBY, UK

I WAS THERE: IAN ROBERTS

I was living in Rugby when the Rugby Jazz and Blues Festival took place. The location was on the Ashlawn Road, just to the south west of the Onley Lane crossroads. I was just starting sixth form and not yet driving, so Coventry was usually out of reach. Myself and three friends went to day two of the festival for the sum of £1 and it absolutely poured all day. Glastonbury at its wettest had nothing on Rugby in September 1969! We managed to find a length of polythene sheet from somewhere and huddled under that. The power generator started to fail just before The Nice came on, and Keith Emerson ended up playing a piano with no amplification.

Pink Floyd were last on the bill and, due to all the problems with the wet, came on hours late. They must have had their own power supply because their set was faultless, with light show, crashing aircraft, etc. We had managed to get to Mothers Club in Erdington in the April before, where Floyd recorded some of *Ummagumma*, but we were not that impressed. I was amazed at the outdoors show in Rugby and have been a Floyd fan ever since. Goodness knows what time we got home but I remember we cycled. My

Clockwise from top left: Roger Waters lets rip during 'Careful With That Axe, Eugene' (Tony Gavins); Tony Gavins recalls the aliens who were part of the Pink Floyd experience didn't go down well in Yorkshire; Graham Gunns thought the sound effects were 'eerie'; Michael McFaul saw the Floyd three times

Clockwise from top left: Peter Royle remembers a gorilla appearing in the audience, or thinks he does; Peter De Moncey-Conegliano found himself at Oxford despite being a working-class lad; Catherine Coulson dressed to the nines to see Prince Charles and Pink Floyd; Paul Dawson loved the free form music the Floyd played mother was not pleased with all the dripping clothes dumped in her pristine kitchen. Yet another serious telling off and I probably ended up grounded again!

My friend Dave Stroud was with me at the show. He went on his Lambretta, including 30-odd wing mirrors, a Union Jack on an aerial and him dressed in his obligatory Parka, proudly sporting his grandfather's Boer War medals; absolutely the height of fashion. This all caused great interest from the Hell's Angels who were there as 'security'. Dave says it was like a scene from *Quadrophenia*, but it all ended happily. Sadly, we didn't take any pictures as we couldn't have afforded to develop them; our priorities were finding enough money for a bit of petrol for the Lambretta and a few beers. Dave's wife, Yvonne, remembers her father would not let her go to the festival as she was 'too young'. She was absolutely furious.

It's a great shame that we cannot see the band live anymore. I have to make do with Aussie Pink Floyd. They are brilliant but the songs are not theirs.

THÉATRE 140
26 – 28 SEPTEMBER 1969, BRUSSELS, BELGIUM

I WAS THERE: DIRK HERMAN

I was 17 or 18 when Pink Floyd appeared at Théatre 140 in Schaerbeek, a municipality of Brussels. We had never heard of them and the 500-capacity room was only half full. When they started, they were surrounded by baffles front and back, and had a screen with some kind of colourful chemical reactions projected onto it. We were open-mouthed. The performance started with a huge bang on a gong. We went home quietly after the performance, realising that we had witnessed something very special.

EDWARD HERBERT BUILDING
10 OCTOBER 1969, LOUGHBOROUGH, UK

I WAS THERE: JANET MCVICAR, AGE 18

I was in my first year of a Computer Studies BSc course. It was the first year that girls had been at Loughborough Uni and there was only a few of us. The Union had many great acts that year – Free, Mott the Hoople, Pink Floyd – all for about ten bob (50p) a ticket. We were all amazed at the psychedelic images projected on the backdrop and walls... Wow!

I WAS THERE: ROGER THOMAS, AGE 19

It was a night to remember. It was the Fresher's Hop at Loughborough University. I remember it as being in Cayley Hall of Residence, which had a big dining hall, but I may be wrong here. I went with a group of people, including my first wife (having spent the first couple of weeks of term looking for a girlfriend, girls being in very short supply – the ratio was about 1:20). I don't remember anything about the gig itself except it was black tie. The date has stuck though – I'm much better with numbers than names! I think I was still in *Piper at the Gates of Dawn* territory, 'Interstellar Overdrive' being a favourite.

UMMAGUMMA RELEASED
25 OCTOBER 1969

Reaching No. 5 in the charts, Ummagumma *is a double album, the first disc comprising live recordings from two UK concerts; Mothers Club in Birmingham on 27 April 1969 and Manchester College of Commerce on 2 May. The album's title supposedly comes from Cambridge slang for sex, commonly used by Pink Floyd friend and occasional roadie, Iain 'Emo' Moore, who would say, 'I'm going back to the house for some ummagumma.'*

ACTUEL FESTIVAL
25 OCTOBER 1969, AMOUGIES, BELGIUM

I WAS THERE: RICHARD DIXON

In 1969, I left school and was staying at home on an army base near Mons, Belgium. In the autumn, the so-called Paris Pop Festival, also referred to as the first continental festival, had its venue moved to Amougies, just over the border from France, because of fears from the French authorities about drug-taking. I joined a small group of kids from the base and camped there for a few days. A number of big names were on the bill – Yes, Ten Years After, The Nice, Alexis Korner, Frank Zappa – and, headlining, the Pink Floyd. The festival took place in a huge marquee and I do not remember it being very full so I am not sure how financially successful the event was. The Beatles' 'Come Together' was played incessantly over the loudspeakers between acts and one French hippy dressed in purple velvet ostentatiously walked through the crowd holding a bloody swab on his arm, so drugs were certainly available.

We were a naive bunch, although cannabis was freely available on the base from the American GIs. Someone told us that morning glory seeds were hallucinogenic so we spent some time in a hedgerow collecting and consuming them and were photographed by *Paris Match* whilst so doing. We had a mass panic in case our parents saw the photo but I don't think they had any effect! One American boy, Tod, who was still at school, was not allowed to come but, being desperate to see the Floyd, he waited until his mother was asleep before creeping out and pinching her Mini. Driving hell for leather down the narrow roads, he clipped a warning sign before some roadworks and broke a side light. Nothing daunted, he came to the festival before returning home in the early hours. He parked the car in the garage and hoped that his mother would not notice the damage when she parked the car the next day in the works car park. The gods were smiling on him when she returned that night, cursing someone who had hit her car in the car park and not left a note. Apparently, Frank Zappa joined the Floyd on stage for 'Interstellar Overdrive' but I can't remember it and, apparently, neither could he!

ELECTRIC GARDEN
27 OCTOBER 1969, GLASGOW, UK

I WAS THERE: JAMES BADDOCK

The second time I saw them was in Glasgow where, once again, they were late arriving. I think they were touring pretty much constantly at the time, notching up something like 200,000 miles in a year on the road. The support band this time were The Stoics, who were actually pretty good (their lead singer was Frankie Miller, who later had a short stint with Robin Trower), playing standard rock tracks like Spooky Tooth's 'Evil Woman'. The problem was that they had to prolong their set because Pink Floyd hadn't arrived, so they ended up having to repeat some of their songs, which didn't go down too well with Floyd's fans, even though it wasn't really their fault. It also meant that Pink Floyd's set ended up being curtailed. As far as I can remember, it was 'Astronomy Domine', 'Interstellar Overdrive', 'Careful With That Axe, Eugene', 'Set the Controls for the Heart of the Sun' and a very shortened version of 'A Saucerful of Secrets'. The management had told them that they were switching off the power at ten o'clock, or something. As when I saw them in Dunoon in 1967, no light show.

The third time was in Glasgow, again, at a venue that was something to do with Glasgow University, and this time, they were already there when the gig started. I think the support band were a Uni act with some strange name that basically played free form jazz (they consisted of sax, keyboards, bass and drums) with pieces lasting fifteen to twenty minutes. Roger Waters and Nick Mason were actually sitting against the wall reading newspapers during this, trying not to be noticed. The Pink Floyd set list, when they came on, was the same as the previous Glasgow gig, but they spent more time on each song and there was a light show, although nothing compared to their later shows. I had the impression that they were more comfortable with their performances, perhaps because there was no time pressure, but, as before, there were no encores. Back then there weren't any generally, because there was a definite cut off point for gigs from the management's point of view but also for the audience – when last buses or trains in Glasgow were often at 10.30pm or thereabouts and because you couldn't go on much after ten o'clock anyway.

Looking back, I suppose I had a different experience then to those who saw Pink Floyd later on, with their elaborate stage productions – crashing airplanes, walls being built, etc. What I saw was just Pink Floyd and their music. They were distinctly non 'show biz' in that they came on stage and simply played their instruments. The most expressive moments were when Rogers Waters leaped around while he was hammering a huge gong during 'Sun' or 'Secrets'. You barely noticed Richard Wright behind his keyboards, while David Gilmour would often sit with his back to the audience while producing the slide guitar effects and Nick Mason was possibly one of the most undemonstrative drummers ever. To put it bluntly, they probably weren't that exciting in concert then, even though they were already doing their best to get the sound right but, in retrospect, it wasn't that surprising that they wanted to develop the visual effects for their live performances – they wanted the audience to focus on something else so they could just get on with playing the music. It was almost as if they were hiding behind a wall even then.

For all that, it was Pink Floyd which for us was amazing, because not that many 'underground' bands ventured north of the border back then, so these gigs were something to be treasured. There was also the feeling of being in on something special, a band that was pushing the boundaries but hadn't yet achieved the superstardom that would later come their way, so they were still 'our' band, something only a few of us knew about (or so we told ourselves).

UNIVERSITY
1 NOVEMBER 1969, MANCHESTER, UK

I WAS THERE: SIMON PHILLIPS

First term at university and the list of bands up to Christmas was published… big (at the time) names, every Saturday night… Blossom Toes, Chicken Shack, Duster Bennett, Soft Machine, Ten Years After, Fairport Convention, Pink Floyd, Family (being the ones I remember) and possibly Colosseum and Keef Hartley too. The Main Debating Hall was on the top floor of the student union building, about four or five floors up. It was rectangular, about 120 to 150 feet long, with quite a high stage at one end. The support band was always set up to play on a low stage either at the back of the room or on the right-hand wall. The support band that night was Stone the Crows, with Maggie Bell on vocals and Les Harvey on guitar (sadly, he was killed a couple of years later, whilst she went on to bigger, but not necessarily better, things).

Whilst I don't particularly recall details of many individual songs that night, I remember thinking it was the first 'proper' concert I'd been to by the Floyd. It was a relatively small, intimate venue (as well as the bands listed above, I also saw Led Zeppelin there a year or two later). It was standing only and, not being packed, it was fairly easy to get from the bar out the back to a position about 20 feet from the stage. It was the first time I'd been close enough, and with a good straight on view, to see all the WEM amps and speakers with their little red lights in the darkness, and also being close enough to see everything that they did. The one song that does stick out in my mind is 'Set the Controls' because a) it was the first time I'd seen Roger go ape with his gong and b) the quiet spacey passage in the middle was so ethereal. I don't think they had a light show but they played this in near darkness with just the hall's stage lights sweeping around. Also, they'd ditched the surround sound quad system and the Azimuth Co-ordinator just controlled left and right from the PA on the stage. A great show.

WALTHAM FOREST, TECHNICAL COLLEGE
7 NOVEMBER 1969, WALTHAMSTOW, LONDON

I WAS THERE: ROBIN ATKINSON

I had a girlfriend who used to go and see them at the Roundhouse and the UFO. I was at boarding school so I wasn't able to get to see them until 1969. But I saw them several times, and perhaps the most interesting time is when I was introduced to them. I went to Queen Mary College, which was part of London University, and they had played there the previous summer. The social secretary was connected to Pink Floyd somehow and I was quite well known for being a big Pink Floyd fan, and I knew this chap quite well. So when they played up the road at one of the technical colleges, I was introduced to them at the interval. They were quite affable. We were chatting for about 20 minutes. I can vividly remember talking with Roger Waters, Nick Mason and Rick Wright. David Gilmour had a bit of a bad first half – I think there was a problem with his guitar – so he was in a bit of an uncommunicative mood.

UNIVERSITY
27 NOVEMBER 1969, LIVERPOOL, UK

I WAS THERE: SIMON PHILLIPS

Three weeks after seeing them in Manchester, we went over to Liverpool to stay with an old school friend who was at university there and who'd thoughtfully got us all tickets to see the Floyd – happy days! I can only vaguely remember the hall where the show took place. I seem to think it was a fairly modern building with a square hall with a large lowish stage at one end. I don't recall whether or not it was seating or standing. I assumed that they'd just do the same songs as three weeks earlier and it started out that way.

Then, and I don't recall any announcement, they went into *The Man*. Our friend hadn't seen the tour earlier in the year so was unfamiliar with some of the songs. I'm pretty sure they didn't bother with a tea break, and the hammering wood section was dropped for something more percussive (I can picture Roger playing timpani or kettle drums) so it was a more restrained, more musical rendition of *The Man*, possibly done on the spur of the moment and hence no props. I recognised a new piece as coming from their new LP, *Ummagumma*, but couldn't place what it was. It turns out it was 'Sysyphus'. My overall feeling was that this was a less relaxed performance than three weeks earlier – maybe it was the hall, maybe the audience, maybe the material – but I enjoyed Manchester slightly more than Liverpool (despite the historically rarer material played).

LYCEUM
30 NOVEMBER 1969, LONDON, UK

I WAS THERE: VAL DITTON
I saw Floyd at the Lyceum Ballroom. It was the most amazing experience. I loved it just sitting on the floor right in front of them. It was my first introduction to Floyd and I still love them. I've never forgotten that gig!

AFAN LIDO INDOOR SPORTS CENTRE
6 DECEMBER 1969, PORT TALBOT, UK

I WAS THERE: LEN SAUNDERS
Floyd are my favourite band and I saw them twice, once at the Crystal Palace Bowl in 1971 but before that at the Afan Lido, in my home town of Port Talbot. This was an all-dayer with the other bands being East of Eden, Pentangle and Sam Apple Pie. It probably cost me ten shillings. They were dreadful and were booed before they even started. It was in a sports hall and the acoustics were naff. The equipment they had was massive gongs, etc, but they spent more time setting up than they did playing so we all felt let down. There was another all-dayer at the Lido with bands such as Rory Gallagher, the Groundhogs and the Keef Hartley Band. My memory of this one is of a 50-a-side football match behind the Lido and watching Keef Hartley and Tony McPhee kick lumps out of each other.

1970 sees Pink Floyd continuing to gig around the UK and Europe until April.

IMPERIAL COLLEGE
6 MARCH 1970, LONDON, UK

I WAS THERE: ALAN BUTCHER
This was one of my favourite ever live gigs. The college was full and students were eating cold baked beans out of cans. You could hear a pin drop in the place and the

huge amount of equipment gave their sound a rare quality. The set the band played was similar to the live set on the *Umma Gumma* album. I sat cross-legged on the floor like everyone else as the sounds of 'Astronomy Domine', 'Set the Controls for the Heart of the Sun' and 'Careful With That Axe, Eugene' filled the air.

 MOTHERS
8 MARCH 1970, ERDINGTON, BIRMINGHAM, UK

I WAS THERE: SIMON PHILLIPS

If I could travel back in time to just one Floyd show that I attended, it would be this one. (Well, maybe after the '67 show with Syd, which has to be number one; I mean, Syd 30 feet away and 'Interstellar Overdrive' and a decent light show). I can't separate this show from the venue and it was probably the latter that made it so special. Yet another school friend was living in Birmingham and had become a regular at Mothers Club, somewhere on the outskirts of Birmingham. All the big names were playing there and the Floyd had recorded some of *Ummagumma* there. My friend contacted us and said they were back… did we want to go? There was no hesitation and tickets were duly bought. A couple of us hitch-hiked down from Manchester and stayed over with him.

The outside wasn't what I expected of Britain's premier music venue. To be honest, it was a bit of a dump. Once inside, it was up a flight of stairs to a small L-shaped room with a small bar at the back. The stage was about 18 inches off the floor and very compact (read 'tiny'). Immediately in front of the stage were two rows of 15 seats. In my mind I can picture theatre-type seats fixed to the floor, but they may have been free-standing school-type seats. Apart from that, it was all standing. The place might have held a couple of hundred people tops and the optimum places were either those seats or standing at the bar. We didn't hesitate; the front row was already taken so we grabbed some beers and sat in the middle of the second row, about four feet from the edge of the stage. Perfect!

When the band came on, they were about six feet in front of us. It was like watching them in your own front room. The 200 people standing behind us weren't in our line of sight; it felt like the Floyd were playing just for us 30 or so sitting in the seats! The stage was small so they were pretty packed in on it. Roger was in particularly good form, chatting and introducing each number – I got the impression that he enjoyed the venue. Being so close we could really see everything they did. I remember Dave sitting down by his foot controls for an incredible version of 'A Saucerful of Secrets' (was it really incredible or was it just because it was all so close up?). Even though we were right up against the stage, the sound was very clear, despite being loud. Had we had a tape deck it would have been a great recording.

'Atom Heart Mother' was again the highlight of the show. It really was a great version and this wasn't just because we could see Dave and Rick performing it right in front of us – we were all buzzing about it when we came out. Roger said it would be on their next LP and I'm sure he gave it a name but it wasn't 'Atom Heart Mother'; maybe it was 'The Amazing Pudding'? 'The Embryo' was also a more polished, tighter, version than the one in Manchester and I started to warm to it (although I can easily take it or leave it these days). I have no other real memories of individual songs but my abiding memory is of a superb show, great sound, extremely close-up, in a very intimate atmosphere. Oh, and the beer wasn't bad either…

I WAS THERE: RICHARD KILBRIDE

In the mists of time reality becomes a bit blurred, as it did then from the occasional joint, but I do remember seeing Pink Floyd a few times, the first time at the Coventry Theatre, when they were part of a tour by the new high energy bands. The only other place we got to see them was at the fantastic Mothers club in Erdington, where we were regular customers. I remember on one occasion getting to that venue early. It was above a warehouse and sat at the bottom of the metal staircase was a short wheelbase Transit. Inside our heroes were eating fish and chips. We exchanged a few words of praise to them but I don't recall any further contact with them, other than being very close to the front whilst they played. My band, Asgard, also got to play at Mothers on the Thursday night John Peel showcase nights a couple of times. Peel took us under his wing for a while and our manager, Paul Padun, became his good friend. Paul sadly died quiet young but did tour with Pink Floyd as part of the road crew on several tours and was responsible for launching the plane into the wall on the *Wall* tour.

I WAS THERE: LYNN PIMLEY, AGE 14

I went with my older sisters and other friends. I remember the unprepossessing frontage of the carpet shop and queuing to get inside and up the stairs. John Peel passed us on our way in. They played most of the tracks from *Ummagumma* and had a light show projected on the black walls. The club was noisy, stuffy and full of people but this was the first time I'd seen a light show or been in such 'senior' company. I must have been one of the youngest there… The music I already knew, but to see a group using so many instruments and so much percussion was, in those days, very rare. I don't recall them having any stage presence or even introducing their songs. They let their music do the talking for them. The scream in 'Careful With That Axe, Eugene' was spine-chilling. I think we all knew we'd witnessed something special.

I also saw them at the Town Hall in Birmingham. That was a very different sort of set up. You had seats, and you didn't lean on the corridor walls like in Erdington. There was no light show either. I was jealous when I later learned that at least one of my sisters saw a live performance of *Atom Heart Mother* with a choir and orchestra and possibly a performance of 'Echoes'. I didn't. But those were the best years and the best music, right up until *Wish You Were Here*.

April finds Floyd embarking on their third North American tour, playing 18 shows. The tour is cut short and the band return to the UK when their equipment is stolen in New Orleans.

FILLMORE EAST
9 APRIL 1970, NEW YORK, NEW YORK

I WAS THERE: THOM LUKAS

The Beatles came to America and I watched them arrive on the TV news. As soon as that segment was finished, I switched to another station and watched them arrive again. I got to watch them arrive about six times! I decided I was going to go and be a part of those screaming girls. I took the subway and went to Penn Station. I thought I was going to find them. I never did.

In June 1964, I snuck into Carnegie Hall through the basement to see the Rolling Stones. I found a ticket stub on the floor and I went to that seat. 15 minutes later, this girl came and said 'what are you doing in my seat?'. I said, 'I think you're mistaken, I have my ticket.' She said, 'Well, I don't know how you got that but if you want you can sit on my lap.' I was eleven years old and this 17-year-old girl was saying I can sit on her lap. I thought, 'This is my world. I want to be part of this.'

In the summer of 1967, I saw all kinds of bands - the Byrds, the Doors, Cream. I said to myself, 'I need a camera to document this. Nobody is going to believe me.' In early '68, I got the opportunity to buy a secondhand camera from a professional freelancer for $125. He used to come into the candy store where I worked and he said, 'You know anybody who wants to buy a camera?' He wanted to upgrade his equipment.

Some of my photographs were used by a new magazine without crediting me and without paying me so I called up and I complained about it and then I found out it was a mistake at the Fillmore. The guy came in and was told 'take any photo you want' and they didn't realise it was my photograph for one time use and so forth. So it was just a mistake.

After we stopped shouting at each other, the guy remembered my name and six months later my mother took a message saying that 'Anne-Marie from *Rock* magazine called and please call her back'. I called back and she said they needed a photographer to photograph Pink Floyd at their hotel in Times Square and was I available? I said sure, even though my Nikkormat had been stolen. A friend let me use his Minolta, so I was operating equipment I wasn't familiar with and I only had a normal 50mm lens. I really got close to those guys.

I didn't have any Pink Floyd albums and I'd never seen Pink Floyd before only in photographs, I knew they would be cool because a good friend of mine had told me they were one of his favourite bands. And I read the British music magazines, *Melody Maker* and *Rave*. But I wasn't in awe of them. If it had been Jimi Hendrix, I'd have been shaking.

They were doing an interview with a writer I didn't know. I got there a little bit late and it was a rainy, overcast day. I called up to the room and I said, 'I'm Tom Lukas from *Rock* magazine,' and a British voice answered, 'Whoa, wait a minute, you're from *Rock* magazine? There's a guy here says *he's* from *Rock* magazine! You'd better come up. We gotta straighten this thing out.' He was joking. I got up there and was like I was interrupting the interview. I felt a little embarrassed until I realised they were kidding with me.

I just started photographing them while they were being interviewed. The conversation was over my head. These were very intellectual guys and I was just a working-class kid. They were very erudite. They weren't high at all. They were totally straight, with soft drinks. Roger and David were really kind of animated most of the time, but Nick and Rick were laid back for most of it. I was able to shoot off 36 shots and they didn't flinch. I guess they accepted the fact that I knew what I was doing. I was a fly on the wall. There were very few shots where they were staring at my camera, and those are probably the ones that worked the least best for me.

There was a guitar in the room and when one guy was talking, eg. Roger, Dave was in the corner playing his acoustic guitar. It was a Gibson J-45, a 1969 model. It had a slightly unusual bridge. I read something about him buying a guitar at Manny's (West 48th Street). He has it on his lap in one of the shots. I think they stayed at that location because it was close to the music shops on 48th Street.

As we were wrapping it up, I said, 'Can I get some shots of you guys together?' and I popped off maybe five shots. But I could tell they weren't that into it, particularly Roger and Dave. Roger was the first to get bored with it and I felt like I had pushed my limit there.

I got invited to go and see them at the Fillmore the following night. Seeing Pink Floyd perform live after being in a hotel room with them was interesting. It was amazing. I'd never seen a band like that before. The bands I'd seen were more animated and full of life – The Jeff Beck Group with Rod Stewart, the Stones, the Animals. These guys were kind of mellow and it was like going to a séance. They had the footsteps in the speakers as though they were walking around the room. They looked so good. They were wearing the same clothes they'd worn in the hotel, although maybe David had velvet pants on. They had the greatest boots!

It was hard to get a shot where you could see each of the guys. I had a photo pass for the Fillmore but it didn't guarantee you anything. You got in for free and could you show it to the guy and he'd say, 'Yeah, but you're in the way. Could you get on the side?' I developed the film and brought the contact sheets to the art director at the magazine. He circled a few that he wanted blow ups of. He wasn't that happy with the stage shots but he picked one out in which you could see everybody. And he said, 'Can you do something with this shot, make it look psychedelic or something?' He wanted me to crumple up some cellophane, like a cigarette pack wrapper, and put it in front of the enlarger lens or something. I tried that and it didn't work. So I wound up tilting the easel as I printed to make it look like the band had longer legs. I heard that they did that with the cover for *Rubber Soul*. It looked pretty good.

ELECTRIC FACTORY
17 & 18 APRIL 1970, PHILADELPHIA, PENNSYLVANIA

I WAS THERE: ALAN NEWMAN

I had family in the music business and spent most of my life in it and a lot of time around music, entertainment and sports people, so I was never starstruck. In 1967, while still in high school, I went with my record promo guy brother-in-law to a taping of Gene Kaye's TV show at Willow Grove Park. We were with Billy Harner, who was out promoting 'Sally's Sayin' Somethin'', which was out nationally and a hit in Philly. The other act on the show was Pink Floyd. They did a lip sync of 'See Emily Play' while wearing matching pink suits and riding the ferris wheel. It was strangely funny as their sound on the song didn't quite match the setting, but got my ears perked.

The next time that I saw them was in 1970 when they played the original Electric Factory in Philly. I was a backstage regular. I don't remember who I was talking to but I was invited into their dressing room as I looked like I belonged, wrote for the *Philadelphia Daily News* and had primo smoke. I was handed some LSD. Everybody seemed to be tripping. We were trading stories and I brought up the pink suits and ferris wheel, which turned the mood into hysterical laughter. I don't remember much else and do not remember if I even watched the show. I can't really elaborate as I was in outer space.

Back in the UK, Pink Floyd play the showcase Bath Festival.

WISH YOU WERE HERE

BATH & WEST SHOWGROUND
27 JUNE 1970, SHEPTON MALLET, UK

I WAS THERE: IAIN WOLSTENHOLME

After the Syd-centred line up, the next incarnation of Pink Floyd was for me rather plodding. I saw the first performance of 'Mother's Amazing Bread Pudding' aka 'Atom Heart Mother' (the 'trended-up' title!) at the Bath Blues and Progressive Music Festival. At 3am on Sunday morning, it was enlivened by choir, brass orchestra and fireworks including impressive red Very light distress flares, but I never bothered to buy the album, which sums it up despite the esoteric cover. I think all were disappointed with the recorded version when it came out.

I WAS THERE: DAVID HORSFIELD

I fell asleep during Canned Heat's set (no mean feat) after about 36 sleepless hours of great bands and music. My companions temporarily thought they were sharing a muddy space with a corpse. I resurfaced in the early hours of the morning. Clouds of green-lit smoke, origin uncertain, swirled around, 20 feet above the crowd, while pipe organ swirled with reverb, about 20 miles up in the ether. Lights streamed skywards from the stage. A choir of schoolchildren, neatly ranked and uniformed, sang angelically, opposite a full string section, while six men in black antique undertaker outfits carried a black coffin off stage. It was the first performance of *Atom Heart Mother*, I believe. Quite a way to wake up. And it had stopped raining.

I WAS THERE: PETER CLINICK

I was also at the 1970 Bath Blues Festival. I was not awake for them at 3am when they came on. Back then, festivals ran 24 hours to fit everybody on, allowing for the often long pauses between bands. I did meet Freddie Bannister who was the promoter for all the Pav (as we knew it) gigs. I happened to get beaten up by one of his bouncers whilst queuing for a gig after the previous week's gig with the Edgar Broughton Band where I was also assaulted by bouncers when on stage with the band at Edgar's (Rob's) request). Freddie took me to hospital in his Alfa Romeo Spider, waited for me and then let me into the Pav for free as his 'guest' (as he put it) to see Principal Edwards Magic Theatre.

While sitting in A&E, Freddie asked which bands I would like to see at his upcoming three day festival. I mentioned Pink Floyd, High Tide, Canned Heat and Led Zeppelin (at his previous one day festival on the Rec in Bath, alongside the Pav) and Edgar

Broughton. He said he would never hire the Edgar Broughton Band again. He also asked what I thought about his friend Maynard Ferguson opening the festival. I said I didn't like the big band sound. As it turned out, he did open the festival.

I WAS THERE: SIMON PHILLIPS

Ah, the Bath Festival in 1970! What a wonderful event that was. An even better line up than Woodstock the year before, in my humble opinion. The best of the UK and the best of the US, together over two days. My main recollections of the Floyd were just not being able to wake my friend (who'd been with me to most of the Floyd shows since 1967) when they were who he'd gone to see; and the orange/red smoke and fireworks at about three in the morning as they premiered *Atom Heart Mother* with choir and orchestra. A fantastic weekend, although I wish we'd also had Soft Machine who played at the sister festival in Kralingen the same weekend.

I WAS THERE: JOHN MANUEL RHODES

This was the first time I ever saw Pink Floyd. Floyd came on very late, it was well past sundown and possibly well past midnight, the perfect setting for what we were about to hear. I seem to recall that Johnny Winter had been on stage pretty recently before. I remembered the weather for this festival as being by and large perfect, but on doing some research I found, and indeed remember vaguely, that the weather on the Saturday was bad to begin with. Because of that, an unprecedented number of fans turning up and a monumental traffic snarl up in the whole area, the bands couldn't get to the venue and so everything was running late.

While Pink Floyd played, the stars were out and all across the audience of 150,000 plus there were small fires, which had been lit to keep kids warm in the chill night hours. This was before the era of waving lighters. Once they launched into 'Careful With That Axe, Eugene', the whole experience for me was perfect. There was no one else on the bill who remotely resembled Floyd musically and the music, along with the ambience around us, combined to produce a feeling of being in space, up there in the stars as it were. I was new to Pink Floyd at the time and what really blew me away was *A Saucerful of Secrets*, which just seemed to get the audience, at least those around me, spellbound. I was only 16 going on 17, not yet really into drugs and stuff, but the whole experience created a natural 'high'. If anyone only knows Floyd from *Dark Side* onwards, then they don't know anything about just how innovative and original they were at the *Ummagumma/Atom Heart Mother* stage. It was apparently one of the first times, if not the first time, the band performed *Atom Heart Mother* under that name, having given it the previous working title of *The Amazing Pudding*.

After we'd seen Pink Floyd, my friends and I went off to find a hot dog stand to sleep under. I woke up on the Sunday morning to see Canned Heat still doing their set!

I WAS THERE: HENRY RACE, AGE 16

I only ever saw them once, and that was at the Bath Festival in 1970. It was after my 'O' levels. I was 16 in the January of that year and decided to hitch down from Sunderland with my pal Micky Wright, who was in the same class as me at school. That was a fair hike. My mum and dad didn't really understand. 'Whereabouts are you going?' 'Bath.' 'Where's that?' '300 odd miles away.' We used to hitch backwards and forwards to Sunderland when we missed the last bus after going to see bands, but to go down to somewhere like Bath was a serious undertaking for 16-year-olds.

The guy who used to help our milkman volunteered to my mum and dad to give me and Micky a lift down to Scotch Corner, the main staging point, the big junction to go across to the Lake District. 'I'll give them a lift down to Scotch Corner just to see them on their way.' We headed south, taking one of those little white canvas toy tents that you give to kids to camp in the garden with. I had the most primitive sleeping bag in the world that my uncle had given me. We ended the day camped in the corner of a field somewhere, just off the M1. We were woken really late at night by a policeman who just wanted to check that we were all right. He asked to see how much money we had, and asked for our names and addresses because we were that young. And we didn't even lie!

We didn't have tickets in advance. We never used to get tickets to see bands at the Mecca Ballroom in Sunderland and we thought, 'We'll get them on the way down somewhere.' We eventually bought tickets at The Diskery in Birmingham. The shop's still there.

The second night, we arrived in Bath and camped in one of the public parks near the Pulteney Bridge, where we'd arranged to meet our friends who were also going down there. And the next day we got the bus down to Bath and West Showground. I think they were running special buses down.

We were really, really, really excited because everybody was there – Zappa was gonna be there and we were big Zappa fans, Led Zeppelin were on, Santana, The Moody Blues, John Mayall, Peter Green, The Byrds, Fairport Convention, Steppenwolf, It's A Beautiful Day – all the big guns. Jefferson Airplane were on, and even at that age I was quite smitten with Grace Slick.

We weren't allowed to get into the ground itself until the first day of the festival, which was maybe the Friday. So we camped outside, in the holding pen. We didn't pitch the tent, because we wanted to be able to make a quick dash into the arena first thing in the morning.

As it happened, we met up with our friends; Harry Errington, Alison Davies, who wasn't my girlfriend at the time, and Yvonne Stewart. They were 15 and had driven down in this black Ford van that they'd stolen. We just happened to meet them. I don't know how many people were there. 150,000? It was huge. I've never seen anything quite like it. If truth be told, I was a little overwhelmed by it all. I was just a working-class lad from the coalfields of County Durham seeing all these proper hippies, proper grown up guys, with proper long hair rather than us school boys pretending we were hippies for the weekend.

We'd met these guys and we just ended up sitting together in the same place. We couldn't put our tent up. Once you'd staked your claim for your little spot in the arena, that was it. You stayed there. I remember the first night I slept there in the arena, it pissed down with rain and my sleeping bag got absolutely soaked. It was a cheapie sleeping bag and that was it. I didn't have anything to sleep in for the rest of the weekend, which is pretty miserable when you're 16. We hadn't really taken any camping stuff down and I don't think they had the infrastructure for all the punters down there. The only thing I can actually remember buying to eat is a big chunk of bread and a big chunk of blue cheese. They didn't have vegan curries or any coconut smoothies or anything. I was cold, wet, hungry and quite overwhelmed by it all. But there was just band after band after band!

Country Joe and the Fish were on. I remember him doing that 'Give me an F!' I don't think the *Woodstock* film was out by then but we'd got the soundtrack album, so we knew Country Joe and we knew 'Give me an F!' (The 'Fish' Cheer/I-Feel-Like-I'm-Fixin'-To-Die Rag').

I think the running order had just gone all to hell. This was the first really super big festival apart from the Isle of Wight, so all the bands were just coming on as and when. And the order in which the bands were supposed to play was shot to shit on the first day. Donovan played on the afternoon that Pink Floyd played. He played for hours. I'm guessing now it's because they didn't have any other bands arrive and they didn't have any other bands who were set up.

Because we didn't have anywhere proper to sleep, you'd try and get 20 minutes or half an hour's sleep. That's what it was like. One of the guys I was with nudged me and said, 'Pink Floyd are coming on. Pink Floyd are coming on.' I remember they did 'A Saucerful of Secrets', 'Set the Controls for the Heart of the Sun' and 'Careful With That Axe, Eugene'. They had one big black and white screen at the right hand side of the stage. We were quite a way back so you couldn't really see it. I can't remember being able to see what kind of lights they had. But I remember kneeling on the ground sheet that we had, watching a close up of Nick Mason and being transfixed, and I remember the big close up of Roger Waters screaming during 'Eugene'. He put his hand on his ear.

The set list was 'Green is the Colour', 'Careful', 'Saucerful', 'Set the Controls' and 'Atom Heart Mother'. 'Green is the Colour'. What an odd song to open the set with.

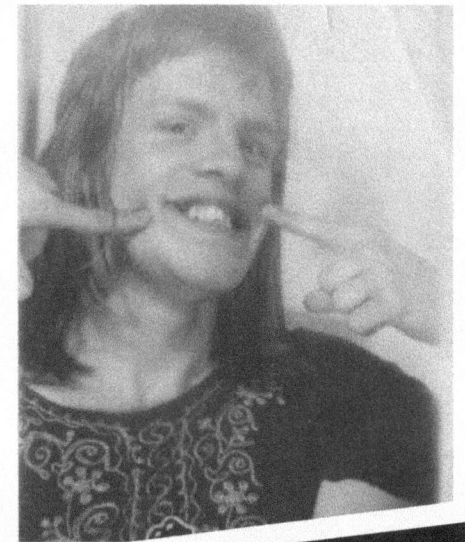

Clockwise from top left: Floyd in action at Birmingham Town Hall in 1970 (Gareth Jones); Alan Newman was in outer space in Philly; John Manuel Rhodes watched Floyd at the Bath Festival and then slept under a hot dog stand; Henry Race rode home from Bath in a stolen van with a Guinness label serving as a 'tax disc'

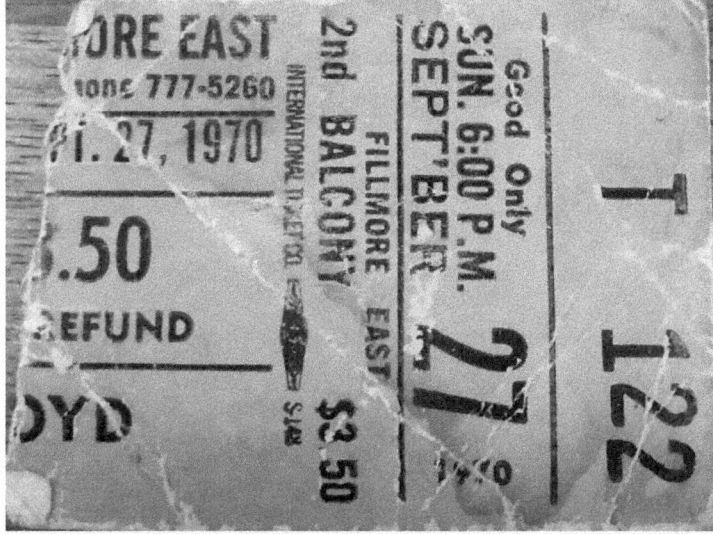

Clockwise from left: Ken Fuller was allowed to take albums into school for music lessons; ad for *Ummagumma* from Fillmore East programme (Philip Simmons); Derek Maddock remembers the sights, sounds and smells of the Floyd's appearance at the Free Trade Hall; Ron Geesin worked with Pink Floyd on *Atom Heart Mother*; Philip Simmons' Fillmore East ticket

That's probably one of the most laidback songs that they had at the time. And 'Atom Heart Mother' – it was only the second time that they'd played that. I think maybe they'd debuted it at the Olympia gig three weeks earlier.

We had a reel-to-reel tape my friend Yvonne had made of the BBC *In Concert* where they did that, which we'd played that. And I'm fairly sure that the album was out by that time so we knew it. I remember the bizarre choral arrangements. Even though, with hindsight, it's not really the Floyd's finest hour, we all declared ourselves to be thoroughly impressed and our minds were thoroughly blown and wasn't it the most amazing thing ever? But if I could press the little button back to the Bath Festival, I'd be more interested in seeing 'A Saucerful', 'Careful With That Axe, Eugene' and 'Set the Controls'. It was in the early hours of the morning, and because of not being able to sleep it was a bit hazy, almost a bit psychedelic, because it was all a bit fragmented by the time they got to that. It was really late at night. After they were on, we just hunkered down. I think somebody had a little groundsheet and we pulled it over the three or four of us that were there and slept as best we could.

Even though me and Micky Wright hitched down, and the other guys had come in this stolen van, we managed to get a lift back to the North East of England with them. Harry had a Guinness label instead of a tax disc, because to the casual observer it was kind of the same and obviously they didn't have any automatic number plate recognition then. We had to give them a couple of quid for petrol for the ride back.

When we got to the North East of England, Harry dumped the van about three miles away from home because he was getting all paranoid and was sure that the police were following us. So we'd driven all the way back from Bath but, when we got home at six or seven o'clock in the morning, we had to walk the last couple of miles back home to our house.

That was the first proper adventure that I had, and the only time I ever saw Pink Floyd. After *Ummagumma*, which is the last album I actually bought when it came out – I lost interest. I didn't buy *Dark Side* when it came out. After *Piper* and *Saucerful* and *More* – my girlfriend Alison Davies had that one – I thought they got a bit up themselves. I have still never heard *Animals*, *The Wall* all the way through or *Wish You Were Here*, although I know 'Shine On'. I've got no interest, really. They became significantly less interesting when Syd Barrett left. *Piper* is still my favourite Floyd album, because there's nothing else like it. I'd like to time travel and go back and see them.

I WAS THERE: PETER DE MONCEY-CONEGLIANO

I had got a job as an international telephonist in the GPO in London. It was the perfect job, as you got plenty of breaks and although it was only £1,000 a year there was plenty of overtime at double time if you wanted to buy, for example, a new guitar. The best thing at that best of all times was that it was full of hippies, dropouts, armchair revolutionaries, closet (and out-of-closet) queens, and resting actors. Despite our differences, we all had two things in common – music and soft drugs. At any time of the day or night, you would find a group of telephonists smoking dope up on the roof! A few of us talked about forming a group (which never actually happened) but we did all decide to go together to the Bath Festival that summer.

There was an incredible atmosphere. It was perhaps the highpoint of British hippiedom. I remember a fat hippie girl who would make you a velvet hippie bag with your star sign embroidered on it and then would not accept any payment for it. She did it out of love and to feel part of a movement. Most people went to Shepton Mallet by train – a tiny little country station – and both coming and going you recognised your fellow passengers by the way they dressed as fellow 'heads'. It was like a mini Woodstock, as several of the American acts that had played Woodstock were also here, such as Jefferson Airplane, Canned Heat, Country Joe, etc.

Nobody had any tents or anything in those days. You just arrived in the clothes you stood up in (for two days!). In my case, it was an army surplus greatcoat and a hat with a feather in it. People were most excited about a brand new group called Led Zeppelin, but I personally found them rather pretentious. For me, the highpoint of the festival was definitely Pink Floyd – especially when they did the world premiere of *Atom Heart Mother* at night followed by fireworks! This was an exciting new direction for the Pink Floyd with a brass band and choir, fusing rock music with classical music. (In the 1990s, when my wife was at Glasgow School of Art, I actually met Ron Geesin who had made all the brass/choir arrangements on *Atom Heart Mother* and a solo album with Roger Waters, *Music from The Body*.)

There is some great video footage of the Bath Festival on YouTube, centring mainly on Led Zeppelin. All that exists of the Floyd's performance is a very grainy black and white video of 'Atom Heart Mother', filmed at night with minimal lighting and where you can barely make out who is who. But it still brings goose pimples to me when I watch it. I was there, man!

I WAS THERE: GUY PIERCE

I saw them twice. Well, once in fact, as the first time their Hyde Park gig was rained off. Then I saw them at Bath, accompanied by the accidental trip from hell. Never again. It was back to beer for me after that.

WISH YOU WERE HERE

HYDE PARK
18 JULY 1970, LONDON, UK

I WAS THERE: KEITH BRADFORD

I turned on to psychedelic music at an early age. I was about ten or eleven in the early Sixties and was excited by 'Telstar' by The Tornados and the *Dr Who* theme. I remember hearing Pink Floyd on a John Peel show and looked out for their music from then on. I was given the 'Point Me at the Sky' seven-inch single by a classmate and played it to death. I bought *A Saucerful of Secrets* a few weeks later and the hairs on my neck tingled when I played it. A week after that, I bought *Piper At The Gates of Dawn*. I was hooked.

I saw the Floyd four times. The first time was at Hyde Park and they played *Atom Heart Mother*. I went with Nelly, a French girl I was seeing. She was on an exchange visit and the guy whose family she was staying with wasn't happy about me dating her. All through the concert, she was swooning and shouting 'my Pink Floyd! My Pink Floyd!', annoying me and several people around us. We were a long way from the stage and the sound was faint and blowing around, but at least I'd seen them.

I WAS THERE: ALAN BUTCHER

I had always loved the music of Pink Floyd but this was out in the open air and they were playing the whole of the *Atom Heart Mother* album. 'Echoes' flowed into the wind as the band played and the fans lapped it up. This was before *The Dark Side of the Moon* and *The Wall* but it was still epic in every way. Set the controls for the heart of the sun.

I WAS THERE: MAT WATKINSON

We travelled down to Hyde Park in my schoolmate's car. In those days, you seemed to be able to park anywhere. I'd bought a new sleeping bag and, in case it rained, I put the plastic packaging over the lot. I woke next morning soaked in sweat. It'd been like sleeping in a roasting bag!

We sat maybe halfway back from the stage. Jeff Dexter deejayed and I bought the Stones' *Get Yer Ya-Ya's Out* on the strength of hearing 'Midnight Rambler' that day. In front of us, a hippie with a hamper ate foot-long smoked salmon sandwiches and smoked foot-long joints, passing the roaches back to his mates.

The Edgar Broughton Band did their 'Out Demons Out' stuff and we chanted. Dear, too soon departed, Kevin Ayers sang his love song to 'Lady Rachel', Roy Harper sang and handed out spliffs and then, on this gorgeous day, Ron Geesin's brass ensemble filled the air as *Atom Heart Mother* swelled across the park. I learnt later the experience all but destroyed him, albeit temporarily. You couldn't tell when he played Scarborough's Penthouse several times throughout the Seventies. We loved him.

Being there at the (almost) premiere of *Atom Heart Mother* was amazing. And because I deejayed with the likes of Bowie, Roxy Music and Mott the Hoople for ten years after that, I wouldn't hear 'Fat Old Sun' live, with its blistering guitar and blissful Englishness until I went to see David Gilmour in Verona in 2015 – with Phil Manzanera on guitar duties.

Going home, I got arrested for hitchhiking on the motorway after my mate's car broke down. I got travelsick and kept taking tablets, so I was off my head when the cops got us.

I WAS THERE: PHIL CARTER

Pink Floyd's music can be divided into three periods – the Syd Barrett era, the David Gilmour/Roger Waters era and the David Gilmour era. In my opinion, the David Gilmour and Roger Waters era is when the band were at their most creative and productive. I tend to think in albums rather than dates, from *Ummagumma* to *The Wall*. I know Gilmour played on an earlier album and there was a later 'Pink Floyd' album called *The Final Cut*. For me, *Ummagumma* encapsulated the best of the earlier Barrett period and the beginnings of the Waters/Gilmour collaboration. This album was released in late 1969. I was 16 in December of that year.

Memory can play games with you and it is very easy to gloss over the negative, and present perhaps a more romantic notion of those times. I can't remember what happened first. Discovering the Floyd or discovering LSD. I think it was the latter. Someone said to me to 'listen to the Floyd, it's amazing while on acid' – and they were right. It was one of the best pieces of advice I was given as a teenager! (It was also suggested I should watch the last part of *2001: A Space Odyssey* and Walt Disney's *Fantasia*.) It's a terrifying thought, thinking about it now, 15-year-olds taking LSD. But in the late Sixties and early Seventies there was a different atmosphere, a different feel about things. The culture felt new, fresh and optimistic. Taking LSD was seen as a quest, a search, a different experience – and it was certainly that!

My first LSD experiences were with my friend Harry. He was my best mate. Both of us lived in the 'nice' part of industrial Coventry in private houses on the edge of the Warwickshire countryside. At some point in our experimenting, I must have bought *Ummagumma* and we did what was suggested. Egg and chips, cheese and pickle, acid and Floyd. Both of us just lay there in my mother's living room (I think perhaps my mum was away) and put on the album. As a visually-orientated person, I was astounded by what happened. My eyes were shut but the music created the most beautiful patterns in my head, which ebbed and flowed with the music. When I opened my eyes, I could see the music coming out of the speakers. Synesthesia, I think you call it. Different colours drifting out. It was truly a revelatory experience. To cut a long evening short, it was a revelation to both Harry and I. It was their soundscapes – 'Astronomy Domine', 'Careful With That Axe, Eugene', 'Set the Controls' and 'Saucerful' – that did it for us and which set us both, or at least me, on some sort of road of discovery.

I was and still am very fond of nature – walking, sitting by rivers, having sex in meadows. Much of Floyd's music mirrored my situation – 'Granchester Meadows', 'Fat Old Sun', 'Green is the Colour', 'Cymbeline' et al. So, again taking LSD, we would set out for the countryside, sit by rivers, wander through fields and, yes, have sex with my girlfriend, Charlie, in meadows.

The pastoral and the soundscapes were both synonymous with the Floyd around that time. I was also into my spiritual quest. 'LSD takes you nearer to God', and I believed it. Perhaps it really did. It certainly opened up my *Doors of Perception* even though I struggled with that book. One aspect of the Floyd's music that hardly gets a mention was their religious/spiritual side. Anyone who listens to the last section of their song 'A Saucerful of Secrets' will know what I am talking about. (On the BBC recording from that time, the DJ John Peel comments on it).

The organist, Richard Wright, always created a wonderful warm atmosphere which underpins so much of Floyd's songs; his style is littered with choral, anthem or church-like references. In their final (final) album, *The Endless River*, there is a small section where Wright is playing the organ at the Royal Festival Hall and it brings tears to my eyes. So manna from heaven – soundscapes, pastoral and spiritual – the three main reasons I loved the Pink Floyd.

The first gig I saw was Hyde Park where they performed *Atom Heart Mother* for the first time. I suspect that's why I went. To hear some new Floyd music for the first time was always a serious highlight for me. I can't remember who I was with or how I got to London from Coventry. Maybe I hitch hiked or got a train. I was proud that our local band, The Edgar Broughton Band, were playing on the same bill. I can't really remember much about the Floyd's set. We were quite far back and I don't remember it being that loud. Although I love *Atom Heart Mother* now, perhaps at the time I did not quite get all this brass playing with the Floyd. It was not psychedelic enough for me! I suspect also, because this was the first time I had been to London independently of my parents, I found the whole experience of a big, big city a little overwhelming.

I WAS THERE: KEN FULLER, AGE 15

Becoming a Floyd fan was inevitable. I was one of the grammar school boys that books about progressive rock suggest were where most of the initial fans came from. We had an enlightened music teacher and would have 'lessons' where you could bring in an album to play to the rest of the class. I was aware of songs like 'See Emily Play' (my first daughter is named Emily) but it's in those sessions where I first heard the longer songs like 'Astronomy Domine'. It got to where I would carry around a copy of *Ummagumma* and play it to whoever I could get to listen.

I saw Pink Floyd play at the Radio One Club in the BBC Paris Studios on Lower Regent Street and play the free gig in Hyde Park. There was a bootleg LP floating around school some time after but it was terrible – it must have been recorded standing next to the bass speakers! I don't recall going with anyone to Hyde Park – I don't think anyone else shared my enthusiasm for Floyd. I recall enjoying the songs that I was familiar with from *Ummagumma* but was not sure what to make of *Atom Heart Mother* – that would take a few more listens.

Although I now live in the US, I was thrilled to be able to go to the Floyd exhibition at the V&A during a visit to my family. I was also delighted when my other daughter – not Emily – bought me a copy of *London '66–'67* on vinyl for my birthday.

I WAS THERE: COL TURNER

Floyd were once again back in the park to do it all again and all for free. This time we were better prepared, and just as well. The first Hyde Park gig in 1968 had attracted perhaps 5,000, maybe 8,000 – I'm not good at estimating crowds. The second concert attracted a reported 200,000. It was chaos! We had noticed when arriving that Floyd's equipment had grown remarkably. They now had speakers set up at the rear of the crowd as well as on the stage to give a 'surround sound' effect. Exactly what was played that day is not all that clear to me save for one song. I believe it was as the second set was opening that it happened… 'Wha wha wha!' The sound of a baby crying. The crowd turned around almost in unison as the crying seemed to be coming from behind us. 'WHA WHA WHA!' It was now at the front. People were looking at each other, wondering where this baby was. Then they began. *'All is love, is all I ammmm, a ball is allll I am.'* It was the first and only time I heard 'Embryo' live and it was a sensation. People had tears in their eyes, including me. I don't think I have ever heard anything so beautiful as that song on that day. (And I wonder why they never used it as the keystone for a concept: birth, growing, death.)

I WAS THERE: GRAHAM DAY

In July 1970, my friend Dave had graduated from his Lambretta scooter to a white Ford Anglia 100E Popular. At last, we had four wheels, meaning we could go to concerts outside our area. This was in an era of huge free open-air concerts in Hyde Park, including the Rolling Stones and the short-lived 'supergroup' Blind Faith, featuring Eric Clapton, Ginger Baker, Steve Winwood and Rich Grech. We were also avid readers of the music press, notably the *New Musical Express*, and saw that Pink Floyd would be playing in Hyde Park. We liked both Pink Floyd and Soft Machine. Dave's mum differentiated between the two by saying that Floyd were the 'nice row' whilst Soft Machine, being more jazz-based, were the 'awful row'!

On a hot Saturday morning, we left our home town of Ipswich early along with our friend Kevin. Dave parked the car at Gants Hill Underground station, with its distinctive semi-circular bus station canopy, and we caught a Central Line Tube straight to Marble Arch. We arrived at the park at about 11.30am. It was not long before an amazing sight greeted us. People were sat on the grass, watching the musicians on a stage some distance away. It is only now that I realised the extent of what was later estimated to be a crowd of 120,000 at the event. We managed to find a space on the ground and sat down near a tousled-haired older man with glasses from Stratford Upon Avon; a world away from our experience at the time. People were drinking and smoking different 'cigarettes', including a young couple a few feet away.

Of particular interest amongst the support acts were Kevin Ayres and the Whole World. Herne Bay's Kevin was enigmatic but entertaining. I enjoyed 'Clarence in Wonderland'. In his band that day were Robert Wyatt of Soft Machine, and Mike Oldfield who was to become famous in his own right some three years later.

d effortlessly across the crowd and created a relaxed atmosphere, occasionally punctuated by the revving motorcycles of the Hell's Angels who acted as unofficial security. We were blissfully unaware of what happened when the Angels performed the same role at a Rolling Stones concert at Altamont, California; had we known we might have been more concerned.

I was also interested in seeing the Edgar Broughton Band, who memorably performed their signature song, 'Out Demons Out', and who kept us well entertained. Due to some acts not being able to perform, Roy Harper did an overly-long set which droned on somewhat. And saxophonist Lol Coxhill was also on the bill. He performed a song called 'Two Little Pigeons' which our friend Clint's dad considered dreadful!

Eventually, Pink Floyd took the stage to applause and a huge cheer. They had just released the album *Atom Heart Mother*, the forerunner to *Meddle* and the song 'Echoes'. It was superb. They also had an orchestra and choir, taking their music to a different level; a real fusion of different musical styles and far removed from our favourite album, *Ummagumma*. We had not experienced anything like it before and were in awe of the complexity and the different sounds. The Floyd seemed to be like artists, composing a pastoral painting in different colours, hues and textures. We were glad we were there to witness such a seismic event. The Floyd also played 'Set The Controls to the Heart of the Sun' and 'Care With That Axe, Eugene', both of which became firm favourites, although 'Axe' had more disturbing content.

But it was not the music that made the headlines the following day. The couple a short distance away from us stood up and embraced each other. Then, due to the music (and probably other reasons), they gradually removed their clothes and stood naked, totally oblivious to where they were. There was then a rush of press photographers to get the best picture! I recall seeing the photograph in the *Sunday Mirror* the next day. My parents knew we had been at the concert but I did not say that we were sitting near where the picture was taken, although you could see the head of the man from Stratford-upon-Avon.

Suddenly, there appeared in the crowd near us an elderly man in a suit and cloth cap. who looked open-mouthed at what was going on in front of him in his park. Another photographer turned up and photographed him saying 'this is the picture they should be taking', but I never saw that one in the press. We did not move all day, and I am not aware that we had very much to eat. We retraced our journey home, stopping for a drink in the Army and Navy pub in Chelmsford to reflect upon an interesting and historic day in musical history. Memorably, we knew that 'we were there'.

A few weeks later, whilst on holiday in the 100E at Torquay, we managed to run the car over some concrete blocks on the campsite late on the Monday night, distorting the tracking. We spent three days of the holiday repair it so that we could get home!

I WAS THERE: ROB RUCK, AGE 16

My first proper gig was in the summer of 1970, a free concert starring Pink Floyd in Hyde Park. Also on the bill were the Edgar Broughton Band and the Kevin Ayers Band, with an up-and-coming guitarist called Mike Oldfield. Floyd were showcasing their new album, *Atom Heart Mother*, which was due for release in the autumn. Apart from the great music, two things stick in my mind. The first is the roar of what sounded like thunder to our rear, which got louder and louder. It turned out to be a band of Hell's Angels riding their bikes through the crowd to get to the front, and at the time it was quite scary at the time. The other thing I remember is an announcement that a man was looking for his son and wanted to make an appeal. He got up and started to berate the crowd that we were all a bunch of drug-taking hippies who should be locked up, etc. Someone shouted out, 'Pass him to the back!'

CHARLTON PARK
31 AUGUST 1970, BISHOPSBOURNE, UK

I WAS THERE: DAVE RADFORD, AGE 18

I was at the *Great Medicine Ball* show. A friend of mine says he saw Edgar Broughton walking about but they didn't play, and yet everybody says they did play. But Pink Floyd definitely did. There were only about 200 people there. It was only advertised on the previous Friday in the *Kentish Gazette*, and if you took the newspaper with you, you got in free. But you didn't even need a newspaper. It was the same weekend as the Isle of Wight Festival. I was 18 and went with my wife. We had just had a baby and we were going backwards and forwards so we could feed the baby, because it was quite newborn and she didn't want to take it with her. There were loads of people on *Easy Rider*-type motorbikes riding around. There was free food. All of the stage was tie-dyed. It was brilliant. We were sitting cross-legged on the floor. It was very open. Everything was free, but there was just nobody there. I don't know why. It was a really lovely atmosphere. I think Floyd thought it was the best gig they played that summer.

ATOM HEART MOTHER RELEASED
2 OCTOBER 1970

The fifth studio album by Pink Floyd is the first to reach No.1 in the UK. The original album cover, designed by art collective Hipgnosis, shows a Holstein-Friesian cow standing in a pasture with no text or other clue as to what might be on the record, baffling the managing director of EMI's record division, who had to sign off on the album art. Storm Thorgerson, inspired by Andy Warhol's cow wallpaper, had driven into the countryside and photographed the first cow he saw. Her name was Lulubelle III.

I WAS THERE: RON GEESIN

At that time in Notting Hill, there were many artists of all persuasions, people involved in the music business as well as visual artists, and everyone was bumping into everyone ese. Rick Wright was walking distance away from our basement flat at 34 Elgin Crescent, between Portobello Road and Ladbroke Grove. I don't remember how I met Sam Cutler, who introduced me to Nick Mason, but I was doing a lot of live performances so he may have seen me in a live performance.

  Nick came down to the basement to meet me and he jumped about, asking me, 'What's this? What's that? That's a funny looking thing.' I was using makeshift gadgets to make sound, not just standard electronics, and we hit it off immediately. Musicians usually have something to exchange, whether it's jokes or something to do with music such as 'what composers do you like? What are you listening to these days. How do you do that?' We were all at an age where we were trying to make a living doing what we liked to do without joining some horrible company and be minced in a machine. That was the common bond.

I didn't know much about rock bands. I didn't need to and I didn't want to. I was doing my own thing. There's a piece on my first album that I made in the basement at 34 Elgin Crescent called 'A World of Too Much Sound'. Nick said he didn't like it because I was criticising the whole idea of getting money 'to make more powerful amplifiers'. He said, 'Why don't you do something a bit more commercial and make more money?'

I was the court jester, being entirely rude about the whole rock, electric music scene in my performances around that time, from '66 to the mid-70s. Pete Townshend's an old mate and he said of me 'he's a terrorist, he was unbelievable'. Because I opened for The Who a couple of times at big concerts. I remember one at Reading University where I went down too well and I got a real scragging from Roger Daltrey in the dressing room. He said, 'You can't do that, mate. *We've* got to get out there and be big.' Then he said, 'We had an opener recently and she just managed to make the half hour and get off.' That told me a lot about the ego side of rock music.

It was all a rush. We were all young sports. Rushing was part of being. You didn't hang about on anything. There was all that energy at that time and one thing was feeding off into another thing. Tony Garnett, the producer for the film, *The Body*, contacted John Peel and said 'who's hot on the scene for doing music?' and John Peel, being a particular fan and supporter of me said, 'Go and talk to Ron Geesin.'

If you got three weeks to do a feature film you were lucky. The money's very good so you don't say, 'I can't do that in three weeks – it'll take me two months,' because they'll say, 'Well, thank you very much - we're off down the road to the next man, who *can* do it in three weeks.' You don't think much; you just get on and do it. There's a serious point there to do with the creative world. If you don't get a subconscious flow going as an artist, your stuff won't be much good. You've got to let the subconscious come out, because it's you that you're exposing. Think too much about it and it won't be any good. Some of my best stuff has been done under extreme stress.

Tony and the film's director, Roy Battersby, came to see me in my fifth floor studio in Ladbroke Grove and listened to some stuff I'd been doing. They said, 'That seems to fit alright. What you're doing and how you're doing it is good. But can you do songs?' I said, 'No, I don't do songs, but I know a man who does.' And that was Roger Waters, because we were particularly close friends at that time, playing golf and socialising together. Roger and I worked completely separately on *The Body*. He did the songs and I did all the fancy, intricate stuff that was in the film and then we put it together.

So Roger would have had an extra feeling that I could do something. He and Nick came to me and said, 'We've got this thing and we don't know what to do with it yet. We're a bit stuck.' They were knackered from touring and were being pushed to get the next album out. They didn't work creatively with many other people ever, but they approached me because I was particularly enthusiastic and a bit different. Floyd obviously knew that I had creative ideas and could do something. They didn't think, 'We'll have to look at this fella and poke him to see if he can do it,' because they didn't know what they were doing with it either.

A high profile person or group need to keep their high profile. They don't want someone climbing over it. A perfect example of this was in comments David made in (possibly) a BBC documentary. He was filmed sitting in a window, and when he was asked about *Atom Heart Mother*, he said, 'Ah yes, we got Ron in to do some arranging,' and I thought 'you bastard'. I did a John Cleese and said to myself, 'Right, that's it. You've had it now.' That's the main reason I wrote my book, *The Flaming Cow - The Making of Pink Floyd's Atom Heart Mother*.

David and Rick designed the chord sequences and David his great solos, but they had not much else to do with it. They had their introductory drone but I thought, 'I'm going to push your cart off the road here for a bit.' So I entered with a brass drone, the most non-harmonic drone against theirs, an anti-introduction, which is coming in at 90 degrees to their track and the way they're travelling.

And then I go into the main theme, which is that chord sequence (that Roger had said was like a cowboy Western theme) and which they used several times. And I'm going through and going through, and we're getting into the cello solo section and then through the whole choral sections, and then that fucking chord sequence comes again, and I'm going, 'Oh God, not that theme again – I can't stand it!'. So I wrote a completely different melody for the last two choruses. It's the same chord sequence, but you wouldn't recognise it, because the whole brass structure and everything is completely different. I had to do that because I was fed up with this repeating thing. And the reason for the repeating was that they didn't have anything else to put on the tape to make something else. I think David would admit that now.

When we recorded the 'Funky' section, I had misinterpreted the bar positions so Nick said, 'That's not beat one, it's beat two, we need to put it on beat one,' and I said, 'But that throws all my inflections out relative to what's going on in the track.' That mistake in the studio in the heat of the moment, was all in the rushing of the brain.

I don't remember why I didn't go to the Bath Festival. I'd done what I'd done and it was over to the conductor, John Aldiss, to get on with it with them. I might have started working on something else – I was doing a lot in 1970. There was the recording at the BBC's Paris Cinema for the John Peel *Sunday Concert*, on 16 July and that was okay because it was in a controlled environment at a reasonable time of day. The Hyde Park performance, two days later, took place later on in the evening. The organisation and John Aldiss, the conductor, had got other players – deps – in. They'd got the dots in front of them but there was no rehearsal. The deps didn't have a clue what they were supposed to be doing. It's a difficult piece to play. You need to know the game and the conductor needs to know that odd mix of the rock and the classical elements, making it a properly homogeneous piece of music. Hyde Park was a mess. I left Hyde Park in tears.

It's now that I've analysed what I did with Floyd's original piece of music – coming in at right angles, going along with it, going in all different directions – creating that energy and that contrast, the dialogue between what I was thinking and what they were thinking, that I see the heat that makes the work appealing to a lot of people. So anything that was said by Gilmour and Waters is now annulled, defunct. I think they need to revise what they said, although of course they don't have to because they've done so much else.

It's there and it still goes around and, after 50-odd years, it still puzzles some people. I think that's great. The arrangement by the Japanese Morgaua Quartet is a jazzy piece of music by a string quartet. I don't know what they've got out of the actual *Atom Heart Mother* or where they've got it. I can't hear it. But that's alright.

The 2012 performance at the Théâtre du Châtelet in Paris was fantastic. The cellist wasn't that amazing but the choir and the brass were absolutely superb. Some dyed-in-the-wool Floyd fans would criticise the group because they weren't a Floyd tribute band. They were professional musicians who had learned the parts and didn't make mistakes or go flying off at tangents.

Last August, the biggest Italian tribute band, Pink Floyd Legend, wanted me in Rome for the opening of their tour and *Atom Heart Mother* was the highlight of the performance. For the 2008 performance at the Cadogan Hall in Chelsea, with David guesting on the Sunday night, I had devised what to do on the piano through the 'excursion' section in the middle, with the electronics and the distant wailing, plucking single strings with a plectrum and caressing all the strings with soft beaters. In Rome, I was amused to get applause for that and the piece a standing ovation from 2,500 people and I thought 'this is good'. The conductor was fantastic.

If Roger and David knocked on the door now and said, 'We've made up and we're going on the road with *Atom Heart Mother*. Will you come and play with us?', I'd say yes.

In October 1970, Pink Floyd embark upon their fourth tour of North America.

FILLMORE EAST
27 SEPTEMBER 1970, NEW YORK, NEW YORK

I WAS THERE: PHILIP SIMMONS
I saw Pink Floyd at the Fillmore East before they became a huge commercial success. *Dark Side of the Moon* was not created yet. I remember the repeated ad for *Ummagumma* in the Fillmore programmes as I saw around 30 shows at the Fillmore East before it closed, including Traffic, The Allman Brothers, Derek and the Dominoes, Jefferson Airplane and the Grateful Dead. Pink Floyd was possibly the most unique of all of them. I was familiar with them on a limited basis from the underground FM station in NYC, WNEW, so decided to get some tickets with some friends. The promoter Bill Graham owned the two Fillmores at the time and booked them on an 'off' night, not the usual Friday or Saturday. It was presented as something special, and it sure turned out to be the case. What I remember most is how they set up speakers all around the auditorium and cranked the sound around the room. The musicianship was great as well. Those details have always stood out in my memory, even if I can't remember too much else. After all, it was 53 years ago!

CENTRE OF THE ARTS
11 OCTOBER 1970, REGINA, CANADA

I WAS THERE: DANA SCOTT
I was not a big fan and won the ticket(s) from CJUS-FM the University of Saskatchewan station (now defunct). I remember it was in a lecture hall on campus and they had speakers set up all around the room which allowed for effects like making a fly buzz around the room. I don't remember specific tunes but it was long jammy stuff, like on *Ummagumma*.

CIVIC AUDITORIUM
23 OCTOBER 1970, SANTA MONICA, CALIFORNIA

I WAS THERE: GREG MASTROGIOVANNI

My friend Rudy, who was a big fan of Floyd, drove us to the Santa Monica Civic Auditorium. We got there early and stopped in the restaurant called Sambo's (which later became a Denny's) for something to eat. Three members of Pink Floyd – David Gilmour, Nick Mason and Richard Wright – were sitting in a booth eating dinner. We walked up to their table and said 'hello'. David said hello back to us. Nick and Richard started laughing hysterically at us and pointing at us. We said 'nice meeting you' and left.

The show was amazing. 'Careful With That Axe, Eugene' was creepier than the *Ummagumma* recording. The band was fantastic, with the full orchestra playing 'Atom Heart Mother'. Later, the audience kept screaming 'Interstellar Overdrive!'. There was a long pause and I think it was Roger Waters who said, 'We're going to do 'Interstellar Overdrive',' which the audience cheered. It was a fantastic show.

Years later, I was working at the Hard Rock Cafe in Los Angeles and David Gilmour was walking through the restaurant. I called him over and told him the story about when we met him, and asked why Nick and Richard were laughing at us. He said, 'Oh, we were probably really high.' He smiled and walked away…

November 1970 sees the Floyd touring Continental Europe.

ERNST-MERCK HALLE
14 NOVEMBER 1970, HAMBURG, WEST GERMANY

I WAS THERE: WILHELM WELZIN

Yes, well I saw them. Not the first time around, though. I was in jail when the legendary first show happened in the Big Hall of Hamburg University, organized by the students' council. All my friends were there, or so they told me. At an admission fee of four (!) deutschmark it was what one could call quite an opportunity. All their monumental sound equipment was put to tremendous use and all the great songs were to be experienced, but not by me. I was serving three weeks in juvenile detention for alleged possession of harmful substances.

When, sometime later, the band did their second Hamburg show I was in drug therapy. When the second show was scheduled, it was a foregone conclusion that all of us ex-junkies would attend. The ticket prices reflected a certain growth in popularity, as did the location: a rather lofty exhibition hall, with room for thousands of those kids who were in the know. Money, however, was no concern of mine; it was paid in this special instance by the State of Hamburg. The band was not mainstream back then. We had rather good places to stand, at the balcony rail with a superb view. And, of course, the music worked its magic. I was engrossed.

I clearly recall the suspension when they played 'Careful With That Axe, Eugene'. Would they surprise us all by omitting the terrible scream? When that ominous scream finally did explode I had not expected it any more. There was a huge gong in the middle of the stage and it burst into flames at that exact moment. I had a sudden wish to make myself heard above the din my contemporaries were producing to send a tiny signal that I approved of the show. Since I have never mastered the art of whistling and since I could not shriek like a girl, I decided to utter a very strident 'eh' (like the e sound in 'guess'). Over and over. I had forgotten that I did this until, many years later, I discovered a bootleg recording of that concert. Someone must have brought a tape recording device to the show. The quality was low and converting it to MP3 had not helped at all. But – my unaccountable attempt at yelling methodically was there, crystal clear. I had become part of music history.

Their third Hamburg show also produced a bootleg and I owned the vinyl recording back then without really appreciating it. Just a few months ago I found it again. Lo fi is the best word to describe it, but compared to *The Endless River* it is just so raw and vital.

THE ROUNDHOUSE PUBLIC HOUSE
12 DECEMBER 1970, DAGENHAM, UK

I WAS THERE: PAUL DAWSON

They played a concert at The Roundhouse (Dagenham – I'll get to the Camden Town venue next) in December 1970. There was a miner's strike taking place. They came onstage wearing miners' helmets to show support. During the first half, Roger announced that there were indications of a power cut looming, so they played *Saucerful* early saying that, if the power remained, the finale might be a little less dramatic than usual. In fact, the power continued and they ended with the group-only version of *Atom Heart Mother* which was pretty good.

I got to the Camden Town Roundhouse at 9am on a Sunday morning, for a gig which was due to start at 3pm. There was something of a line, but it was all very social and the time passed pleasantly enough. This time, they performed *Atom Heart Mother* with choir and brass band.

I saw them several times when they were touring *Dark Side* prior to LP release. There was no real indication that this was going to propel them to become superstars, but personally I disliked the increase in lyrics and decrease in music. In that early version, one of the taped sound effects was Malcolm Muggeridge complaining about students wanting pot. I was sorry that this didn't make the recorded version.

I belong to that strange group of fans who like the pre-*Dark Side* stuff very much more than the remainder. For me, it was all about the music. The lyrics didn't seem to matter very much before *Dark Side*. The *Dark Side* lyrics clearly captured the *zeitgeist*, but to me they came across as sixth form poetry and the later stuff was too much Roger ranting on about his dislikes. I got to many concerts of theirs, but I always came away thinking what a pity it wasn't up to the first gig of theirs that I saw.

TOWN HALL
18 DECEMBER 1970, BIRMINGHAM, UK

I WAS THERE: GARETH JONES, AGE 16

It was the *Atom Heart Mother* tour and I had just bought the album. My first Floyd album was *Ummagumma*. It was the first record I had bought by anyone (unless you count the single of 'Maggie May' by Rod Stewart – which, clearly, we shouldn't). I was 16 years old and this was my first gig of any kind. Talk about starting your gig-going life at the top! My uncle drove me into Birmingham and to the famous old Town Hall. I was seated some four or five rows back in the left of the audience, just in front of Dave Gilmour. I took a camera and used flashbulbs to take a few photos (which sadly have got lost in the passage of time and following too many house moves). I remember the band playing 'Alan's Psychedelic Breakfast' with, I presume, a roadie on stage actually cooking breakfast (I could smell the bacon) on a camping gas stove. 'Marmalade, I like marmalade…'. It was the only time I saw that piece being performed, and excellent it was too. I guess that gas stoves on stage are not necessarily a good idea.

I also remember 'Set the Controls for the Heart of the Sun', which was magnificent, and which I have seen them do many times, with Roger giving the gong real welly! And, of course, *Atom Heart Mother* in all its glory, with Ron Geesin, brass orchestra and singers. I thought then and still do now that *Atom Heart Mother* is my favourite Floyd music (after Saucerful of course!). It has the same range, scope and intensity that I find in Gustav Holst's *The Planets*. I left the gig a happy bunny to be collected outside by my uncle. Great times and a great start to my Floyd life.

 FREE TRADE HALL
21 DECEMBER 1970, MANCHESTER, UK

I WAS THERE: DEREK MADDOCK

I have seen Pink Floyd at least three times, once at Manchester Free Trade Hall in 1970, once at the Bath Festival (1970) and once at Maine Road football stadium in 1988. They say that if you remember stuff from the Sixties or Seventies then you weren't really there and, frankly, I don't remember all that much! One thing I do remember, however, is possibly the most surreal and bizarre event I have ever witnessed at a concert. This was Pink Floyd performing 'Alan's Psychedelic Breakfast' from *Atom Heart Mother*. This consisted of one of the roadies actually cooking bacon and eggs and preparing cereal and milk (it must have been Rice Krispies). All the food was 'miked up' and you could hear the bacon and eggs spitting and crackling, and the Rice Krispies snap, crackle and popping! And, to make matters worse, the auditorium was filled with the most delicious, appetising aroma of bacon and eggs, complete with blue smoke from the frying pan. I daresay a lot of concertgoers made straight for the local Wimpeys or other snack bars at the end of the concert!

I WAS THERE: SIMON PHILLIPS

The Free Trade Hall, a neoclassical building, was the home of England's Halle Orchestra. All that's left now is the façade behind which is a modern hotel. I'd seen Frank Zappa there about a month earlier, with seats on about the sixth row. For the Floyd, we had seats up in the circle and round to the left, so we looked down and to our left towards the stage. I only have hazy memories of the performance of 'Alan's Psychedelic Breakfast'. Part of the stage was set up as a kitchen. There was definitely a huge box of Kellogg's cornflakes and I seem to think everything else might have been oversized too – a bottle of ketchup, a radio, a bowl and spoon and maybe the table and chairs too? That's my abiding memory of this show, looking down onto this 'large' breakfast scene. I know that the box of cornflakes was enormous and the other things were there, so they must have been large too or it would have just looked stupid. I've listened and listened to a tape of the show, but I can't dredge up any memory of what was happening on stage during this song.

Breakfasts aside, this was of course a show with a full choir and orchestra for *Atom Heart Mother*, which had been premiered at the Bath Festival and subsequently released on LP. I didn't welcome the additions to this piece because I loved the band-only version so much. Nonetheless, it was stirring to see and hear the choir and the brass. I do remember feeling that it seemed to inhibit the band, as they had to keep strict time with the rest of the ensemble, who were working to musical scores.

REFECTORY HALL, UNIVERSITY OF LEEDS
23 JANUARY 1971, LEEDS, UK

I WAS THERE: LES LAMB

After seeing them at Leeds Town Hall in 1969, my next concert was at the Uni in 1971 when they played *Atom Heart Mother* all the way through, again an amazing sound system with the noise of a train going round the speakers in the hall. Next up was the *Animals* tour in 1976 at Stafford Bingley Hall, by which time the side show and effects were as good as the music. The last time was in 1991, when they played Earl's Court for several nights, I had tickets for the second night but the stage collapsed on the first night and that show was cancelled, so I saw the first live show the following day. I miss them and still try and see Gilmour and Waters when possible and, of course, the Australian Pink Floyd. I've just got back from a friend's funeral – he was piped out to 'Comfortably Numb'!

QUEEN MARY COLLEGE
20 FEBRUARY 1971, TWICKENHAM, UK

I WAS THERE: ALAN HOLLIS

I was at Queen Mary College. I purchased four tickets so that three of my ex-school mates could come down from Loughborough for the weekend. They all slept in my college room. There didn't seem to be any restriction on the number of tickets you could buy; I think the student union was just glad to sell them all. Tickets were only £1, but bearing in mind that at the beginning of that year you could buy eight pints and a good night out for

£1, some sacrifices had to be made. The theatre probably held no more than 500 and was packed. Fire and health and safety regulations now would restrict attendance to something like 300. We were standing on the right-hand – ie. Gilmour's – side as you faced the stage and people were sitting at the front. I think this was so those at the back could see properly rather than because it was a relaxed atmosphere. The stage was only a platform about two steps high, so it was more of a drama workshop than a theatre. The wall of speakers was impressive compared to what we'd seen used by other groups. The playlist was based around *Ummagumma* and the finale was 'Careful With That Axe, Eugene' and 'Set The Controls...', which were brilliantly reproduced in a live setting. There was no encore that I remember but it would have been difficult to follow that ending.

I WAS THERE: DAVID LAWRENSON

Growing up in Lancashire in the 1960s I, like many other teenagers, became besotted by the changing culture, particularly the music. Unfortunately, the Swinging Sixties wasn't really happening where I lived, a typical Northern industrial town. Bands didn't come to St Helens. Increasingly, all the best ones were playing the college and university circuit. One of my favourites were Pink Floyd. I loved their psychedelic sounds. 'Arnold Layne' was great and I went out and bought 'See Emily Play'. On leaving grammar school, I was determined to get away, preferably to London where everything was happening. In September 1970 I arrived at St Mary's, a teacher training college in Strawberry Hill, Twickenham. Although I had no great desire to be a teacher, I could be a student for three years and – more importantly – see a lot of great bands. Imagine my excitement when, after just a few months there, it was announced that Pink Floyd would be playing in the college theatre. I couldn't believe it. Tickets were £1 and soon went but I made sure I got one!

The theatre only held about 500 people. There were no seats, we just sat on the floor. The first thing I noticed was the speakers arranged around the back of the hall, which I'd never seen before. As the concert got underway, I soon realised what they were there for. The band were using something called an Azimuth Co-ordinator, which sent the sound around the theatre via the speakers! Amazing. I can't really remember the set list. Me and my mates just sat there and let the whole experience wash over us.

After teaching for just a year I changed careers and became a journalist, spending three years writing about rock music. St Mary's University now run journalism courses and I'm often asked in to talk to the students. I tell them about when I was a student there and always mention seeing Pink Floyd in the theatre for £1 – they're amazed. For most of my life, I've lived around St Mary's, about three miles down the road in Hampton. Dave Gilmour has his recording studio on his houseboat, Astoria, moored nearby on the River Thames.

In 2017, I went to see the *Their Mortal Remains* exhibition at the V&A. I was pleased to see a list of Floyd's 1971 gigs, with St Mary's College proudly featuring. At the end of the exhibition, there was a room showing concert footage of the band. There were no chairs so I sat on the floor to watch it. I was immediately transported back to 1971. It was a bit more difficult getting up off the floor afterwards than it was all those years ago!

 GREAT HALL, UNIVERSITY OF EXETER
3 FEBRUARY 1971, EXETER, UK

I WAS THERE: MIKE WATTS

Pink Floyd playing Exeter was very much a booking at short notice. I was rung one afternoon in January 1971 by an agent that we often booked through, Don Kingswell at Bron Agency, and asked if the Great Hall might be available for a mid-week date two weeks later. Floyd had started on an *Atom Heart Mother* world tour and Don said the band wanted to play a handful of colleges before they went to Europe and they knew the hall had great acoustics. I'd been looking at booking The Incredible String Band for that week, but Floyd was a better bet. Their fee would only be £600 and they were stipulating that we couldn't charge more than 50p per ticket. We did the maths and with the cost of paying for the hall, security, printing tickets, and hospitality for the band, it was just possible. There'd be no money for posters but we figured distributing handbills around the residence halls and bars would be enough.

We announced tickets would go on sale a few days later and sold out straight away. We'd just been through the difficult experience of the Faces cancelling a booking at 24 hours' notice, so there was a degree of cynicism amongst the student body that Floyd would even show but the day went without a hitch. They arrived early afternoon because the sound crew needed to set up PA speakers around the perimeter of the hall so that the band could do a full sound check. Social committee members that were on hand to hump equipment had the unexpected treat of the band sound checking their way through an extended twelve bar blues, with Dave Gilmour channelling his best Muddy Waters. It was all very relaxed, and before the gig got underway the band happily chatted backstage with student journalists and posed for photos. As well as the title track and 'Fat Old Sun' from *Atom Heart Mother*, I remember the setlist included 'Astronomy Domine', 'Set the Controls for the Heart of the Sun' and 'Careful With That Axe, Eugene'.

The purpose of the strategically placed speakers around the hall became evident halfway through the set as echoey footsteps could be heard circling around the audience which, my fellow Exeter alum Phil Mercer tells me, was Rick Wright playing an Azimuth Co-ordinator. It was probably the first time any of us had heard surround sound!

TOP RANK SUITE
16 APRIL 1971, DONCASTER, UK

I WAS THERE: IAN DOUGALL

A group from Doncaster Grammar School for Boys, we used to listen to Floyd, Cream and Jethro Tull round a friend's house after school; he had a music centre and a good collection of records – both items were to be envied at the time. Less coolly, we ate toast and Marmite until we went home around 6pm. Significantly, the nature of the music appealed to males. From memory, those more successful with girls pragmatically went to the Top Rank on Tuesday evenings, where The Isley Brothers and The Four Tops played to a mixed teenage audience.

I attended the Top Rank suite for the above *Atom Heart Mother* concert. It remains one of my favourite albums, and was the piece I remember most from the concert, which was well attended. It seemed to be mainly young men, who sat reverentially around the stage, legs crossed, heads nodding. I happened to take a girl with me, but sadly she was not impressed, thinking the evening was rather dull. Shortly after, she clearly thought I must be rather dull too and dumped me for a bloke with an impressive Tamla Motown collection.

I suspect there was a level of intellectual snobbery around going to progressive rock concerts, and maybe punk chose to blast what they considered to be pseudo-intellectual indulgences. However, the music of *Atom Heart Mother* still has the emotional power to move me to this day, lasting a life far in excess of the span of a teenage crush... and the cover is up there with the best.

THE LADS CLUB
22 APRIL 1971, NORWICH, UK

I WAS THERE: STEVE HOWES, AGE 16

At the age of 16 I saw Pink Floyd for the first time at The Lads Club in Norwich where they performed 'Echoes' for the first time under the original title 'Return of the Son of Nothing' amongst other gems. I then went on to see Pink Floyd another nine times over the years. I was probably 15 when I discovered their music. I was into Led Zeppelin at the time, and a mate of mine at school said to me, 'Why don't you listen to this?'. It was *Ummagumma*. That was the first album of theirs I ever heard and I thought 'this is fantastic'. I was a fan of Ten Years After, the Edgar Broughton Band and Hawkwind and things like that, and Pink Floyd went to the top of the tree.

It was a Thursday night. My dad worked for himself so me and two of my mates took the afternoon off school – I don't think anybody's going to condemn me for that now – and he took us in his old Vauxhall Victor. It was a run through Thetford Forest, 60 miles from where we lived in Huntingdon. My dad always wished he'd gone in there because he went on to like 'em as well. One of Floyd's roadies was at the door of the venue. My dad must have been in his mid-forties at the time and he walked up to the roadie and said, 'Are Floyd here tonight, mate?' and the roadie looked him up and down and said, 'Yeah, they're here tonight.' So we cleared off and I remember we went and had some egg and chips, and then we turned up and went in there. We got some funny looks because we were quite young. Most of the people who were in there were in their twenties.

We shouldn't have been there, really. It was a student thing at the University of East Anglia, so really the gig was behind closed doors. But there was a tobacconists called Bristows and they advertised several tickets in the *New Musical Express* so we chanced our arm and got them. The UEA used to have a major band on every month during that era. I think the one booked after the Floyd was Yes.

There were only 500 people in the hall. They started off with the band version of *Atom Heart Mother* and then they did 'Careful With That Axe, Eugene'. They did a track called 'Embryo' which was never put down on album, apart from a studio version that was put out on a Harvest sampler, and then they did 'Cymbaline' and that was quite epic, because they had quadraphonic footsteps going around the room. This was the sort of thing that attracted me to Pink Floyd, because they were different. Rick Wright used to operate the Azimuth Co-ordinator from his keyboards and it all went quiet and these steps went around and around the hall, and kept opening doors. You had to be there to experience it. It was fantastic. They also did 'Fat Old Sun' and they encored with 'Careful With That Axe, Eugene'.

Of all the Floyd concerts I've ever seen, that one stands out because it was the first time I saw them and it was quite a novelty gig. They did 'Echoes' for the very first time under the original title, 'Return of the Son of Nothing'. It hadn't even been put down on an album at that stage. Roger Waters said, 'We've never done this before.' When it ended and there was no reaction from the crowd, because they hadn't heard it before, Dave Gilmour just nodded. He said, 'That's it.'

CENTRAL HALL, LANCASTER UNIVERSITY
7 MAY 1971, LANCASTER, UK

I WAS THERE: SIMON PHILLIPS

Home turf! The university campus had been built from scratch during the Sixties and, as a consequence, was something of a concrete jungle but they did put on some good shows. The hall was a low square building with a square concert hall and an outer area with bar and seating. My brother and a couple of friends and I arrived about an hour before the show. If there was a support band, I can't remember seeing them.

We wandered into the hall and there was all the familiar equipment set up on stage. I think they were still using the WEM amplification and speakers. It looked reassuringly familiar. There weren't too many people there, so we went out to the bar where there were eight to ten round tables, each about three feet in diameter and accommodating four people comfortably, more if people squashed in. We got beers from the bar and sat at one of the tables. The place was still fairly empty but people were starting to trickle in. A few people came and sat at the next table to us and got some beers in. I glanced round idly, people-watching as you do, and there was the whole band plus a couple of others. Roadies, perhaps. They were sitting there with pints of beer, only a couple of feet from our table, just chatting and laughing.

Now, a quiz. What would you have done back then? a) ignore them, b) pester them for autographs, or c) take a selfie with them? (We didn't have mobile phones back then, thank God). We did a) because it seemed the most cool thing to do. We said absolutely nothing to them.

It was a stunning show, with plenty of room to move around. Just imagine that now. The highlight was my first hearing of what was to become 'Echoes'. I think they introduced it as 'The Return of the Son of Nothing'. This is still one of my all-time favourite Floyd numbers – there's an elegance in its simplicity. I'm pretty sure that they also did 'Atom Heart Mother' (for my fourth and final time).

CRYSTAL PALACE BOWL
15 MAY 1971, LONDON, UK

I WAS THERE: PHIL CARTER

The line-up was Mountain, Rod Stewart and the Faces, and the Floyd. This was a ticketed gig and I came down to London with Harry and three beautiful girls, Hilary being my favourite. They were all convent girls, well spoken, coolly dressed and up for a day out. Harry and I could not believe our luck. Harry and I had already decided to take some acid. The girls chose not to partake. They were convent girls after all!

We got there nice and early and were able to watch most of the acts. There were probably about eight to ten thousand people in attendance. Harry and I starting flying when the Faces came on. I got totally confused when, in the middle of their gig, the rugby league commentator Eddie Waring was heard talking about the rugby league cup final through their speakers and, at the end of the Faces show, Elvis Presley appeared on the stage. Both of these had a simple explanation, we found out later, but we were flying by then.

Mountain were loud and some of their stuff suited our mood. By the time the Floyd came on and started playing, the heavens started opening and there was heavy, heavy rain. The girls departed for shelter, but Harry and I just smiled at each other. We were listening to the Floyd live while on acid – nirvana! I would say that at least half of the audience were also tripping. Like us, they were mesmerised by this whole experience. I think there was thunder, lightning and even more rain. Some inflatables appeared in the pond at the front of the stage while others were swimming in it.

The Floyd played beautifully that afternoon. They premiered 'Echoes' which is now considered a classic. The climax of the show was *A Saucerful of Secrets* with an impressive firework display which was truly wonderful on LSD. Harry and I were high as the proverbial kite, blissed out. It was fucking glorious. Afterwards, we had to get home and got on the wrong train out of Crystal Palace heading for Brighton, but that's another story.

I WAS THERE: PETER DE MONCEY-CONEGLIANO

By 1971, I was jamming a lot with a guitarist called Stevie Pomorski I'd met when we both lived the hippie dream (and the nightmare) in a north London commune. We jammed on an old harmonium and electric guitars and wrote a lot of Pink Floyd-type songs. And the more we jammed, the less we were actually interested in forming a band or playing in public. That's the way it went in those days. Anyway, when we heard about it we decided to go to see Pink Floyd at the *Garden Party at the Crystal Palace Bowl*.

It was great to hear them and they were really good in the open air, with loudspeakers strung up in the trees and an Azimuth Co-ordinator projecting the sound around the area. It was a beautiful day and you could just lie in the grass and listen to the sounds moving around.

What put me off this otherwise hippie dream was the sight of Rod Stewart in a pink velvet suit and arriving and leaving by helicopter. LSD is wonderful on a nice warm day in a park but we were getting the definite impression that these people – Rod 'the Mod' Stewart and the Floyd themselves – were now something else, rich superstars who no longer could be thought of as our equals as human beings or musicians. As soon as they finished, they would jump into a helicopter and leave the poor acid freak fans in the mud and the cold. Have you ever tried to cross a busy road on LSD? Heavy, man.

Pink Floyd ceased to interest me after *The Dark Side of the Moon*, and when they started to be a stadium band producing mainstream musical wallpaper for yuppies that was the end. I wish I had been there in the very, very early days, at Middle Earth and the UFO Club, when they were new and fresh and truly underground, and truly part of the alternative society and genuinely musically and verbally creative. While Floyd produced some great early albums, their last truly great album was *Meddle* and the group that was once a tight unit, full of enthusiasm, ended in acrimony, ego trips and – worst of all – as bread heads.

REFECTORY, UNIVERSITY OF EDINBURGH
19 MAY 1971, EDINBURGH, UK

I WAS THERE: RICHARD DIXON

After seeing them in Belgium, I next saw the Pink Floyd when I was at Edinburgh University in the early Seventies. They performed in the 'Cavern' that was the health centre. Memories of that gig were of the light show that accompanied it. Up until then, light shows did not feature in concerts. At one point, an aeroplane appeared on the big screen and the sound of it taking off seemed to travel from one side of the room to the other. It was a totally new experience for us and a real talking point.

Many years later, I was invited to the wedding of my second cousin's daughter in France and who should be there but Nick Mason and his son. The connection between them was vintage cars, as my cousin's husband rallies an old Jaguar. Another of the guests used to go to a flat in London, when he was at art college, where the band stayed, but neither of us had the courage to go and reminisce with Nick. An opportunity missed which I have regretted ever since.

June sees Floyd play European shows and then fly to Japan and Australia.

FESTIVAL HALL
13 AUGUST 1971, MELBOURNE, AUSTRALIA

I WAS THERE: COL TURNER

Less than ten months after the last time I saw them, I was to see them again, this time in Australia where I'd emigrated to from England in October 1970. They were booked to play one gig. I was looking forward to seeing Floyd in my new country with eager anticipation but near disaster struck on the day of the concert when I went down with a severe sore throat! I felt like death all day but that night mustered up the strength to get out of bed and take my girlfriend (now my wife) to see her first Pink Floyd show. We arrived at Festival Hall about 45 minutes before the advertised start. There were not many booking agencies in those days, so you got to the venue early and took your chance on buying a ticket at the door. Floyd had not yet 'cracked it' in Australia and I was hoping to get a reasonable seat.

'Two tickets please,' I croaked to the girl behind the counter. We then entered the hall to be shown our seats… wait for it… seventh row centre! I estimate the crowd as about 500 and Floyd probably lost money that night but what a show. Not many people in Australia were aware of the show. Even today people do not believe that Floyd toured that early. That is why I refer to this as 'the 1971 forgotten show'. A while ago, I was lucky enough to receive a bootleg of this show (audience recording) and this has helped me remember what a brilliant show it was! The set consisted of *Atom Heart Mother* (without orchestra), 'Green is the Colour', 'Careful With That Axe, Eugene', 'Set the Controls for the Heart of the Sun', 'Echoes' (planetary version), 'Cymbaline' and *A Saucerful of Secrets*. Not a bad selection, I think you will agree. They casually walked onto the stage, picked up their instruments, tuned up a bit and then launched into the sweetest version of *Atom Heart Mother*. Beautifully done, with Roger using his scream and some backing tapes, I suspect, to fill in for the orchestra. Nick was on his mettle that night, really giving the skins a thrashing on this number. For a change of pace, they played 'Green is the Colour', which Dave found a tad difficult in places! He missed a few of the higher notes, but hey, who's perfect? Then the tension started to build as they crept into a very haunting 'Careful With That Axe, Eugene'. Roger's scream was at its best and the hairs on my arm tingled as the

Clockwise from top left: David Lawrenson couldn't believe Pink Floyd were playing his college; Tim Marshall was at the Bradford Uni concert which has since appeared on bootleg; For Ian Dougall, the Seventies meant prog rock and Marmite; Richard Dixon saw the Floyd using sound effects and visuals at their Edinburgh show

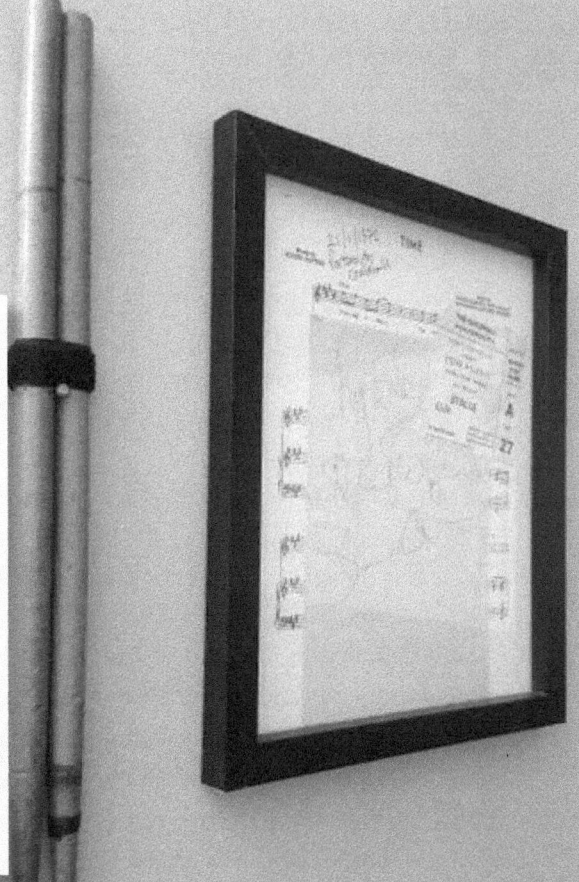

Clockwise from top left: Rick Crossley was at Hunter College; Robert Rearick remembers seeing Pink Floyd despite ingesting various substances during the show; Steve Hudson (centre) has the Floyd's autographs framed on the wall

music cascaded around the almost empty hall. It was like a private Pink Floyd concert for the select 500 or so, and a bit like the old UFO days!

Roger then announced that they were intending to play 'Echoes' but, because of equipment failure, they would do 'Set the Controls for the Heart of the Sun' next instead. After a lot of messing with the equipment, Nick's cymbals reverberated as the intro begun. Rick's playing was also at its peak that night as his fingers danced across the keyboards. Nick was now going berserk on the drums, thrashing and crashing away, and Dave and Roger were totally involved as they contributed to a song I had heard them perform many times before but never as good as then. Roger then announced that one of the 'Leslies' (speakers) had burnt out but they were going to do 'Echoes'. I think this was the only time I saw them do this number live. A bit of 'Rick's Turkish Delight' before ping… ping… ping… A slow beginning, some beautiful soaring guitar from Dave and then the vocals. Now I suppose I could look it up and transcribe the words here but that is not what this is all about. Suffice it to say they sang the 'Planetary' version. That is, the song this night was not about albatrosses but instead about planets. It was an absolutely glorious version, with delightful vocals and guitar work. Rick seemed to me to be slightly out in the first part and his organ seemed a bit heavy-handed, but when it came to the seagulls bit… man, were they together! Sensational, and I wish I could put into words how good it was.

Next came an old favourite in 'Cymbaline', which Dave sang to perfection. He hit every note in a very difficult song. Very nicely done by everybody, an extended version, with delicate keyboards by Rick and Nick doing some nifty work on the cymbals again. They then played the 'Footsteps' tape (from *Man* and *The Journey*) which I found pretty boring and the rest of the audience were getting restless as well. Fortunately, it only lasted a couple of minutes and they found their way back into the end of 'Cymbaline'. I was hoping they might do 'Embryo' but instead got to hear 'A Saucerful of Secrets', which I was pretty pleased about. Roger's guitar and Nick's drums could be heard as they eased into a cacophony of sounds, all going off doing their own thing, just like the old days. I could see a few people with their fingers in their ears as the sound got louder, but the guys were all having a ball. Nick let fly again with pulsating drums, Rick's organ was screaming and Roger and Dave let loose. Then it was all over.

Even though it was a very small crowd, Floyd had given it their all. My memories have been assisted by the tape I have of the show, but I can still remember the sounds they made that night, even after all this time. They had changed from the 'experimental' band I had seen some four-and-a-half years previously into a polished and professional outfit, still prepared to try something different but now in control of their musical wanderings. (As a silly aside, there is one part of the tape where I can actually hear myself whistling! All these years later and still a Floyd nut!) I have been very lucky with what I have witnessed with the birth of Floyd. I sadly would not get to see them again for another 17 years, in 1988.

RANDWICK RACECOURSE
15 AUGUST 1971, SYDNEY, AUSTRALIA

I WAS THERE: JEAN-PAUL

This was an outdoor concert, but still memorable. The opening act was a Sydney band called the Pirhanas who played a Santana-like kind of music. Floyd's set list was very close to the set they had played in Hakone, Japan a few days earlier. They started with 'Atom Heart Mother', with no choir or brass. There was a technical problem that didn't last long, although a large speaker nearly toppled over the stage. That was followed by a 'Green is the Colour'/'Careful With That Axe, Eugene' medley. Then we were graced with 'Cymbaline' before Roger moved to Rick's keyboard set up after announcing a new track that was barely played live. It was 'Echoes', of course, with the famous 'ping'. The finale was the second live side of *Ummagumma*, 'Set the Controls' and 'A Saucerful of Secrets'. There were no encores, although I was secretly hoping for 'Interstellar Overdrive'.

When they landed in Sydney, they went straight to the airport bar. A friend of mine worked there as as barman. The band and their manager (probably Steve O'Rourke) ordered four beers and a scotch. Who knows? Maybe Mason was the 'scotch man'!

They did Pompeii two months later, minus 'Atom Heart Mother' and 'Cymbaline'. I drove 1,000 kilometres in a Volkswagen Beetle with a reconditioned engine to get there. It took me ages. The Floyd were not very well known then. It all changed after *Dark Side*. I also saw them in Paris in '89, where they played an unusually long version of 'One of These Days'.

PAVILLION DE MONTREUX
18 & 19 SEPTEMBER 1971, MONTREUX, SWITZERLAND

I WAS THERE: GIANCARLO VERGANI

I saw Pink Floyd for the first time at the Pavilion in Montreux where they gave two concerts (the first with the choir performing *Atom Heart Mother*) as part of the *Festival de Musique Classique*. In the afternoon, after rehearsals, I managed to meet them for an autograph. I was amazed at the quality of the quadraphonic sound. The second time I saw them was at the Hallenstadion in Zürich in December 1972, where they played

Dark Side of the Moon. As in Montreux, the concerts developed in two parts, where the second began with 'Echoes'. In Zürich, the stage scenery was enriched by the huge circle behind Mason and a carpet of fumes. It was hypnotic. Concerts then did not have the technological riches of today but lived on the spontaneity and happiness of involving their audience.

In early October 1971, the band flies out to Pompeii in Italy to film a concert in the ruins of the village destroyed by the volcano Vesuvius following an eruption in AD 79. Directed by Adrian Maben, Pink Floyd: Live at Pompeii *was released in 1972 and is widely regarded as groundbreaking, not least because it captured the band in such an exotic setting and performing to an empty Roman amphitheatre.*

ROMAN AMPHITHEATRE
4 – 7 OCTOBER 1971, POMPEII, ITALY

I WAS THERE: BRADY MENTZ

I was just a boy living in Naples, about eleven or twelve years old. Some of the other local boys and myself saw trucks heading out to the amphitheatre, so we decided to go and have a look. I recall my friend commenting on the 'shaggy-looking men' unloading the trucks with 'PINK FLOYD LONDON' spray-painted on all the cargo. They initially tried to shoo us away once they saw us but one man – who I later discovered was the film director, Adrian Maben – told us we could stay and watch as long as we were quiet while they were recording. As the sun rose into the sky, it wasn't long before most of the Brits removed their shirts. I was unfamiliar with the material at the time, but later saw the footage and recognized what was the first half of 'Echoes'. As the sun started to set, my friends and I decided to head back home, and we happened to cross paths with the band and crew as they were out doing the landscape shots that were later used in 'Careful With That Axe, Eugene'. Suffice it to say, that day as a whole was what introduced me to Pink Floyd. About a year or two later, I found a copy of *The Dark Side of the Moon*, remembered seeing that group at the amphitheatre and so I picked it up. It's been love ever since.

GREAT HALL, UNIVERSITY OF BRADFORD
10 OCTOBER 1971, BRADFORD, UK

I WAS THERE: TIM MARSHALL

My brother Peter was attending the university, I was visiting him and Floyd were playing. It was a Sunday night, and the gig had been rescheduled after the original date was postponed, and this was the first date available. Tickets were £1. My memory is that I got in for free, as my brother was involved with the university theatre as a lighting and sound technician, but he says that he had to pay for our tickets. It was a fabulous gig, starting in total darkness with red amp lights that were barely perceptible once your eyes adjusted. Then the awesome quad sound effects began, starting with a jailer in heavy boots jangling his keys, locking and opening creaking doors, and slamming them shut and walking around the theatre behind you. I can't remember the track list (Peter remembers they played the whole of *Meddle*) but hearing 'One of These Days' with its thumping bass line prompted me to purchase *Meddle* as soon as I got home to the Midlands some days later. This was the only time I saw Floyd live, but I have been a fan ever since 1967, when a classmate asked the music teacher if he could bring his electric guitar into school and went on to play 'Arnold Layne'. Some music lesson that was!

TOWN HALL
11 OCTOBER 1971, BIRMINGHAM, UK

I WAS THERE: PHIL COOPER, AGE 18

I got tickets from the Town Hall and went with my mate from Stourbridge, Mick Simmons. They played with two huge banks of speakers. They played 'Echoes' and other songs. It was just prior to *Meddle* being released. It was a great night. It was great to see them before they went global. What a band. I remember Roger Waters lit the gong up on 'Set the Controls for the Heart of the Sun'.

The Meddle *tour is the fifth North American tour by Pink Floyd.*

WISH YOU WERE HERE

CIVIC AUDITORIUM
16 OCTOBER 1971, SANTA MONICA, CALIFORNIA

I WAS THERE: IRA KNOPF

I saw Pink Floyd eight times in all. The first time was at Santa Monica Civic, where the setlist was 'Atom Heart Mother', 'Fat Old Sun', 'Set the Controls for the Heart of the Sun', 'A Saucerful of Secrets', 'One of These Days' and 'Echoes'. During 'Set the Controls', Rick Wright's synth went out. David Gilmour started improvising a blues song, with Roger Waters and Nick Mason joining in, until the problem was fixed. The show continued with no further problems.

I then saw them at the Hollywood Bowl in September 1972. The first half of the show consisted of an early version of *Dark Side of the Moon* and the second half 'One of These Days', 'Careful With That Axe, Eugene', 'Echoes', 'A Saucerful of Secrets' and 'Set the Controls for the Heart of the Sun'. There was a great light and video show to go with the performance.

April 1975 saw them performing the entire *Dark Side of the Moon* at the LA Sports Arena. This was another great light and video show, including an airplane flying over the arena. They encored with 'Echoes'. In 1977, they visited Anaheim Stadium on the *Animals* tour and did the whole of that album and *Wish You Were Here*. One highlight was a flying pig going over the stadium from one end to the other.

February 1980 saw them back at the LA Sports Arena, performing *The Wall* in its entirety. The wall was constructed as the band played their songs, and the highlight was David playing 'Comfortably Numb' above the wall. They projected graphics onto the wall which ended when the wall came tumbling down. On vacation in London in June 1981, I got the opportunity to see one of the final performances of *The Wall* at Earl's Court. The show was the same as had been performed in Los Angeles.

In November 1987, the revamped Floyd (minus Roger) again played the LA Sports Arena. Song selections this time were 'Shine On You Crazy Diamond', 'Learning To Fly', 'Yet Another Movie', 'Round and Around', 'Sorrow The Dogs Of War', On The Turning Away, 'One of These Days', 'Time', 'Wish You Were Here', 'Us and Them', 'Money', 'Another Brick in the Wall (Part 2)', 'Comfortably Numb' and an encore of 'Run Like Hell'.

The last time I saw Floyd was on April 16th, 1994 at the Rose Bowl Stadium in Pasadena. The first half comprised 'Shine On You Crazy Diamond', 'Astronomy Domine', 'What Do You Want From Me', 'Learning to Fly', 'Keep Talking', 'Coming Back To Life', 'Hey You', 'A Great Day For Freedom', 'Sorrow', 'High Hopes' and

'Another Brick in The Wall (Part 2)' while the second half was *The Dark Side of the Moon* and then 'Wish You Were Here', 'Comfortably Numb', where a gigantic lotus flower opened up and sent bright lights swirling around the stadium, which was visually stunning to see, plus an encore of 'Run Like Hell'.

I had the pleasure of meeting David Gilmour on April 14th, 1987. He was sat behind me at an Eric Clapton concert at the LA Forum. I asked if he was going to join Eric on stage and he said that he was just there to enjoy the show and was in LA to do some recording, which later turned out to be *The Division Bell*. We had a nice chat about music and a general discussion. Tony Levin was with him who I also got to chat with. And I also got to meet Nick Mason at Virgin Records; he autographed his bio, *Inside Out*, for me.

ARMORY AUDITORIUM
21 OCTOBER 1971, SALEM, OREGON

I WAS THERE: GREGORY SCHERZINGER

The first time I heard Pink Floyd was while in high school and their minor radio hit 'See Emily Play'. It was entertaining enough, but somehow the album never made it into my collection. It was *Ummagumma* in 1970 that opened my ears to Floyd. I was late into my freshman year in college when I first heard it. Today, *Ummagumma* is dismissed both by critics and the band themselves as rubbish, but I still stand strong in its defence. The live disc of the double album contains four seminal recordings of their live experience. Anyone who has never seen them in concert should have the album for those cuts alone. The studio cuts seem to be the bone of contention. Because it is being viewed in retrospect it is an easy target, especially from fans who were introduced late to Pink Floyd. In 1970, it was an eye-opener. 'Grantchester Meadows' remains one of my favourite songs. That and the opening to 'Narrow Way' represented acoustic sounds not heard in evidence anywhere else in their discography. The middle of 'Narrow Way' laid heavy metal open and bare on the floor, while part three provided a lush and satisfying niche.

In those hippie smoke-filled rooms, *Ummagumma* was required listening. 'Several Small Creatures...' was both wacked out and humorous, while 'Sysyphus' was dark and beautiful and worthy of the journey it took you on. Richard Wright evoked beautiful classical piano (I always wanted that section to go longer) and also produced the most chilling note ever recorded. Even Nick Mason's 'Vizier's Garden' piece was a perfect accompaniment to giggling over Zap comics. And then the live cuts... all of them elevated the mind into aural bliss. 'Astronomy Domine' remains one of my favourite and most listened to cuts.

WISH YOU WERE HERE

Nobody was doing what Pink Floyd did on that album. Groups could get into long, psychedelic jams, but Floyd were performing a composition. They did live what other groups couldn't accomplish in the studio. There were other bands featuring complex compositions, such as Yes or Genesis, but they had a more technical approach, like hearing Mozart instead of Tchaikovsky. In those recordings, and live, it felt more like the 'Rick Wakeman' exposition with a heavy dominance in keyboard. With Pink Floyd the song was everything. The balance of Gilmour's guitar and Wright's keyboard propelled the music forward. I never felt David's guitar solos were showcase bridges, but integral to the music, the story being told.

In 1971, there was no *Meddle* album, nor *Moon* nor *Wall*. They were a band heard on the fringes and playing small venues. I wanted to 'see' *Ummagumma* live, a concert experience of 'Astronomy Domine' and 'Set the Controls…'. They played in the Salem Armory, an arena little bigger than a basketball gymnasium, complete with bleacher seats. Even then, they didn't pack the house. It was festival seating and I'm not sure there was even a thousand people there, all of which meant the arena was free to roam, from stage to back bleacher. There was no security or screens and I could walk up to Gilmour and Waters, just a few feet away. I spent most of the concert staring at Gilmour's guitar work.

The concert was an event for which I reserved a rarity for me, a bit of acid. A small dose was enough for me, a sliver of Orange Owsley. I was driving four of my mates down to the concert from Portland, Oregon, just 45 miles away. We dropped just as we left town, anticipating the effects wouldn't begin until we were safely parked at the Armory.

It is too far past the event now to describe the set list, nor every song that they played. They certainly played everything from *Ummagumma* and I would have been disappointed otherwise. Just the four of them were a sonic *tour de force* and capable of taming any crowd with their music alone. I can think of no other concert I've been to where the quiet passages left the entire audience enthralled, as if collectively holding their breath. At any other concert, there would be odd hoots and cheers and background rhubarb. When Floyd brought the sound back to earth, they brought the audience with them, rapt for the next moment. It was the first time I heard 'Echoes', though it wasn't called that at the time. The band never announced any of their songs, just thanked the audience and played. There was no mistaking the signature beginning… the raindrop 'plunks' of Wright's keyboard. It was a magnificent piece that never seemed to end, Gilmour both rhapsodising and thrashing on guitar, while Wright's space interlude had people sitting down on the floor (remember, it was not crowded at all) and communing with their souls.

Most of the recorded interlude sounds like it's all Wright, but I remember Gilmour standing to the side near his amp heads, working the neck of his guitar and fiddling with knobs, creating the most surreal sounds that blended flawlessly with Wright's key moment. By the time the concert was over, I was convinced that Gilmour was the finest guitarist in rock music. There were others faster and more flamboyant, but none that could coax emotion and melody out as he did, every note appropriate and felt from the heart.

There was another element to the concert that I can't overlook: quad sound. This was a venue a little larger than a gymnasium, with tiered bench seating surrounding an open floor on three sides with an area devoted to the stage on the fourth. There were a couple of speaker columns placed at the rear and both sides of the Armory. Wright had a lot of things going on his keyboard decks, but as my memory recalls it, there was a box with a joystick and he could move the sound around the quad set of auditorium speakers, effectively swirling the room. The effect wasn't always used, and it may have been some unseen soundman controlling things, but Mason's drumming in 'Set the Controls...' was all over the place, and many times throughout the concert Gilmour's soaring guitars were taking off across the room. Yes, I know that partly it was the bit of acid I took, but it was what made the concert special. They didn't have much of a light show to speak of, or maybe they didn't want to unpack it all for Salem, but it hardly mattered. They had a soundscape that was as genuine as the astral planes they sang about.

The revelation of the scream in 'Careful With That Axe, Eugene' was another moment that was clear for me. I was standing very close to the stage, ten or 15 feet away, when he started the sequence. I was expecting a wrenching scream, but instead, Waters just had his mouth open, no more than a squeak coming out. If not for the mic effects, I doubt if he'd have been heard more than a couple of feet away, but the effect was astonishing, hair-raising.

They had a gong! What band had a fucking gong? It got a few whacks now and again in the concert, and Waters had his way with it at the beginning of 'Saucerful' and, somewhere in the course of the concert, the rim burst into flame!

MONTREAL UNIVERSITY
23 OCTOBER 1971, MONTREAL, CANADA

I WAS THERE: GORDON PHINN

When we trooped excitedly into the only downtown theatre in Toronto showing *Pink Floyd at Pompeii* in 1973, knowing that in a couple of weeks it would be gone, just like any of that first wave of rock movies then trying the market, I had no idea, and wouldn't for decades, that it had been filmed within a couple of weeks of my journey from Toronto to Montreal to catch them live at the University in October of 1971. No TV screenings, no VHS tapes, no PVRs. Those were the days, let me tell you. *Meddle* had yet to be released, but *Atom Heart Mother* had been played with that devoted attention to the detail in stereo imaging that only a marijuana high can provide. With its musique concrete sounds and textures subtly woven into the mix, it often felt like some coded message from another dimension, an esoteric missive looking to rearrange our molecules. *Ummagumma* was a long-standing treasure, with Richard Wright's 'Sisyphus' ranking as a fine contribution to twentieth century classical music. *More* was a treasure trove of mystical atmospheres and delicate melodies. The friend I was driving with had long declared that *Piper* could only be properly understood when high on LSD. An initiate myself, I was still not ready to embrace that pronouncement, despite hearing the scuttlebutt on Syd's vast intake in the months of *Piper*'s composition, the information that would only be convincingly conveyed decades later in Julian Palacios's *Dark Globe* and Rob Chapman's *A Very Irregular Head*.

The venue was a university gymnasium/basketball court with the steepest bleachers I had ever sat in. We peered down on the band from a great height, swamped by the reek of the hashish we could not afford, having spent most of our cash just getting there. Let's just say the contact high was unmistakeable. As was the silence after each piece was completed. The audience was listening, the audience was transfixed. We were soon inhabiting a magical realm where moods beyond description were evoked in texture and rhythm, a self-enclosed nirvana of sonic transcendence. Tapes of that North American tour are plentiful at this point, and all of them point to a band at the peak of their powers. With such classics as 'Fat Old Sun', 'Embryo', 'Eugene', 'Atom Heart Mother' and the then new 'Echoes' enchanting our already altered states, how could it be anything less than marvellous? Despite seeing a colossally talented and technically brilliant performance by King Crimson that December in Toronto (the *Earthbound* tour), I still consider this the most magical musical performance of my life. In my heart, 1971 is a year I shall never leave.

FIELD HOUSE, UNIVERSITY OF TOLEDO
31 OCTOBER 1971, TOLEDO, OHIO

I WAS THERE: RICHARD B KELLEY, AGE 14

In 1971 I had been collecting rock and roll records for a couple of years. I owned about 15 LPs, which I played relentlessly, and was fascinated with recording music from the radio and

A PEOPLE'S HISTORY OF PINK FLOYD

TV using a portable Magnavox cassette recorder and microphone my mother had given me. As a mid-sized town in a secondary market, national touring acts rarely passed through Toledo and groups from overseas almost never did. But in the fall of 1971, posters began appearing around the University of Toledo which were printed in black on pink card stock with a pencil rendering of the Pink Floyd members. The poster advertised an appearance by the group on Hallowe'en, Sunday, October 31st at the University of Toledo Field House. Tickets were $1 for University of Toledo students and $2.50 for everyone else.

$2.50 wasn't hard to scrape up, even for middle schoolers in 1971, so the show became the destination of choice for those of us who were too old to trick-or-treat. My parents were not terribly enthused about my attending, but my friends were all going and the University was a mere six blocks from our front door. I didn't own any Pink Floyd records and neither did many of my friends. The older teens and collegiate types had adopted *Ummagumma* as a pot-smoking soundtrack but we had yet to advance to that stage. We just knew Pink Floyd were a cool band from England and they were coming to our town. To our neighbourhood. We also knew a lot of their songs were long, weird and spooky - perfect for Hallowe'en.

I had recorded a Ritchie Havens show at the university the previous year but it had come out abysmally so I decided to record the Pink Floyd concert to see if I could do better. I had a US Army surplus musette bag which my veteran father explained was a sort of secondary knapsack that infantrymen used to pack extra gear. It held my portable cassette recorder beautifully. It was green canvas with straps and, as Army surplus clothing and gear was an ironic fashion statement at the time, didn't draw the attention of security personnel when I presented my $2.50 ticket to enter the concert.

Built in the 1930s, the Field House held about 3,500 and primarily hosted Toledo Rockets basketball along with graduation ceremonies and the like. The stage was set at what would have been centre court for a basketball game and pushed towards the bleachers on the east side of the building, the floor and the bleachers on the opposing side providing 'festival seating'. The four-channel sound system was quite large and included PA speakers at each corner of the venue.

As was their wont, Pink Floyd made sure the sound was loud, clear and dramatic. The stage was no more than four feet from the floor and barely large enough to hold the band and their impressive arsenal of instruments and equipment, which included gongs and large cymbals. I remember the band being murkily lit in pinks, blues and purples, mostly from the rear and sides. They did not present themselves in rock star fashion but blended, ghost-like, into the dark lighting, which was dimmed and dispersed by tobacco and marijuana smoke.

I had one 90-minute cassette on which to record Pink Floyd and absolutely no idea what I was recording. I watched and listened and recorded, sometimes fading a song early if I thought it had gone on too long. I moved around the large room several times, recording from at least four different positions. I experienced most of the show, including the five to six minutes of sound effects that oozed through the quad sound system in a recorded portion of 'Cymbaline'. Mostly footsteps and horror movie screams and laughter, the effects were perfect for Hallowe'en night.

The last song on my tape was the final portion of 'Echoes', which I faded out before turning off the recorder to head home. I may have heard a bit of 'More Blues' reverberating through the campus but I didn't record it. More blues was what I'd have if I didn't get my butt home by 11pm. (My time at the show was limited as next day was a school day.)

My recording came out marginally well, although I'd allowed the input to be too high resulting in distortion in some parts. I shared the tape with friends, most of whom responded with 'that sounds like shit' or words to that effect. I stored the tape with others I'd made in the era and promptly forgot about it for 25 years.

In the mid '90s, I was attending a local record show where I always checked the stock of a dealer who always carried a large array of classic rock bootlegs. I was shocked to find he was selling a two CD set of the same Toledo show I had attended and recorded. Could these CDs somehow be sourced from my recording? I got the set home and played the first disc, which began with 'Set the Controls for the Heart of the Sun'. The remainder of the first CD captured the show without interruption. I realised this couldn't be my recording as I had faded and edited several songs on the fly.

I was disappointed to find the bootleg dealer had accidentally put two 'disc ones' in the case he'd sold me so had to wait three months for the next show to make an exchange. The following spring, I came home with my 'disc two' and played it, realising this could also not be my tape as the recording was likewise uninterrupted. At this point, I pulled my 25-year-old cassette out of storage and decided it was too fragile to be fussing around with. Using a dual-well cassette deck, I made a real-time copy of the old tape. In the process the old tape broke at the leader, but fortunately after I'd been able to copy both sides – or so I thought.

I now had a fresh version of the recording on a sturdy new cassette. I transferred the recording onto a Sony Mini Disc and played around with my new copy, using equalization in an attempt to improve it but only succeeded in making it sound different. I put the project away and forgot about it for another 25 years…

Fast forward to the autumn of 2021. Still an ardent music fan and collector, I'm a member in (mostly) good standing of an online forum where all manner of recordings, artists and equipment are discussed. Floyd had, for copyright reasons, recently released a dozen old concert recordings from 50 years earlier. Some were copies of radio broadcasts and some were clandestine audio recordings like mine. None were official.

A PEOPLE'S HISTORY OF PINK FLOYD

As part of my contribution to the discussion I related how I'd seen the 1971 tour and recorded a show. My thinking was I'd finally be able to hear the band on the tour I saw, playing the songs I'd heard but now in better quality thanks to the newly-issued cache of other old recordings. What other readers heard was, 'Damn! You've got an unheard, 50-year-old Pink Floyd recording!' I explained that it wasn't very good (in fact it was ghastly by modern standards) but that didn't matter.

A New Yorker named Phil desperately wanted to hear it. I dusted off the now 25-year-old digital version and divided it into three segments, which made it easier to transfer to Phil and, eventually, his fellow Floyd aficionados.

While I had my recording handy, I decided to again compare it the better-known version of the Toledo show which had been making the rounds in collectors circles for over 20 years. Both recordings start with 'Set the Controls for the Heart of the Sun' (or so I thought). My tape faded up and into the droning intro of the song. The better-known tape pauses and starts several times during the drone, barely getting underway as the band comes in.

For at least the first half of my tape I was apparently sitting near the other taper as the same audience 'whoops and hollers' are audible, albeit at different levels. Eventually my 50-year-old cassette of the 1971 Toledo show meandered its way across the pond to noted British Floyd aficionado Ian Priston, who had heard my digital version and contacted me, desperate to work with the original. Ian used his skills to disassemble the cassette and put the delicate tape into a new shell. My tape was broken at the leader and elsewhere, resulting in two repairs to rejoin the old tape. Thereafter Ian and a friend performed electronic voodoo to draw as much detail from the old recording as possible.

The results were astounding. Ian and his friend found about 20 minutes of the show on my recording which hadn't made it onto the much better-known tape that collectors had been swapping back and forth for decades. They were able to merge my 'newly discovered' recording with the other, resulting in a virtually complete version of the show. I had captured the first three songs while the other unknown recordist's efforts began at 'Set the Controls for the Heart of the Sun', the fourth song in the show. I had also caught most of the recorded segment that was a part of 'Cymbaline' while the other taper caught part that I did not. The other taper apparently didn't have a curfew, as his recording adds the last ten minutes of the show, which I missed.

By putting my mono recording in the right channel and the better-known mono recording in the left, these ardent Floyd-o-philes were able to create a faux stereo that is actually quite listenable. As both recordings came from the audience, snippets of anonymous, 50-year-old comments float through the songs, adding an air of very Pink Floyd-like mystery and whimsey.

MEDDLE RELEASED
5 NOVEMBER 1971

The sixth album release by Pink Floyd gets to 3 in the UK charts and No. 70 in the US.

HUNTER COLLEGE ASSEMBLY HALL
5 NOVEMBER 1971, NEW YORK, NEW YORK

I WAS THERE: RICK CROSSLEY

The band suffered a couple of equipment failures but not enough to distract from their playing. The setlist was comprised of highlights from *A Saucerful of Secrets* and *Atom Heart Mother* plus 'Echoes'. Much of what we heard were the moody, pastoral elements of their work. It was stately and elegant, foreshadowing what was to come. But late in the set they played 'One of These Days'…

The auditorium went completely black as they turned out the houselights. The backing tape brought up the wind sounds on the PA from the album's introduction to the song, with the echoed bass. Waters, coming in on another bass, tucked it into the mix and they were off and running. Waters was spotted in the darkness with a pulsing red light as he pumped out the notes. Every time Rick threw in a keyboard accent, he was briefly lit up with a golden lightning blast of colour. And Dave, covered in green light, played the first slide solo. The song went into the descending riff before the climax and the lights went out again. The thundering bass sounded loud enough to dismantle most people's nervous systems. We heard Nick's distorted voice roaring 'One of These Days' and then…

The goddamn auditorium exploded in a barrage of lights, dry ice machines and blazing white light, showing all the band members playing like bastards. I was up in the balcony but at that moment I could see the entire first floor was crowded with jumping, screaming fans. It was by far the most electrifying moment in the show. The Floyd noticed and extended the ending with additional searing slide work from Gilmour. I started gasping for breath. I'd been frozen in my seat, unable to breathe from the dramatic impact of that moment.

I've seen multiple classic rock concerts, but I have never seen such a galvanizing assault on the senses and the immediate effect it had on the crowd. The rest of the show, albeit good, paled in comparison to that particular performance. I'll never forget it.

A PEOPLE'S HISTORY OF PINK FLOYD

CASE WESTERN RESERVE UNIVERSITY
6 NOVEMBER 1971, CLEVELAND, OHIO

I WAS THERE: S R JABORSKY, AGE 20

Sometime in the mid-summer of 1971, I was a 20-year-old drummer, machinist and ne'er-do-well, a dedicated follower of progressive rock, and broke as hell in my hometown of Painesville, Ohio, about 30 miles east of Cleveland. I could be found in the local convenience stores on Saturdays searching for 'cut-out' albums. Back then, these were albums that did not sell well enough in record stores (whatever they are) and a piece was cut out of the corner of the record jacket to denote that the albums would be distributed to different low-end retailers to sell at, usually, $1.00 an album.

My friend had mentioned a group called Pink Floyd and a tune called 'See Emily Play' that he had heard on the local FM station's underground midnight broadcast. Well, there it was in front of me in the bin, an odd-looking album titled *Ummagumma* by Pink Floyd. The array of equipment displayed on the cover was impressive. However, since it was a double album, it was $2.00! Damn! I searched my bellbottoms and managed to find enough change to buy the album.

I emerged from my Koss headphones, Pioneer turntable and Fisher 504 receiver a day later (yeah, even then, I liked crystal clear tunes pumped directly into my cranium and that's the reason that I was generally broke from buying the latest audio stuff), a bit dazed and somewhat incoherent. My friends suspected chemical enhancement but I explained I had listened to the album numerous times, playing certain tunes over a few more times. I had never heard anything like it! The studio album was fantastic and the live album superb. I became a Pink Floyd fan for life. I soon cranked the album through speakers for everyone who came to my house. Many more fans were created…

Jump ahead to the fall. Pink Floyd were touring, and they were coming to the Emerson Gym at Case Western Reserve University, brought in by the CWRU Student Union. A few of my friends and I were in front of the gym at 4pm in anticipation of the 8.30pm concert time. There were fold-up chairs on the gym floor when we finally got in. Tickets were $3.50 advance, $4.50 at the door!

The first thing we noticed was various large speaker cabinets throughout the audience section against the walls with 'Pink Floyd' stencilled in white on the cabinets. There was a sound pit in the rear with more panels, lights, meters and switches than I had ever seen at a concert. I remember they started with 'Embryo'. Also, they did 'Set the Controls for the Heart of the Sun', tunes from *Atom Heart Mother* and an incomplete version of 'Echoes'. The internet reminds me they also did 'One of These Days' and I remember distinctly 'Careful With That Axe, Eugene' because of a certain visual effect. They did very few visual effects compared to their later concerts. They had a screen with projections, swirls, oil in water, coloured lights… stuff like that. They also must have controlled the house lights as they dimmed to darkness and then brightened during sections of different tunes. That was rare stuff for concerts back then.

I mentioned a visual effect during 'Careful With That Axe, Eugene'. When the tune slowly built in low light, we all anticipated the Waters' 'scream'. The audience was firing up in anticipation, all eyes glued to the stage. When the scream came, they set off a huge flash pot on stage that lit the entire gym. There were gasps as the guitar cranked, people were looking away and at each other in surprise and a few who may have been 'enhanced' stumbled around and headed for the exits. Applause and cheers soon erupted as the audience realised they had been gotten by Floyd! A flash pot is nothing unique today. But in the fall of 1971, it had the desired effect.

I realised why there were speaker cabinets throughout the gym; the legendary Floyd-designed Azimuth Co-ordinator, more than simple stereo, swirled the music around our heads and senses. I knew then, at the end of this concert, that this band wanted to grasp not just our ears but our minds and thoughts, to get into the deepest reaches of our psyche and destroy any preconceived notions of what music can evoke. No, you probably wouldn't dance to it. And, mesmerised, you probably couldn't.

I WAS THERE: ROBERT R REARICK

We had been fans of Pink Floyd since *The Piper at the Gates of Dawn*, so when we heard they were playing in the area we had to go. Having done the usual preconcert herbal inhalation therapy (it was the Seventies!), we (Rob, Tom, Jack and I) piled into my 1967 metal flake blue cougar, The Beastie, and growled our way across town to CWRU. We arrived, paid our $4.50 and found ourselves in a large gym with the bleachers folded back and a tarpaulin covering the basketball court with a stage at the far end.

There were speakers on both sides at the rear of the hall, on the top of the bleachers halfway down the hall and on the stage. We found seats in the centre of the hall where we could see the stage very well. There we met up with our east side friends from the Cat City Commune. My (late) friend Rob was a master modeller and had created a disposable pipe out of poster-board. It was about three inches in diameter with a regular brass bowl screwed into the center. It had 'PINK FLOYD MEMORIAL PIPE' arching across its top. This got filled with the 'Killer Jamaican' which we had reserved for the occasion. The couple sitting to our right (he introduced himself as Star) had brought, oh, about half a pound or so of absolutely stunning herb himself.

As Pink Floyd took the stage, the little enlightened memorial pipe was passed all the way to the bleachers on the left, up a row, all the way to the bleachers on the right and back to our row, where Star or one of us would refill it, relight it and send it on its way to continue its' journey – as it did for most of the concert.

The reason for all the speakers became clear very quickly as Pink Floyd were performing in quadraphonic stereo which allowed them to position sounds anywhere in the hall. Rick Wright had a chrome shift knob, the Azimuth Co-ordinator, which allowed him to pan the sound around the hall. The Azimuth Co-ordinator was used to great effect during 'Set the Controls for the Heart of the Sun', 'One of These Days' and 'Echoes'. The overall performance was just stunning.

One of my most vivid memories of that concert is 'Cymbaline'. By that late in the concert, the little pipe having continued its' journey, had done its work well and we were holding on to the tarpaulin for fear of floating away. The full moon was magically shining through the high windows of the gymnasium. In the middle of the song, the music faded out and the lights went off. In the darkness, it sounded like a fellow entered the back of the hall, walked across the hall, climbed up some stairs, opened the door and a lady laughed hysterically. He slammed the door, ran down the stairs, turned the corner, walked along the side of the hall to the front of the stage, turned the corner, walked to the middle of the stage, opened the door and the band started again. All in all, one of my favourite and most enjoyable concerts ever!

Some years ago, I went to a concert at the Winchester Music Hall in Lakewood, Ohio on a whim. The act I saw was Acoustic Side of the Moon, an unplugged version of Wish You Were Here, a Pink Floyd tribute band who have been performing the 'Sight and Sound of Pink Floyd' and selling out North Eastern Ohio venues for over 20 years. I approached them after the show and said that they had given me the same vibe as when I had seen Pink Floyd in a gym back in 1971. The bass player, Eric 'Eroc' Sosinski, thanked me and said, 'You know, that concert is available online!' It was – I've now got it!

IRVINE AUDITORIUM
12 NOVEMBER 1971, PHILADELPHIA, PENNSYLVANIA

I WAS THERE: DENNY HORN, AGE 19

I first saw Pink Floyd at the 1,260 capacity, all-seated Irvine Auditorium on the Drexel campus in Philly. I was working for Arby's and the sales rep from Click Root Beer dropped off some schwag to give to customers. As my buddy and I 'readied' for the show, we took a huge bag of the clickers to the show. We stood at the entrance and handed out around 300 clickers to concert attendees. The audience was noiseless throughout, and during a quiet moment between two songs, we decided to click our clickers. Within seconds, the entire hall sounded like a forest of insects, and when it subsided after a minute or so, David Gilmour went to the mic and said 'thank you' to the crowd.

During set up, an announcer asked us to look for a watch or bracelet that one of their roadies had left in the upper balcony. Being curious, we looked behind us and saw a huge stack of speakers, which was replicated on the opposite side of the auditorium, enabling the quad sound they utilised then. With the toggle control, they had the monster from 'Eugene' walk to an exit door, bang on the door to get in and, having failed to gain entrance, walk across the ceiling to another exit door (lit by an exit sign) where it tried again to bang down the door. Were we scared? Yes!

I remember Rick Wright operating the house pipe organ on one song. And, at one point, the guy next to me handed me a thread from a spool. He said to pass it on, which I did. As the thread was being passed around, each person holding the thread could feel it moving through their fingers until, like magic, the spool emptied and the feeling ended. Very odd...

January 1972 sees Floyd touring the UK, with the show at the Dome in Brighton on 20th January being the first performance of The Dark Side of the Moon.

DOME
20 JANUARY 1972, BRIGHTON, UK

I WAS THERE: PAUL JOHNSTON, AGE 15

That was the original Mark II four piece line up. Obviously, when they last toured 15, 20 years ago, they were augmented by another five musicians. The Brighton Dome holds about 2,500 people and it's a circular venue, so no matter where you sit you get a fantastic view. I remember, as an 11-year-old, 'See Emily Play' was being played a lot, and 'Arnold Layne', and I was really struck by them at the time.

In 1970 or '71, I managed to blag a Saturday job in a tiny little record store called Expansion Records in Brighton. It's now a barber's. I got a job in there on Saturdays, probably only because I was a bloody nuisance and used to hang around there on Saturdays. They probably thought, 'Well, we might as well pay him to do something.' If you've read the David Hepworth book, *Never A Dull Moment*, it's like reading my diary from 1971, because I remember all those albums arriving in the shop and us selling them. They were great times. Thanks to this particular shop, I had a real introduction to music.

One of the first albums I remember seeing in the shop and which I played incessantly was *Ummagumma*, a double album, half of which was live and half studio. And they had half a side each to do their own thing. I got into them through that. Then I heard live versions of 'Astronomy Domine' and 'Set the Controls for the Heart of the Sun' and stuff like that, so I was really into the psychedelic side, which prompted me to go to the concerts – the January and June ones at the Dome. I had longish hair, although it wasn't quite Dave Gilmour length!

I remember at the first gig in January they played a lot of that psychedelic stuff, *Meddle* and then snippets of what became *The Dark Side of the Moon*, although at the time you didn't know what it was. More of it was played in the second concert a few months later.

I had seen them at the free concert in Hyde Park in 1970 as well, with Edgar Broughton, Kevin Ayers, and maybe even Roy Harper. It was a showcase for Harvest Records, and it was organised by Blackhill Enterprises, their management company run by Peter Jenner. They played all of *Atom Heart Mother*.

GUILDHALL
21 JANUARY 1972, PORTSMOUTH, UK

I WAS THERE: STEVE HUDSON, AGE 16

I had just turned 16 and after buying 'Echoes' on vinyl I was excited to be going to see Pink Floyd live for the first time at Portsmouth Guildhall. Little did I, or probably anyone else, know that we were going to witness the birth of one of the most iconic and timeless albums ever produced that evening. I took my place in Seat 27 Row A with my two friends and we were treated to the very first successful performance of *The Dark Side of the Moon*. I don't remember many specifics of the concert itself apart from the fact that everyone just sat transfixed, listening to this incredible music. Unlike every other concert I had been to, no-one stood up or shouted for the entire performance.

After the concert finished, me and my two friends went round the back of the Guildhall to the stage door hoping to catch a glimpse of the Floyd as they left. Almost immediately, the door opened and a roadie asked us if we wanted to meet the band! We went inside and directly to the right there was a small and shabby dressing room with about a half a dozen people in it – including Dave Gilmour, Roger Waters and Rick Wright. I was totally unprepared for this scenario and I didn't even have a piece of paper to get their autographs, so I left the room, turned right and went on to the nearly empty Guildhall stage, down into the stalls and into the front foyer, where I found a rack of concert flyers. I took a Tony Bennett flyer and made my way back to the stage (stopping to pick up a couple of drum sticks on the way), and then to the dressing room where I got the three band members' signatures, but not that of Nick Mason. Nobody seemed to know where he was, but someone said he might be in the auditorium. I then went back up on the stage and, in the dim light, I could see someone sitting in the stalls. Sure enough, it was Nick Mason, 'chatting' to a girl. I tapped him on the shoulder and asked for his autograph, which he duly signed on the Tony Bennett flyer. Unfortunately, I didn't notice that the ink in the pen was running out, so his signature is lighter than the others, but readable nevertheless. I still have the signed Tony Bennett flyer, the ticket and the drum sticks. Maybe, if Nick Mason reads this story, he might re-sign his dodgy signature!

CITY HALL
27 JANUARY 1972, NEWCASTLE-UPON-TYNE, UK

I WAS THERE: PETER SMITH, AGE 15

I went the week before, not knowing the gig had been postponed by a week or so, and returned on the correct night without a ticket for the sold-out gig. I managed to buy one outside for face value. I'd read in the music papers about Floyd's quadraphonic sound system and noticed immediately the four large PA speakers set out in the corners of the hall. They introduced their new composition, 'Eclipse (A Piece for Assorted Lunatics)' and played it in full during the first half of the concert. 'Eclipse' was to develop into *The Dark Side of the Moon* in the coming months, and the titles of the tracks changed during that period. (A few of the tracks were apparently played as instrumentals in some earlier concerts.) Roger introduced it as 'Eclipse' and I recall the voice 'I've been mad for fucking years' swirling around the hall, as well as the clock, the heartbeat and that laugh reverberating around us. I nearly jumped out of my seat when I heard the laugh come out of a speaker at the back of the hall behind me, and at very high volume.

After the interval the Floyd returned to play a set of classics, starting with 'One of These Days', a favourite of mine at the time, from Meddle. Roger's bass vibrated through the hall. This was followed by lots of screaming in 'Careful With That Axe, Eugene'. The elevated lighting rig which stood at the back of the stage behind the band was unlike anything I had seen before. Towards the end of the show, it swirled up to the ceiling, drowning the hall in myriad coloured lights, very effective and actually quite spooky. By today's standards it was pretty basic but it was state-of-the-art stuff then and all added to the mystery of the Floyd in concert. The second half closed with the beautiful 'Echoes' and the haunting 'Set the Controls for the Heart of the Sun', with its heartbeat drum beat, and closing with Roger beating a fire-lit gong.

I bored everyone at school for weeks afterwards telling them how great Pink Floyd were!

TOWN HALL
28 JANUARY 1972, LEEDS, UK

I WAS THERE: MARTIN SANDFORD

I first became aware of the band around the time of the release of *Dark Side of the Moon*. Having just mourned the loss of Jim Morrison, I moved on to another great sound and, as a student in Leeds, I went to see them at Leeds Town Hall. As we sat down in an auditorium slowly filling up, we were all feeling cold from a strange draught that was loud enough to be heard blowing into the concert hall. It blew louder and swirled around the entire room, making everyone wonder what was happening. It went on for some time until the lights dropped and Waters and crew struck into 'One of These Days', which began with swirling wind sound effects enhanced by their new quadraphonic sound system. A great concert was to follow and my love of their sound was cemented.

Several years later, I took a holiday in Rhodes and spent about seven days in Lindos, a world heritage site but in those days frequented by musicians, actors and artists. Like all guys, my interest in ancient Greek history was dwarfed by my interest in women, wine and sunshine, more or less in that order. Come the evening we witnessed England's finest, the student graduates from our best universities, relaxing and pissing off the locals as they crashed through tables and the sensibilities of a usually welcoming local populace. We found a bar. A bar like we'd never seen before, one that didn't have a till but a hole in the rough wooden counter. The atmosphere was contemplative but with overtones of quiet threat. It made you feel like you wanted to look around and study people but daren't look in case you stared a moment too long. In the corner were two guys, one with long hair down his back dressed all in white linen, and his buddy with shoulder-length hair. It was David and Rick, although we didn't recognise them immediately. Both were playing backgammon. Behind the bar was a character from Greek mythology, a handsome, fit-looking Greek Adonis serving drinks who told us he owned the place and that we were welcome. 'Yamas.' His name was Socrates.

Trying our best not to intrude on the Floyd guys and to appear cool (and probably not succeeding) we stood, drink in hand, listening in the most surreal of circumstances, wondering why we recognised the guys in the corner and why it somehow tied in with the music playing on a very basic sound system (their album *Meddle* was playing).

Even as all this was going on, we were accosted by a large man with a heavy Scots accent who was well acquainted with the local brew and wanted to impress us with his prowess at arm wrestling! The Scot (Nicol Williamson) was loud on the inebriation plateau due to personal problems (his wife had just left him for a pop star) and wanted to reenact some of his great roles, and to prove it he burst into as many different accents as he could fit in, in between wrestling one of us to the floor. In all of this, we soaked up the music and tried to put some sense into our surreal Socrates experience. We spent several evenings in this place with various strange types, but always with either one of the Floyd guys and Nicol wanting to beat us English at some bar sport or other. Williamson was a very talented guy who showed some extra talents when he stole my American girlfriend. (I forgive you, Nicol.)

LOCARNO BALLROOM
3 FEBRUARY 1972, COVENTRY, UK

I WAS THERE: BOB MANSFIELD

We were at the Locarno during the Lanchester Polytechnic Rag week to see Pink Floyd (it was the same night that Chuck Berry recorded his only UK No 1, 'My Ding-a-Ling'). We also went to see and meet up with them at the New Bingley Hall in Staffordshire, an agricultural showground that had bands on in their massive indoor shed. We attended the final *Wall* concert in London, where the original wall was destroyed, and our manager went on to tour with Pink Floyd as one of their road crew during their first tours of the USA.

I WAS THERE: GARETH JONES, AGE 17

Having passed my driving test only a couple of months before, I drove my Morris Minor 1000 to Coventry with a carful of five Floyd fans. The gig was part of the local college festival and the preceding band was Chuck Berry. Mr Berry kindly over ran his time slot and the Floyd fans were let in after midnight (the ticket was for Floyd only). Apparently, the gig started at 2am. I can't remember that but I guess if it did then we coped somehow! We sat on the floor (something we did a lot of back then) and in the first half they played a number of songs which were destined to become *Dark Side of the Moon* – and what I now know was just its seventh performance.

Then it was half time and, as I had brought my copy of *Meddle* with me, I thought I would have a go at trying to get their autographs. I went to the side of the stage where there was a door to the back stage area. There was one security guard on the door and I said to him, 'Can I please go through and meet the band?' (It's always a good strategy to be polite.) Amazingly, he said, 'OK, yeah, if you like.' So I went through the door, walked down a short corridor, opened the door at the end and, wow, I was in the inner sanctum of the communal dressing room – and there they were, large as life!

I asked if they would kindly sign the inside spread of *Meddle* and Nick asked me to sit next to him on the sofa, with Dave on the other side. Gosh! Nick did a small drawing of 'Best Wishes Pink Floyd' and then Rick came over and teased me by saying he would sign over Roger's picture! But then did the decent thing and signed his own image. Roger was his challenging self and asked me what was my favourite Floyd number and I said, 'Atom Heart Mother'. Roger's reply was, 'Oh, we don't like that one!' I didn't explore with him why not, as it was getting time for the second half.

I shook hands with all of them, they are really nice guys (if you cut Roger a little slack) and it was moment I will treasure.

I WAS THERE: LIZ WOLSEY

On Sunday 8th March 1970, Pink Floyd were playing at Mothers Nightclub in Birmingham. This was a fantastic small club which was voted number one venue in the world by America's *Billboard* magazine. Sadly, it was only open from 1968 to 1971. I was the glass collector on that night, even though I was only 17 and shouldn't have been allowed in. More and more people crammed in and there was no thought of health and safety then. Eventually there were so many people that no one could move so I couldn't collect glasses. Sadly, I couldn't actually see Pink Floyd either, only hear them! But in February 1972 I finally got to see Pink Floyd, in Coventry. I remember the psychedelic light show and a huge model aeroplane flying over our heads. It was a great night out.

I WAS THERE: MIKE CORNER

I attended Lanchester Poly from '69 to '72 and, with others, did the majority of the lighting for countless gigs, including Elton John, the Who, Free, Peter Green, Yes, Taste and Jack Bruce. It was the time of oily bubbles projected onto the stage in addition to the floods and spots – and bands were still known as 'groups'! Pink Floyd had their own lighting console at the Locarno, so I and three others were operating follow spots. All of these were positioned on the balcony, and the follow spot I was operating was on Roger Waters.

At some point, there was a break and all stage lights were off. For the next song, my job was to aim my spot at Roger and there were be a prompt through the headphones to turn it on. 50 odd years ago, the technology was a little different to today. Turning the spot on required someone to put in a plug, and I co-opted someone next to me to do so when prompted. Bearing in mind that the stage was in darkness, it wasn't too easy to aim the spot. I could make out Roger's form so could position it laterally, but not so easily vertically. I was requested to have a small aperture aimed at Roger's hands. The prompt came through and I told the 'plug man' to plug it in. He did and there was the spot, shining brightly on Roger's feet. A small movement of the spot was required to move up to his hands. I slightly overdid this, which probably resulted in a blinded bass guitarist. Having overcome this faux pas, things went smoothly until another prompt wanted a change of colour gel. This was simply a frame sliding in the front of the light and swapping one for another. At the prompt, I removed the old one and slid the new one into place. Unfortunately, the frame wasn't correctly in position and this piece of metal dropped onto some poor individual below. I quickly grabbed another that luckily went into place, saving me from any further embarrassment. I must admit I do not remember much of the music, as I was concentrating on preventing any further catastrophes.

I WAS THERE: PAUL FOX

I was a student at Lanchester Polytechnic when I saw Pink Floyd in 1972. The schedule at the Locarno Ballroom was something like Slade followed by Chuck Berry for the early show, then Billy Preston followed by Pink Floyd for the late show. We opted for the late show starting at 10.30pm to find the low-ceilinged ballroom already heavy with debris and smoke. I wasn't a mad Floyd fan myself – The Who were my band – but soon got into it, largely due to the mesmeric music and post-pub, smoky atmosphere. I may even have dozed off at one point. I don't remember Billy Preston playing (a slightly less aged pal confirms that Pink Floyd appeared on their own) so perhaps he appeared as part of the early show). In the days afterwards, most of the talk was about the Chuck Berry concert. From what I could hazily recall of the Floyd concert, they might have been right. It was a memorable night nonetheless.

COLSTON HALL
5 FEBRUARY 1972, BRISTOL, UK

I WAS THERE: JOHN MANUEL RHODES

This was the *Eclipse* tour. Filing into the auditorium for this gig, everyone found an A4 four-page lyric sheet on their seat. The paper was yellow, basic copier quality and the format was simply just words, mainly the lyrics, with the title on the front page reading *Eclipse – A Piece for Assorted Lunatics*. They played the suite in its entirety and it was the first time anyone had heard it. In those days, to premier a new piece, especially one that lasted for three quarters of an hour, was risky, but I seem to recall enjoying it. After a short intermission, they came out and played a set of known songs, including 'One of These Days' and 'Set the Controls'. Once they'd played what they told the audience was the last song, the usual clamour for an encore got under way. They hadn't done 'Careful With That Axe, Eugene' and everyone was calling out for it. It was very apparent from the band's demeanour that they'd had enough of playing this number and really didn't want to do it. Some of this mood seeped out into the audience and there was a degree of irritation since, as far as we were concerned, they ought to remember who paid their wages (as it were), and so we were entitled to hear our favourites – and 'Careful With That Axe' was at the time the top favourite for fans.

After a delay which was just long enough for the band members to express with their body language that they didn't want to play it, they launched into it anyway. Oddly enough, it was a really good rendering of the piece, even though throughout they all tried to look bored. Once they'd done 'Careful With That Axe' they immediately launched into a laidback blues jam, seemingly to make a statement, like, 'Okay, if you want old stuff, cop a load of this!'

When the album came out (I'd pre-ordered it from my local record store in Bath and so got it on the first day of release), I was at first not aware that *Dark Side* was in fact the recorded version of *Eclipse*. I kept that yellow lyric sheet from the gig for many years. I only wish I still had it.

 DE MONTFORT HALL
10 FEBRUARY 1972, LEICESTER, UK

I WAS THERE: NEIL HARRIS

I had been looking forward to seeing Pink Floyd live for many years. And this was the first opportunity to do so. My fear was that the industrial troubles at the time – power outages, frequent blackouts – would kill the concert before it even stated and, if it started, would it even finish? I had heard about the new Pink Floyd revolutionary sound system and the light shows were already a key feature of all of their performances, so I was really up for this one. The show began with the Pink Floyd heartbeat travelling around the concert hall and wrapping around the audience – this was really impressive and left the audience in anticipation for what was to follow. I then sat amongst a full house of loyal followers eagerly braced for all my favourite tracks to be belted out. This didn't happen.

Floyd were taking an innovative new work out on the road. This soon-to-be album was being road tested in performance throughout this tour, and refined as the tour and performances progressed. In hindsight, it would now be cool to say that I was immediately won over by this new offering and knew it would set the standard for the next two decades, but sadly that was not the case. The reality was I felt a little cheated. Where was all the good stuff? Who starts a concert with a completely new work? There was no sign of anything I wanted to hear or recognised until the end.

The piece finished, and afterward some of the tracks I knew well and wanted to hear were played splendidly. The sound system (I think it was quad sound) fired out some wonderful musical and abstract sound effects throughout the whole evening. I don't recall any significant power issues but maybe some small issues.

The musicianship of the band was as always superb and the concert in hindsight unique – a real major event. The new piece being played and refined was *The Dark Side of the Moon: A Place for Assorted Lunatics*. At the concert, a set of lyrics was left on each seat to give the audience some sense of what they were about to see and hear. Since the concert, I have played this album more than any other I possess and now feel quite guilty for my original indifference.

Sadly, in those days there was rarely any visual or even audio evidence of rock group concert performances apart from the occasional dodgy bootleg. It would be great to replay the evening to see where I went wrong!

I WAS THERE: JOHN LANGHAM

I guess this concert was one of my most memorable. The tour was promoting their latest release, *Meddle*, but they were trying things out at their one and only appearance at the De Montfort Hall. The current hi-fi trend was for quadraphonic record releases – using surround sound with speakers to the rear as well as the front and also maintaining clearly defined left and right sound channels. While this may be straightforward to produce in the studio, Pink Floyd wanted to go that step further and performed the surround experience in the theatre, so there were speakers behind the audience as well as the front of house.

Having performed excerpts from the *Meddle* album and the classic 'Careful With That Axe, Eugene' (complete with a screaming, axe-wielding girl in a nightdress running across the stage), an intermission followed. During the intermission, lyric sheets were distributed for a new piece of music in preparation for their next album. The title had not been finalised, nor had it even recorded yet. They wanted to call it *The Dark Side of the Moon*, but a band called Medicine Head had beaten them to it with that title. So they had a plan B – a title of *A Piece for Assorted Lunatics*. They ultimately determined that Medicine Head seemed a one-hit-wonder and proceeded with their first choice of title when they recorded the album later in 1972.

So the De Montfort Hall was treated to an early performance, in full quadraphonic sound, of *The Dark Side of the Moon* before it had even been recorded. I particularly recall the track 'Money' was performed with a soundtrack of Malcolm Muggeridge, the journalist and TV social critic, spouting a section of a sermon about the evils of money from the front, whilst the quadraphonic soundtrack depicted a church collection plate being passed down the rows from left to right. The sound passed right through you as the chink of money dropped into the plate and passed to the rows behind. This was changed to become cash registers ringing on the final album recording.

I was granted an interview with the band and was also able to obtain a full set of autographs on my cassette sleeve of *Meddle*. The cassette was slipped into a flip-top packet and inserted into a seven-inch laminated mini albumsleeve – a short-lived method of packaging, which obviously became too expensive to continue marketing that way. It was a truly memorable experience and historic event.

I WAS THERE: KEVIN HEWICK

I was in the fourth row of the stalls with my dad and my uncle, who got a cassette recorder in and taped it! They took ages tuning up between songs, with no stage chat, wearing long hair jeans and t-shirts and looking like roadies. 'Echoes' was over 28 minutes and truly astounding.

I WAS THERE: DAVE HARRIMAN

I was there at this fantastic show. They did 'Careful With That Axe, Eugene' as an encore. A big orange revolving light to the left of the stage went off to coincide with the scream. I nearly fell off my seat!

I WAS THERE: HENRY DOYLE

I was fortunate in the late Sixties and Seventies to see many groups and solo acts at the beginning of their careers who went on to become stars and, in a few cases, megastars – The Nice, Jethro Tull, Ten Years After, Wishbone Ash, Emerson, Lake and Palmer, Free, Deep Purple ,Captain Beefheart, Colosseum, Taste, Derek and the Dominoes, etc. Pink Floyd were very different from many other groups at that time, or indeed since, insofar as not only was their music very different – and some of it was very weird – but many of the pieces were long in an orchestral style instead of the usual three or four minutes, although other groups also performed long pieces in their acts but in a completely different style of music, eg. Cream playing blues.

Even then, Floyd had a big following and from my recollection there was a good attendance at the hall. As with other groups, it was quite cool to follow Pink Floyd and other bands who were not in mainstream pop but were underground before they came to the surface and became more successful commercially. Many people felt much of their music was a load of old twaddle and or very pretentious – *Ummagumma*, 'Furry Animals Grooving With a Pict' – but their fans ignored all that and believed that much of their music was groundbreaking and very, very special.

I WAS THERE: ANDY KOWALSKI

We had a sixth form room with a record player on which which we used to play records during lunchtimes and after classes were finished. Other social events were also held there. Pink Floyd were keenly followed by a lot of us, as were other bands as it was the beginning of the rock era. I saw them in the early Seventies, when a group of us from De Lisle School's sixth form went to see them and we had seats in the stalls. They were brilliant.

FREE TRADE HALL
11 FEBRUARY 1972, MANCHESTER, UK

I WAS THERE: SIMON PHILLIPS

This was (literally) dark days of the early Seventies, with the miners' strikes and power cuts everywhere. We had tickets to their show at the Free Trade Hall and had heard that they were premiering an even longer new piece than 'Echoes' on this tour. The power cuts were, at least, predictable. Local radio stations would broadcast 'such-and-such an area will be blacked out between 4pm and 6pm and then the next area between 6pm and 8pm, etc.' We used to do our university coursework until 15 minutes before we'd be plunged into darkness, then stop, jump into a car, and drive to the next district, which was now just having its electricity restored, have a couple of pints, and return to our house just as the power came back on. Happy days – not!

Come the night of the gig, the Free Trade Hall was in line to have a power cut part way through the Floyd's show. As a result, they came on stage on time and announced that there was a high probability of a power cut during the show and so they would reverse their sets. Instead of doing their long piece and risking having to stop part way through, they'd do short numbers until they were forced to stop, in which case, if we kept our ticket stubs, we could come along on a rearranged date. Which was no good to my friend, who couldn't come back to Manchester. I don't recall what they did – probably 'One of These Days', not my favourite song from that era and maybe a couple more – before they stopped, mid-song, and said the power would go off in about 15 or 20 minutes and could we all leave the hall in an orderly manner. Of course we could – we were British after all! We were front circle so were among the last to leave. As we shuffled out, I looked back and they were playing a fairly elementary blues number to an almost empty hall. Fast forward to…

RAINBOW THEATRE
17 – 20 FEBRUARY 1972, LONDON, UK

I WAS THERE: KEITH BRADFORD

I got tickets to the Rainbow. It was a Thursday, a few days after my 18th birthday. I took my first steady girlfriend, June, whose parents were Mormons and a bit wary of me, with my worldly ways, taking their daughter to a London gig. I was worried the electricity might fail (was there a miners' strike?) and, when the lights went off and the band walked on in miners' helmets with lamps, I feared the worst. We were centre front balcony and this was the debut of *Dark Side*, months before its release. We were perfectly placed for the quadraphonic system and the intro drum/heartbeat went round and round. I'm gutted now that I didn't get a programme then. A couple of years ago, a relative of my partner was visiting from the US. He gave me a retro/repro t-shirt of that gig and was amazed when I told him: 'I was there!'.

I WAS THERE: GARY MARSH

We went up to Waterloo Station and walked across London in the middle of the night, getting to the Rainbow Theatre in the early hours of the morning to queue up to get tickets. In those days, you had to go to the box office. The ticket office was meant to open at 10am and it didn't open until about 11.30am and we were tired and a bit pissed off. Fortunately, it didn't rain. That's how I got my first ticket to go and see Pink Floyd.

At the actual gig, we were sat to the left hand side of the stage, about twelve rows from the front, so we had quite good seats. I was rather in awe, obviously. They did 'Eclipse', which was *The Dark Side of the Moon*, and 'Echoes' quite different to how they did latterly. They were on for a good couple of hours. Afterwards, upon leaving, we dashed around

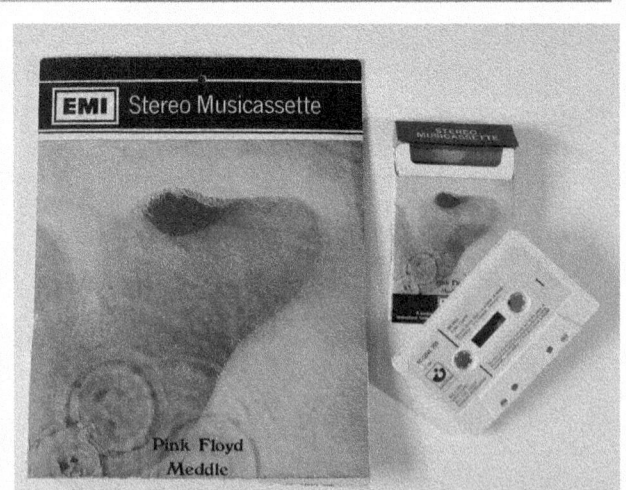
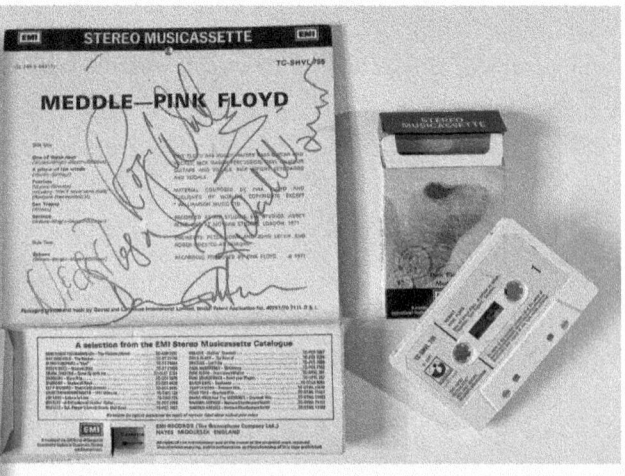

Clockwise from top left: Martin Sandford saw Pink Floyd in Leeds and, later, David and Rick in a bar in Greece; Paul Fox remembers the smoky atmosphere and possibly nodding off; Gareth Jones got backstage and still has the autographs from the band; autographed Pink Floyd cassette in its original packaging (John Langham)

Clockwise from top left: Henry Doyle knew it was cool to like Pink Floyd; copy of the early *Dark Side* lyrics (Neil Harris); Mark Hoffmeister, putting his best foot forward; Paul Sherman kept his programme from the Rainbow to the stage door and met them all as they came out, every single one. I said to them, 'I thoroughly enjoyed a wonderful evening. Thank you so much' and I remember Gilmour being very civil about it. He said, 'I'm pleased you enjoyed it.' They were no other fans there.

The album that really got me into Pink Floyd was *Ummagumma*, which remains my favourite album to this day. Nick Mason told me he didn't agree with that and said 'it's a load of rubbish'. So they don't hold it in very high regard, and I know a lot of fans don't either.

I WAS THERE: PAUL SHERMAN

I saw Pink Floyd at the Rainbow, Finsbury Park. I had seen them before and loved the music. They played some of the old stuff and some new stuff, called *Dark Side of the Moon*. We had very mixed views on the new commercial stuff, because they stopped playing small venues and lost their esoteric edge. But this was the fate of many of the groups at the time.

March 1972 sees the Floyd in Japan and Australia for a total of eight shows, before a return to the UK for the rearranged Manchester date.

FREE TRADE HALL
29 MARCH 1972, MANCHESTER, UK

I WAS THERE: SIMON PHILLIPS

My last 'proper' Pink Floyd show. From now on, I'd be sharing them with the world… stadia, sports grounds, queues, tightly packed crowds, etc. But their music was changing too. It had become more predictable, more precise, every show the same. I liked unpredictability… if a band flubbed it and you could hear them laugh but recover, that was fine. The Grateful Dead did that most shows, but the Floyd were becoming too polished, too rehearsed for me. Why see them more than once a year when each show would be identical? Or so I thought back then.

The show was fine. I've no particular recollections of *Dark Side of the Moon* other than it was 'long'. We were about a third of the way back in the stalls so had a pretty good view. I'm pretty sure they did 'Echoes' which, for me, would have been the highlight. My friend recorded the *Dark Side of the Moon* set so we got to hear it a few more times before he recorded over it!

I stopped going to the shows (and, for a while, I also stopped buying the records). I can't remember if it was a conscious decision or not, or maybe because I left university in 1973, moved out of the city, got married and had a different sort of life. I bought *The Wall* and caught two of the Earl's Court shows in 1980, the last time I saw them, but they'd moved on – no longer the 'local band', they were now megastars, the gigs had become huge spectacles, and I felt as though I was sitting half a mile away. I hardly listened to them for the next 25 years and, really, it was stumbling across recordings of the early shows that I witnessed that re-ignited my passion. I now listen to their early – pre 1972 – stuff regularly.

In April and May 1972, Pink Floyd embark on another North American tour (taking in 18 shows) and then four European dates.

SYRIA MOSQUE THEATER
20 APRIL 1972, PITTSBURGH, PENNSYLVANIA

I WAS THERE: MARK HOFFMEISTER

My older brother saw Pink Floyd before I did. He was more of a jazz listener, but turned me on to them. I bought *Ummagumma* and then Pink Floyd were coming to town soon after that. My first Pink Floyd concert cost about $4 at the Syria Mosque in Pittsburgh. The music was mainly from *Ummagumma*, *More* and *Atom Heart Mother*. And I remember all the speakers behind the audience, up both balconies behind the audience and with speakers facing backwards behind the band. Richard Wright had these devices on his keyboard and he could put the music through the speakers in a figure, right and upstairs and around, for sound effects like in 'Grantchester Meadows'. When they were doing a quiet song, the audience was noisy, so the band left the stage and came back and did a loud blues jam. I saw them again at Syria Mosque a year or so later and had a similar experience, but *Meddle* was the new album and 'Echoes' was fantastic. Next time I saw them was at Civic Arena for *Dark Side of the Moon* when they had additional singers and sax, plus even more speakers. They performed all of *Dark Side* plus some *Meddle* and a few songs from *Obscured by Clouds*.

I WAS THERE: PAUL STAUFFER

I saw them in concert four times and I wish I had photos of some of those shows but the people on the door usually didn't let anyone in with cameras in those days as there was no such thing as iPhones back then! At the Syria Mosque in Pittsburgh, they did excerpts from their new album, *Dark Side of the Moon*, one year before the release of the album. The rest, as they say, is history.

FORD AUDITORIUM
26 & 27 APRIL 1972, DETROIT, MICHIGAN

I WAS THERE: ROB THRASHER

I have been a huge Floyd fan since I heard 'A Saucerful of Secrets' on WABX in Detroit. The Ford Auditorium was a 5,000 seat place in Detroit. We were sitting in the back row, with speakers behind us. They started playing 'Careful With That Axe, Eugene'. The flash pots went off, the famous blood-curdling scream came out of those speakers – and my buddy and I screamed like little girls. It was the best!

CARNEGIE HALL
1 MAY 1972, NEW YORK CITY, NEW YORK

I WAS THERE: MICHAEL NOLAN

Pink Floyd came on and said, 'We're going to play something new.' It was *The Dark Side of the Moon*. The whole thing, I think, from start to finish. They ended the night with 'Careful With That Axe, Eugene'. There was a speaker in our box where we were sitting. You would hear chicken and animal sounds coming out of it!

OBSCURED BY CLOUDS RELEASED
2 JUNE 1972

Only reaching No.6 in the UK, Obscured by Clouds *reaches 46 on the* Billboard 200.

Back from Continental Europe, Pink Floyd play two shows in Brighton before heading back to North America in September for their seventh tour there.

THE DOME
28 JUNE 1972, BRIGHTON, UK

I WAS THERE: PHIL BURTON

Me and a couple of friends had bought tickets for £1 each. The first couple of seat rows were taken up by the engineers – the Brighton Dome wasn't a large venue. I can remember them playing most if not all of *Dark Side of the Moon*, which of course was not released until 1973. Memories dull over the years and I saw many big bands at that time, not only at the Dome but also at the Big Apple Club in North Street, Brighton. It was relatively easy getting the Floyd tickets as they were still an up-and-coming until *Dark Side* exploded on the scene.

VANCOUVER GARDENS
27 SEPTEMBER 1972, VANCOUVER, CANADA

I WAS THERE: KELLY HUGHES

I was there for the *Dark Side of the Moon* tour. Me and my buddy Vince, back in the shag rug, black light days. We were getting primed for the show in his bedroom, listening to tunes. We had four hits of purple micro-dot to share. I was starting to feel the effects of the first two and decided to do the next two. Vince dropped them on the rug, yes – the purple shag carpet. You can well imagine. Still, it was one of the greatest shows of my life. The first half of the show was a lot of their early psychedelic stuff. Then we had the intermission and then *The Dark Side of the Moon* – the full album. I'll never forget it. And, no, we never did find those two other hits. Probably a good thing!

MEMORIAL COLISEUM
28 SEPTEMBER 1972, PORTLAND, OREGON

I WAS THERE: GREGORY SCHERZINGER

Seeing them again in 1972 was a different experience altogether. It was fall of my senior year in college. There was none of the relaxed intimacy of the small venue. *Dark Side of the Moon* was the tour title, although the album had not yet been released. The light show was in full effect. The concert began with a dark stage, a single red light thumping with a heartbeat and from there the *Dark Side* suite unfolded for the first time. It was performed without a break, one long continuous song. The band was still the four of them, no sax nor female vocalists. The performance was Floyd at its best. I remembered 'Echoes' being played, for it was on vinyl by that time. They also did 'Careful' and 'Set the Controls…', which were so distinctive in their performance with Waters screaming in the one and ailing on the gong with the other. I would have to bet 'Astronomy Domine' was in there too, though I can't really remember.

Once again, the quad speaker columns created a surround sound effect. I can't say the band was better or tighter during that concert than before, but the grand venue and light show made them seem larger than life. They had the power to fill the Coliseum with the same hypnosis, dipping into quiet passages with scarcely a peep from the audience. *The Dark Side of the Moon* came out shortly afterward. It joined the pantheon of *Ummagumma* and *Meddle*. I never had the opportunity to see them live again. As an avid fan, I bought their subsequent albums, although as they got further from the astral sounds that had attracted me, they became less interesting. Even so, they produced songs on those last few albums that still resonate strongly today.

The late Sixties and early Seventies included many opportunities to see seminal bands that still impact music today and I saw many remarkable acts over the course of my life, including the Jimi Hendrix Experience. The two Pink Floyd concerts remain the highlights of my concert career.

 EMPIRE POOL
21 OCTOBER 1972, WEMBLEY, LONDON, UK

I WAS THERE: RON SHEPCAR, AGE 17

So what was my first taste of Pink Floyd like? Rewind to 1972 and a chilly early autumn evening. At the very impressionable age of just 17, for my eagerly anticipated first date with the ever so lovely new girl at work, Lory, I chose to show her the bright lights of Old London Town. The main event of the evening promised to be a special treat; a screening of a new film, *Pink Floyd: Live at Pompeii*, at a bijou cinema (somewhere close to Russell Square, I vaguely recall). The underground music press and my new more-worldly friends in metropolitan Kingston-upon-Thames had steered me to their diverse output, ever since I bravely moved away from sleepy provincial Lincoln, less than a year earlier. I was (and still am) much more into experimental sounds, so me and Pink Floyd seemed like a match made in heaven. Bedecked in loon pants and cheesecloth shirt, I was ready for a night to remember – I couldn't afford the Afghan coat! Following a swift tour of a couple of iconic London landmarks, the excitement was building as we arrived at the cinema and slowly edged nearer and nearer to the front of the queue. Within sight of the main entrance our dreams shattered. Very apologetically, we were turned away, as the woefully undersized venue was sadly deemed to be bursting at the seams.

Mercifully, Lory and I really hit it off big time, especially in the sense of humour department. I recall so vividly to this day the madcap evening we spent in The Swan at Hammersmith, most of the time with tears in our eyes. Tears from all the joking, laughing and crying, as we produced our own wildly imaginative script for what we'd just missed seeing. Monty Python was by far the biggest thing on our incredibly small television at the time. In that vein, cue images of a very serious Roger, Dave and Rick avidly seeking musical inspiration from the wonder and majesty of the archeology, history and mythology of ancient Pompeii. Conversely, somewhere not-too-distant, roguish Nick was in his best seaside holiday attire, trousers and shirt sleeves haphazardly rolled up, complemented by traditional gumboots and the ubiquitous knotted handkerchief, frantically lost in a tacky Italian souvenir shop, seeking out a psychedelic tank top. Think Eric Gumby on acid. My brain hurts, man! For those old enough to care. Oh, to be young, innocent and overly immature again.

So my first bite of Pink Floyd was really of my own making. And fairly wide of the mark, as I was soon to realise only a few weeks later at the Empire Pool, Wembley. So what was my first taste of Pink Floyd really like? Another chilly autumn evening. I arrived on the back of my new best friend's somewhat rapid motorbike. Excited? Yes! But a little frozen and with my nerves slightly shredded. Thank goodness he hadn't bought that big Norton yet! It was, after all, my first time on the back of a fast bike.

Having spent the last month or so with *Atom Heart Mother*, *Meddle* and *Obscured By Clouds* all constantly gracing my shiny new transcription unit, I really thought I was ready for this. I could not have been more mistaken. Maybe it had something to do with the intensifying effect of the unfamiliar exotic smoke billowing from the group of older, wiser post-psychedelia Summer of Love hippies seated right in front of us. Or perhaps it was just the sheer impact of experiencing a mind-blowing, slowly evolving version of a new sequence of songs, tentatively labelled 'Eclipse', many months before they were committed to tape and released as what would become the favourite album of millions of unsuspecting listeners. Either way, I was truly stunned. The ride home was just a crazy, hazy blur with my ears still ringing joyfully in awe of what I had just witnessed. Possibly the best night of my life.

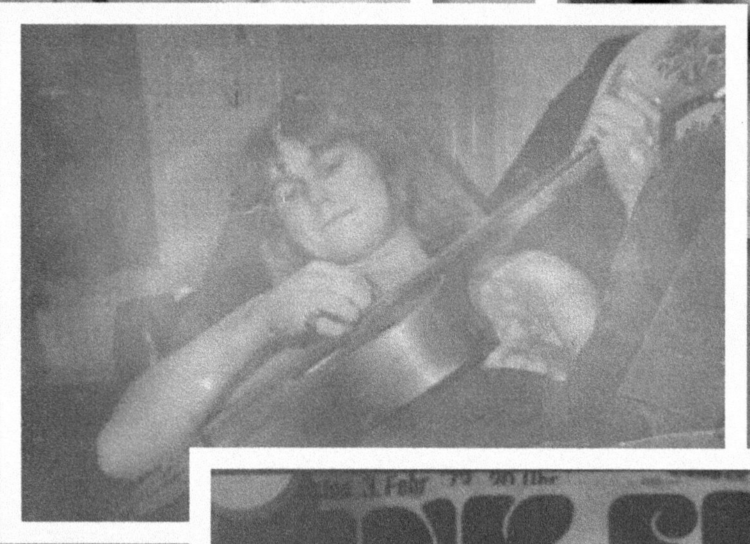

Clockwise from top left: Rob Thrasher and his friend were a little spooked by the scream in 'Eugene'; Ron Shepcar remembers seeing the Floyd in October 1972 as possibly the best night of his life; Phil Burton remembers getting Pink Floyd tickets as being 'easy'; Gary Dycus saw the speakers and thought 'wow'

Floyd in action in Belgium in the 1970s (all photos Gaston Sonck)

 FESTHALLE
16 & 17 NOVEMBER 1972, FRANKFURT, WEST GERMANY

I WAS THERE: GARY DYCUS

I didn't care too much for the early Pink Floyd but my Army buddies convinced me to go see this concert. When we got there, a huge mob of fans was storming the gates. Inside was a wooden bicycle track and we had to sit on the floor. Whilst sitting there, I noticed these huge speakers in the upper deck and thinking 'wow!'. All of a sudden, the house lights went out. The next thing I heard was the loud sound of a cash register running; it was the song 'Money'. They played songs from *Dark Side of the Moon* before it was released in 1973. Many bands tried their new tracks out in Europe to see if they were successful. I've been a fan ever since.

THE DARK SIDE OF THE MOON RELEASED
1 MARCH 1973

The Dark Side of the Moon *eclipses the performance of all previous Floyd releases and sells 45 million copies worldwide, including 560 weeks on the UK album charts, a consecutive 736 weeks on the Billboard 200 and platinum-certified sales in 14 countries.*

March 1973 sees the Floyd touring The Dark Side of the Moon.

 MAPLE LEAF GARDENS
3 MARCH 1973, TORONTO, CANADA

I WAS THERE: GORDON PHINN

The dreaded hockey arena with the usual lousy sound. Many ascending bands had graduated to such ignominy and many fans would subject themselves to the tortures of such soulless empty shells for years to come. Still *Dark Side of the Moon* was on display, so how could we resist? The album was steadily gaining in popularity, although still miles from the planetary fame of later decades when every café guitarist from Tel Aviv to Caracas and Kyoto could strum and sing 'Wish You Were Here' with fake conviction. The old Floyd devotees had been replaced with a rock crowd, who would soon know the bitter truths of 'money – it's a gas'. At the back row on the ground floor, we watched as tiny figures far away projected the giant thundering sounds of that first piece from *Obscured by Clouds*, 'When You're In', a raunchy slow rocker inheriting the proto-metal raunch of *More's* 'The Nile Song'. As always with these echoey barns, the attack was diffused throughout the hall, looking in vain for its signature thrust. I recall a fine, but not fabulous, rendition of *Dark Side*, the highlight being the three ladies' take on 'Great Gig in the Sky', which more than transcended the arena's sound deficit. I recall trying to explain to a friend's classically-trained wife my impression of the singing style that she was about to hear, and I think I got as far as 'gospelly'. We now can see just how innovative Clare Torry's original studio improvisation, at the behest of the lads who didn't really know what they wanted, was: gospel preaching the cosmic orgasm.

Until checking in with the archives I had forgotten the first half's 'Eugene', 'Set the Controls' and 'Echoes', linking us to the glory days of hippies in clubs and stoner college students, helping to forget the bleak industrial ambience of the arena. Fortunately for my friends who had missed the glory of 1971's magic, this show brought joy to their hearts, despite them only having heard the new album once or twice since its March 1st release. I would have played my copy several times in that fortnight, letting it burn a hole in my psyche, as did its predecessors. Little did we know, as we marvelled at our cult band breaking out into what sure looked like fame, that we were hearing the birth of at least two of Gilmour's legendary solos, the ones that would set the gold standard for all rock guitarists (except for Beck and Clapton) for decades to come. Tapes from the era reveal passionate but rough-around-the-edges performances trying to come to terms with backing tapes and light shows, distracting them from the musician's first duty: listening to each other.

COBO ARENA
5 MARCH 1973, DETROIT, MICHIGAN

I WAS THERE: MARK REID SNR, AGE 19

I have seen Pink Floyd five times – the last being the *Division Bell* tour in 1994, which was my favourite tour ever and which was totally unreal. I first saw Pink Floyd in 1973, on the *Dark Side* tour. I had never heard of them before and a good friend asked me to go. Being 19 and into all music, I said 'great, let's do it!' Tickets were $6.50 and very affordable and from the first note I was mesmerised. The highlight of the show was

'Echoes', which made me a fan for life. In the second half, they played *Dark Side* in its entirety. Please believe me when I say I'd never heard one of their songs in my life but I ran out of that concert and bought everything they had released up to that date.

I'm not a big Syd Barrett fan. I thought his music was kinda hokey, but that was the beginning of Pink Floyd. My favourite album is *Division Bell* post Roger, but *The Wall* with Roger. Roger in August 2017 was the third time I saw him in his solo career. I've never seen David Gilmour live. He hasn't toured solo in Michigan in 20 plus years but I would love to see my all-time favourite guitarist.

KIEL AUDITORIUM
6 MARCH 1973, ST LOUIS, MISSOURI

I WAS THERE: BONES

Just as the Gateway Arch in St Louis came into view the local rock station, KSHE, was talking about *Dark Side of the Moon* being released that day and then played 'Money' as my friend and I crossed the bridge in my '68 white Mustang and headed to the concert to meet up with friends, indulge in some psychedelics, sit back and be amongst the first to enjoy *Dark Side of the Moon*. Needless to say, the concert was great and blew everyone there away.

ST LOUIS PLANETATRIUM
1970s, ST LOUIS, MISSOURI

I WASN'T THERE: SUSAN STEWART

My husband Rob and I would would go listen to Pink Floyd music with friends at the psychedelic video shows held at the St Louis Planetarium. A really neat production of wild designs that went along with their music would be shown on the ceiling of the planetarium dome and I guess it would be as close to a trip you could get without drugs. The place would always be packed, and many smoked pot before the show in order to get a more 'engaging' experience. Unfortunately, we never got to see them perform live.

RADIO CITY MUSIC HALL
17 MARCH 1973, NEW YORK CITY, NEW YORK

I WAS THERE: DANIEL TRIFAN

This was the most impressive stage show I have ever seen. The sound was mixed in 360-degree quad. Radio City has niches along the walls, and each niche had a PA speaker stack in it. This enabled the band to do some amazing things; sounds travelling around the room, sounds jumping across the room at high speed, etc. They could make the vocals emanate from any point in the hall – a mesmerising experience. The coordination between the lighting crew and the sound technicians was the best I have ever witnessed. It was a thoroughly unforgettable experience.

HAMPTON COLISEUM
22 MARCH 1973, HAMPTON, VIRGINIA

I WAS THERE: STEVEN BURGESS

I saw them 50 years ago on the *Dark Side of the Moon* tour. Just as the scream in 'Careful With That Axe, Eugene' came, there was a wall of flame behind the stage. It scared the crap out of everyone. My seats were probably 20 to 25 rows back and I could feel the heat from the flash.

MUNICIPAL AUDITORIUM
24 MARCH 1973, ATLANTA, GEORGIA

I WAS THERE: TENDER LEE, AGE 21

I saw them twice and both concerts were unforgettable. I was 21 the first time, on the *Dark Side of the Moon* tour in Atlanta, and 25 when I saw them at the Omni in Atlanta in April 1977 on the *In The Flesh* tour. They had a great light show for the era and the back up singers wore huge pink and purple Afro wigs. I'm thankful I had the opportunity to be there both times.

WISH YOU WERE HERE

May 1973 finds Floyd playing two benefit concerts at the 19,000 capacity Earl's Court in London for the homelessness charity, Shelter, before returning to the USA in June.

EARL'S COURT EXHIBITION HALL
18 & 19 MAY 1973, LONDON, UK

I WAS THERE: ROB PASCOE

In 1972 I left home at the age of 16 to work and live on a farm in Buckingham. There was a really good pub scene in Buckingham and a really good bus service to Oxford and Aylesbury, where I was able to see a great number of gigs. I had recently purchased *Dark Side of the Moon* and contacted a friend, Chris Crooks from Bristol, to ask if he wanted to go to see Pink Floyd at Earl's Court, I had seen the advert in *New Musical Express* some weeks earlier. Chris came to stay with me at the farm where I was working. On the morning of the 18th May, we were expecting a large quantity of ready-mixed concrete to be laid into paths and ramps for the farm. After we had finished the work in question, we showered and changed and the farm owner took us into Oxford to catch the train to London. We eventually arrived at Earl's Court and there was a small ticket office to the side of the hall. We got our tickets, which cost the princely sum of £1.75, and then went off for something to eat, eagerly anticipating the evening's performance.

The evening came and we were certainly not disappointed. The set started with 'Obscured by Clouds' followed by 'When You're In' and then an absolutely stunning performance of 'Set the Controls for the Heart of the Sun' followed by 'Careful With That Axe, Eugene'. The first half was finished off with 'Echoes'. There was then a 20 minute intermission before we were treated to the most amazing performance of *Dark Side of the Moon* finally followed by 'One of These Days' as an encore. We were both absolutely buzzing by the end and I think that we were both aware that we had witnessed a significant moment in music history.

As we left the venue, it seemed as if everyone was trying to get on to the same Tube train. We eventually made it back as far as Oxford and we arrived at stupid o'clock in the morning to find no further connections to Buckingham. After a short discussion, we decided that we would try to hitchhike and headed off towards Buckingham. As we were walking along the road, we saw a police car approaching. It slowed down to get a good look at us as it went past, and about half an hour later the same police car came past us again, this time in our direction of travel. The same police car passed us by another six times before they decided to pick us up and take us to the police station in Bicester for questioning, after we had walked through the night for over eleven miles.

After a short period of questioning we were eventually released and given a lift to the bus station in Bicester, where we caught the bus back to Buckingham. When we eventually arrived back at the farm, we were both absolutely exhausted and all we wanted to do was go to bed. The farmer's four-year-old daughter couldn't understand why Chris and I were going to bed when she was just getting up.

It was without doubt one of the best concerts that I have ever had the good fortune to attend. I still have the ticket, the programme (which cost the princely sum of 30 pence) and the copy of *New Musical Express* with the advert for the release of *Dark Side* and Tony Stewart's review of the album.

I was fortunate to see Pink Floyd again two years later, for the *Wish You Were Here* tour at Wembley, which was another superb performance. But that *Dark Side of the Moon* expedition remains one of my all-time favourite experiences.

In 2008, I was doing some shopping in Sainsbury's in Chippenham when I just happened to bump into the legend that is Nick Mason. I was completely taken by surprise, but I just so happened to be wearing a *Dark Side of the Moon* t-shirt from the Roger Waters' performance of *Dark Side* in Hyde Park, on which Nick had played percussion. I was subsequently invited to his house in Corsham for one of his fundraising events, raising money for the Wiltshire Air Ambulance and the Wiltshire Bobby Van Trust.

I WAS THERE: KEITH BRADFORD

I got tickets for Earl's Court and *Dark Side of the Moon*. I got Friday tickets, by post I think, but when we were getting tickets for Bowie from Earl's Court box office, which was a caravan outside, tickets for the Saturday Floyd show had just gone on sale. The three of us got a ticket each in the centre stalls, Row 6. Needless to say, we were blown away. During 'Echoes', I put my arm out and couldn't see my hand, the dry ice was that dense. I'm afraid *Dark Side* put me off Floyd eventually. Everyone was playing it. I even heard it in a supermarket a couple of times and I hate the alarm clocks! The raw excitement of their early psychedelic era was over and the secret was out.

I WAS THERE: MIKE BAESS, AGE 15

My love of Pink Floyd really started with *Atom Heart Mother* in 1971. 1972 was spent borrowing albums such as *Ummagumma* and *Relics* from my local library in Swiss Cottage, north London. But everything took a seismic leap forward in early 1973 when I read in *Melody Maker* and *NME* of the imminent release of *Eclipse*, their new album. Then, in about January 1973, the album title was changed to the even spacier-sounding *Dark Side of the Moon* and a release date was given. The first Saturday after release, me and a friend ventured down to Virgin Records in Oxford Street in central London and paid £2.15 for the said album. It was the first Floyd album I actually bought with my own money and, as soon as I got home, I marvelled at the brilliant cover with its gatefold sleeve featuring the lyrics and its two posters and two stickers and superior pressing with triangle motif on the label. It was the start of the love affair with Floyd. I hoped that I would soon be able to see them live and I didn't have to wait too long.

A week or so later, an advert went up in the music papers advertising two charity gigs – for Shelter – they would be playing in May at Earl's Court. I went to the second show on the Saturday night and they were unbelievably good. The gig still stands as one of the best I have ever seen and is in my top ten gigs of all time. The first two numbers were 'Obscured by Clouds' and 'When You're In' and they then played 'Set the Controls for the Heart of the Sun' and 'Careful With That Axe, Eugene' – the last time they ever performed those numbers, as far as I know.

The next section of the gig was *The Dark Side of the Moon* in its entirety, and in sequence. What I didn't know was that they had a quadraphonic sound system, so as 'Speak to Me' flowed into 'Breathe in the Air', laughter echoed all around the hall. Absolutely brilliant! Then during the next number, 'On the Run', a plane on a wire was run high from the back of the hall to explode into Nick Mason's drum kit. I was mesmerised. But there was more magic to come. For 'Time', they started showing a fabulous film of cartoon clocks cascading and falling through the sky. I'd never seen anything like this before, and for a 15-year-old rock fan this was far, far more than anything I'd come to expect from the Floyd. I was solid sold – a fan for life. But it didn't end there. After more films and the dreamy second side of the album, the band came back for one final encore. But what an encore it was – a 25-minute version of 'Echoes'. The show set an extremely high benchmark for future gigs.

I WAS THERE: STEVE HOWES

I went on to see them another eight or nine times after I first saw them at Norwich Lads Club. I never looked back really. I've got a big bootleg collection. I've got most of the stuff they did plus a lot they never put on album. In 1973, I saw them again at Earl's Court. I was about 20 by then. It was a concert in aid of Shelter. We were quite a long way from the group and we had to have these little binoculars. It was just after *Dark Side of the Moon* came out and they played the best version of 'Careful With That Axe, Eugene' I ever saw. The whole stage was covered in dry ice and a statue rose behind Nick Mason and had piercing green eyes.

A PEOPLE'S HISTORY OF PINK FLOYD

I WAS THERE: DAVE HILLIER

A particularly groovy teacher brought *A Saucerful of Secrets* into an English lesson, played the title track and asked us to write about what the song made us think of. I said 'mountains'. I bought the album. I was 14. That was the start. My teenage years at college saw me buying *Dark Side*. I still have it – the solid blue version complete with stickers and poster. I got tickets to see them at Earl's Court. I went with several college friends. I was completely blown away.

I then saw them perform *Wish You Were Here*, and still remember hearing 'Shine On…' live for the first time. I saw them perform *Animals* with my then new wife. We are still together 40 years later.

I saw *The Wall* twice and finally *Momentary Lapse…* in 1994. This was again in London, a few days after a section of seating had collapsed. My claim to fame is appearing with my 14-year-old son in the pages of the booklet in the *Pulse* album that was recorded as part of that tour. We are on the bottom of page 31 on the bottom left. That's me in the blue shirt!

I've seen Roger Waters a couple of times live. He did *Dark Side* and also *The Wall*. Good; very good, but not the same as the whole. I have a Dave Gilmour solo album but, despite loving his guitar playing, I'm yet to see him perform live.

I WAS THERE: PERRY RIDLEY

I discovered Pink Floyd as a 14-year-old in 1972, when I saw 'One of These Days' played with a curious old film on the BBC's *Old Grey Whistle Test*. I spoke the following day with my school friends and we agreed we were all blown away by this record. My friend, who was three years older than me and who was working at WEA Records, saw it as well and he told me he had the LP which contained this track. He lent me the LP, *Meddle*, and I was immediately hooked on Pink Floyd. I used to buy *Sounds*, *Melody Maker* and *NME* every week and so followed them in print. I'd see comments about the work in progress at the time, and kept the cuttings in a small scrap book. I eagerly awaited the release of the next LP, which was, of course, *The Dark Side of the Moon*.

I bought the LP on the day it came out and, without being funny, it changed my life. I still have a cutting advertising the LP one week before its release, inserted in the sleeve of the original LP. The original LP itself is a valuable item, as the first pressings had a solid blue triangle, with some copies now changing hands at £1,000. Subsequent re-pressings only had the outline of the triangle. When I first heard the album, I then wanted to learn to play the guitar, and 40 plus years later I still play guitar. I can play most of the songs on the LP and have played several of them live in pub bands over the years.

My friend at WEA managed to get tickets for the Friday night show at Earl's Court in May 1973. It was a vast arena with a very high roof and I had a seat in the upper tier about two thirds of the way back. My recollection of the show is quite good, remembering the effects they had like the plane flying from one corner and crashing over the stage. I still have my ticket and programme for this show, both in mint condition and framed in my home.

I WAS THERE: PHIL DAVIES

I first became aware of Pink Floyd, at the age of 14, via my older sister in 1971, when she brought home *Meddle*. Played on our parents' Phillips portable single speaker (mono) record player, we didn't know yet what we were missing. I remember thinking how different and strange 'Echoes' was, but liking it very much. I soon headed off to the library to see what other albums they had and found *A Saucerful of Secrets*. And so began my lifelong relationship with Pink Floyd.

By 1973 and the release of *The Dark Side of the Moon*, their concert at Earl's Court was very much a 'must see' for me. It was my first ever concert. I was not quite 16 but my parents allowed me to go along with my sisters and their boyfriends, who were 18 and 19. Up until this point, I had only managed to hear some of Floyd's music in stereo by going to the record shops and stealing ten minutes in the listening booths with stereo headphones on, which was amazing, so I was in for a pleasant surprise.

We learned that the band had invested in a very high-tech quadraphonic sound system (to be honest, I didn't really know what that meant) and, together with huge flags draped from the ceiling of the metal-roofed arena, the sound quality was absolutely amazing. Our seats were high up the back which, although far from the band, allowed a terrific view of the whole show. I remember the massive gong for 'Set the Controls for the Heart of the Sun', the enormous moon hanging over the crowd and the huge circular projection screen. On the seats was a little piece of paper on which was written 'towards the end of the show flaming rockets will be projected on wires above your heads - no cause for alarm'. I suspect most of the audience did not see or read this notice (the only reason I did was that it was stuck to my back and someone else told me it was there), as there was much alarm when the rockets were fired from tubes that seemed only three or four feet above us.

Follow spots chased around the audience and all converged on one person for a short spell and then onto another, and then the aeroplane zoomed into the back of the stage with an almighty explosion at the end of 'On the Run'. It was fantastic. The first set consisted of well-known material, followed after the break by the entire new album (*Dark Side*) with 'Echoes' as the encore.

I WAS THERE: ROB (RINGO) STARR

I couldn't wait to see Pink Floyd after buying *The Dark Side of the Moon* when it first came out. I went with my friend Les. We had both decided to take some LSD, as people did at such times – especially with a band like Pink Floyd – and we got into the arena at the start of the trip, with the buzzing sound of the crowd all around us like a hive of bees. Our seats were in the middle of the arena on a slight incline (well, it felt like it was an incline...) with a great view. When they came on, the quadraphonic sound was amazing, starting with 'Obscured by Clouds', 'When You're In', 'Set the Controls for the Heart of the Sun', 'Careful With That Axe, Eugene' and 'Echoes'. Then we got what for us was the first live performance of *Dark Side of the Moon*. It was just such an outstanding experience. Certain parts of my memory are a bit hazy, but the overall sound and feeling was marvellous as that kind of show was completely out this world to me and never seen before. It was so new...

The concert was so good that we were completely dazed by the end. Exiting the arena, we were confronted by trucks with searchlights on the back and beams of light crisscrossing the sky. We were blown away, thinking this was part of the show. On that same night, England played Scotland with Scotland losing 5-0. We were trying to find where Les had parked his Mini as the Scots were causing havoc, with fighting breaking out and shop windows being broken. We found the car and I said to Les, 'Let's get the fuck out of here!'.

ROOSEVELT STADIUM
16 JUNE 1973, JERSEY CITY, NEW JERSEY

I WAS THERE: DENNY HORN

The stage was dead centre field and the grass field was standing room only. 24,000 seats were filled. The first two songs were from the *La Vallée* soundtrack and it was an absolute mind melt. During *Dark Side of the Moon*, they launched a 20-foot long paper mache airplane from the uppermost centre bleacher with Pink Floyd emblazoned on the tail and shooting sparks from its exhaust. It came over everyone's head on a guide wire and landed inches from Nick's drum kit in a huge ball of smoke. As the smoke cleared, there stood a tall astronaut, surrounded by a ring of flames.

Clockwise from top left: Gordon Phinn recalls the 'usual lousy sound' of a hockey arena; Susan Stewart and her husband enjoyed tripping to the Floyd; Rob Pascoe bumped into Nick Mason outside Sainsbury's & still has his Earl's Court programme; Mike Baess paid £2.15 for his copy of *Dark Side of the Moon*, the start of a long journey into Floyd fandom

Clockwise from top left: UK television show *The Old Grey Whistle Test* was Perry Ridley's introduction to the Floyd; Bob DeLeonardis only bought tickets to see Floyd because Led Zep were sold out; Wayne Bob Moist admits to being 'slightly toasted' when this pic was taken; Richard Lyon saw an acid casualty; Tommy Bush remembers that Floyd managed to brown out Jacksonville

CIVIC ARENA
19 JUNE 1973, PITTSBURGH, PENNSYLVANIA

I WAS THERE: BOB DELEONARDIS, AGE 16

I went with a friend a month or so before the concert to buy tickets for the upcoming Led Zeppelin show in Pittsburgh but they were sold out at the head shop we went to. The guy behind the counter said he had some Pink Floyd tickets available. We had no clue really, having only associated the band with the single 'Money', and we really wanted to go elsewhere and find Zeppelin tickets, having only enough money for one concert. But the guy at the head shop looked at us and simply said 'trust me, you will not regret it'. Tickets were $5 each.

We showed up that night not knowing anything about the band and hoping we didn't make the 40-minute drive for nothing. The Civic Arena has a dome that opens. We did not know this. For the first half of the show, it was closed and the Floyd were playing older material (as I learned later) but we were naturally blown away and pretty much in heaven at our luck. The crowd was great, the energy was great, and the place smelled like a pot field at harvest time.

We filtered back into our seats for the second half, the lights went down and I remember thinking how stuffy and hot it was inside. Then came the heartbeat... 'I've always been mad...' and, all of a sudden, there was cool night air slowly filtering in and the ceiling seemed to be twinkling. I thought they had little twinkly lights on the ceiling, but it was the Pittsburgh skyline slowly coming into view as the roof began to open.

I don't know if they timed the song for this effect, but as soon as the dome was fully open, the skyline fully in view and the arena filled with fresh, cool night air, I heard the words 'breathe, breathe in the air...'. I thought it was simply the most astounding thing I'd experienced. It was magical. The band went on to perform the entire album, and that was the night I fell in love with Pink Floyd. I saw them again in 1975 in Pittsburgh for the *Wish You Were Here* tour, 1977 in Oakland, California for *Animals*, 1988 in Oakland for the *Momentary Lapse of Reason* tour, and for the last time in Oakland for the 1994 *Division Bell* tour, all because of that night in 1973 as a kid.

And, to pass it along, I took my 13-year-old son to see Roger perform *The Wall* in San Francisco in 2012, and we went to see Roger again in 2017 in Sacramento. Sitting there watching old grey Roger, feeling a bit old and grey myself, I looked over at my son and I knew he had been given two lifelong Pink Floyd memories.

I WAS THERE: PAUL STAUFFER

The first set started out with music from *Obscured by Clouds*. The second set was *Dark Side of the Moon* in its entirety. The Civic Arena had a retractable roof. I will never forget this to this day. Right when the Floyd went into 'Breathe', they opened the roof of the Civic Arena. There was a natural full moon right above the stage. Everybody thought it was a stage prop. Nope, a natural full moon. I freaked. I absolutely loved this show.

MEMORIAL AUDITORIUM
22 JUNE 1973, BUFFALO, NEW YORK

I WAS THERE: RICHARD LYON

I was sitting in the very upper levels. A group of guys were seated in front of me, visibly high on what I thought were psychedelic drugs (LSD), when all of a sudden one of them became very restless and dove over a row of people seated in front of him, all the way down to the people below, both seated and standing.

OLYMPIA STADIUM
23 JUNE 1973, DETROIT, MICHIGAN

I WAS THERE: WAYNE-BOB MOIST

I have vivid memories of the *Dark Side of the Moon* tour. They played the whole album and then 'Careful With That Axe, Eugene' blew our eyes out when the rim of the gong was set ablaze. There was so much dry ice you couldn't see five rows in front, but all the churning, swirling lights cut through the haze with that primal screaming piercing above it all. Now, I really don't know how much of that was the Floyd and how much was the chocolate mescaline we had dropped an hour earlier, but it was the absolute best show I think I have ever seen!

WISH YOU WERE HERE

BLOSSOM MUSIC CENTER
24 JUNE 1973, CUYAHOGA FALLS, OHIO

I WAS THERE: S R JABORSKY

The next time I saw them was at Blossom, an amphitheatre in Cuyahoga Falls, Ohio situated in the middle of a wood actually within a few miles of where I live now. It's a beautiful venue. It was called the *Dark Side of the Moon* tour. They did the title track and other cuts but also older tunes, including 'Set the Controls for the Heart of the Sun', 'Brain Damage', an incomplete 'Echoes' and an encore of 'One of These Days'. However, it was 'Careful With That Axe, Eugene' that I waited for. Remembering the first concert, I brought a 35mm single reflex camera with me and situated myself stage centre half way back in the crowd. At the appropriate time, I opened the lens and let the flash pot trip the camera. The picture came out better than expected. The entire interior of the amphitheatre shell was illuminated and on stage there appeared silhouettes of Gilmour and Waters, guitars in hand, and of Richard Wright and the black hat he was wearing. Now the sad part. The picture is long gone. Oh, it may exist in some of my ex's stuff or in the corner of some house or apartment I lived in, but gone it is.

I WAS THERE: JOHN NACE

I saw Pink Floyd twice on the *Dark Side of the Moon* tour. It's the greatest show I've ever seen.

VETERANS MEMORIAL COLISEUM
27 JUNE 1973, JACKSONVILLE, FLORIDA

I WAS THERE: TOMMY BUSH

This is the best concert I've ever seen – to this day! The band's use of a massive quadraphonic PA and light show display caused the city of Jacksonville to brown out during the show. That left local city engineers to scratch their heads and wonder how a rock band could do such a thing. That said, no band since has ever been allowed to use that much fire power for a concert here.

RAINBOW THEATRE
4 NOVEMBER 1973, LONDON, UK

I WAS THERE: IAN NICHOLSON

My introduction to Floyd was through a schoolmate, Ray Reilly, who played me the album *Meddle* sometime around 1971 or '72. That album is still my all-time favourite Floyd album, particularly because of the tracks 'One of These Days' and the sublime 'Echoes'. Some of my mates had managed to get to see the Floyd at Earl's Court in May 1973, but my first Floyd gig was to be the Robert Wyatt benefit gig at the Rainbow Theatre in London. Two shows were played, with Wyatt's ex-band mates, Kevin Ayres and Soft Machine, also on the bill. John Peel compered the shows. Kevin Ayres kicked things off with a short solo set, and then Soft Machine, with Pink Floyd topping the bill. I attended the first performance at 5pm, and my ticket cost the princely sum of £2. This gig was a great introduction to seeing Floyd live, as they played the whole of *Dark Side of the Moon*, and encored with 'Obscured by Clouds' and 'When You're In'.

I remember the visual impact of seeing Floyd live, the amazing lighting that worked so perfectly with the music and, from what I can remember, the sound was good at these shows. My mates said that had not been the case in the cavernous Earl's Court earlier in the year. These shows were highly significant, as they were the last theatre shows played by Floyd in London, before going on to arenas and stadiums. They did play theatres outside of London in 1974 but by then, they were playing the Wembley Empire Pool for their London shows. I therefore feel honoured to have seen them in such a relatively small venue. Even my seat in row Z in the stalls did not seem too far back!

I WAS THERE: MIKE BAESS

The next time I saw them was during my final months of school – in November 1973 and another charity gig – this time in aid of Robert Wyatt, who had become paralysed after breaking his back falling out of a window. The show was at the Rainbow in north London and tickets went on sale a few days before the show. In those days you had to queue to get tickets and I bunked off school and queued from the morning, finally getting a circle seat at about 2pm. This time they were supported by the fantastic Kevin Ayres, who played a song called 'Oh! Wot a Dream' about Floyd founder Syd Barrett. Next on were Soft Machine, a band I now love, but they were a little too jazzy for me at the time.

But Floyd played another blinder, the whole of *Dark Side* in sequence and encoring with 'Obscured by Clouds' and 'When You're In' – about a 90-minute set. They played two shows that day and this was the later one.

I became more and more fascinated by the band and started collecting music mag clippings of them as well as bootlegs, bought from a tiny little hole-in-the-wall shop off Carnaby Street called Straight Ahead Records. It was run by another Floyd freak, a Welsh guy called Derek who was one of the main bootleg sellers in London at the time. I also started visiting their design studio, Hipgnosis, and became friends with the owner, Storm Thorgerson. I was asked if I would appear on a few album sleeves – which I did – and in return I got some free tickets, for Floyd at Wembley '74 and also for Led Zeppelin the next year at Earl's Court.

I WAS THERE: RON SHEPCAR

I thought my first time experiencing the majestic wonder of Pink Floyd, at the Empire Pool in Wembley the year before, could never be topped. Well, that was before the unfortunate Robert Wyatt came a cropper. I recall fervently rushing up to Finsbury Park to join the many brave souls prepared to pull an all-nighter to ensure they could help wish the hapless Soft Machine drummer well by bagging a golden ticket for one of two special and hastily arranged performances by the aforementioned Mr Wyatt's band mates and, of course, Pink Floyd. It was a chance also to make some new like-minded friends, all crazy enough to spend a cold autumn night queuing outside the Rainbow Theatre. The night went eerily swiftly, with the morning bringing the delight of what we had all been lined up for. I just couldn't wait for that big November night in 1973.

As I breathlessly made my way towards the front of the theatre, my plush velvet seat was bathed in stark white light. Front row! A dream come true. I was so damn close you could reach out and touch them – and what a gig. My view was appropriately sometimes obscured by intermittent clouds of dry ice gently cascading over the front edge of the stage but I didn't care one little bit. I was also totally consumed by the latest incarnation of the *Dark Side of the Moon*, the one we all now so fondly love, cherish and obey. Having previously witnessed the 'newly committed to vinyl' version live for the first time at Earl's Court a few months earlier, we were truly blessed this time with the surprise addition of the irreplaceable Ms Clare Torry for a very rare live appearance. Her pitch perfect rendition of 'The Great Gig in the Sky' was especially moving and really made it a night to remember. It was another glorious evening that has lived long and bright in my memory. This really was the best night of my life.

1974 sees Floyd in France in June, playing seven shows in total, before embarking upon a 20-date UK tour in November and December.

USHER HALL
4 NOVEMBER 1974, EDINBURGH, UK

I WAS THERE: ROB MULLEN

I saw the *Dark Side of the Moon* tour at the Usher Hall. In the first half of the concert they played a few new songs. I remember one of them was 'Shine On You Crazy Diamond'. The second half was *The Dark Side of the Moon* in its entirety. It was an excellent concert. None of the band spoke during the concert until the end. After *Dark Side of the Moon*, they left the stage and returned after lengthy applause for an encore. At that point, Roger Waters said, 'Thank you. A song called 'Echoes'.' Those were the only words addressed to the audience the whole evening.

ODEON
8 & 9 NOVEMBER 1974, NEWCASTLE-UPON-TYNE, UK

I WAS THERE: JOHN WATSON

I was a Stones and Faces fan at the time. I first heard of Floyd through my Chemistry teacher, who often played *Ummagumma* during lessons (it was the early Seventies). I lived in Newcastle so it was only a short bus ride to the venue. Because I'd just left school and started college, my mum queued up for the ticket for me – there was no internet then! They came on with a version of 'Shine On You Crazy Diamond' that seemed to last a bloody eternity and eventually did *The Dark Side of the Moon* from start to finish. I think 'Echoes' was the encore. After the bonhomie of the Faces, I remember thinking they were a bit of a miserable bunch. I also think that Yes were playing at the City Hall the same night – big prog rivalry!

I WAS THERE: PETER SMITH

Pink Floyd did a short winter tour of the UK in late 1974, stopping off for two nights at Newcastle Odeon, and I attended the first of the two nights. The first set consisted of three songs of new material; a lengthy version of the unreleased 'Shine On You Crazy Diamond', which sounded amazing on first hearing, and early versions of 'Sheep' and 'Dogs'. The second half was a performance of their then latest album, *The Dark Side of the Moon*. Floyd said little to the audience; they wandered quietly on stage and performed the music, illuminated by an impressive light show and with a large circular screen showing a series of videos recorded to accompany each song. They were technically perfect, although the band appeared distant. The programme took the form of a great little 'The Pink Floyd' comic subtitled 'A Super All-Action Official Music Programme for Boys and Girls!' and featured stories about each band member, who became 'Rog of the Rovers', 'Captain Mason RN', 'Rich Right' and 'Dave Derring'.

EMPIRE POOL
14 - 17 NOVEMBER 1974, WEMBLEY, LONDON, UK

I WAS THERE: MIKE BAESS

1974 was another great year for Floyd and they set off on a European tour in the summer before playing a short UK tour from whence a high-selling bootleg called *Tour 74* was released. They were now a pretty big deal and slotted in four shows at the Empire Pool in November. I got tickets for three of the shows and also recorded one of them in what has become a highly rated collector's recording.

I WAS THERE: STEVE HOWES

In '74 I saw them at the Empire Pool at Wembley, when they first did the stuff that went on to be *Wish You Were Here* and *Animals*. They were under different titles in those days. I think 'Sheep' was called 'Raving and Drooling' and 'Dogs' was called 'Gotta Be Crazy'. 'Pigs' kept the same title.

I WAS THERE: PERRY RIDLEY

The next time I saw them was on their British tour in November 1974. My ticket was very good, about a quarter of the way back and central on the arena floor. They started with three unknown songs, which at the time were met with a lukewarm response, The songs were 'Shine On You Crazy Diamond', 'Raving and Drooling' (an early version of 'Sheep'), and 'You've Got to Be Crazy' (an early version of 'Dogs'). These ended up on *Wish You Were Here* and *Animals*. They played *Dark Side of the Moon* as the second set, with 'Echoes' as an encore. My biggest memory of this show is when Roger Waters broke a string on his bass guitar and everything just stopped!

Soon after these shows, I had the pleasure of meeting David Gilmour and Roger Waters for a few times when they played football for the WEA Records football team. I recall Roger being a very competitive forward and David a mediocre right back. Roger avoided talking to others in the team as much as he could, but David was altogether different. I chatted with him and said I was learning to play the guitar. He gave me some handy tips, plus corrected me when I said the opening chord on *Dark Side of the Moon* did not sound right when I played it. He advised me it was an up-stroke, which obviously made it sound perfect! He gave me a lovely autograph, which is framed on my study wall, 'Good Luck Wiv Yor Guitar Playing – David Gilmour'. The others at school did not believe I was mixing with music royalty, until my girlfriend at the time produced a photo to back my story up.

I WAS THERE: IAN NICHOLSON

My second Floyd gig was on the 1974 UK tour, an afternoon gig starting at 3pm. This was a busy weekend for me, gig-wise, with Jethro Tull at the Rainbow on the Thursday, the Faces at Lewisham Odeon on the Friday and Saturday and Floyd on Sunday. But the second Faces show was postponed until Monday because, if I remember rightly, Rod had a vocal issue.

The 1974 Floyd tour included three new unreleased songs, 'Raving and Drooling', 'You Got To Be Crazy' (both would end up on *Animals*, as 'Sheep' and 'Dogs') and 'Shine On You Crazy Diamond'. After the tour, the songs ended up on the bootleg *Pink Floyd 1974*, which went on to sell so well that it would have charted if the sales were official. This tour also had one of the best and most original programmes, in the form of a boy's comic like *The Hornet* and *Hotspur*. Each band member was a character in the comic with a story about them such as Captain Mason RN, Rich Right, Rog of the Rovers and the exploits of Dave Derring. Sadly, I no longer have my copy.

My seat was in the south arena, to the right-hand side of the stage and on the main arena floor. It was no more than a few rows deep, and I was sat at the end of an aisle, next to the access to the arena floor. Part way through the first half of the show, my mate's girlfriend, Suzanne, nudged me and pointed to my right. I turned around to see Paul and Linda McCartney standing next to me! They were looking to get to the sound and lighting desk in the middle of the main arena floor to watch the show. Which they then did, joining another well-known musician, Brian Eno, who was already there, extravagantly dressed in a French stripy top and a bright red beret. (Coinincidentally, I got to see the McCartneys again on the Monday, as they appeared on stage with the Faces, providing backing vocals on a song Paul had written for Rod Stewart's *Smiler* album).

The second half of the Floyd show was the whole of *Dark Side of the Moon*, but for me the highlight was the encore of 'Echoes', my favourite Pink Floyd track. It more than made my day to see that performed live. This was my favourite of the Floyd shows that I saw. Great set, great memories, and seeing the McCartneys there was a bonus!

WISH YOU WERE HERE

I WAS THERE: ANDY GIBBONS

In the winter of 1974, the Pink Floyd Wembley shows were the hottest ticket in town. So I was disappointed, but not surprised, when my cheque was returned by the box office without a ticket. Luckily, a friend who didn't want his tickets gave me a pair. When we got to the venue, I picked up a copy of the programme, which was set out like a comic book. It also included lyrics for new songs with unfamiliar titles: 'Shine On You Crazy Diamond', 'Raving and Drooling' and 'You've Gotta Be Crazy'. They were dark and tinged with madness.

Our seats were high up, stage left rather than on the floor of the auditorium, so the view was narrow. Looking around, there were four sets of speakers packed round the arena as well as the big PA stacks at the front. The lights dimmed and the four members of the band came on stage. A synth echoed eerily round the darkened hall. A ghostly voice sang the line, 'Wouldn't you miss me at all?', from Syd Barrett's 'Dark Globe' and then Dave Gilmour played four reverberating notes over and over: had he forgotten what came next? A pause, then the band crashed in with a driving crescendo. The next twenty minutes unfolded a new piece, built around a slow blues with a stately, haunting chorus. This was one of the first ever performances of 'Shine On You Crazy Diamond'.

The next song sounded like a re-working of 'One of These Days' but with lyrics and in a much more aggressive style than *Dark Side of the Moon*. It seemed to be meandering along, going nowhere in particular, until Gilmour came in with a descending guitar run, filling the space with chiming chords. At this point, there were shouts from the audience for 'Set the Controls', but Roger responded defiantly 'this is 1974' and got a ripple of applause. He then pointedly said, 'This is another new song.' This was another lengthy piece, opening with urgent, shifting chords segueing into a melodious guitar theme. Again, the lyrics were about death and madness: 'You Gotta Be Crazy' closed the first set.

A quick visit to the bar and merch stalls was shortened by the unmistakeable sound of a heartbeat. We rushed back to our seats only to find the light still up in the arena. Eventually a small dot appeared on the screen, growing larger as the sound grew louder. Once again, the lights dimmed and the immortal phrase 'I've been mad for fucking years' came from the speakers. Supplementing the four-piece band were Dick Parry and a group of female backing singers. The next hour brought an excellent performance of *Dark Side of the Moon* which was rapturously received by the crowd.

The band returned for the encore but the stage was still dark. Pressed for time, they played the opening note of 'Echoes' with the stage still dark. This continued through the first few minutes of the song, but eventually the lights came on to a round of applause. Images of waves from the surfing film *Crystal Voyager* were projected on the screen. Dick Parry played a sax solo on the track as a variation on the LP version and the backing vocalists filled out the sound. The seabirds section was impressive, with dry ice flooding the stage which was bathed in green light.

It was a spectacular ending to a concert of two halves: interesting but raw new material and inspired performances of recorded tracks. It was a privilege to have seen the band at the height of their powers, even though some press reviews were less complimentary.

I WAS THERE: MICK MORGAN

I had been waiting to see them after missing out on their Rainbow gigs in London in February 1972, when I'd gone to get tickets and it had turned into absolute chaos. After arriving in our seats at Wembley, I remember hearing the sound checks going on and thinking 'wow'. It was quadraphonic, with sounds coming from all four corners of the arena. They came on and said, 'We would like to play our new record,' and went on to play 'Shine On You Crazy Diamond' from *Wish You Were Here* and some of 'Sheep' and 'Dogs' from *Animals*. I had never heard a gig in quad before and the sound was awesome. Then came what I was waiting for, the whole of *Dark Side of the Moon*. Wow again! I had only heard the LP before and not the music played live. It was awesome. They finished off a superb evening with 'Echoes'… Two and a half hours of Floyd. I remember talking to my mate Dave Toomey and saying that it was nothing like the LP and he replied 'it's not supposed to'.

I WAS THERE: CHRISTINE NEWEY

This was my first big concert experience which, because of my love of Pink Floyd and especially *Dark Side of the Moon*, was eagerly awaited. Our appetites were whetted by 'Shine On You Crazy Diamond', and warming up to the quadraphonic sound was memorable. I still remember the feeling of the crowd, all so eager for the sounds that were indelibly imprinted on our minds after playing the album time and time again. We were not disappointed. The feeling in the arena was electric, the whole audience all feeling the same vibe. I remember looking around at fans grinning from ear to ear as we became enthralled. The girls were faultless in their vocal ranges, sending shivers down my spine. The feeling that everyone was so in tune with the band was palpable and just enhanced the total hypnotic joy of 'feeling the music'. I have seen them perform it since in the UK and where I now live in Sydney, Australia (minus Roger), and it was still as enthralling, but 1974 at Wembley was truly special.

I WAS THERE: RUPERT BOBROWICZ

Having treated my brother to front row tickets for Tull's A Passion Play, he returned the compliment with Floyd tickets for *Dark Side of the Moon* at Wembley, not on the front row but near the back of the auditorium. Yeah, we were there and I remember the music, the group with hair and instruments, the lighting, the flying plane through the auditorium to explode, the films… It was a magnificent performance which was then supplemented by 'Shine On You Crazy Diamond', 'Echoes' and a few other previously unheard tracks. On the underground after the show, I was playing my bootleg cassette recording to the amazement of those in the carriage. Sadly, the tapes are long gone but the memories linger on, and the concert was eventually released on CD – so I must get a copy!

I WAS THERE: DYLAN WHITE, AGE 16

As part of growing up and leaving my Glam rock years behind, I discovered Pink Floyd. I was an only child, but I had a couple of friends who had older sisters, and you get a lot of stuff from older brothers and sisters. Through one of these sisters, we discovered *Dark Side of the Moon*. It was number one in the album charts. You got into this more album thing with Floyd, Led Zeppelin and Deep Purple. And then Pink Floyd had this concert. We were quite a way back and I can't remember much about it but they had these green lasers that shone to the back of the arena. It was considered 'wow' at the time but it wasn't particularly amazing. The band were just there, on the stage some way away.

Getting into them later on, I'd have bought *Atom Heart Mother* and albums like that, probably in a secondhand record shop. Going to a secondhand record shop on a Saturday was a sort of pilgrimage, because you could buy records that had been out quite a while and they were cheaper than buying them new. That's how I built up my collection of all the old albums that had been out in the Sixties.

Then they decided to do Knebworth. It was a big adventure, going to this place somewhere north of London. Two or three of us went. It was a nice day and we just sat around having joints. This was pre-punk and we're very much talking Long Hair Central. It was just the summer of love, peace and sitting around, smoking joints. I suppose we ate some food. I remember you couldn't work out the difference between the members of pink Floyd and the roadies. They were all in jeans and had long hair. Floyd didn't come on in platform shoes or anything like that. We were quite a long way away, looking at this stage and going 'are the band on yet?' Eventually, it became apparent that the roadies had plugged them all in and off they went.

It was packed. And then we had to walk back to Stevenage station and sat around attempting to get a bit of sleep, waiting for the trains to start running the next morning. 1975 was just one of those hippy days out, when Floyd were the kings of long-haired music. It was them, Emerson Lake & Palmer and Genesis.

PALACE THEATRE
9 & 10 DECEMBER 1974, MANCHESTER, UK

I WAS THERE: DAVID BELL, AGE 19

I had heard a bit of early Pink Floyd in the sixth form at school in 1970 to 1971. I became a big fan when I heard *The Dark Side of the Moon* for the first time. It blew me away. I only saw them the once, unfortunately. It's a bit hazy now, but I remember I went with a schoolmate called Kevin and two of his pals and Floyd did the whole of *The Dark Side of the Moon* and encored with 'Echoes'. That's always been my favourite song and the *Live in Pompeii* stuff was exceptional.

HIPPODROME
14 DECEMBER 1974, BRISTOL, UK

I WAS THERE: PETER REYNOLDS

For the princely sum of £1, I got to see Pink Floyd at Bristol Hippodrome. The concert was unbelievably good. They began by performing *The Dark Side of the Moon* in its entirety, followed by three new tracks, including 'Raving and Drooling' and 'Gotta be Crazy', which were to emerge in the future renamed and tweaked on the *Animals* album. They then did 'Shine On You Crazy Diamond', enhanced by flooding the auditorium with smoke and bouncing lasers off a disco ball which created weird effects like being surrounded by, and pierced by, bars. (I hadn't taken any mind-expanding drugs, honestly!) If that were not enough, they finished with 'Echoes' as an encore. If ever there was a better concert, and a better value for money one, then I would be surprised! One of the bonuses of a Floyd concert is that on top of the peerless music there are special effects and films to enhance the occasion. One final memorable thing about this gig was the programme. It cost about 10p and took the form of a comic. Sadly, my mate's mum threw it away when I lent it to him!

WISH YOU WERE HERE

ABBEY ROAD STUDIOS
JANUARY 1975, LONDON, UK

I WAS THERE: JANE GRAHAM

I was born in October 1952 into a comfortable middle-class family, when life was still getting back to normal after the war and new music was coming out of the dark days and creating new sounds. My first memory of Pink Floyd was at the age of 15, when 'See Emily Play' was released. I can remember buying the 45 and playing it on my Dansette record player until I drove the family crazy. I was always a bit of a creative wild child and began my love of progressive music at an early age. This was especially during the US Summer of Love period in 1967, when bands such as The Doors, The Byrds, Jefferson Airplane, Grateful Dead and Hendrix and then Cream, Pink Floyd, The Moody Blues and The Who, to name but a few, came into their own...

My next encounter with Pink Floyd was at the Bath Festival of Blues and Progressive Rock at Shepton Mallet in June 1970. Again, there was a big US presence including Santana, Canned Heat, The Byrds, Steppenwolf and Jefferson Airplane along with Led Zeppelin, Pink Floyd and more. It was the first big festival in the UK since Woodstock and none of us had ever experienced anything like it before. I was 17 and went with some college friends armed with tent, sleeping bag, plastic sheeting (very necessary) and a toothbrush! We soon realised the impact of 150,000 people descending into a large field with not many facilities took its toll, but who cared? We had another joint, drank wine and just went with the flow and expectation – and smiled a lot! It was the first time a big stage had side screen projection and a decent PA. The only thing was it took ages between each band to set up, hence Pink Floyd didn't come on until the early hours of Sunday morning. By this time, we were all rather bleary-eyed and damp – it rained all day (hence the plastic sheeting) – but the atmosphere was expectant and we were ready for anything. They didn't disappoint and debuted *Atom Heart Mother* and I remember there was a choir and a brass band. The song that stuck with me was 'Set the Controls for the Heart of the Sun' and I was, along with everyone else, completely mesmerised by the hypnotic drumming. I can't remember much after that. I wonder why? Little did I know that, four years later, I'd be their PA!

I began my career in the industry by temping for Bell Records (the Bay City Rollers' label) for three weeks in September 1974 and was hooked. Then, through a specialised agency, I landed the job of PA to Steve O'Rourke and the band at Emka Productions at the end of October 1974 for six months up to April 1975. The offices were in Bond Street, London and we had Tony Howard Management (T.Rex) on the first floor, us on the second and Bill Curbishley management (The Who) on the top floor. I recollect coming to work every morning and fighting my way through young girls skipping school, hanging round the front door most of the day desperate for a possible glimpse or news of Marc Bolan!

Although not there very long, it certainly was an experience I'll never forget, including being totally dumbstruck when introduced to the band. My duties were very varied and sometimes bizarre and you never knew what was coming next. They were recording *Wish You Were Here* and I was privileged to pay a visit to Abbey Road Studios one afternoon during sessions and have some Polaroid keepsakes of the day.

Brian Humphries was the engineer and it was just amazing to see how it all worked. I remember Roger Waters experimenting by playing and singing something he'd created, then playing it backwards and trying to replicate it in real time - very bizarre! They did a UK winter tour and I went to the Empire Pool, Wembley in November 1974 as part of the team. I was blown away by the enormity of the project, both backstage and in the crowd, and I sat mostly at the mixing desk throughout the two sets and marvelled at how the road crew pulled it all together like a well-oiled machine. The expectancy and atmosphere of the crowd was electric when it all kicked off with 'Shine On You Crazy Diamond' and it just kept coming… The special effects were beyond anything I'd ever seen, especially when an aeroplane flew down a zip wire over everyone's heads onto the stage. Tracks from *Dark Side of the Moon* were the best, with 'Money' and 'Great Gig in the Sky' my favourites, enhanced by two great backing singers, Venetta Fields and Carlena Williams, who were larger than life and such fun. I also went to a Bristol gig but I don't remember much about it – apart from the aftershow party at the hotel where they threw Harvey Goldsmith into a bath full of water. He wasn't too pleased!

Going back over the years, it's been very sad to see how many people have passed that I used to know, including Richard Wright, Steve O'Rourke, Storm Thorgerson, Tony Howard, Bryan Morrison, Mick Kuczynski (road crew), Pete Watts (road manager), to name but a few… Sadly, it didn't work out for me working for Steve O'Rourke and I left after six months. The band, however, were gentlemen and although I didn't have too many one-on-ones with them, Nick Mason took me for a drink to say 'sorry and thank you', and I will always cherish the time I spent there. I went on to work in the music industry for another 20 years and even now still have a strong connection to music and a lot of great memories. Those were the days…

Floyd play a two-legged North American tour in 1975, with 13 dates in April and 15 in June.

Clockwise from top left: John Watson's introduction to the band involved chemicals but not in the way most Floyd fans used them; Andy Gibbons recalls the lyrics for the new songs weren't exactly joyous and uplifting; Ian Nicholson's ticket for the Empire Pool at Wembley; 'Echoes' is David Bell's favourite song

Clockwise from top left: Peter Reynolds was at the Hippodrome in '74; Jane Graham at the Bath Festival in 1970 and with Nick Mason and David Gilmour at Abbey Road Studios

WISH YOU WERE HERE

LOS ANGELES MEMORIAL SPORTS ARENA
24 – 27 APRIL 1975, LOS ANGELES, CALIFORNIA

I WAS THERE: RANDY DIXON

I saw Pink Floyd a number of times and would go again to see *The Final Cut* less one player – so sad. The first show I saw was *Dark Side of the Moon* in 1974 in LA. At the end of the first set, they played 'Set the Controls for the Heart of the Sun' and the light wheel stopped and beams of light shot out. One hit my left shoulder and, as I turned to see it, it went through and hit the guy behind me.

I WAS THERE: DAVID KAUFMAN

Back in 1975 everyone was into *Dark Side of the Moon* and Floyd were coming to Los Angeles. Police Chief Ed Davis of LAPD didn't want all of the drugs that were permitted in Inglewood at The Forum, so he made a big deal about it. I was excited to see *Dark Side*, with *Wish You Were Here* not yet having been released. I had good floor seats to the show, back in the day when the true fans and not cash got the best seats. Chief Davis had so many police outside the arena and many inside to intimidate the crowd. Floyd hit the stage with the unheard *Wish You Were Here* from start to finish. Whoa! Then they did *Dark Side*, with 'Echoes' as an encore. What can I say? At the end of the show, I realised that I hadn't even pulled out my pot – the show was that good! This show in LA was known as the *Ed Davis Bust-O-Rama* show.

SPECTRUM
12 & 13 JUNE 1975, PHILADELPHIA, PENNSYLVANIA

I WAS THERE: SAM MCCLAFFERTY

Pink Floyd's *Wish You Were Here* tour in 1975 was the best concert I ever saw. They played *Dark Side*, *Wish You Were Here* and a few other gems. But the stage show was like nothing I ever saw, with movies on a big circular screen that was in sync with the songs, a laser show and an airplane that crashed into the stage. It was mind blowing. Plus there was the music… I also saw the *Animals* tour two years later, which was very good. Sadly, they didn't play Philly for *The Wall* tour but I did get to see Roger Waters do *The Wall* a few years ago.

BOSTON GARDEN
18 JUNE 1975, BOSTON, MASSACHUSETTS

I WAS THERE: MIKE CARPENTER

I saw Pink Floyd in concert twice in Boston, once in 1975 and again in 1977. I remember them being one of the loudest bands I ever heard, particularly at the '75 concert in the old Boston Garden. They played 'Raving and Drooling', 'You Gotta Be Crazy', 'Shine On You Crazy Diamond' and 'Have a Cigar' for the first set. The second set was *Dark Side of the Moon* in its entirety, and 'Echoes' for the encore. The old Boston Garden had no air-conditioning and it must have been 100 degrees in there, but it didn't affect the Floyd at all. They were flawless. A lot of people were stoned on LSD and other stuff, and I noticed some people looking around a little freaked out because of the decibel level. All in all, it was a great concert, as was the one in 1977. Security was quite lax back in those days, particularly in '75. They'd check you out going through the turnstiles, but once in, it was a free-for-all. I remember people lighting off fireworks in front of the stage before the concert. It was memorable however. The music, lightshow, the airplane crashing on stage… totally phenomenal…

THREE RIVERS STADIUM
20 JUNE 1975, PITTSBURGH, PENNSYLVANIA

I WAS THERE: STEVE DRURY

My first road trip was to go from my hometown of Canton, Ohio to see Pink Floyd at the original Three Rivers stadium in Pittsburgh. The tickets were $13, the first time we ever paid double digits for a show. It was between *Dark Side* and before *Wish You Were Here*, which they played several cuts from, plus the whole of *Dark Side*. The things that stand out were the crossover in 'Money', it being a large round football stadium. It was mind blowing at the time. The second thing of course was the infamous airplane from the top of the back of the stadium coming down to crash behind the stage.

It was festival seating and my friends and I had staked out two blankets worth of real estate, a cooler full of fruits and water, and some booze in bota bags. To cap off the night, we each had three of the double-long rolling paper joints that were rolled in a rolling machine made for them, making them the width of about a nickel. We stingily didn't share them with anyone, much to our neighbours' displeasure, but we had staked our claim and intended to experience the night the same as one amongst thousands in that stadium.

I WAS THERE: BRIAN FOWLER, AGE 19

They played *Dark Side of the Moon* and some of *Wish You Were Here*, which is my favourite. I think there was a screen with money flying, and maybe an inflatable pig? One thing I do remember was we didn't have any weed that day (bummer!).

I WAS THERE: S R JABORSKY

In June of 1975, we ventured to the old Three Rivers Stadium in Pittsburgh. I only remember it as being one of the worst Pink Floyd concerts. Not Floyd, but the crowd – 50,000 shirtless, drunk and rowdy folks with fireworks. Most of the women were not shirtless, unfortunately. At one point, Waters was pleading with the crowd to quiet down. Screams for 'Money' and other tunes rang out. They eventually did 'Money' but I could barely hear it. I also remember them doing most of 'Echoes' as an encore. I was glad to get back to Ohio.

I WAS THERE: VALERIE ROLLAND

Once Pink Floyd got into my blood all those many years ago, they never left! I am also a huge Genesis fan and they were the band that first got me into prog rock. That was a little unusual for a female in the late Sixties but what can I say? I'm a proud progger! My first husband was a drummer and in the very early Seventies he started to bring bands to our area. On the list of bands was Pink Floyd for around $9,000. He didn't think the area we lived in was ready for Pink Floyd and instead he brought George Clinton and the Funkadelics (Maggot Brain) to town. I was heartbroken!

The very first time I saw Pink Floyd was at Three Rivers Stadium in Pittsburgh, Pennsylvania, about three hours away from where I live. I was working for my brother-in-law at the time and some of the bus boys were huge Pink Floyd fans and were going to the concert, so my sister and I went along. It was festival seating and we were right in front, sitting on the ground. It was the most amazing thing I had ever seen! It was *Dark Side of the Moon* and when the pig came over the stadium the whole crowd was stunned and I think we all just watched it in awe. Even though I knew the album, I was blown away to see them live. It was amazing, fantastic, incredible and unlike anything I had ever seen before. It amazed me that even though the seating was festival, the people were there to see and more importantly to listen to this phenomenal band, and no one caused any problems. That was also the first time I ever tasted moonshine. A gallon jug was being passed around – I didn't like it!

The plane at that concert? We had heard about it but being there and watching it explode into the stage was unbelievable. I have been to literally hundreds of concerts in my life and have seen all the top bands, and I have still to this day never seen anything that comes close to that concert. A *Dark Side of the Moon* cassette or CD has been in my car ever since and I listen to it almost every time I'm in the car.

I WAS THERE: TRACY STEVENSON, AGE 16

I had been a huge fan of the band since *Dark Side of the Moon* came out a couple years before. I knew every note and had worn the grooves off the record. I lived in a small rural town 100 miles north of the concert and caught a ride with a bunch of friends in a van. It was a daytime concert. The thing I remember most was the giant floating pig. Like all the girls, I was very excited to see the beautiful, young David Gilmour. Hearing *Dark Side of the Moon* was fantastic. It was the first time I heard 'Pigs (Three Different Ones)' and 'Shine On You Crazy Diamond'. Those two really stood out.

OLYMPIA STADIUM
23 & 24 JUNE 1975, DETROIT, MICHIGAN

I WAS THERE: TOM RUSH

I grew up in West Michigan, normally a pretty sleepy and somewhat backward and late blooming conservative area, especially in the late Sixties and early Seventies. But we had a pretty active and hip music scene including some great local bands that cut albums, such as The Fredric and Phlegethon. I discovered Pink Floyd's music along with other prog rockers such as Yes, Genesis, King Crimson, etc. while in high school. King Crimson played at a local church and did a large section of their *In the Court of the Crimson King* album which led me to discovering certain mood enhancing substances and more great music to listen to whilst enhanced. While I was at college, the *Dark Side of The Moon* album came out and I was blown away by the music and knew that if Pink Floyd ever came around anywhere close to home, I was going to get to see them, whatever it took. I had a friend named Kevin who was into going to concerts and seemed to have a knack for finding out in advance who was on tour and where they would be playing, etc. He was also a good source for herbal enhancement! My girlfriend, who later became my wife, was not a big fan of my partying but she tolerated it. Juggling college, studying, work and her wasn't easy but I was young, 19 or 20, at the time so that helped.

I recall going to a number of concerts along the way – Genesis, Queen, Styx, Journey, Rush – all at the peak of their careers and I don't think I ever paid more than ten to twelve bucks a ticket, prices people would die for today. Gas was less than a dollar a gallon back then so the cost of a two-hour car ride out of town was very reasonable too.

Pink Floyd played at the old hockey arena in a very sketchy part of Detroit. It was June of 1975, late in the month, and it wasn't a weekend show either. Kevin had scored us general admission tickets and some three part blotter. The show was amazing; they played the entire *Dark Side of the Moon* album and some newer stuff like 'Shine On You Crazy Diamond'. During 'Echoes' the lights danced off a fog. I had not seen anything like that before. And there was the plane that came from behind, flew over the crowd and crashed on the stage with quite the explosion. They were doing stuff that is the norm nowadays for a lot of acts, like a large round-shaped screen behind them with a slide show going continuously with the lights and music. Genesis were pretty good at doing this type of thing too, but Pink Floyd really had them beat by a country mile. It was exhilarating, with a good-sized crowd of maybe 10,000 people. I would rank it right up there with the best shows I have ever seen.

As I look back fondly at those carefree times, almost living the *Cheech and Chong*-type of lifestyle, I realize now that I was a lousy student, a bad boyfriend and I wonder how I ever made it to my sixties, with kids, grandkids, etc. who all turned out to be normal.

It's a shame that Richard Wright passed away at such a young age and that Roger, David and Nick are not together. I love the last release, the tribute to Richard, *The Endless River*. Their music will live on.

 AUTOSTADE
26 JUNE 1975, MONTREAL, CANADA

I WAS THERE: JEAN-FRANÇOIS LAFERTE, AGE 18

I was a prog music lover from the age of 13. The first prog album I bought was *Ummagumma* by Pink Floyd. My parents were quite different from each other in every sense but particularly musically. My dad was into classical music and jazz (think Beethoven and Stan Kenton) while my mom was more of a French lover, with tastes ranging from Léo Ferré and Barbara to Jacques Brel. *Ummagumma* was a combination of all that… 'Careful With That Axe, Eugene' was 'my' song, revolving around the organ and a slow pace. All my further acquisitions were targeted in that prog direction – King Crimson, Genesis, Gentle Giant, Tangerine Dream, Kraftwerk et al. But Pink Floyd were at the top of my list. Then came *Meddle* and, in 1973,

The Dark Side of the Moon, the record of my life. I have bought every version of this album since it came out and still listen to the vinyl, CD and digital versions today.

When the group came to the Autostade, a football field just outside downtown Montreal, it was their third visit to Montreal. I went with ten of my friends in an old Chevrolet and several plates filled with good weed joints, ready to witness a live performance out of the ordinary. The security guards were at the entrance with their German Shepherd dogs, which gave us a weird kind of feeling before we entered the stadium.

The gig revolved around songs from *Animals* and *Wish You Were Here* for the first part and, after a break, they came back with *Dark Side of the Moon*. The show was packed full of people waiting for the 'wow' moment, and it came when the rocket hit the screen, followed by 'Time'. The night was falling, with just enough heat to give us the chills of the sound that came from the surround sound in the stadium. The music was clear and we could hear the lyrics. It was a perfect night and a perfect show that I still remember very well today.

I WAS THERE: BRIAN STEWART

I saw Floyd for the first time at the Autostade, a football field where the Alouettes played football. There I was, standing on the grass in sweltering heat of 90F, in a three-piece suit after just getting out of work. But after all that, I was still a hippy bum freak. And it was a great show!

IVOR WYNNE STADIUM
28 JUNE 1975, HAMILTON, ONTARIO, CANADA

I WAS THERE: HOLLY GALLETTI, AGE 17

I lived in Burlington, Ontario, which is located between Toronto and Hamilton. This concert was a very big deal at the time because the only places that got big name artists were either Toronto or Buffalo, New York which was further away from me – Hamilton was only about 20 minutes from our house. My mom got the tickets. I didn't even know they were coming to town – she was in line for tickets to something else, and the guy at the ticket booth asked her if she was getting Pink Floyd tickets. She said she had never heard of them and he asked her if she had teenagers, and if so, he was pretty sure we'd want them. Thankfully, she listened to him and bought four tickets.

I believe this was the first concert ever at Ivor Wynne stadium and the newspapers said the next day that it would be the last concert there! What did they expect? The

Hamilton Spectator had an article in their paper that said the police would not be checking concert goers for drugs – the only thing they were checking for was glass containers. They basically said you could bring in drugs and alcohol. Now what could go wrong there? And they were true to their word.

We didn't get checked and were allowed to bring our booze in because it was in a thermos camping jug – a cop even tasted it and let us in. At the time, *The Dark Side of the Moon* was the only Pink Floyd album I owned (I loved it from start to finish and still do) so the highlight for me was that they played the entire album – I don't know of any other band that ever did that.

It was an outdoor concert and hot as hell that day. I remember their pyrotechnics blowing up the scoreboard and, of course, seeing the big pig floating over the stadium. I was the only girl in our group so, after waiting in line for the bathroom for what seemed liked hours, the guys had quit waiting for me. That is not what you want to see when you have festival seating tickets and can't remember where you sat, so I sat with strangers for the entire concert. Luckily, I found my brother in the parking lot after the show or there would have been hell to pay when he went home without me!

Needless to say, a great time was had by all. I also saw the *Division Bell* tour, which I enjoyed, but it paled in comparison to the *Wish You Were Here* tour. I still listen to Pink Floyd and get my fix by going to see Roger Waters. Hands down, *The Wall* tour was the best concert I've ever been to. I went to Roger's 'Us and Them' concert and enjoyed hearing the old tunes again. But the concert at Ivor Wynne will always hold a special place in my heart as it reminds me of the fun times of my youth.

I WAS THERE: JOHN MCFARLANE, AGE 12

It was my very first concert. My parents made my older sister, who was 19, take me on her date. My sister had introduced me to them in 1973 with the *Dark Side of the Moon* album. 'Time' caught my attention at first but gradually the whole album took me over. My favourite track is 'Wish You Were Here'. When my best friend Paul passed in 1986, I cut out lyrics from the album sleeve and taped them to his place of rest.

I saw them again, without Waters, at the National Exhibition Stadium for the *Division Bell* tour in 1988. I don't remember much about it because I was too wasted, but the lighting was awesome. And my most memorable Floyd moment was their reunion for *Live 8*. Up until then, I never thought they would play together again.

I WAS THERE: GORDON PHINN

A classically beautiful summer's afternoon in the heart of an old industrial town, about 30 miles from my country home. I'd driven down excitedly, wondering what new music might be in store for us. We'd heard a new album was being road tested, and by this time *Dark Side* was world famous, its' melodies and addictive arrangements transcending all tastes and boundaries, holding up what seemed like an impossible challenge. The Beatles would never top *Abbey Road* and I suspect Floyd feared the same fate. The stadium was located in an unfamiliar part of town but I finally found a parking spot on a residential street that I thought was close to the stadium. I was rewarded almost immediately by the unmistakable sting of a Gilmour solo seemingly charging across the blue sky and enveloping the neighbourhood. Locals seated on porches as I walked past, none of them young, seemed charmed by this sonic assault. Yes, I was late, but not for the sky or the heavenly serenade.

Tapes reveal that I was hearing David at about five or seven minutes in on a positively demented 'Raving and Drooling', although one now realises that Richard's synth, dueting with David's Strat, could easily be mistaken for it. They also reveal Roger's introduction as 'raving and drooling, I fell on his neck with a scream', definitely indicative of his provocative mood. The crowd, happy in the sun, were excited and chatty, perhaps at being unenclosed and free to move as I did, strolling about enjoying the vibes.

'Tell you what, we'll carry on and you just talk amongst yourselves,' was Roger's scathing intro to their second piece, 'You Gotta Be Crazy', as new to the crowd as the first. But, as a completist collector, I had somehow survived the atrocious sound of the previous year's boot, *British Winter Tour 74*, and was somewhat familiar with the, ahem, tunes. 'This a song about not being here, it was written partly for Syd Barrett, who I'm sure some of you remember… good old Syd.' Roger's last three words were dripping with sarcasm at the onset of his homage to the man show the love/hate paradox at the heart of his own creative enterprise. Of course, we now know it was the early version, including 'Have a Cigar' but not 'Wish You Were Here' or 'Welcome to the Machine'. But it did include Dick Parry's sweet sax serenade, now as iconic as any of Dave's signature solos. Later we would be shocked, at least I was, by his solo in the middle of 'Echoes' and his dueting with David on the coda. Bloody sacrilege at the time, but one's purity mellows with age.

I WAS THERE: RHONDA O'BRIEN

I first saw Pink Floyd on the *Wish You Were Here* tour. I attended the concert with my boyfriend John Hubbard, my best girlfriend Judy Rodgers and a friend of ours, Don Goddard. We are all from London, Ontario and we drove to the concert in John's souped-up Ford Mustang. I don't remember how we got the tickets. I do remember that there was a very colourful plane that flew overhead and then landed on the stage and blew up! I also remember my friend Judi wanting to get right up to the front and climbing over all kinds of people to get there and pissing everybody off! The song 'Money' also sticks out in my mind because I remember the big screen on the stage behind the band showing cash registers and money flowing out of them.

Clockwise from top left: David Kaufman with former Genesis front man Peter Gabriel; Mike Carpenter remembers Floyd being loud; Steve Drury paid double digits for his ticket and had double long rolling papers too; Brian Fowler can't remember the stage effects but he does remember being out of weed

Clockwise from top left: Valerie Rolland got Pink Floyd in her blood; Tom Rush's introduction to hip music was via the mighty Phlegethon; Brian Stewart was at the Floyd show in a three-piece suit

The whole album is outstanding and I was already a huge fan, but this concert absolutely sealed it for me! I was hooked and forever until this day I am a confirmed Pink Floyd fan. I have since seen the *A Momentary Lapse of Reason* and *Division Bell* tours. And I saw Roger in 2017 doing a remake of *The Dark Side of the Moon* tour.

I WASN'T THERE: DAVID CLAYTON

In June 1975, a Toronto appearance was unexpectedly cancelled and the Floyd were detoured to Hamilton's Ivor Wynne Stadium. This was considerably smaller than the arenas Floyd were now playing in and the audience overflow pushed people outside the stadium and into the streets. Accounts of happy people flooding the sidewalks and lying in people's front yards were widespread, with the air filled with clouds of pot smoke and the unmistakable sound of Pink Floyd. It was the last show of the North American tour, and the road crew decided to go out with a bang and use up their remaining pyrotechnics around the stadium scoreboard for the plane crash on 'On The Run'. The explosion at the show's climax blew the scoreboard to pieces and shattered windows in neighbouring houses. The city forbade any more events at Ivor Wynne after that, with only Rush and The Tragically Hip appearing there before Ivor Wynne closed in 2012.

I WAS THERE: PHIL DAVIES

The second time I saw Pink Floyd was in Hamilton, Ontario, one day after my 18th birthday. The concert was taking place on the Saturday, and due to the unreserved seating and size of the stadium, some friends and I went down to Hamilton on the Wednesday prior to ensure prime seating. Somewhat amazingly, we were not the first in line! By the time Saturday morning arrived, there were tens of thousands of fans (with no facilities) all along the road of the main entrance. It was mayhem, but enterprising locals did a roaring trade in hot dogs and beer.

Once the gates opened, we rushed to just in front of the mixing desk, as great sound was most important to me. The show was to start at 8pm and there were many people milling around on stage at that time. Suddenly all but four people left the stage and Roger Waters introduced 'Raving and Drooling'. It was brilliant and I loved it straight away. The rest of the first set was all new material, and all terrific.

After intermission, darkness allowed the light show and the video on the circular screen to play along to *The Dark Side of the Moon*. There was a tremendous roar from the crowd when the screen lit up with hundreds of alarm clocks at the beginning of 'Time', as many thousands of alarm clock blotter LSD hits had been sold before the start of the show and were no doubt providing their full force at about that time. The end of show pyrotechnics were spectacular, but I was so sad it had ended. It was three hours of pure bliss.

Floyd's live performances in 1975 conclude with an appearance at the Knebworth Festival.

 KNEBWORTH PARK
5 JULY 1975, STEVENAGE, UK

I WAS THERE: MIKE BAESS

My next Floyd show was Knebworth in July 1975. They were huge by this point – along with the Stones, Zep and The Who – one of the biggest bands on the planet. And what a bill they offered up – Roy Harper, Captain Beefheart and Steve Miller. We got down there the night before, pitched up a tent and then stayed up the most of the night. That summer – and the next – were brilliant, really hot for long periods and that Saturday was no exception with temperatures in the seventies. Oddly enough it wasn't the greatest Floyd performance and they seemed to be on autopilot as they more or less played the same set as on their 1974 tours, with the exception of Roy Harper coming on to sing 'Have a Cigar'.

WE WERE THERE: CHRISTINE NEWEY & ROB (RINGO) STARR

We were not too far from the stage, on the right-hand side. The crowd was enormous and most of us had flags so that our group of friends could find each other when returning from trips to the toilets, etc. It was a warm sunny day with the sweet smell of cannabis floating above the crowd. The anticipation for Pink Floyd built throughout the day. An idiot climbed the tower that had the rocket ready to go and he was jeered down by those nearby. Other fans were clinging to the scaffolding either side of the stage but eventually descended when they realised their view would be impeded. Then the Spitfires flew over. The yells from the crowd couldn't outdo the sound of the aircraft but they gave it a good go, the sound of 'oohs' and 'aahs' carrying on long after the Spitfires had passed. When the rocket was finally released and headed for the stage, everyone was craning their necks to see it pass overhead and then eventually hit the back of the stage in a firework-like explosion. It was absolutely brilliant. It was such an immersive experience and Roy Harper joining the band for 'Have a Cigar' was a huge bonus.

WISH YOU WERE HERE

I WAS THERE: PAULINE ISAACS

It was a lovely sunny day, and Captain Beefheart and Linda Lewis (of 'Rock A Doodle Doo' fame) were also on the bill. As dusk approached, two World War Two spitfires flew over the crowd to herald Floyd's imminent arrival on stage and a massive roar went up. They played *Dark Side of the Moon* in its entirety, with the circular screen behind them showing film accompanying each track. In the second half, they played tracks from what was their new album, *Wish You Were Here*. I was fortunate, too, to hear one of the first live shows of *Dark Side of the Moon* at Wembley and since then I have been to many Floyd concerts, mostly in London. My two sons, who are now in their forties, like to tell people that they too have been to a live Floyd concert. When they were aged only 21 months and two months, we took them to the 1975 Knebworth concert. We will never see the great Pink Floyd play live again, but to hear their incredible music played well is the next best thing and we are big fans of Aussie Floyd and Brit Floyd and regularly attend their concerts. I have been a die-hard Floyd fan for an incredible 50 years and their music never wanes for me. They are still the greatest. We attended the Floyd exhibition at the V&A in London. It was brilliant.

I WAS THERE: JOHN PEAKE, AGE 24

I still have the programme and a couple of posters. My school friend, Rob, was doing a PhD at Reading and one of his mates was working for the promoter, Fred Bannister. He got us in for free, 'us' being me, Steve Jackson and Ian Livingstone. All old school friends... me (John Peake), Steve and Ian had just started *Games Workshop*, but that's another story!

There was a huge crowd. I remember we were quite near – perhaps 20 metres from, and just in front of, the tower that supported one end of a steel cable, the other end of which disappeared somewhere into the stage about 200 metres away. The cable was maybe ten metres above the heads of people at the tower end, but much higher at the stage. There was a model aircraft with perhaps a six-metre wingspan suspended on the cable at the tower end. I think it was dusk. We'd done several spliffs, as had everyone else. There was a sense of anticipation as we waited for the band to appear. There was a large circular screen, centre stage, raised up above stage level, in the back of the stage.

As we were waiting for them to come on, I had this premonition of aircraft buzzing the stage. Then, almost without warning, two or three Spitfires flew in quite low and fast in tight formation from the left and buzzed the stage. Wow! It was all over in a few seconds but what an amazing sight. The gig started pretty much immediately, I think, though it's all a bit of a blur now. We were unaware of the technical problems they were apparently having with sound equipment or, if we were, then I've forgotten.

History tells us that they played several pieces that would be included on their soon-to-be-released album *Wish You Were Here*. But for me it was hearing many of the songs from *Dark Side of the Moon* that really made it special. The circular screen worked well, and at some point during the show the aircraft, with various lights flashing, was released to run down the cable (which couldn't be seen as it was now dark) at ever increasing speed, to climax by crashing into the stage as appropriate smoke and lighting effects were triggered. At the same time, a film was projected onto the screen, showing the view from the cockpit of a plane as it accelerated towards the ground and to its' inevitable demise. Great gig.

I WAS THERE: OVE STRID, AGE 17

It was May 1973 when me and a friend hitchhiked to our nearest town, Ostersund in the middle of Sweden, to buy records. I was looking for records by the likes of Alice Cooper, Deep Purple and Black Sabbath. We were in our favourite record shop when my friend handed me a record and said, 'You should listen to this one. I heard it last weekend at my cousin's and it's something special.' I looked at the record and thought 'nice sleeve', bought it, listened to it and… From that moment I was a total Pink Floyd fan! The record was *The Dark Side of the Moon*.

I soon bought all the Floyd records and my walls were quickly covered with posters and pictures of Pink Floyd. I read everything I could get my hands on that included a single word about them. I looked at the posters where you could see them on stage with all that mystic smoke and dreamed about how fantastic their concerts would be. So, in the spring of 1975, I read in the *New Musical Express* that Pink Floyd would be previewing a new album at an outdoor gig in England. I don't remember where I got the tickets from, but we managed to get tickets for the Knebworth festival by post. When I held that ticket in my hand I thought, 'Wow, am I really going to see the Floyd? Is this really true?'

Me, and my friends Anders and Hans booked inter-rail tickets and began our journey from the middle of Sweden through Norway, Denmark, Germany and Holland to England and Stevenage, the nearest town to Knebworth Park. We brought just our sleeping bags and a cassette player that I remember weighed a couple of kilos. We must have played *The Dark Side of the Moon* 100 times on that trip. We arrived in Stevenage the day before the concert and it was amazing. The town was already filled with fans and you could hear Floyd music everywhere. Shop windows were filled with Pink Floyd records, posters and memorabilia. People were drinking beer and enjoying themselves and some of them took a bath in a fountain. I will never forget the guy who came by when we were sitting next to a wall having a beer and shouted 'tomorrow!' at us before ripping his shirt open to reveal the Pink Floyd tattoo on his chest.

Clockwise from top left: Jean-François Laferte's ticket for the Montreal show; a ticket for the Ivor Wynne Stadium show, at which Phil Davies was an early arrival

Clockwise from top left: Rhonda O'Brien's friend Judi climbed over fellow gig-goers to try and get down front; Peter Reynolds was at Knebworth with all the beer and still has his Knebworth flyers

WISH YOU WERE HERE

We spent the night just outside one of the big tents. It was a magical evening with a campsite full of Pink Floyd fans. I was in heaven. I drank beer and walked around the tents talking to other fans, listening to the music that was playing everywhere. Very early in the morning, they opened the gates and we went in and got a fairly good spot right in front of the stage. As we were a bit tired, we jumped into our sleeping bags and fell asleep. I woke up very abruptly because I heard loud music and I immediately sat up thinking, 'Oh my God, they have begun.' But it was hours before the first act. What I had heard was the first song being played over the PA, which was Jethro Tull's 'Aqualung'.

I don't remember much about the other acts that performed apart from Floyd, although I do remember one of the Monty Python guys being there and getting the audience to shout 'get off', and off he went. And Captain Beefheart was throwing records out into the audience.

While we were waiting for Pink Floyd to appear, my friend Anders ran into the branch of a tree near us and got lots of laughs and a round of applause from the crowd. The guys in front of us were smoking lots of joints and burned loads of holes in my sleeping bag.

Two Swedish hippies came stumbling through the crowd carrying five litre beer cans and shouting 'vilket jaevla drag' ('this is fucking heavy') as they passed us. Logs were being passed through the crowd, handed from person to person, and it was very funny, just like big worms crawling over people's heads.

There were camp fires in the outer part of the arena and I think a couple of tents got burned down. There was a guy sitting at the top of one of the towers, dancing, and the guy on the PA (who might have been John Peel) said, 'If that guy won't get down from there the Floyd won't go on stage.' Suddenly a couple of spitfires flew over the arena. (It wasn't until I read the review in the *Melody Maker* about a month later that I realised this was meant to be part of the show.) In that moment, Pink Floyd were on stage.

I don't remember much from the first part of the set ('Raving and Drooling', 'You Gotta be Crazy' and 'Shine On You Crazy Diamond') except that they seemed to be struggling with the sound and Roger Waters seemed a bit angry. Then the *Dark Side* part came and I was totally stunned. This was my big dream coming true, to actually see Pink Floyd playing *The Dark Side of the Moon* live with all the films and effects. I can still feel how I felt right then, with the quadraphonic sound, the clocks in the 'Time' film, the waves in 'The Great Gig in the Sky', the fantastic guitar solo on 'Money', etc. It was so good!

And I will never forget when they came back on stage for an encore and Roger said, 'This is called 'Echoes'.' This piece of music is one of my all-time favourites and it was just magic to sit there in the dark and watch this fantastic band perform it live. How many times had I been laying on my bed at home listening to 'Echoes'? Now it was for real. It still sends shivers down my spine when I think about it.

Afterwards, we stumbled around in the dark until we found a place in the forest where we could put our sleeping bags down and spend the night. One of the highlights of my life!

I WAS THERE: PETER REYNOLDS

My next Pink Floyd concert was at Knebworth in July 1975. Having enjoyed a stellar support cast (including the Monty Python boys getting a singalong started with 'The Lumberjack Song'), as the evening drew in the unmistakable sound of 'Speak to Me' wafted across the packed field and yet another wonderful concert began. It cost an extortionate £2.75 to attend the whole festival. Unfortunately for our friends, my mate Phil Wozencroft (sadly, no longer with us) and I got separated from them – and I had all our drink in my rucksack. It was rather heavy, so Phil and I felt we had to lighten my load! My diary for that day records that the set was largely the same as at Bristol the previous year.

I WAS THERE: PETER SMITH

A group of mates had organised a coach to take us down. It left on the Friday night (after closing time!) from outside the Londonderry pub and got us to the site in the early hours of Saturday morning. The line-up for the day was pretty strong and the attendance seemed bigger than for the Allman Brothers the year before. We were all there to see the Floyd play *Dark Side of the Moon*, and the ticket price was a bargain at £2.75. There was a long wait after the second-billed Steve Miller before two Spitfires flew overhead to herald Floyd's arrival on stage. The show was similar to Newcastle Odeon a year previously; they had their large circular screen and the first half of their set featured new songs which would ultimately appear on *Wish You Were Here* and *Animals*. The second half was *Dark Side of the Moon*, with 'Echoes' as the encore. Just before the start of *Dark Side*, a plane flew down over the crowd (travelling down a wire from the lighting tower) and crashed into the stage. And then came the familiar opening voice, 'I've been mad for fucking years, absolutely years', and the haunting laughter and we were off, witnessing what was to be the last complete performance of *Dark Side of the Moon* by the Floyd with Roger Waters. The sound wasn't great from where we were sitting, but it was amazing to see them perform their classic album in a field on a cool summer's evening, and 'Echoes' was the perfect closer for the day. Then it was out of the field through the crowds and campsites (and chants of 'Wally', a favourite festival chant), back on the bus and up the A1. We were missing one guy from our party and the coach driver decided he would leave without him. We then saw the guy hitching at the side of the road and picked him up. We were back in the early hours of Sunday morning, tired but with the sound of 'Echoes' still running through our heads.

WISH YOU WERE HERE

I WAS THERE: MICK MORGAN

This was a huge outside gig with Floyd, the Steve Miller Band, Captain Beefheart, Roy Harper and Linda Lewis. Lots of us went from Borehamwood and we took a large number of cans of alcohol with us – that people around us then wanted to buy from us! We positioned ourselves about halfway back, to the left of the rocket launch tower. Steve Millar was excellent and my friend Linda Lewis looked so small on that stage but she did a great set. With all that alcohol we took many trips to the toilets at the back of us, and it was about an hour's trip there and back. Before Floyd came on, some idiot had climbed the rocket tower. There was an announcement on the tannoy that Floyd wouldn't come on stage until this guy came down. Well, he got the bum's rush from the crowd and he soon got down. It was time for Floyd to come on when a brace of Spitfire fighter planes swooped over the crowd from the back of Knebworth House and then flew over the stage. Then we were off on another superb Floyd set. Their set was in two halves, with *Dark Side of the Moon* and their next album, *Wish You Were Here*, and then an encore of 'Echoes' that was played flawlessly. I found out later that the set was beset with technical problems but it really didn't stop us having a fantastic day on what was the last time I saw Pink Floyd live.

I WAS THERE: GARETH JONES

I was at the University of Sheffield and a group of us travelled down in a minibus and camped for a couple of days. Looking at the pictures now of the state of the festival site and the campsite, I am amazed we put up with it, but it's what you did back then! I don't remember a huge amount about the Floyd set other than the model aeroplane which flew into the stage at the climax of 'On the Run'.

My memory is more about what I went through to get away from the gig. I had decided, as I was in Stevenage and my parents lived in Stratford-upon-Avon, that I was going to try and get home from the festival by hitchhiking, which again was something one did in those days which we don't do now. It was surreal; as the concert finished, a large amount of smoke or fog obscured the grounds ('obscured by clouds'?) and, as the crowds were heading for the exits, a herd of deer suddenly galloped across the field and people scattered to get away from them. Knebworth has a deer park and I guess someone must have let them out! I managed to get out of the grounds, but trying to hitch a lift at 1am turned out not to be such a good idea and I ended up sleeping under a hedge, waking at 5am and eventually getting a lift to the A1 from which I eventually made it home. The things I did in those days to get to see the Pink Floyd!

ISLINGTON
SUMMER 1975, LONDON, UK

I WAS THERE: MIKE BAESS

In the summer of 1975, my best friend was having a clandestine affair with the wife of one of the Floyd's inner circle. He was 17 and she was 29. Knowing how much I loved the Floyd, one evening he called me and asked if I wanted to come over and visit him and his girlfriend who were staying the night – as secret lovers do – in a safe house, not far away from where I lived, near Essex Road, in Islington, which just happened to belong to Judy Trim, wife of Roger Waters. I couldn't believe my ears, and bolted over to my mate's house where his girlfriend gave us all a lift in her car. Roger and Judy had just split up and, as Judy was on holiday, my friend's girlfriend was looking after the place for her. This was in the last week of August and the Floyd's latest album was set to come out in a few weeks' time.

The house was relatively modest and the first thing I noticed when we walked into the living room was the hi-fi system – a Bang and Olufsen which was a top notch, state-of-the-art system. Being a music nut, I immediately went to look what was in the album collection and amongst the records was a copy of the unreleased *Wish You Were Here*. I froze. It was as if a thunderbolt had struck me and my eyes felt like that had popped out on stalks just like a character in one of those *Merry Melodies* cartoons. Other records of interest in the collection included albums by the Steve Miller Band, The Beatles, Leonard Cohen, Dylan and some classical recordings.

Well, after a few glasses of wine, my friends sloped off to enjoy each other's company in private and I was left to my own devices. I felt like a child on Christmas morning. I almost shook, crossed with both fear and great anticipation, as I placed side one of *Wish You Were Here* on the Beo System turntable, reclined on a lovely sofa and let the beginnings of 'Shine On You Crazy Diamond' guide me to an absolutely wonderful place. I felt like I'd won the lottery, and so lucky to be hearing this epic work before it had even been released.

Those great, bluesy notes echoed around the living room, which ran from the street to overlooking the small stone garden at the back. I'd never heard a hi-fi as vibrant as this before and the next song, 'Welcome to the Machine', made me feel as if I'd been transported into the future with those incredible, industrial-sounding metal shafts of sound making the whole room come alive.

My friends were obviously enjoying each other's company so much that they forgot about me but I didn't mind, as I was having a whale of a time checking out what I presumed was Roger's album collection. The next album I put on was Steve Miller's brilliant *Sailor* album and it made me realise why Steve had been asked to support the Floyd at Knebworth the previous month.

In the early hours, I decided to brave the patio garden and ventured into what was obviously Roger's studio shed, which had his Fender Precision bass and a Revox reel-to-reel machine. It was great enough to be able to listen to the new album but having a look at his home studio was even better. I went back into the house to while away the small hours listening to more albums. The whole evening was magical and it is experience that I will never forget.

WISH YOU WERE HERE RELEASED
12 SEPTEMBER 1975

Floyd's ninth studio album, including the tribute to Syd Barrett entitled 'Shine On You Crazy Diamond', reaches No.1 in the charts in the UK, US and six other countries. On 5 June 1975, the band were in the studio completing the final mix of when an overweight man with shaven head and eyebrows entered the room. Roger Waters didn't recognise him. Richard Wright was also mystified by the identity of the visitor and presumed he was a friend of Waters' but soon realised that it was Syd Barrett. The sight of his former bandmate reportedly reduced Roger to tears.

I WAS THERE: STEVE BURROWS

Everyone remembers where they were and what they were doing at certain poignant events in history: eg. 9/11 and the fall of the Berlin Wall, but I remember the first time I actually listened to Pink Floyd. Born in 1969, I always thought I was born ten years too late when it came to my musical tastes. I grew up with one younger brother and with Chris, the older brother with whom I shared a bedroom. Being nine years my senior, Chris influenced my musical direction by playing Led Zeppelin, Slade, The Sweet and Deep Purple. I was seven years old and doing the usual seven-year-old stuff – Action Man, colouring in, Subbuteo – when Chris called me in to show me the big black Pioneer headphones with a curly lead he'd just bought as Dad was forever complaining about 'that bloody racket!' from when he was playing his albums. He placed them on my head and said 'it's about time you listened to this' and I heard the sound of the organ, the space age goings on in the background and the tinkling of some unknown instruments in my ears. 'Shine On You Crazy Diamond' was playing and I closed my eyes as Chris turned out the lights. The guitar sound and THAT key change made the hairs on my neck stand up. I listened to the whole song with my eyes closed and when it had finished, Chris said 'that is Pink Floyd'. I couldn't get enough of them.

Chris taped his Floyd albums so I could listen to them on the single speaker player I had and I devoured them all. I had a very trendy ex-hippy teacher with a massive OMZ motorbike who was a massive Yes fan and at the age of ten I was having conversations about Gilmour being a better guitarist, the songs being more influential and Floyd's effect on music. I never got to see Pink Floyd live. I remember Live at Pompeii being on a late night BBC2 show in the early Eighties, begging my dad to let me stay up and watch it, and being blown away by 'Echoes'.

I managed to get to see Roger Waters on his last tour of *The Wall*. I stood there with Chris and witnessed not just a concert but a life event. I don't get particularly starstruck, but that night I saw a boyhood hero play an album live on stage that I knew off by heart, every word, every note. I welled up a few times that night, as did many around me. 'Comfortably Numb' finished me off. I was in the presence of musical genius, musical history, and it took me back to that moment, as a seven-year-old with my brother's headphones on, in a dark room listening to 'Shine On'. I had seen greatness and nothing compares.

After a quiet 1976, gig-wise, Pink Floyd begin 1977 with a 29-date European and British tour which takes the band through to the end of March.

ANIMALS RELEASED
21 JANUARY 1977

Pink Floyd's tenth studio album reaches No.2 in the UK, No.3 on the Billboard 200 and tops the charts in five other countries. The album sleeve cover image, of a pig floating between two chimneys on Battersea Power Station, involved a three day photo shoot. 'Algie' escaped on day two, floating off over the skies of London. He was recaptured and photographed again on the third day, lashed to the towers of the power station.

OLYMPIAHALLE
27 FEBRUARY 1977, MUNICH, WEST GERMANY

I WAS THERE: MIKE QUINN

I was stationed in Augsburg, West Germany in 1976 and 1977. I saw a lot of great concerts in Munich, which was an easy train ride from where I was based. We always got a bottle of great German wine for the ride and to fill up the bota bag! This concert was actually the *Animals* tour, even though the ticket showed the *Wish You Were Here* cover. I went with my friend Mark, who is one crazy guy. We got to the Olympiahalle and the doors were not open. There was a huge crowd outside the front area and, as more people came to the entrance, we were all getting pushed together. All of a sudden, this cute fraulein right in front of me starts kicking backwards at my shins. I was like 'WTF?' I look down and I see Mark's hand pulling back. He had been reaching past me and grabbing her ass and she thought I was doing it!

Finally, we all got in. Mark and I had decent seats and another group of our buddies were partying down on the floor. We smoked a lot of hashish there in Germany and that's what Mark and I did at the show. It was a great concert. 'Pigs' was so incredible. The big floating pig came out and floated over the crowd! We learned the next day that our friends that were down on the floor were doing some acid and that when the big pig floated over, one of our crazy buddies passed right out. Too intense, I guess!

EMPIRE POOL
15 – 19 MARCH 1977, WEMBLEY, LONDON, UK

I WAS THERE: IAN NICHOLSON

Gig number three for me was the 1977 *In The Flesh Animals* tour. The show I attended was the Friday show of their five-night run there. My seat, in block A of the arena floor, was only 14 rows from the front, the closest that I've been for a Floyd gig. This was another show split into two halves. The first half was the complete *Animals* album, and the second half the complete *Wish You Were Here* album. It was a fantastic set, complemented by the band's excellent lighting and visuals projected on to the huge circular screen that towered over the band. We also got to see the use of inflatables on this tour, including the famous flying pig, so we had a glimpse of what was to come with the *Wall* tour three years later.

Another thing about this tour was that the band were augmented by an extra guitarist, Snowy White, plus Dick Parry on sax. Dick, of course, had toured with Floyd before, his work on *Dark Side of the Moon* being so memorable. It did seem odd having an extra guitarist, but Snowy did an excellent job, playing both lead and bass guitar. I think the encore was 'Money'.

I WAS THERE: VINCE GROOME, AGE 17

It's March 1977 and I was off to Wembley to see Pink Floyd on their *Animals* tour. Quite an experience for a fresh-faced 17-year-old sixth former from a sleepy

Northamptonshire shoe town to go to my first big gig. Correction – my first ever gig, beyond pub bands!

Looking suitably cool and sporting voluminous long hair in staunch resistance to the onslaught of punk, and being thrilled when offered some acid (having established what that actually was – and opting to decline), we entered the auditorium to experience two and a half hours of prog rock bliss. Floyd were at their imperial best; totally assured in what they did, including the aloof, distant presence on stage. No 'let's hear you, Wembley!' whoops for Waters and co. Just getting down to business in front of a largely sedentary audience.

But what a show. The set was *Animals* first half, *Wish You Were Here* second, all played straight through as if listening to the LPs, with an encore of 'Us and Them' to follow. Superb fare for an angsty-arty teenager...

The sound was produced by an exquisite quintaphonic system that swirled around the auditorium, making every note crystal clear. Then there was the massive circular screen that became a trade mark, displaying sublime images and animations to accompany the swelling Rick Wright synths and stunning Gilmour guitar licks. The inflatables are often spoken about but I was never a huge fan – and in later years I could see that they were only a smidgeon away from a Spinal Tap parody. But that was probably just me.

Hours later, we spilled into the cold London night, elated by the experience – even without the benefit of LSD – and feeling even more validated in defence of prog. Not bad for a first ever concert and I wondered how on earth I could follow that. Fortunately, the Genesis *Seconds Out* and Yes *Going for the One* tours followed that year, so my concert going life wasn't entirely ruined. Great days!

I WAS THERE: PETER SMITH

The UK leg of the *In the Flesh* tour took in five nights at Wembley's Empire Pool and four nights at Stafford Bingley Hall. I went to the third night at Wembley, leaving Newcastle by train around 3pm and taking the Tube across London to arrive at Wembley by 7pm. The show followed the two-part format that had become the norm for Floyd in the '70s: the first set featured the new album, *Animals*, and the second showcased their last release, Wish You Were Here. The encore was 'Us and Them' although some nights it would be 'Money' and one lucky audience in the States got the last ever performance of 'Careful With That Axe, Eugene'. The tour featured large inflatable puppets, including the famous inflatable pig which flew over us and around the Empire Pool during 'Pigs on the Wing'. I enjoyed the gig but found the band somewhat distant, and distant in a literal sense from my seat way up in the tiers. I'd seen the Sex Pistols live a few months before, and was starting to get interested in punk, and as part of that I was losing faith in bands like the Floyd. I missed the Wall shows at Earl's Court, which in hindsight I regret.

WISH YOU WERE HERE

I WAS THERE: IAN TANDY

I have been a Pink Floyd fan for 50 years. I recall bringing *The Dark Side of the Moon* vinyl into school in the days when we all brought our new albums into school to brag and prove how grown up we were. My economics teacher borrowed it and kept it for two months! I was beside myself with excitement when I read in *NME* that Floyd were touring the *Animals* album. There were details of the tour dates and promoter, and where to apply. I wrote my cheque and posted it off first class the same day. Several weeks passed before I read that a stamped addressed envelope should be forwarded with payment. Distraught I applied again, this time with an SAE. A few weeks before the concert, I received my ticket. It was from my second application with the SAE. It was a seat far back from the stage and for a date two days later than I had originally applied for, but it was a ticket nonetheless. My original application appeared to have been ignored. The cheque had not been cashed.

A couple of days before the first gig, I received in the post a response to my first application. The ticket was for a seat four rows back from the front of the stage, right in the middle and on the opening night, just behind the press and the celebs. I was so close to the band during the performance that I could see them relaxing with a beer, sitting around a table, while Richard Wright played a solo during 'Sheep'. But the best bit happened a few hours before the concert. I turned up early and sat outside the venue. Suddenly I could her Floyd practising 'Pigs' and then 'Sheep'. I cannot put into words how thrilled I was. It was the first time I had heard the band live, and all these years later the memory of those magical sounds coming through the closed doors of the arena are as fresh as if it were today.

I WAS THERE: MICK MORGAN

Back then you could rock up to Wembley Empire Pool in your Ford Cortina, park right outside and nip into the box office to buy your tickets days before the gig. We arrived on the night well excited that we were gonna see another Pink Floyd gig, and on a Friday too. We went straight to one of the bars for a few beers, then realised – oops! – that we had forgotten to get a programme so went back for one. Then it was off high up to the North Upper Tier. The sound was being tested, with it flip-flopping around the arena in quadraphonic. Floyd did five numbers from the new *Animals* LP and five from *Wish You Were Here*, along with 'Us and Them' for the encore. It was a 'typical' Floyd arena gig, with puppets each side of stage and pigs slowly flying around. And as it was a Friday night, off we went to Dingwalls in Camden Lock after the concert.

NEW BINGLEY HALL
28 – 31 MARCH 1977, STAFFORD, UK

I WAS THERE: ALASTAIR CALDER

It was late March 1977 on the *Animals* tour at Stafford Bingley Hall. A group of about 20 of us took the train and bus from Coventry and got to the venue very early as Bingley Hall was just that, a huge open seatless hall, and we wanted a good spot on the floor. It was freezing outside and if I remember they took pity on us and opened the doors earlier than advertised.

The PA kicked in with 'Echoes' and possibly even 'One of These Days' and then the band walked on and started with *Animals*. They stopped for a break and then played *Wish You Were Here* and 'Money' for an encore. In truth, *Animals* and *Wish You Were Here* were note perfect renditions of the albums and worthy versions. Only on 'Money' did they improvise, but everyone was dancing by then anyway. It was an awesome show, and I still listen to a lot of early Floyd to this day.

I WAS THERE: PETER LONGTHORNE, AGE 19

They played all of *Animals*, then all of *Wish You Were Here*. The encore was 'Money'. The highlight of the show for me was 'Wish You Were Here', the radio tuning intro picking up the England vs Luxembourg score (England won!) and a lovely blues improvisation at the end of it from Gilmour. I also later saw Roger Waters on the *Pros and Cons* tour at Birmingham NEC in 1983, with Eric Clapton playing guitar. The first half was all Floyd songs and the second half all of *Pros and Cons*. My highlight? 'The Gunner's Dream'. Great memories.

I WAS THERE: IAN MCCORMICK

Bingley Hall was a cattle shed or exhibition hall, but except for the fact that there was a giant pig over the stage and I think I went with a friend from Teeside Polytechnic, I can't remember too much about it!

I WAS THERE: ROB BOOTH, AGE 15

My first ever live gig, and the day before my sixteenth birthday. We lived in West Bromwich and had to bunk off school for a day. Me, Tony (known as Badger due to an unfortunate black and white cardigan he wore… just once), Robert Duncan and an Afghan-wearing, patchouli oil-scented hippy fella whose name I cannot recall caught the

74 bus to Birmingham and hopped on the first available train to Stafford. Arriving at our destination at around 11.30am, we quickly sought the seediest rundown boozer available that didn't mind serving alcohol to school kids. We left there at around 3pm and acquired half bottles of whisky, rum and vodka from an equally seedy, above the law off licence and made our way on foot as fast as we could stagger to the venue, which was still around three and a half miles away. We joined the queue about 50 to 60 people back from the entrance door and still had to wait nearly three hours before being let in. It was a good job we had our beverages to keep us company… But the gig was absolutely amazing, with the whole *Animals* album, most (if not all) of *Wish You Were Here* and an encore of a good 20 minutes of *Dark Side* offered up for our consumption.

I WAS THERE: ANDREW MORRIS

I was blown away by them. I was in my early twenties. Edwin Shirley Trucking did the trucking, because I can remember the great big lorries outside the concert. Edwin Shirley was a massive company that used to truck round all the bands at the time. That was the first time I'd been to an enormous concert. They were really hitting the big time then. What was remarkable about that concert was that it was the *Animals* tour, with the giant flying pig that would fly down towards the stage. It had little beady eyes that glowed in the dark and it came out the back of the hall and slid down a fly rope towards the stage. (During the tour, I believe the pig escaped at London – or the roadies let it – and it floated over Battersea power station.) I remember a great big chrome fan that came up at the back of Nick Mason and all the lights shone on it, throwing the spotlights all over the hall.

The atmosphere that night was full of cannabis. You couldn't help but breathe it in. It was one of those gigs! And although I didn't smoke the stuff you couldn't help it. It was part of the gig, because everyone was smoking it at the time and the hall was that thick with it.

They were absolutely amazing. I really enjoyed it. It's one of those gigs that'll stick in my mind forever. They were way ahead of their time.

From April through to July 1977, Pink Floyd take the In The Flesh *tour to North America, playing a total of 26 shows over two legs.*

JEPPESEN STADIUM
30 APRIL 1977, HOUSTON, TEXAS

I WAS THERE: MICHAEL HUTCHINSON

I was not a fan but was dragged along by a girlfriend who was really into them. It took place at Jeppesen Stadium, previously a high school football stadium in the Houston school district. All I remember after 40 something years is that it was pouring down rain and we were covering up with trash bags that some enterprising person was selling for maybe $1 each. I believe the band made a valiant attempt at playing but I really don't remember if they were able to finish the show. More than 40 years later I now believe Pink Floyd are one of the greatest bands of all time.

ANAHEIM STADIUM
6 & 7 MAY 1977, LOS ANGELES, CALIFORNIA

I WAS THERE: CHERYL HOWARD

It was almost rained out. But we stuck it out, sitting out the rain for over two hours. I just knew they would perform for us and we got the concert and more. They outdid themselves! It turned out to be one of the best concerts I've ever seen. They put on a great show that went on into the night, and then followed that up with 'Shine On You Crazy Diamond' and the whole *Dark Side of the Moon* album. The night ended with fireworks and an exploding pig hanging over the audience in the ball field. I went to a lot of concerts in those years and kept all the stubs as souvenirs. It was worth the rain. It wasn't cold – it was California!

I WAS THERE: BRIAN HUNTER

I was a senior at Valencia High School in Placentia, California. I had my first part time job that school year, my first money to spend as I wished. That led me to spend more time in the record store. Some great records found their way into the house – The Eagles' *Hotel California* and *Greatest Hits*, Tull's *Songs From The Wood*, Fleetwood Mac's *Rumours*, ELO's *Out of the Blue* and *New World Record*, Meat Loaf's *Bat Out of Hell*, Aerosmith's *Rocks*, Boston's *Boston*, Bob Seger's *Live Bullet* and… Pink Floyd's *Animals*. It was *Animals* that made me buy my first headphones. I remember falling asleep with head phones on and *Animals* on repeat. Trippy!

WISH YOU WERE HERE

By April of 1977, I had money, a driver's license and what turned out to be a lifelong music addiction. Friends invited me to Jethro Tull's show in April, my first real concert. The energy, the sound and just being at the event was such a rush. The next day I was checking on other shows coming near and was thrilled to find out the *Animals* tour, *In The Flesh*, was coming up in May. I can't remember where I got the tickets, but I had two before I knew who would go with me. I didn't have any Floyd friends at the time, but I got the girl (next door to) next door to agree to go. Sometime before the show, I bought *Wish You Were Here* and *Dark Side of the Moon*. If I was awake and at home, Gilmour's guitar would be leaking from my room. I didn't know what they would play, but I was as ready as I could afford to be. I just hoped they would play some tracks off the three records I owned.

The concert was in 'The Big A', Anaheim Stadium, home of the Anaheim Angels baseball team. It was a pretty standard stadium at the time, with an opening in the outfield where there was, well, a big A. My tickets were on the third base side near the field, and the stage was out in centre field. I remember being sad at the distance, but I think we could see better than people on the field towards the back. I was also worried about the sound. How could it compare to my headphones?

The lights dimmed and Floyd came out and launched into 'Sheep'. The lead in is a perfect way to start – keyboards and bass. I realised they set up speakers around the stadium and were spinning the bass around. So cool. Better than my headphones! Once the music grew with vocals and guitar, I was in a spinning trance. How could this be more epic? Balloons! The large animals showed up behind the stage. Nice touch.

Soon it became apparent that they would play all of *Animals* with extra long solos. When they were near done, playing 'Pigs (Three Different Ones)', the pig balloon came out. It was over the crowd near home plate and moving toward the stage, with red eyes and advancing with that song swirling. Then the thing blew up! There was a fireball above the crowd that started to drop. I was actually afraid it would reach the crowd but then it went out. Crazy!

I couldn't imagine how they would follow that, when 'Shine On' started. The show switched from the balloons to a large screen with images and the animated machine. They played all of *Wish You Were Here*, the sound still swirling which fitted that record even better. Every single song on two of my three Floyd records was played, but the show was ending. I was hoping for *Dark Side of the Moon* songs when they came back for the encore. The crowd loved the opening bass notes of 'Money'. The plane flew with sparks. It was a good way to close. It was a great show.

The only other thing I remember from that night is that my date was a complete bust. We went to an all-night joint and my neighbour, who I had hoped to impress, ordered a glass of water only. Turns out I may have been a bit preoccupied with the show, and she only knew the last song. Heh… I didn't care. Best. Show. Ever.

I WAS THERE: JOHN L SMITH

It was 40 years ago, the *Animals* tour, and a spring day with some patchy clouds. We had some light rain as we were pre-partying in the parking lot, and as we made our way into the stadium trying to find a good seat on the outfield grass. The stage was located in the centrefield opening and was flanked by the upper seating levels on each side. We were settling in for a great show when the sound of sheep, cows and pigs seemed like it was coming from a distance. The excitement was growing in the crowd and the farmyard sound kept getting louder and louder. As we all looked up to the stage, we saw two big, bright rainbows on each side of the stage, going all the way over to each end of the stadium seats as the music continued to grow and get louder. The natural rainbows appeared to get brighter and then, as the sun started setting, they disappeared as the band went full swing into the opening song. That was the best opening to any to any concert ever.

 COLISEUM
9 & 10 MAY 1977, OAKLAND, CALIFORNIA

I WAS THERE: LEON FRENCH

I saw the Floyd 14 times, starting in '68 and through to the *Division Bell* tour, only missing the *Wall* tour. My friends and I went down to the *Dark Side* show at the Ford Theatre in Detroit in 1972 after dropping some very nice acid. For the final segment of the show, the fog machines went into high gear and fogged up the Ford Theatre real good. When we went out to our car to go home, a thick fog bank had rolled into the area along the Detroit River. Naturally, we figured the Floyd had magically fogged up the entire metro area... On the way home on the freeway, it was so thick we had slowed down to 10mph and the only way we could tell where we were on the road was for me to hang out the side window to watch the white line on the side of the road to make sure we were still on it.

A couple of years earlier, I was at the Detroit show when the roadies had overloaded the flash bomb and during the 'Axe, Eugene' scream, it went off and blew the PA and some amps off the stage, injuring a couple of roadies. The show was halted and it was 40 minutes before they restarted.

In 1977, I got tickets for both nights. I had a very good and very attractive British friend named Lola who worked at the Trident in Sausalito, where a lot of big groups would come to hang at. The Floyd came in and I think it was Snowy White who chatted her up and gave her a backstage pass for the second night. Knowing I was a

Floyd fan she came out from backstage and we traded our tickets. So the first night I watched from out front and the second night I watched from backstage. During the intermission Dave, Rick and Nick chatted with me for about 15 minutes in a relaxed and friendly manner. Then Roger came over and told me to scram so he could talk with the boys.

The high point of any Floyd show was always 'Echoes', their finest piece of music.

I WAS THERE: RON BENDORFF

They performed 'Careful With That Axe, Eugene' during an unprecedented second encore after much of the crowd had exited. We had persisted and were rewarded. It was a fantastic show!

MEMORIAL COLISEUM
12 MAY 1977, PORTLAND, OREGON

I WAS THERE: JOHN CASPER, AGE 22

I saw the *Animals* tour for a whopping ten dollars. With no opening act it was three hours of Floyd. I particularly remember Roger Waters holding up the transistor radio at the end of 'Welcome to the Machine'.

FREEDOM HALL
17 JUNE 1977, LOUISVILLE, KENTUCKY

I WAS THERE: JOHN CONEY

I was with two younger brothers, the youngest being 17, and a couple of friends. My next youngest brother and I were (and are) diehard Floyd fans. We would call every record shop in town when a new album came out to find out who had it, so that we could be the first to spin it on the turntable. We would play the new albums over and over and have the whole thing memorised in hours.

We had to drive about 70 miles from Lexington to Louisville for this show. We had some good acid with us and set off around 4pm. We were going in two cars and, having left first, we stopped on the freeway to let the other car catch up. We sat there for a few minutes and I emptied the ashtray out right beside my driver's door. About three minutes later a state trooper pulled up behind us to see if we needed assistance. We weren't messed up yet and he was about to walk away when he looked down and saw the cigarette residue on the ground. He asked if I had done that. It was pretty obvious that I had. I said 'no' but got a ticket for littering. A nice start to the trip. A big truck blew by about a minute later and the cigarette mess was blown away by the wind.

Our friends showed up and we proceeded to Louisville. On arrival, we headed for the front of the stage. The floor was general admission back in those days and to get up front required a bit of finagling and manoeuvring through the crowd. We wound up no more than 20 feet from the stage, dead centre. We waited for what seemed an eternity. The acid was kicking in. Some sort of sound test was being performed, a super loud wind noise that lasted a long time.

There was no support band. I don't recall the exact setlist, but Floyd started with songs from *Animals* and had the pig floating around for a while. Gilmour had a cold or a sore throat and was having a bit of trouble singing but he was still great. They then started in with *Wish You Were Here*, playing the album front to back. I was totally blown away by this point. During one of the quiet parts, some asshole threw a pack of firecrackers up on the stage and they landed right on the keyboard. Richard Wright didn't miss a beat and simply brushed them off whilst still playing. The band had an AM/FM portable radio on stage to do the radio interlude between 'Have a Cigar' and 'Wish You Were Here'. The show finished and they came back for one encore, 'Money'.

I will never forget that show. It's burned into my memory. Oh, and I got out of my littering ticket.

I WAS THERE: DOUG DELANEY, AGE 20

This is the only time I saw them with Roger Waters. Needless to say, the show was epic and one I will never forget. The burning airplane flew across the stadium. They had the pig floating above us and the plane dive bombing toward the stage. I'd never seen anything like that before at a concert. 'Shine On You Crazy Diamond' was the opener, and they played most of the *Animals* album plus a couple of songs from *Wish You Were Here* and a good part from *Dark Side of The Moon*. The show lasted for about three hours. Freedom Hall was primarily a basketball arena and not really big enough to house a Floyd show but the place was packed and you could really feel the emotions.

KEMPER ARENA
21 JUNE 1977, KANSAS CITY, KANSAS

I WAS THERE: ED HERNANDEZ

I was just a sophomore in college; my two older brothers had turned me on to Pink Floyd. They opened up with *Animals* and then got straight into 'Wish You Were Here' and finished off with 'Money'. They only played eleven songs but each song was five to ten minutes long. They turned off all the lights and the strobe lights went on upstairs and showed all the inflatable animals floating from the ceiling. A spectacular, wonderful night.

RIVERFRONT COLISEUM
23 JUNE 1977, CINCINNATI, OHIO

I WAS THERE: JOHN W ROSE

I was introduced to Pink Floyd by my oldest brother via the *Relics* album. I saw the *In the Flesh* tour in Cincinnati with a school mate. We saved up our school lunch money to buy our $8.50 tickets. It was absolutely the greatest concert I've ever seen, and I have seen a few! Even though the whole show was fantastic, my favourite song from it was 'Welcome To The Machine'.

I WAS THERE: KEN SMITH

We climbed up on one of the quadraphonic speaker stands for a better view and nearly got blown off about every fourth note. The flying pig seemed right at home in Cincinnati.

MUNICIPAL STADIUM
25 JUNE 1977, CLEVELAND, OHIO

I WAS THERE: S R JABORSKY

This was one of the legendary *World Series of Rock* shows at the old Cleveland Stadium. Everyone in the world says they were there but I definitely was, with a pregnant wife.

Their plane buzzed the stadium to start the concert. *Animals* was out and they did 'Sheep', 'Dogs' and 'Pigs', with pigs filling the air above the stadium. 'Echoes' was, I think, the encore. Great concert, great album.

I WAS THERE: WILLIAM RUSCHLER

I was a fan from the first time I heard them, at age twelve, listening to a friend's copy of *Atom Heart Mother*. I still love that album but I also liked their early music as well as the even more progressive Seventies albums. I am from the Buffalo/Rochester, western New York area. The tickets came from a friend in my senior class who drove to Cleveland to get them – it was a sold-out show at concert time. I went the same week as I graduated high school with four others in one vehicle.

The old Cleveland Municipal Stadium was nicknamed 'The Mistake by the Lake'. Cleveland was rather dumpy back then, especially in that neighbourhood. We paid extra to park in a secure garage a 20-minute walk from the stadium. The size of the crowd was apparent, blocks away. We had general admission, which meant we didn't have a seat, but a space on the main field. The stage was set up in the outfield, if you can visualise a baseball game. The tickets were $9 each. The feeling was electric and exciting. We were maybe 20 metres from the stage on the left side, and that is the best we could do and still be comfortable.

When the lights went down, there was a roar and then the lasers and back scene visuals came on while the band took stage. I had never seen anything quite like it. It was a bizarre cartoon movie with farm animals and effects. I would say my favourite track was 'Pigs on the Wing (Three Different Ones)' At that point, the giant inflatable pig with the laser eyes came over the crowd, with the lasers and lights shooting everywhere. I had never witnessed anything close to it. The Who in Philadelphia the year before was the first time I had seen lasers, but this light show and animation backdrop on the band was better. The sound was decent too, and not as loud and painfully piercing as The Who. We could see just enough to know who was who on stage. They did the entire *Animals* album, as well as most all of *Wish You Were Here* and a couple from of *Dark Side of the Moon* for the encore.

I WAS THERE: MICHAEL MCFANN, AGE 15

We lived in Columbus, Ohio. Having an older brother, I was already hanging with an older crowd so I had been introduced to Floyd early. In June of 1977 I turned 15 years old. My mother wanted to know what I wanted for my birthday. Having found out that Pink Floyd were going to play Cleveland and that my brother and all his friends were going, I told my mom I wanted to see Floyd. Right away it was a 'no'. A couple of days later, she asked again, 'What would you like?' I didn't budge and she didn't either. But, a couple of days later, she caved and said that, if I found a driver she trusted, she would buy me two tickets. I found a friend of my brother's who fitted the bill, so Mom took me to Sears Ticketron outlet where she purchased two tickets to see Pink Floyd – 25 bucks.

Fast forward to early morning, 25 June. We're heading north to Cleveland. We had beer and some weed and a little money. We showed up at the stadium around 7.30 in the morning and found a parking spot. We partied up a bit and met the folks around us. I noticed a van a row up and down a bit from us which was selling Dixie Cup shots of keg beer for a quarter, plus other stuff. I mentioned to my buddy that I didn't like the vibe but he checked them out. I went looking around the lot, and sure enough I found my brother and his friends.

We hung for a while and then I split back to our car. It was time to go in, and me and my friend headed up when my friend said, 'Hey, I want to see what these guys have for sale out of that van.' I said, 'Dude, fuck them, it's time to go in!' He insisted, and went to them. They were motioning me to come also. I saw him get dragged in the van and then be tossed out. They took his ticket. I told him if he wanted to leave, I could probably get home without him. But he hung out and waited for me – with a black eye!

Once inside, at my first concert of any kind, I was down by the stage looking in the stands. After about 20 minutes, I saw my brother and his friends in the upper grandstand. It took me another 20 minutes to get to where they were, but they were surprised that I had found them out of 100,000 people! They smoked me out and I headed back to the stage area. Then I met some people from PA who, finding out I had no party goods, gave me a half flagon of Yago sangria and a hit of mescaline. (Yes, I was 15.)

It had been raining, but when the show started it stopped. People were actually holding the infield plywood over their heads and lots of people were sheltering under them from the rain. A huge jet plane flew over and Floyd took the stage. My buddy was waiting. I made it home.

I WAS THERE: SCOTT DEMORE

Everyone that was going from my small town was meeting in the stadium, under the Golden Arches flag we had stolen from McDonalds. We went the night before and camped out in the stadium parking lot, already jammed with partygoers, even though the concert was 24 hours away. We partied our asses off all night and the next morning, got in line to enter the stadium and made our way in around 1pm. A friend had made a watermelon bong, so we partied all day in centre field, right in front of the stage. About 8.45pm, a man came out on stage and said Floyd were ready to come on, but needed 15 minutes of silence in the stadium. Everyone became quiet, and for the next 15 minutes, all you could hear coming from the loudspeakers was pigs grunting.

The stadium was right next to Cleveland Burke Lakefront Airport, where the Rock & Roll Hall of Fame is now. A 707 took off from the airport and buzzed Cleveland Stadium. Everyone looked up to see the 707, and after the jet flew away, everyone looked back at the stage to see that Floyd had taken the stage. (I later learned that Floyd were heavily fined for doing this.) They performed the entire *Animals* album, took a break and then did the entire *Wish You Were Here* album, before taking another break and coming back to do 'Money' and 'Us and Them'. I've been to hundreds of concerts and this one was by far the best.

I WAS THERE: JAMES SIATRAS

It was totally awesome when the jetliner flew from behind the stage out over the top of the stadium. Seeing the laser lights and the sheep on parachutes was a trip, as was watching the giant pig get shot to pieces by skyrockets and then the band stopping the show and threatening to leave because someone was holding on to the cable for the pig and they couldn't pull it back in.

Lots of people passed out from different substances and were being rescued by the medical teams all afternoon, including one of my friends who rode up on the bus with us hippies from Wadsworth and drank too much tequila. He sat in the hot sun before the band started to play, puking and passing out. When the medics came for him too, we convinced them he would be all right. By showtime he was up on his feet. The group of us from the bus ended up in a centrefold in the *Akron Beacon Journal* entitled 'The Day 83,000 Got Zunked'.

I WAS THERE: JIM RAMOS

We were outside the gate at 10am along with several thousand others. We sat in the box seats, above the dugout at first base. I remember the business jet from Burke Lakefront Airport diving straight down at the stadium. Everyone had their eyes on the jet, which looked like it was going to crash into the second base area, but it made a quick pull up into the sky. And, as it did so, Pink Floyd were on stage playing the first notes of the first song.

I remember a very large pig sliding on a wire across the whole field, from the centre field bleachers to behind home plate. The parachuting sheep were strange, but then again, I had done some blotter, so I wasn't too surprised. It was crazy, insane, wild – and a fantastic time!

I WAS THERE: ED FOX, AGE 15

I had no drugs and no alcohol, other than maybe a contact high! Someone slipped my ticket out of my hand right as I was coming to the entrance. Luckily for me, the guy admitting people into the stadium saw it happen and let me in. I remember the crowd, the loud firecracker someone threw from the upper deck, and people pulling up the artificial turf and plywood to make 'tents' during the rain. It was an amazing show and weed was everywhere. Oh, and the Red Line Rapid going home was packed with people when it went dead. We were sat in the pitch dark and sitting on the tracks for over half an hour.

I WAS THERE: MARK SHAHEEN

I stood on someone's cooler to see over the crowd and the people who owned it never came back for it. They probably looked for it the whole show, and we never looked to see what was in it! People were shooting bottle rockets at the pig. And I'll always remember the beginning, when the plane came over the stadium and, when it was gone, the band was playing the same sound on their instruments to open what was an outstanding show.

I WAS THERE: GRANT A WOLFE

Sitting in the upper deck of the old Cleveland Stadium behind home plate, I could see the runway at Burke Lakefront Airport through the open end of the stadium. Shortly before the show started, I noticed an older propeller-driven passenger plane taking off from the airport. It headed east only briefly, quickly turned around and then headed back towards the open end of the stadium at a low altitude, where Pink Floyd's stage was set up. Very soon, it became apparent that it was going to fly over the stadium. As it approached, the noise from the plane became very loud. As the plane started flying over the open end of the stadium, an explosion went off on stage, the lights came up and the plane released numerous pig parachutes that came floating down. Suddenly, the band was on stage and started playing the *Animals* album. Almost 46 years later, I remember it clear as a bell.

I WAS THERE: MICHAEL WHALEN

On the bootleg CD, you can hear all the announcements regarding the pig being held up by fans, some medical warnings about drugs and (something you don't hear today) fireworks going off. I believe they were more than bottle rockets, as people were bleeding on the infield. But hands down it's the best show I have ever witnessed.

I WAS THERE: JOHN NACE

My memory is that someone grabbed the wires to the pig and started pulling it into the crowd. They announced that the show would stop unless the pig was released!

A PEOPLE'S HISTORY OF PINK FLOYD

I WAS THERE: RICHARD B KELLEY

Promoters Michael and Jules Belkin – in tandem with WMMS-FM (Home of the Buzzard) radio – created a summer run of concerts they dubbed the *World Series of Rock*, all-day Saturday music events headlined by the Eagles, the Stones and other top acts of the era with second tier support acts such as Todd Rundgren and REO Speedwagon. Floyd were on their way to setting the record for the highest ever attendance. My best friend, G, came to this concert with me, as he had to see Floyd six years earlier in Toledo. He enjoyed his music but enjoyed mind-altering substances more, and when we learned that Pink Floyd tickets were $9.50 each, he offered to offset the cost by bringing the best lysergic acid diethylamide money could buy. We (naturally) had pot but a supply of what helped push poor Syd Barrett off the deep end seemed like a good idea. The two-hour trip to Cleveland in my not air-conditioned Dodge Challenger was very hot so the beers went down quick. Arriving in the parking lot, G dipped into his goody bag and we all swallowed a hit and made our way through the gates. We got seats in a lower tier parallel with first base and settled in just as our trip got underway. We laughed, we marvelled at the massive crowd on the field and we exchanged a plethora of the astoundingly profound observations that LSD inspires. Then it wore off and we realised we'd been there for hours and nothing had happened.

There were no warm-up acts to pass the time, just a world record crowd of 78,000 broiling in the sun and Great Lakes humidity, taking drugs and flinging the occasional cherry bomb. The others decided to do more acid but I passed. One out-of-body experience was enough, plus the increasingly unruly and impatient crowd lent itself to the possibility of a bad trip. The one bit of entertainment we had whilst waiting for Pink Floyd to start was watching as many as five small airplanes circling the stadium towing advertising banners for car dealers, radio stations, beer, etc. At 7pm, the sky had almost emptied, making it easy to spot a small business-size jet circling lazily far out over the lake and then moving closer. After perhaps ten minutes, it had gained the attention of the crowd. It took a turn, headed far out over the lake and then, turning 180 degrees, accelerated straight towards the stadium and the centre of the crowd.

A collective, screaming gasp came from 78,000 Floyd fans, their heads figuratively exploding. Seemingly at the last second, the little plane pulled up and rapidly rocketed away into the night sky. Everyone swore they could see the pilot's face. The trick was on us. As the shouts and excitement created by the plane started to die away, we became aware of a Roger Waters' signature one-note bass line emanating through the stadium - in tandem with the sounds of sheep. Pink Floyd had walked on stage, in broad daylight, and begun the show!

We settled in for the next hour to hear the *Animals* album performed while a variety of four-legged inflatables floated over the crowd or parachuted from the sky. One such creature was the pig, whose control ropes were apparently hijacked by audience members as the first set ended, much to the chagrin of stagehands and organisers. For the second set, *Wish You Were Here*, played in its entirety while animated variants of the album's logo were projected on a circular screen behind the band, was lost in the massive stadium. But the show regained some momentum with a trio of tracks from *Dark Side of the Moon*, re-energising the crowd for their ride home.

I WAS THERE: ROB BRITTON
Floyd had to pay a fine for flying so low over a sold-out stadium.

BOSTON GARDEN
27 JUNE 1977, BOSTON, MASSACHUSETTS

I WAS THERE: EMMY SMITH
My favourite band. I wish I could remember all the details, if you know what I mean. I used to go to the Providence Civic Center, only ten minutes from home, every time they were in town. I would buy tickets for two nights. My boyfriend lived 15 minutes from the Boston Garden and we would get two tickets to the shows there too. We never ever missed a tour. We were wealthy, spoilt and did a lot of drugs, including at the concerts. But we never got in trouble!

My favourite concert was the *Animals* tour because I wasn't tripping but I felt like I was. Pink Floyd were always so much fun! I've also seen David Gilmour solo, and it was a good show but no Pink Floyd – if you know what I mean?

MADISON SQUARE GARDEN
1 – 4 JULY 1977, NEW YORK, NEW YORK

I WAS THERE: ELLIOT TAYMAN
1977 was a landmark year for me. In June, I graduated from High School (like Waters, I loathed school). In July, I saw Pink Floyd perform live on their legendary *Animals* tour...

Animals was released in the US in February 1977. A few months later, Columbia Records staged a publicity stunt in New York City to promote the album. Led by a flatbed truck with a video camera on the rear, live animals were paraded up 6th Avenue to Central Park. On the truck were also loudspeakers blaring out the *Animals* album. Following immediately behind were a few Columbia personnel walking a pig, a sheep and a dog. Following these three symbolic animals were a hundred or so fans, including me. We all believed this event was directly related to the upcoming concerts at Madison Square Garden on July 1st to 4th. So everyone there had the same reason for attending – concert tickets!

Even though we were all fully aware that 1977 was the year of the 'mail order only' ticket sales at MSG (Led Zep, ELP, Yes, Fleetwood Mac, etc.), we all raced back down 6th Avenue to the MSG box office after the parade to see if the tickets were indeed on sale. They were not. We went home that day very puzzled and a bit disappointed.

A week or two later, WNEW-FM began airing spot announcements for another upcoming publicity event. This would be a giant inflatable pink pig launching in Central Park's Sheep Meadow and sponsored by WNEW-FM. The announcements made it very clear that this event was directly related to the ticket sale which, as expected, was by mail order only. The station DJs handed out a 'WNEW-FM Priority Mail Order Form' (these would be given priority by the MSG box office over the regular coupon that would appear in the *New York Times* newspaper concert ad two weeks later). I secured a pile of forms and wasted no time in hailing a taxi to race me to the main post office. There I purchased money orders and mailed off several ticket orders. A few weeks later, I received tickets to three of the four concerts. Better yet, one pair of tickets were for the first night and were on the second row!

The first night, my friends and I arrived at MSG around 7.30pm. Before taking our seats, we walked around the inside of the venue to check out the massive Floyd setup. It was great to see the return of the large round screen (which had made its debut on the previous tour). We noticed that the 360-degree sound system was in place, as well as a long guide wire attached from the stage to the opposite end of the venue. We already knew from reading the concert reviews of earlier shows on the tour that this would be used to carry an enormous inflatable pink pig.

Since the Floyd are known for being a punctual band, we made sure to return to our seats prior to 8pm. A few minutes later, the lights of the near-full venue went out and the familiar opening bass chords of 'Sheep' could be heard emanating from Waters' guitar. Coloured stage lights came on in full force to reveal our four chaps 'in the flesh'. An extra guitarist could also be seen on stage (which we later learned was Snowy White). All during 'Sheep', I could clearly see Waters looking all around the venue. This was, after all, the first time they had played at MSG. With the roar of Gilmour strumming his lead at the end of the song, two mechanical arm-like devices, emitting showers of white sparks, rose from the sides of the stage.

Waters then performed an acoustic solo of 'Pigs on the Wing (Part 1)'. Now it was

WISH YOU WERE HERE

Gilmour's turn to start out with the familiar beginning guitar chords of 'Dogs'. This song won the audience. Not only did we hear Dave sing for the first time that evening, we also heard him break out into some of the best guitar leads of the night. During the long middle segment, several large inflatables were floated to the ceiling – a father, a mother sitting on a couch, a little boy and a car. When the song picked up again, Gilmour sang Waters' first verse (which I noticed immediately). Waters then picked up and crooned the powerful final verse to a standing crowd that was in awe.

Several minutes of applause had passed when Waters, once again, went solo, this time for the second part of the album's acoustical bookend – 'Pigs on the Wing (Part 2)'. However, this live version was different from the one on the album: Snowy White played a sweet lead guitar solo in the middle of the song. Within minutes it was Wright's turn to begin a piece. The beginning organ notes of 'Pigs (Three Different Ones)', the final song to complete the playing of *Animals* in its entirety, drifted out to the crowd. It was during the lengthy mid-section of this song that the pig was finally revealed. With glowing eyes, he travelled along the guide wire from one end of the arena to the other, only some ten feet above the fans seated on the floor.

Predictably, they were throwing things at him and trying to grab his feet (hooves, whatever). After he arrived back to his pen, the song picked up with Wright repeating the opening organ notes. To dry ice smoke flooding onto the stage, Gilmour's brilliant guitar solo finale ended the song and the first half of the show. Waters thanked the audience and announced that the band was taking a twenty-minute break.

Exactly twenty minutes later, the arena went black. I was about to hear my favourite album of all time played live by my favourite rock group. I got goose bumps as I listened to Wright begin what he called 'the band's favourite album'. They performed 'Shine On You Crazy Diamond (Parts I – V)' with Dick Parry making his evening debut on saxophone. During this moment, I couldn't help but think about Syd Barrett, to whom the song was written.

The Floyd moved on to 'Welcome to the Machine', finally using the circular screen. We all watched the most breathtaking animation video we had ever seen! From there Gilmour kicked in and jammed out the opening chords of 'Have a Cigar'. In the absence of the song's original vocalist Roy Harper, Waters and Gilmour shared the task.

It suddenly became quiet in the venue as we anticipated the start of the album's title track, 'Wish You Were Here'. During most of the song the audience sang along, a tradition honoured by audiences since. The song faded into wind sounds that were swirling around the speaker system.

Closing out the second set was 'Shine On You Crazy Diamond (Parts VI – IX)', the better half of the song in my opinion. Dry ice smoke billowed on stage once again. The performance was captivating and the video sequence stunning. This took us to the end of the album, where the band received a deserved standing ovation. They thanked the audience, said their goodbyes and departed the stage.

The fans went crazy until the band returned to the stage ten minutes later for the first of two encores. Waters started playing the all-too-familiar bass intro for 'Money'. The crowd screamed even louder. Gilmour sang, Parry saxed, the famous video was shown, and finally it was back to Gilmour for his electrifying guitar solo. Wright began the second and final encore with his intro to 'Us and Them'. Once again, we heard Parry on sax and watched a video that is still in use by the band today. They played as a true foursome – a unified feeling as they wound their way through a song they all love. I would never again see them perform with that same feeling.

At the end of the song, Waters cursed a local union for insisting the band use the lighting people employed at MSG. Apparently, they didn't do a very good job. I myself could not tell the difference. The band came together at the front of the stage to thank the audience and then calmly left. The house lights came on to a tremendous roar of disappointment by the fans. I wasn't so sad though. I would be seeing it all two more times that week.

I WAS THERE: P DAVID LEVINTON, AGE 16

My first concert. I remember fireworks going off in Madison Square Garden followed by an announcement that unless they stopped, the show would not go on. The fireworks stopped, the show resumed and when the fireworks started again, everybody booed.

OLYMPIC STADIUM
6 JULY 1977, MONTREAL, CANADA

I WAS THERE: ANNA ALEXIOU, AGE 21

I saw them twice. The first time was in Montreal, on the *In The Flesh* tour, where they set an attendance record by playing to over 80,000 people. My boyfriend had broken off with me, and I didn't have a ticket and there was no cell phone or social media – I couldn't get in touch with him so I went to the Olympic Stadium where they were playing, hoping to see him. It didn't happen, but I met lots of interesting people and ended up entering the stadium unnoticed by the garage entry. You couldn't do that today, as security is much different. I saw the last hour. It was a very memorable show.

Clockwise from top left: Mike Quinn got his ass kicked by a young lady who didn't want her ass felt; Andrew Morris remembers the huge Edwin Shirley trucks parked outside the venue; Michael Hutchinson was dragged along to see Pink Floyd by a girlfriend; Ian Tandy felt a sense of triumph when he bagged a ticket four rows from the stage

Clockwise from top left: John Coney (second left) and his brothers (from left) Chris, Rob and Richard – acid was involved; World Series of Rock ticket (Michael McFann); Floyd at MSG in July 1977 (Elliott Tayman)

I WAS THERE: EDDY LEGER

I've never had a visual experience like seeing Pink Floyd at the Big O in Montreal. The band hadn't started yet, and when everyone lit their lighters and held them up, the view of the open sky through the open roof almost made me puke. I could not tell where the lighters ended and the stars began. I don't think I even blinked thoughout the show. I've been in recording studios and I've been at amazing heights (I am a retired steeplejack and been in some pretty tricky stuff), but nothing has ever compared to that feeling of weightlessness. I want that floating feeling again.

Following the conclusion of the North American In The Flesh *tour, Pink Floyd are off the road for two and a half years.*

MAX'S KANSAS CITY
JULY 1977, NEW YORK, NEW YORK

I WAS THERE: MARCO TIKA

I was bartending at Max's Kansas City. Roger came in waving his credit card and said, 'I'm Roger Waters – tell the boss I'm here.' A waitress called Nicole yelled at him, 'We don't give a shit who you are.' I said, 'Roger, I just saw the *Animals* tour – when are you coming back?' 'I'm not.' 'Why not?' 'No place big enough… If you want to see me play, my limo holds seven people. Fly with me to Aspen, Colorado where I'm recording a new album.' I assume it was *The Wall.*

THE WALL RELEASED
30 NOVEMBER 1979

Pink Floyd return to live performance in February 1980 with seven shows in Los Angeles and five in New York, premiering The Wall, *Floyd's eleventh studio album. It peaks at No.3 on the UK album charts but tops the US* Billboard *200 chart for 15 weeks.*

A PEOPLE'S HISTORY OF PINK FLOYD

LOS ANGELES MEMORIAL SPORTS ARENA
7 – 13 FEBRUARY 1980, LOS ANGELES, CALIFORNIA

I WAS THERE: KEN KNOTTS

I got into their music in 1969. The first album of theirs I bought was *Meddle*. I was so sad I missed seeing the *Dark Side of the Moon* tour or 'Welcome to the Machine' with the original line up in the mid-Seventies, but I saw *The Wall* at the Los Angeles Sports Arena in 1980, buying a ticket for $60 from a scalper at a reduced price after the concert had started. That was the only time I saw the line up including Roger Waters and David Gilmour. I later saw David's version of Pink Floyd at the LA Coliseum and at the Rose Bowl in Pasadena a few years later, on the *Division Bell* tour. The show was that good I had to drive over 100 miles one way to see it again in San Diego at the Jack Murphy Stadium a week later!

Then I saw Roger Waters perform the entire *Dark Side of the Moon* and other tunes at the iconic Hollywood Bowl in October 2006 and saw the same show at Irvine Meadows in June 2007. I also saw Roger headline the Coachella Music Festival in Indio, out in the desert by Palm Springs, in April 2008 and perform *The Wall* in Oakland, California in December 2010 and in my home town of Anaheim, California in January 2011.

I am one of only 13 members to be inducted into the American Disc Jockey Awards Hall of Fame. I was inducted in February 2006 at the Sands Hotel in Las Vegas at an annual mobile DJ trade show. Having spent over 30 years as a professional mobile DJ, I have a varied taste in music but one constant has always been my extreme appreciation of Pink Floyd and their music.

I WAS THERE: JOHN RIVERA

The Wall was a Christmas gift from a friend. I played it so much I had to buy another copy. I learned every nuance and sound. When the tour was announced, I sent a money order to the ticket agency and received six first row loge seats. On the day, we drove in from Orange County, parked close enough to hear the sound check and began 'celebrating'. People had come from all over the US, including a guy who had hitched from Minnesota, and two guys from Arizona who ate magic mushrooms with Doritos and drank Michelob beer. We laughed the entire time. A guy in the queue wearing a puffy coat was found to have a huge tape recorder strapped to his back and was escorted away. Getting to our seats, we noticed a partial wall was part of the stage, a plane (with a Red Baron Snoopy on the nose) above three huge movie projectors and speakers either side of our seats and behind us.

WISH YOU WERE HERE

The lights went out and the music started. I saw Mr Screen, which symbolised Floyd playing live. Wow! I still get goosebumps thinking about it. At the end of 'In the Flesh' the plane flew from behind us to stage left and lit up the arena. Did I say 'wow' already? When 'Happiest Days of Our Lives' started, I saw the first of the puppets. Boy, was it a surprise given my 'excited' condition. We just laughed. The Teacher puppet disappeared and the song 'Mother' started. Roger sang 'Mother, should I build a wall?' and roadies began putting bricks in place on stage. In our 'celebratory' state, I mistook the Mother puppet for an animation. Our minds were blown again by the animation for 'Empty Spaces', with the fornicating flowers turning to people and several different shapes. Roger sang the last notes of 'Goodbye Cruel World' through the space left by a single missing brick. He finished the song, the last brick went into place and the house lights went up.

The second part of the show saw the band playing behind the wall, which was used as a screen and then as a stage within a stage when Roger sang 'Nobody's Home' from an outcrop, complete with TV and chair. The sound was so clear and exact. The music sounded just like the recording I had heard at least a thousand times before on my stereo. 'Comfortably Numb' saw David Gilmour sing his part and play his solos from atop the wall illuminated from behind. The band came from behind the wall and played 'The Show Must Go On'. Then 'In the Flesh' was belted through the speakers with the hammers on either side of the wall. Roger was left on stage singing 'The Trial' while an animation took up the entire wall before we heard a loud rumble and the wall crumbled to the floor before us. The crowd went nuts! As the rumble eased, we heard the acoustic instruments for 'Outside the Wall' and the entire band slowly marched out from the side to play the song. The back up musicians then walked off stage to leave the four members of Pink Floyd standing in front of the remains of the wall, taking their bows. My friend Chris and I still talk about that show. I have seen a great many concerts since. This was the magnum opus.

I WAS THERE: SHAWN PERRY

It was a bit tricky getting tickets because they were available by mail order only. Pink Floyd could sell out shows just about any way they chose. The mail order concept eliminated the need to stand in line, but it had its pitfalls. I made the mistake of sending a personal check, which was promptly rejected and returned. Frantically, I sent back a cashier's check and miraculously snagged a pair of seats just off the floor. I had a bull's eye view of a stage that spanned the width of the arena with stacks of cardboard 'bricks' at each side, waiting to be hoisted up by the Floyd's wall builders. Their job was simple: they would symbolically and literally construct *The Wall* between the band and its audience. To my way of thinking, this made a front row seat practically worthless.

There were several layers to the tour that were unique. Because of the massive staging, the show only ran in four cities: LA and New York in the States, and Dortmund and London in Europe. This had a great impact on the demand for tickets far beyond the local regions. The big shots and hardcores would be flying in for this one.

Another unusual element of *The Wall* shows was the absence of Pink Floyd material outside of that album, which they played song by song, as it was recorded and with minimal improvisation. Those who went expecting to see the band in peak form, performing a cross-section of their best-known material and extended jams, were in for a big disappointment.

The tour was destined to be the last one for Waters. Despite his gift for turning a lyric, his ego was killing the spirit of Floyd. After a flurry of vicious legal wrangling, he surrendered the name to Gilmour and Mason, who quickly rehired Wright to reaffirm that Pink Floyd – minus one – was back in business. Pink Floyd the band was transformed into Pink Floyd the brand.

By all accounts, *The Wall* was bound for greatness despite the internal friction. Waters apparently drew his inspiration for the piece from a personal episode in which he off-handedly hawked a loogy at some innocent, screaming Eskimo in the front row of a Floyd concert in Montreal, Canada. He had contempt for his audience and his fellow band members, and yet Roger Waters still needed the power of Pink Floyd to transcend his message. Waters is fond of calling The Wall his, but it will always belong to Pink Floyd.

In rehearsal tapes, I've heard from the tour, Waters attempts to direct the entire production while 'starring' as its main character. He bursts into agitated rages with everyone – the wall builders, the sound and video technicians, Gilmour, Mason – anyone who isn't paying attention. To his credit, the shows were massive, unyielding in format, and someone had to take the reins. But at this point, he just couldn't let go. He tried to stretch it out with *The Final Cut*, his last record with Pink Floyd. Then in 1989, he went a step further and restaged *The Wall* with all its trappings, everything in place, without Pink Floyd. We all know how that turned out…

When it was first released, I listened to *The Wall* constantly. I thought it was the most brilliant album of the day. From the opening chords of 'In The Flesh?' to the final notes of 'Outside the Wall', I was sonically transported by Waters' nightmarish tale of alienation and star-obsessed calamity. The entire piece ebbs and flows without becoming stale and uninteresting. David Gilmour's guitar work is exceptional in its sheer density and power. Add in a team of producers that included Waters, Gilmour, Bob Ezrin and James Guthrie, plus Michael Kamen's grand orchestrations and Gerald Scarfe's grotesque, chaotic illustrations that adorn the album cover and inner sleeve, and *The Wall* is more than just another Pink Floyd album. Even by today's standards, It is a vast and complex production, a mellifluous monster, much like The Who's *Tommy*, full of endless possibilities.

With tickets in hand, I went to the Sports Arena on the fourth night of the Los Angeles run. On the first (and opening) night, about two minutes into the show, a stage curtain had caught on fire. Talk about opening night jitters. I imagine the Floyd and their entourage were at their wit's end in LA. I could only hope that by tonight, the bugs were worked out and everything was ready to go without a hitch.

A few rows behind me were a number of cameras, projectors and special effects gadgets. As I was to find out, the projectors would be screening tons of images across *The Wall* while the cameras took it all in. Jim Ladd, then a DJ for 94.7 KMET and later the DJ/narrator on Roger Water's *Radio KAOS* album and tour, stepped out to make a few stage announcements, which, I understand, were actually written by Waters. Suddenly, the strained tones of a Hammond organ started simmering, the drums pounded out the time, fountains of fire illuminated the stage and the crunching chords of 'In The Flesh?' echoed throughout the arena. 'So you thought you might like to go to crunching chords of 'In The Flesh?' echoed throughout the arena. 'So you thought you might like to go to the show…'. The excitement mounted as a small airplane, attached to a wire, hovered over the audience and crashed into the stage. *The Wall* was underway.

 NASSAU VETERANS MEMORIAL COLISEUM
24 – 28 FEBRUARY 1980, UNIONDALE, NEW YORK

I WAS THERE: JIMMY PARTRIDGE

Back in late 1979 *The Wall* was released. My friend John Morton and I were seniors in high school at Royal Oak Dondero, about 15 minutes north of Detroit, Michigan. (The school's claim to fame is that Glenn Frey of The Eagles graduated from there in the late Sixties.) After the release of *The Wall*, we waited for the tour announcement and then heard the terrible news that there would only be seven shows in LA and five in New York, all in February 1980. Well, that was that – no show for us. John would bring up the idea of going to see them from time to time as February approached, but not seriously. Then, the day before the opening night of *The Wall* in New York, John called me and asked 'are we going?'. I asked if he was serious and he assured me he was. So I called my stepmother to ask if I could borrow her Dodge Colt to 'go up north' for a few days. She said it was fine with her so I scrounged up $200 and John $220 (our senior trip money). Once we had the car, we went by the local gas station where our friends worked and hung out. We topped off the tank and asked who wanted to go – no takers. So off we went, just the two of us, and we were on our way late Saturday afternoon!

Now we both knew we should head east and we had a road map, so we were good. With only $420 to last the length of the trip, we ate nothing but chicken nuggets and pop with some Oreo cookies thrown in. Very late on Saturday night, the gas gauge came on saying we were low on fuel. Every station was closed and as we trudged on it wasn't looking good. We pulled into the small town of Sharon, Pennsylvania hoping for an open gas station but it was closed! We stopped at a 7-Eleven hoping to get directions to an open station. The girl behind the counter looked to be our age and asked if we needed help. We explained that we were going to New York for Pink Floyd but we were on empty. She got excited and exclaimed that her mother worked for the city and drove a truck with two five gallon tanks of gas on it for emergencies. She called her mom and soon we were filling our tank up – and I don't believe she charged us!

With cookies secured from the 7-Eleven and a full tank of gas, we were back on the road. We stopped and slept at a rest stop awhile outside of New York. When we woke up it was the morning of the opening night's show.

New York City! Now we were in search of Madison Square Garden. Shockingly, we found it without too much trouble and parked close by and ran for the doors. We were looking all around for a ticket booth to be open when we were approached by a security guard wondering what we wanted. After explaining what we were after, he laughed and said that the shows were at the Nassau Coliseum out on Long Island. He wished us good luck in getting tickets as the five shows had sold out in two hours, gave us directions and we hurriedly rushed back to our car. The next few hours were spent hopelessly trying to get to Long Island. We went through the Lincoln Tunnel three times before John threatened me with bodily harm if I went through it again (he's claustrophobic). We also went over many bridges many times.

Finally, I saw a police officer sitting in his car and made quite the illegal turn to pull up next to him facing the opposite way to him. He was on his lunch break and nearly spat out his food when I stopped next to him. I was lucky he didn't give me a ticket. He was mad and kept asking where I came from, but after what seemed like 20 minutes he let us go, with better directions to Nassau Coliseum.

We got into West Hempstead, New York in the early afternoon. Once we found the Coliseum, we got a room at a hotel located a mile or two from the venue and started walking around the city looking for tickets. After no luck we headed to the venue. Once in the parking area, I wished I had a camera as there were license plates from California, Utah, Texas… everywhere! I told John that we could spend $150 on tickets and still we'd

Clockwise from top left: Jimmy Partridge bought two t-shirts in NYC; Richard Wolff couldn't believe Gerald Scarfe's milk bill; 800809 John was a glam rocker until he discovered the Floyd; Jimmy Partridge thought he wouldn't get to see the Floyd in NYC

Clockwise from top left: Not everyone loved *The Wall* (Peter Reynolds); Aspi Tantra with his then wife Rosie, who needed convincing to go to Earl's Court; David Cookney avoided drugs when he went to see Pink Floyd, & possibly this failure to mass produce cocaine put him off; Peter Reynolds' ticket for Floyd; Dave Long with fiancee Louise and his autographed copy of *The Wall*

have enough money to make it home. Well, it wasn't looking good as tickets were going for $200-$350 apiece when the original ticket price was $15! After a few hours, John found someone with a stack of tickets, all counterfeit, and advertised as such. The man selling them wanted $50 a tickct and guaranteed you getting in, just no seat. I didn't want to do it but, after several more minutes of no luck getting a ticket through other means, gave the okay. But, whoops, we waited too long as the counterfeit tickets were quickly sold out.

Showtime was at 8pm and it was now a little after 7pm. We started back to the hotel to try again the next night. As we were walking, the traffic was lined up to get inside the parking area. I passed by three guys holding a 'need tickets' sign. A passenger in a car that was stopped to get inside the parking area rolled down his window saying he had tickets. I quickly ran behind the three guys. The man only had two tickets, leaving the three guys to look at each other like 'who's out?' They decided they needed three and I quickly shoved $150 at the man for his two tickets. His eyes got big and the deal was made and sealed with a swig from his vodka bottle. I yelled out to John who had no idea what was going down. Waving the tickets at him, we quickly made for the doors. We each bought a programme (for maybe ten bucks?) and got to our seats. Even now, I could still point out exactly where we sat, maybe ten rows up off of the main floor in one of the corners.

The show was unbelievable and I was so glad we hadn't drunk any booze before the show. Each visual, each puppet was seared into my memory. The teacher puppet freaked me out when I first saw it! A rock 'n' roll show with planes crashing, puppets, inflatables, movies playing on the wall – wow! It was perfect.

After the show, there was a man selling bootleg t-shirts, two for $10. They were the three-quarter sleeve baseball-style shirts that were popular back in the day and we had to get them, and in the two different styles on offer.

On the Monday morning we started for home. Having spent more than the $150 limit, I worried things would be tight but John announced that he 'borrowed' his dad's gas card – we were going to make it! After stopping for gas and putting a quart of oil in, we were on our way. John was driving when, all of a sudden, he said that the oil light was on. 'It can't be,' I said, and told him to get off at the next exit, which happened to be Sharon, Pennsylvania! We pulled up to the 7-Eleven and popped the hood. Oil everywhere! I had forgotten to put the oil cap back on. As we figured out what to do, we went inside and were greeted with 'are you the two guys that were in here Saturday night?' Apparently, our story was the talk of the town. The girl asked if we made it to the show and, after hearing we did, she said she'd pass the word along. John was just finishing fashioning a cap out of a can of pop when I spotted the oil cap hung up on some wires – we were saved again! Thank you Sharon, PA!

We got back on the road and it wasn't long before we hit a major snowstorm. A

Dodge Colt weighs about 1,000 pounds and from the steering wheel to the front bumper it's only like five feet (I'm exaggerating, but you get my drift). I could not see the front of the hood. I relied on following the tail lights of semi-trucks ahead of us. When John counted the seventeenth jack-knifed truck, I told him to shut up. We pulled over at a rest stop so John could call home (I think it was in case we didn't make it). We had no money and no credit cards to get a place to stay so we had to keep going. I totally did about three complete spins on the freeway but managed to keep it on the road. John offered me some gum and not a word was spoken for many miles.

We somehow made it home Monday evening. We had seven dollars, some Oreo cookies, some beer and a fifth of Johnny Walker Red left over. Tuesday morning, we walked into the school with our t-shirts on and a smile you could not take off.

I have wondered if the girls in Sharon remember us and if what we went through would be a big deal if done in this day and age. We had no cell phone, no sat nav system, no credit cards – just guts to do something we wanted to do. I still have my t-shirts and actually had Crashious Roadside make a hoodie out of one of them a few years back. It's my favourite hoodie.

I have been to hundreds and hundreds of shows since but nothing will ever top this – ever!

I WAS THERE: ELLIOT TAYMAN

It was shortly after *The Wall* was released when rumours began circulating of an upcoming tour. However, this US. tour would be vastly different from any previous tour as it would take place in only two cities, with seven nights at the LA Sports Arena and five nights at New York's Nassau Coliseum. On a chilly winter night some weeks later, I found myself at home listening to WNEW-FM, as I usually did back then. Suddenly two DJs began talking about a phone call they had just received. The call was from a Floyd fan who said he had obtained a copy of the next morning's *New York Times* and that it contained a full page advert for The Wall concerts bearing a headline, 'On Sale Today at 8am'. I knew I had to act immediately!

I telephoned my good friend Bob, also a big Floyd fan, and convinced him that we must rush to our local Ticketron at once. He agreed. When we arrived, there was already a car parked, with four people in it trying to keep warm. A few minutes after I parked, a guy from the other car came over and knocked on my window. He asked that Bob and I sign a list that they had started, which we gladly did. By doing that, we had secured spots five and six in what I knew would be a very long line by morning. Feeling more at ease, we settled in for a cold night. Needless to say, we had to keep the car running the entire time to keep us from freezing to death!

The morning seemed to arrive quickly, and sure enough a line of about 200 people accumulated before 8am. The clock struck eight, the line began to move and within two minutes Bob and I were purchasing tickets to what would become one of the most historic rock tours ever! Only three of the five shows were on sale then, so we bought tickets to two of them. A few days later, the tickets for the other two shows went on sale, only this time the New York and New Jersey metro area was blocked out of the sale to allow fans from Virginia to Maine a better chance to get these scarce tickets. All that remained was to wait for the last week of February to arrive…

On February 25th, we pulled into the parking lot at 7pm, one hour prior to showtime. While walking from the car to the Coliseum, the first thing I noticed was all the out-of-town license plates, some from as far away as Colorado! I knew that thousands of fans from across the country (and overseas) were desperate to attend these concerts. This was confirmed by the huge number of people canvassing the parking lot asking everyone 'have you got an extra ticket to sell?' Once inside the Coliseum, my eyes were immediately drawn to the enormous stage centred between two partially built sections of a wall. These two sections protruded out from the seating on both sides of the stage and would eventually be joined together, brick by brick, to form one giant wall across the entire Coliseum. Bob and I made our way to the fifth row, where we had two aisle seats directly in front of David Gilmour's microphone.

At 8pm sharp, the lights went out and local DJ Gary Yudman took the stage. He read a list of do's and don'ts (the usual warnings of no flash cameras, fireworks, etc.). Right at the end of his message, the surrogate band (consisting of backing musicians) led by Roger Waters broke into the powerful opening 'In the Flesh?'. Pink Floyd, with surrogate band in tow, proceeded to give us a beautifully played note-for-note rendition of sides one and two of the double album. It was only during 'Another Brick (Part 2)' and 'Mother' that we were treated to a little jamming, with gigantic inflatables of a school teacher and mother were dangling in front of the wall.

Throughout the set, the band gave us all the pyrotechnics and film footage we had grown accustomed to. The large round screen was used for the films, and the flying plane was brought back to crash into the wall. All during the first half, the roadies were slowly building the wall. We were now at the end of side two and the band was completely hidden behind the wall save for one brick-sized opening. It was from this 'window' in the wall that Waters sang 'Goodbye Cruel World'. One final brick was placed in the opening, bringing the first half of the concert to a close.

After a 20-minute intermission, the band played 'Hey You' while completely hidden behind the wall. A few bricks were then removed to give us a peek at Dave while he played 'Is There Anybody Out There?'. A small portion of the bricks were then unfolded to reveal a living room setting on a platform, on which Waters sat in a chair, facing a working television, and sang 'Nobody Home'. After the next two songs were sung by Waters to a host of wartime film footage projected on the wall, we had arrived at the point that everyone had been waiting for. We were about to hear Floyd's greatest hit, 'Comfortably Numb'!

The high point of the concert had to be Dave's first verse and guitar solo, which he performed on the very top of the wall. After a quick rendition of the next song, the band took a short pause to regroup and allow Gary Yudman, the concert MC, to return to the stage. He again rattled off the same do's and don'ts, reprising his role at the beginning of the show, only this time he read them in a deep robotic voice. Within seconds of his finish, the band started up again to the opening chords of 'In the Flesh'. Now the entire band was in front of the wall (now used as a large screen for the films).

Waters introduced the next song, 'Run Like Hell', and dedicated it 'to all the paranoid people in the audience'. During 'Waiting for the Worms', the best animation sequence was used, the infamous 'marching hammers'. After the next short song, 'The Trial' sequence began with Waters singing before a host of animation clips projected on the wall behind him. At the end of the song, with the chants of 'tear down the wall' echoing throughout the venue, the wall fell. It was knocked over by the roadies with the bricks falling harmlessly between the stage and the audience. The group, led by Roger Waters, then paraded in front of the remains of the wall while playing 'Outside the Wall'.

I'm glad that I was 'one of the few' fortunate fans to have witnessed two of these historic concerts. The last week of February 1980 will live in my mind forever.

I WAS THERE: ALDO BUZZI

I'm a big Floyd fan as I started out first by listening to *Meddle*. In grammar school, I made a stop-motion video with GI Joes and had 'One of These Days' as the background music. I never got to see the *Dark Side* tour but I went to every tour after that. I still remember the *Animals* tour with the giant pig and its glowing red eyes, and *The Wall* tour, where I was doing acid sitting twelfth row centre. I was engulfed in sound and sight and watched in awe as the wall was built and came crumbling down. They are gonna take you home to momma in a cardboard box!

I WAS THERE: PETER WYNBERG, AGE 20

The wall was partially built on both sides. The airplane crashed into the wall during 'Another Brick (Part 1)' and someone placed a giant brick centre stage. As they got to 'Young Lust' in the set, everyone except Roger disappeared behind the wall. He had always complained that people would make noise during the quiet moments in a show. When he said the last 'goodbye' and the final brick was put in place, there was

30 seconds of stunned silence. Most of the second half was played behind the wall. They used the wall as a video screen, with the marching hammers, and then knocked it down. Dave played on top of it. He said, 'The audience are all looking straight ahead and down, and I'm up top and no one knows I'm there. And their heads all lift up, and there's this thing up there and the sound's coming out.' I was standing directly across from Dave. The second guitar solo had a spotlight behind him, and all I saw was his silhouette. I saw Pink Floyd four times in total, and this was one of a kind, but for me it just did not have a Floydian feel about it. I went to boot camp the next day.

I WAS THERE: JAY FRANK, AGE 20

That *Wall* show was both majestic and confusing, kinda like life. I'll always remember sitting in the back of the arena and hearing little kids talking before 'Another Brick in the Wall'. I looked around to see where they were chatting and then realised the voices were coming out of the quad system, tucked up in the back of the arena. The 350-mile train trip from Rochester, New York to NYC was… a 'trip'. People from Chicago were already on the train and the party had begun. It was the first time I had been down to NYC but in reality all we saw was Grand Central Station and then the subway to Penn Station to get to Long Island.

The dose was real good and kicked in soon after the show began, but you could feel the anticipation for this show in the arena. We had heard a little about the Los Angeles shows (eg. the curtain catching fire) but since there was no internet back then, the show was going to be a big surprise! I was a little disappointed to find out that no encore would be played. I was hoping for something like 'Echoes', but afterwards I realised that this was a standalone show – a concept, an opus – and, as we would later find out, a swan song of sorts That wall had to be torn down!

Following the US shows, Pink Floyd bring The Wall *to London in August 1980.*

EARL'S COURT EXHIBITION HALL
4 – 9 AUGUST 1980, LONDON, UK

I WAS THERE: GARETH JONES

The original *Wall* concert in 1980 was performed only 31 times: there were seven consecutive concerts at the Sports Arena in Los Angeles, five performances at the Nassau Coliseum in New York and six consecutive shows at Earl's Court in London, with further concerts in 1981. I was there in 1980 for one of the Earl's Court shows.

I do recall being in about the third or fourth row back from the front, right in the middle. Nowadays it would be almost impossible to get such a fantastic seat, and it would cost hundreds of pounds, if not thousands; but in the 1980s it didn't seem to be difficult.

The concert was probably unique in being the only live concert I have been to when there was no encore, not surprising since the entire set was destroyed at the end. Although maybe the short coda, 'Outside the Wall', could be thought of as an encore? Maybe not. What an amazing gig, and still the most dramatic I have been to. I remember looking up at the construction of what seemed to be 'bricks' made of hardboard being constructed in front of us and wondering if it could collapse at any time.

The inflatables, the lighting effects and, of course, Dave's solo on 'Comfortably Numb' played on top of the wall were all magnificent highlights. But the iconic moment for me was when the bricks started to tumble and the wall collapsed in front of us. What a tremendous experience. Trust the Floyd to go beyond anything anyone had done before.

I WAS THERE: STEVEN HARDCASTLE, AGE 17

I saw them do *The Wall* at Earl's Court, one of the early performances. It was amazing. I went with two old school friends. We all liked Sixties music – The Doors, Beatles, Dylan. Obviously, we took a couple of spliffs with us and some guys in front of us got busted so we were wetting ourselves. Fortunately, we didn't. At the end, the band all ran across the stage in jeans and t-shirts, waving at the crowd.

I WAS THERE: MIKE LOMAX

I didn't earn a lot of money as a lad so I didn't get to a lot of gigs, although I liked buying records when I could. But the Pink Floyd concert was extra special. I acquired one ticket to see them perform *The Wall* at Earl's Court. I lived in the north of England and worked in a factory. I couldn't work a full day and travel down to arrive in time for when the concert started, so I went home for my lunch break and got a workmate to say I was sick on the way home... I couldn't drive so I hired a car, and a guy I knew drove me all the way down in time for the concert. He happily went off to a pub until it was over. I didn't mind sitting on my own as everyone was there to see Floyd. I sat to the right of the stage, way up in the rafters. I had a fair view. I thought it clever that a little room with TV, floor laminate and an armchair appeared in the left side of the wall. The music, the lights, the huge puppets and the rest made for an unforgettable night. I managed to see one of the biggest bands in the world and nicked off work to do it!

WISH YOU WERE HERE

I WAS THERE: IAN NICHOLSON

My fourth Floyd gig was the opening night of the run at Earl's Court in August 1980 for the *Wall* shows. Not only did I attend that gig, but I worked in the arena for the run of the shows, selling pizza slices from a concession stall. My girlfriend (now my wife) was in Canada for four weeks, so I was able to take a week off from my normal job. My brother's boss was a bit of a wheeler dealer and he had the concession, so my brother managed to get me the job there. This was great, as not only could I see the whole show on the opening night, but I was able to go and stand at the back of the arena to watch parts of the show on all the other nights when we had a lull in trade at the stall. I made sure that I got to watch the wall come down every night.

It was a real buzz driving into Earl's Court each day in my eight-year-old MGB, roof down, flashing my pass at the gate to get in past the crowds waiting outside. One huge advantage of getting in early was getting to see the band/surrogate band sound checking in the afternoon, and running through parts of the show in an empty Earl's Court Arena.

These *Wall* shows were nothing short of spectacular, and like nothing I had witnessed live before. They really were on a totally different scale. The closest in rock theatre terms were when I had seen Alice Cooper perform his *Killer* and *Welcome to my Nightmare* shows back in 1972 and 1975 and Genesis with Peter Gabriel at Drury Lane in 1974, and when they did their *The Lamb Lies Down on Broadway* shows in 1975. However, Floyd had moved the goalposts, and rock shows would never be the same again.

I WAS THERE: DAVID COOKNEY

About eight or nine guys and one girl set off from the Commercial pub on Huddersfield Road in Stalybridge, Cheshire. This was a bit of a biker/rocker pub – a lot of hairy people. We made the journey to London in a minibus. It was a bit smelly but the girl, who I didn't know, didn't seem to mind. When we arrived in Piccadilly, we all jumped out. The first thing we saw was a man with sandwich board announcing 'the end is coming' or similar. One of the older guys with us commented that he was a pessimistic bastard, which was funny at the time. We had a few hours to kill before concert so we decided to go to Carnaby Street and Soho. I remember struggling to find it because we asked for directions and nobody understood us. I'm not sure if it was our Northern accents or if they were foreigners, but it was a good laugh. In our ignorance we also accidently walked onto a live film set. We pushed through the crowd without thinking and it was a real 'bloody Northerners!' moment. Still, we giggled like children and carried on. We finally made it to our goal and found a pub where we were all very unimpressed – the beer was terrible!

On the approach to Earl's Court later, one of the guys with us was eager to score some drugs (not me – I wanted to remember Pink Floyd as best I could) and he managed to get some acid tabs off some dodgy looking Middle Eastern guy. They cost him quite a bit of cash, which we also thought was funny.

Now it was concert time. We were up in the gallery, very high up, and the stage looked tiny, but I was impressed by the size of Earl's Court. Once the Floyd started, I was mesmerised. I go into a bubble when I'm watching something I like. Now and again, I would have a quick look at the guy who had dropped the acid to see that he was okay. The wall on stage was building up, brick by brick, the sound quality was amazing and the artwork projected on the wall had me thinking 'who needs acid?', with a quick glance to you-know-who.

Us being so high up spoilt some of the special effects, like the war plane zooming down above us. We could see all the wires and runners, but who cares? They were superb. I loved every minute of it, my favourite song being 'Hey You'. Roger Waters is a genius and sings from the heart.

After the concert, the guy on the acid came over to us and said, 'I've been fucking ripped off. Nothing happened.' We all laughed – idiot! I was happy for him that they were blanks, as he got to see a great, great band.

I WAS THERE: KEITH BRADFORD

I was into New Wave, although not really a punk. I was too old anyway but, being a biker, looked a bit punky. A few of us were down the pub on pool night talking and the conversation turned to *The Wall* concerts that were being talked about on the radio a lot. Phil (who's now in Aus), Terry (RIP) and myself decided to throw a sickie and go up the next day to see it 'for old time's sake'. We went up by car in the afternoon, found a cheap private car park and walked to the station to get tickets from the touts. I thought we paid £50 for three but Phil says it was £20. I can't believe the tickets were that cheap, but we were happy with the deal anyway. We wandered round Earl's Court for a drink and food, all bought matching shoes that were in a sale and then went to the gig. We were downstairs centre so had a pretty good view. A fantastic show! Since then, I've replaced the Floyd vinyl I sold/lost/gave away and have most of their albums, but I'm afraid they don't get played much. I'm listening to Arcade Fire, The Kills, Bowie, Dreadzone, etc. these days. But I enjoyed the V&A exhibition and bought the hardback book, which is excellent.

I WAS THERE: ANTHONY MCNULTY, AGE 16

I was inducted into Floyd by my older brother who had *Dark Side of the Moon* and *Obscured By Clouds*. The Earl's Court concerts took place when I was in my O level year at school. Because it was a Monday night, I had to get off school early. I lived in Southport and got the train to Liverpool for the coach pick up. There were lots of older people on the coach who had obviously been into Floyd for years, with pink hats, tie dyed shirts, inflatable pigs and so on. This was very weird for me as a 16-year-old. The trip to London was accompanied by lots of singing, especially Syd songs, which I confess I didn't know (except the ones off *Relics* which I had bought at Woolies).

Earl's Court was amazing, and huge. The stage looked weird with all the scaffolding up and we didn't know what to expect. Then, as the show continued and the wall began to get bigger, we realised at some point we wouldn't be able to see the band. 'Great,' I thought, 'all that effort and cost to get here and I can't even see them half the time.' But all the cut out sections, with David on top of the wall for 'Comfortably Numb' and the inflatables, etc. made it the most spectacular event I could imagine.

After the show, we found our coach and made our way back to Liverpool. The coach got in at about 3am and there were no trains until 6.15am back to Southport, so me and my mate huddled against a radiator in the ticker collector's cabin on Lime Street Station, imagining we were young Beatles after arriving back from Hamburg! The memory of the Earl's Court show has stayed with me, especially as this was the last time for many years that Rick Wright was part of the band.

I WAS THERE: JOHN GARRETT MORTER

As a teenager in the mid to late Seventies. I was well into the glam rock scene. One day I was sat in my cousin's bedroom and he played *Dark Side* and – boom! – that was it. *Wish You Was Here* was next and I have been a lover of Floyd ever since. Even today, my daily play list includes *Dark Side*, *Wish You Were Here*, *Animals* and *The Wall*. My only live experience of Floyd was the last night of *The Wall* at Earl's Court. Gilmour on top of the wall playing the solo to 'Comfortably Numb' was the most memorable moment, and to this day it is still the best show I have seen live. I did see Roger Waters at Earl's Court and in Zurich playing *Hitchhiker's Guide to the Universe*, and in 2016 I succumbed to the Australian Pink Floyd. Well worth a view.

I WAS THERE: ALAN WINROW, AGE 19

I was 13 and still at school when my friend David said to me, 'Have you heard of Pink Floyd? You wanna listen to *Dark Side of the Moon*.' When I went home that night I spoke to my friend Andrew and he said, 'Oh, I've bought that album.' I listened to it and didn't like it. Because it was so different to anything I'd ever heard before, I couldn't get into it. But after he played it to me quite a few times, I started getting into it. Then I absolutely loved it and after that I was hooked. In 1975, *Wish You Were Here* came out and I bought it and loved it from the first note. And then *The Wall* came out and we went to see them live at Earl's Court.

I went with my sister and a couple of mates. We went the first time they did it and while we were there bought tickets to go back the next night, going all the way back to London from Woking on the train to watch it a second time. The following night was the last night of the Earl's Court run and we couldn't get tickets in advance because they were only selling them on the night. So we went all the way back again and queued up for about four hours. Just as we got to the window, and with about 20 people in front of us, they shut it and said there were none left. I remember my mate saying, 'Come on, let's not be greedy. We've seen it twice,' and I said, 'Yeah, but I wanted to see it again!'

Walking into that auditorium, it was all dark and they had the flags hanging up and there was an overwhelming smell of cannabis – I'll always remember that. It was just so fantastic when they built the wall up, and when they flew the plane into it and the flying pig came over. As they started singing, the roadies came on and started locking the big white blocks together. They kept leaving little gaps, and by the time Roger sang 'goodbye cruel world, goodbye', the last track on the second side, they put the last block in and the lights came up and that was the end of the first two sides. And I thought, 'Well, how are they going to do it then?'

In the second half, when they started playing the third side of the album, there was an animated film show on the wall and they played behind the wall and you couldn't see them. All of a sudden, a trap door came down in the top part of the wall and Roger Waters was sitting in a chair singing, with his lamp and his TV. Then they took a couple of bricks out and you could see them moving around behind the wall and then the pigs came over, for 'Run Like Hell'. They painted the pig black and it had laser eyes and it came right over and this aeroplane came over our heads and smashed right into the wall and blew up. Then David Gilmour got up on top of the wall and did his guitar solo for 'Comfortably Numb' and the spotlight was just on him.

At the end, when they did 'Outside the Wall', the whole thing started rumbling and came tumbling down, a mass of smoke and rubble. All four members of the band then walked out in front of the wall, said 'good night, thank you' and walked off. There was no encore or anything. There couldn't be. It was amazing the way they worked it all out.

I WAS THERE: MICK MORGAN

I was there with my brother-in-law Ian for the third night of Pink Floyd's shows at Earl's Court. We had heard a lot about it and couldn't wait to see Floyd again. The venue was huge and we were in the stalls on the right-hand side of the stage, so quite close. The band came on and started up and the crowd went nuts but then the band stopped and walked off. It wasn't Floyd…! But then the real Floyd members came on and the show started. Guys came on with huge bricks and started to build the wall from both sides of the huge stage. The wall was getting bigger and bigger as the band played and they were soon hidden by this huge white wall. Some bricks were left out for band members to appear through and sing. The puppets and pigs with spotlights for eyes were there, hovering low over the crowd. Gilmour did his thing at the very top of the wall, playing 'Comfortably Numb', but while it was a fantastic solo we couldn't really see him from our seats. At the end, and with a very loud rumbling sound, the wall came tumbling down. It was absolutely amazing to watch.

I WAS THERE: PETER REYNOLDS

I was lucky to see them for a third time in August 1980, performing *The Wall*. Ticket prices were rocketing and this one cost £8.50. Mind you, I saw Roger Waters perform *The Wall* a couple of years ago and it was about a hundred quid more – and not as good! I know it sounds almost sacrilegious, but for me the boys had reached their zenith with *Wish You Were Here* and I never enjoyed *The Wall* as much as the wonderful albums that preceded it.

The last occasion I saw Pink Floyd was in 1988 at Wembley Stadium. There was no Roger Waters by then of course, but they put in a good shift, performing many of their best known tracks accompanied by the usual brilliant light and film show. I have seen Mr Waters (as previously mentioned) at the Manchester Evening News Arena performing *The Wall*, and more recently in Hyde Park, where the concert was accompanied by political rants that frankly detracted from the music.

In 2005, to mark the 20th anniversary of *Live Aid*, Roger Waters and Dave Gilmour put aside their differences to reunite with Nick Mason and Richard Wright to perform four songs as Pink Floyd at the *Live 8* festival in Hyde Park. Tickets were allocated via a ballot. I was unlucky but my 17-year-old daughter Lizzy was successful. Insanely jealous as I was, I impressed upon her how lucky she was to be able to see The Who and Pink Floyd, but in the event, her friend's dad collected her and her friend before the end of the concert and she missed them both.

There are many Floyd tribute bands about. I have seen Think Floyd on a number of occasions. The last time I saw them, they dipped into the less played tracks. They don't disappoint.

I WAS THERE: RICHARD WOLFF

When I was at art school in about 1968, a bunch of us art students went to a 'happening' at the Roundhouse in north London. The Pink Floyd were headlining the event. They were less well known then but created a buzz because they were the group that we were going to see. I think the Pink Floyd were the first group, at least that I can recall, to use the word 'concert' in popular modern music.

I attended an early *Pink Floyd: The Wall* concert at Earl's Court. The show was spectacular. I had worked as an animation cameraman on the film special effects that were projected and used within the show. I was given a complimentary ticket to see the concert as were other crew members that had created the filmed elements of the show. In the programme, I was credited as Richard Wolff Productions.

When I was approached to do camerawork on the concert, by Michael Stuart, the show's assistant animation director, I was invited to meet Gerald Scarfe, the cartoonist who was responsible for the animation design and direction, and the art direction. When I entered his Chelsea studio, I looked at some of the extraordinary pieces of animation artwork. The only thing about the artwork that was disconcerting from my perspective was that it was very much larger sized than it is normally in cartoon films. So I was wondering if it was practical while trying to fathom out the answers to the problems that this would entail. Then Gerald Scarfe asked me if it was possible for me to shoot this scene and I heard myself answering 'yes!'. I wanted to work on this show, it was brilliant. And more scenes followed over time.

The meeting was coming to an end when Gerald Scarfe's glamorous wife, Jane Asher, breezed in like the sun when a cloud passes by and said: 'Gerald, can I have a hundred pounds to pay the milkman, please?' I thought to myself, 'These Chelsea people drink a lot of milk!'

After appearing at Earl's Court in 1980, Pink Floyd play eight shows in Dortmund, West Germany in February 1981 and return to Earl's Court in London for a further five nights.

EARL'S COURT EXHIBITION HALL
13 – 17 JUNE 1981, LONDON, UK

I WAS THERE: JAMES LIVELY

I've seen them twice. The second time was at the Canadian National Exhibition Stadium in Toronto in 1994, when I was sat to the right of the large 'hidden lamp' and sound desk. The first was back in 1981 at Earl's Court, on 15th June. It's an easy day for me to remember as it was my birthday. I was at Chelsea College, the same one as John Deacon of Queen went to. The student union was asked if any of the students wanted to do security. A friend of mine at the time, Keith Head, said 'yes'. On the day, he suggested I tag along to see if he could get me in. I skipped out of an exam an hour early and made it to the show, sitting on the steps to watch. Gilmour was warming up on stage when we got there and Keith asked him if I could stay.

I WAS THERE: BRIAN MCATEER, AGE 16

My very first time seeing Pink Floyd. We drove down from Glasgow and stayed a couple of days with friends. I was amazed by the sheer scale of the stage. The emcee came out, and to create tension and atmosphere he was wearing a top hat and suit and spoke in a very low, deliberate, almost deranged tone. 'Good evening, everyone. The band will take to the stage in five minutes. In the meantime, I would like to remind you of the health and safety…'. This was a deliberate tactic to build the atmosphere and tension. It worked, as he repeated himself about four times for around twelve minutes. 'No, they are not quite ready just yet…'. He went on and on.

Finally, the band came out, Roger battered the emcee on the back of his head with the bass headstock and the compere took a dramatic stage dive off the stage. Boom boom! Straight into the first song. I have the bootleg, and it still makes smile.

Just before 'Run Like Hell', Roger said, 'Thank you very much. Do you like our pig? He obviously doesn't like someone out there, so in an audience this size there are bound to be a few outsiders. Are there any paranoids in the audience tonight? Is there anyone who worries about things? Pathetic! If we spend too much time worrying about things, we won't get on. Together we can rule Earl's Court. Anyway, for those of you undiscovered here, this one's called 'Run Like Hell'. This one we can all clap our hands to. Not yet – wait for it'. Meanwhile, Gilmour was building up the extended riff in the background – just brilliant!

I went back for the Wednesday show. It was a very similar show with similar dialogue at the start and before 'Run Like Hell', with Roger saying, 'Thank you, welcome. Are you gonna have a good time? Does anyone here like pigs? This one is for all you weak people in the audience. Is there anyone here who's weak? This is for you; it's called 'Run Like Hell'. Let's have a clap.'

This was the last complete liver show that Roger Waters, David Gilmour, Nick Mason and Richard Wright played together.

I WAS THERE: PERRY RIDLEY

I could not get tickets for Knebworth in the summer of 1975, or the *Animals* tour in 1977. The next time I would see the band was again at Earl's Court for *The Wall* in June 1981. I went with my ex-wife, who did not stop moaning at how loud it was, and 'how could you pay to see a band that play behind a wall?'. I just sat there stunned and open-mouthed at how good the show was, and how they had made a great album sound even better. The images and film work projected onto the wall were stunning.

I WAS THERE: BOBBY COLQUHOUN

I have been a Pink Floyd fan since the mid '70s. As a teenager, buying albums was expensive as was going to live concerts. The first album I bought was *The Dark Side of the Moon*. I also went to the local cinema to watch *Live at Pompeii*. My first Floyd concert was *The Wall* at Earl's Court in London. Myself and two friends drove over 400 miles from a small village between Glasgow and Edinburgh, in a very old car that I had spent the summer getting back on the road. We took a tent with us and it took us two days to get to London.

The show was an experience. Other bands I had seen, eg. Genesis and Yes, had performed in Edinburgh, putting on a traditional concert. Pink Floyd was completely different. The show was spectacular and the huge auditorium held thousands of fans. All sorts of people were there, from young punk rockers to pensioners. The hall had speakers all around and not just at the front of the stage. The sound swirled around and the quality was excellent. All sorts happened, not just the expected wall being built. I remember model aeroplanes on wires coming from the back of the hall to the front, and the sounds and lights following them before they crashed. The light show was spectacular, as was the projections of cartoons, etc. on the wall. Suddenly, a hole would open in the wall and Roger would appear. The highlight for me was Dave appearing at the top of the wall for 'Comfortably Numb'.

All good things come to an end and, like most fans, I am sad they have fallen out with each other. In the early days they worked well together, producing music that will never die.

I WAS THERE: DAVE LONG

When I was 18, I drove in convoy with six friends in two cars from Bristol to London to see the last extra show of *The Wall* at Earl's Court, which were added to film the crowd sequences for the Alan Parker film. We had a half day on Wednesday as the shops where we worked had early closing, so we could leave at 1pm, plenty of time to arrive in time for the evening show... Except that my mate's Avenger blew its head gasket and we limped into Earl's Court half an hour into the show! The aeroplane crashing was a highlight, as was seeing 'old people' smoking joints!

On the way back, the Avenger burnt through more oil and petrol and I was driving up and down the M4 to get fuel from different service stations. We got back to Bristol at 8.30am and I dropped several of our party at school. Then I got to work and asked for the day off. This was not possible, and I was sent to the Bristol International Wine Festival to put up temporary speakers for the show. I lasted about ten minutes before falling asleep in the job and leaving the company! It was a turning point for me, as I changed course and started a degree in Electronic and Electrical Engineering. Years later, I met Gerald Scarfe and he signed my copy of *The Wall*.

The last concert I saw with my dearly beloved late wife Annie was David Gilmour in Stuttgart. 'Comfortably Numb' was one of many great performances, but hearing 'Fat Old Sun' was a lifetime ambition completed. Our son Daniel is now a fan too. More recently, I have attended Nick Mason's *Saucerful of Secrets* shows at Birmingham and Bath with my lovely fiancée Louise. Pink Floyd's music has touched so many of us and the world is a better place for their wonderful music. We are all grateful to them for it.

I WAS THERE: ASPI TANTRA

I recently met with my ex-wife, Rose, to reminisce about this evening. She fondly remembered how I dragged her down to Earl's Court to see Pink Floyd touring to promote their latest album, *The Wall*. In 1980, I was concerned from newspaper articles – this was before the Internet, remember – that this might be the last ever chance to see Pink Floyd live, as band members were reported to be having artistic differences. As far as I was concerned, Pink Floyd were the greatest, but Rose needed convincing to go. I had followed Pink Floyd since 1973 and *Dark Side of the Moon*, and had by now collected all their albums. In my youth, I saw myself as a budding bass player – another Roger Waters in the making – but now reluctantly have to admit that I possess none of his talent.

I am not good with dates but Rose assured me it was June 1981 as our first daughter, Selina, was born in March 1982. It was at the very start of our relationship, with limited finances as we set up a new home, but things were great. We drove down to London from our home in Norwich in an old Mini which had definitely seen better days. The first sight of Earl's Court was awesome. We were soon inside. We originally sat down in the wrong seats and were asked to move. I was glad we did. Our 'new' seats were way up in the gantry but we could see the whole stage.

Either we got there very early or I was impatient for the concert to start, because it felt like an eternity before the band came on. But when they did, I must have sung every song with them at the top of my voice – Rose remembers that people in the seats next to us kept giving me dirty looks, but I was beyond being embarrassed.

During the show, I was a bit confused about a wall being erected and the band members being hidden, only to pop up in different parts of the wall. I wanted to see the band members playing their instruments – my idols performing. It also seemed to me that the whole show was cluttered, with objects flying around, and I found it difficult to concentrate on any one part. It was, however, the music that kept me enthralled and entertained. It was some months later that I grasped the full importance of the performance. I had not gone to see a traditional concert but a theatrical performance. It was telling a story – a concept I had not grasped at the time due to youth and immaturity, but which I later grew to admire.

Taking Rose home from the pub after meeting to reminisce about Pink Floyd, I put the MP3 player on in the car and selected *The Wall*. Ironically the first song we heard from the speakers was 'The Show Must Go On', which we both agreed – it has to.

Driving home after dropping Rose, I was thinking, 'What if the first song that came on was 'Don't Leave Me Now' and would that have got me to think any differently?' I doubt it, but I was nevertheless very pleased that after all these years, Rose and I did at least agree on one thing – that the night we both saw Pink Floyd performing *The Wall* at Earl's Court was a great evening. And our daughter Selina, who was too busy listening to Take That when she was younger, is now a big fan.

I WAS THERE: IAN NICHOLSON

My girlfriend got her chance to see Pink Floyd when we attended what was my fifth and final show of theirs during their second run at Earl's Court in June 1981. I don't remember there being much difference between this one and the show that I'd seen in 1980, but it still struck me as an incredible, completely original piece of rock theatre. You could see it more than once and still be awestruck by it all. The Gerald Scarfe cartoons were amongst my favourite elements of the shows, working perfectly at conveying the meanings of the songs being performed. A particularly powerful image was that of the fore-playing male and female flowers during 'Empty Spaces/What Shall We Do Now'. Even after more than 35 years, I can still recall that image in vivid detail.

There is so much of *The Wall* shows that is memorable: the wall going up during the first half of the show; roadies wandering across the stage, acting like brickies working with the oversized bricks; the moment that the last brick goes in to end part one of the show, as the word 'goodbye' ends 'Goodbye Cruel World'; the inflatables and giant puppets; teacher, mother, wife, the return of the flying pig, now taking on a more sinister look; the hotel room set coming out of the wall for 'Nobody Home'; and, of course, David Gilmour, atop the wall, for THAT solo, spotlight blazing out behind him during 'Comfortably Numb'. Oh, and I nearly forgot – the wall coming down in a blaze of lights and smoke.

The Wall shows showed a different, more edgy Pink Floyd than I'd seen live before, although the roots were there in 1977 for the *Animals/In The Flesh* tour. More memorable maybe, but more enjoyable? I'm not so sure. It certainly marked a point that would eventually become a very messy divorce and a new start for the next stage of Pink Floyd, one that I sadly did not get to experience live.

Overall, the Floyd shows that I've been to have been amongst the most memorable of all the bands that I've seen since starting to go to gigs in 1972, when I was 15. As a live band, Floyd are up there with other greats that I've seen live; The Who, Led Zeppelin, Genesis, Bruce Springsteen, ELP. All are acts that give everything to their performance, who don't just go through the motions and who leave you wanting more.

Some things that always struck me with Pink Floyd shows is that they were always punctual, starting on time. The sound was always good and clear, and they kept an air of mystery about them, keeping communication with the audience down to a minimum. A very professional band. There was nothing slapdash about the Floyd.

I WAS THERE: MICK MORGAN

I was at Earl's Court for the fifth show (and the last night) with my sister Racheal and brother in-law, Micky Pugh. It was the same show I'd seen in August 1980. We were up in the gods, on the left hand side of stage, but right on top of where the wall would end up. It turned out to be quite a good location as we could see the front and back of the wall plus all the huge puppets and pigs flying around. We had Mr Gilmour in front of us for his awesome 'Comfortably Numb' solo. It was a great sight to see the reaction of the audience in the front of the arena to the wall falling down.

Pink Floyd don't perform anywhere in 1982 or 1983, either as a band or as individuals.

THE FINAL CUT RELEASED
21 MARCH 1983

The last album to feature Roger Waters sees Floyd reach No.1 in the UK but only No.6 in the US album charts.

In March 1984, David Gilmour takes to the road to perform in support of his album About Face. *In June, Roger Waters plays his first solo shows, promoting* The Pros and Cons of Hitchhiking.

EARL'S COURT EXHIBITION CENTRE
22 JUNE 1984, LONDON, UK

I WAS THERE: ALEXANDER G MITLEHNER

I was lucky enough to see all the members of the famous four-piece line-up live in concert, though sadly not together. I very nearly got to see *The Wall* shows with my dad back in 1980, but the tickets had all sold out (you had to apply postally in those days, long before the Internet so it was something of a lottery!) and I had to wait until 1984 to see any of *The Wall* played live. Roger Waters announced that he would be touring that summer to promote his album, *The Pros and Cons of Hitchhiking*, including Mr Eric Clapton on guitar! I'd always loved the music of Slowhand so this promised to be quite a show… I went along with two friends from school (it was in the middle of our A level exams, so it provided a welcome distraction from our studies). As wide-eyed 18-year-olds, it was the first time any of us had been to Earl's Court and we were taken aback by its sheer size. It was the largest indoor venue in London at the time. The band were superb, of course, and the programme was designed by Gerald Scarfe so it had a definite *Wall* feel to it and they went straight in with the Floyd numbers! It was magical, with some great tracks, from 'Set the Controls for the Heart of the Sun' and even 'If' from *Atom Heart Mother*, as well as tracks from *Dark Side of the Moon* and *Wish You Were Here* (including 'Have a Cigar', which is rarely performed live). They also performed three from *The Wall*, including 'Nobody Home' which included Roger sat in a bedsit room suspended high up off the stage, as in *The Wall* shows. It was also great so see a track from *The Final Cut* performed live for the first time, 'The Gunner's Dream', which is still my favourite from that album.

1985 and 1986 are again fallow years for Floyd watchers. The A Momentary Lapse of Reason *tour runs from 1987 to 1990 to promote the album of the same name, concluding with a UK show at Knebworth Park. The first Pink Floyd tour without Roger, it's also the first tour in ten years to feature music other than from* The Wall. *Playing 197 shows in total, the tour is witnessed by 5.5 million people and in 1987 and 1988 grosses a combined $135 million.*

A MOMENTARY LAPSE OF REASON RELEASED
7 SEPTEMBER 1987

The first Floyd album not to feature Roger Waters reaches No.3 in the UK and US album charts. Only in New Zealand does it top the charts.

LANSDOWNE PARK
9 SEPTEMBER 1987, OTTAWA, CANADA

I WAS THERE: MARIO LEFEBVRE
I started as a journalist in Montreal for a French language rock newspaper not unlike *Circus* and *Creem*. The paper was named *PopRock* and focused mainly on Prog and major

rock bands like Led Zep, the Stones and solo Beatles. But in Quebec, Pink Floyd were always demi-gods and we covered them extensively, including the 1975 show at the Autostade Stadium where they premiered what was going to be the *Animals* album a few months later. I moved to become a promotional representative for record companies in 1977, and in 1980 I moved to CBS where I got to work with Pink Floyd and their solo projects. When the group called it quits after *The Final Cut*, David toured his *About Face* album and did very well as a solo act. So did Roger with *The Pros and Cons of Hitchhiking*, with Eric Clapton on guitar.

But in 1987, when Pink Floyd reunited without Roger, Canada was home base because of the Michael Cohl connection, him being the global promoter. The band rehearsed for many weeks in Toronto in a huge airport hangar and I was fortunate to be invited to attend one of the last rehearsals for the tour. It is something I will never, never, never forget. I won't forget the wit, charm and class of their manager, Steve O'Rourke, and the entire quality of the production team including lights designer Marc Brickman and the Fisher/Park designing team. David, Richard and Nick were the most pleasant rock stars one could ever meet, as were the rest of the players who complemented their line-up.

The very first show was an outdoor event in Ottawa. It was raining and everything went wrong. The pods were not functioning properly, the band was (obviously) nervous and the crowd was okay but not great. After the show, everybody agreed that the big test would be the three shows at the Montreal Forum, that had been sold out on day one and gave the band the proof that everybody was willing to give Pink Floyd a chance, even if it was Roger-less.

MONTREAL FORUM
12 – 14 SEPTEMBER 1987, MONTREAL, CANADA

I WAS THERE: MARIO LEFEBVRE

Rolling Stone magazine assigned their best journalist, David Fricke, to attend and investigate this new version of the legendary band. When the show ended, the fans went crazy and no one left the venue. Because they were playing the next two nights, no roadie was taking down the equipment. So the fans clapped, yelled and cheered for a good ten minutes. Backstage, Steve and David were asking legendary promoter Donald K Donald and myself what was the next step. David said that there was one song that had been rehearsed in the hangar and which wasn't part of the set list: 'Shine On You

Crazy Diamond'.

We all said 'that seems like a good way to thank the fans', and the band went back on stage and played all 21 minutes of the song. The crowd went ballistic and that night, Pink Floyd v2 was born. Fricke and *Rolling Stone* reported it that way and, as we say, the rest is history.

JFK STADIUM
19 SEPTEMBER 1987, PHILADELPHIA, PENNSYLVANIA

I WAS THERE: CHRIS BRISBIN, AGE 22

I was a big fan of Pink Floyd's since before *The Wall*. I was 14 years old when that album came out. It's all you heard on the radio. Me, my brother and a few friends went to JFK Stadium in South Philadelphia not too long before it closed for good when they played, minus Roger Waters. We were walking to the stadium in the early evening. Dark low clouds were hovering over the stadium, and it looked as if it was going to pour down with rain. During the first part of the show, we stood on the field. Then, at the intermission, we went into the stands to watch the rest of the show. They did two sets. The first one was all new music and the second was all the classics. I remember everyone singing to 'Wish You Were Here', and the final song 'Run Like Hell' which got very loud at the end. There were over 80,000 in attendance despite the light rain.

CANADIAN NATIONAL EXHIBITION STADIUM
21 – 23 SEPTEMBER 1987, TORONTO, CANADA

I WAS THERE: GORDON PHINN

Having turned down the chance to squeeze into a van for the six hour ride to Montreal for the stadium gig that became in Floyd iconography 'the Roger spit gig', my friends who did brave the bumps to sardine themselves into the 70,000 plus audience reported a great show and little rowdiness, and then missing the 1980 *Wall* shows, the closest of which was still an entire country away, I was more than pleased to drive the ten miles into Toronto for these three CNE shows (although I missed the first hour of night one as an extremely rare showing of the Jack Nicholson directed

Drive, He Said was playing for one night at one of our repertory theatres – and hasn't played since). Thus, I arrived late to hear the band in full flight and playing a fine blend of old and new with fire and sophistication.

As the tour progressed, they polished themselves into something like perfection and by the time they filmed the Versailles and New York gigs for *Delicate Sound of Thunder*, they were the very incarnation of it. Some would say they were a little too perfect for their own good. The silk smooth editing is one of the highlights of what of course is a VHS, impressive at the time but somewhat grainy now. Until digitisation is approved, I remain undecided on the matter but their live rendition of the *Momentary Lapse* songs breathed life into their rather stilted studio versions. Having jigged about in delight for three nights (I was only 35!) outside the low gates of the CNE along with many others (the sound spilled over volcanically and accurately), I can assure those too young to have had the pleasure that this was, as *Melody Maker* said of *Animals*, 'killer Floyd all the way', and on all three nights. After years of legal hassle and nastiness all round, the lads were back and Floydheads were delirious.

This was the lawsuit-haunted *Momentary Lapse of Reason* tour, and the threat of Roger's lawyers descending on venues with writs and suits kept many promoters shy until Toronto's own Michael Cohl stepped up to the plate and actually booked the lads, now reunited with the irreplaceable Richard Wright and the intriguing addition of Tim Renwick on second guitar, whom I hadn't heard of since he'd played lead for Al Stewart's band years before. I do recall reading at the time of his Cambridge roots and him being a member of Syd's scout – or was it cub? – pack. In a world of Gilmour copyists, right up to Roger's 2017 touring outfit with Dave Kilminster, Tim's soloing as evidenced on the *Delicate Sound of Thunder* VHS stands out for its originality. All in all, it was a three-day Floydfest to gorge on in the years to follow as they shepherded themselves into another version of the endless world tour.

PROVIDENCE CIVIC CENTER
16 & 17 OCTOBER 1987, PROVIDENCE, RHODE ISLAND

I WAS THERE: STEVE MCGINLEY

I saw the *Momentary Lapse of Reason* tour five times. I think what's interesting about that tour is how the opening changed. The first six to ten shows or so started with 'Echoes' and then went into 'Signs of Life' with the video playing on the round screen of the guy rowing in the channel. It was an awesome opening, and I say opening, because 'Echoes' was played in the dark. I personally preferred it over the 'Shine On' opening. I had been seeing hard rock arena shows for ten years at that point. This was bigger than any show

I had ever seen by a large margin. My favourite effect was the floating and roaming UFO-like light racks they had. I'm not even sure how to describe them.

The next two times I saw them would've been at the Providence Civic Center in Providence, Rhode Island. Providence is about halfway between Boston and New York and it's always had a great music scene and a great nightlife scene. They have some really long-running clubs down there. But it's a smaller city, their arena is probably only 12,000 and when Pink Floyd put that show in there it was incredible! The pig was so low, people could jump up and hit its feet and they had the thing rocking. The band at this point was on fire. On one of the two nights and it being a small arena, me and a few other people were really acknowledging Scott Page's saxophone solos. He ended up being right up front next to Gilmour one night, with Scott getting the greater applause for the *Dark Side of the Moon* pieces he was featured in. And David Gilmour acknowledged that with a smile on his face.

CAPITOL CENTER
20 – 22 OCTOBER 1987, LANDOVER, MARYLAND

I WAS THERE: JEFF ALLEN

I went to two shows – on 20 and 22 October – and my best memory is of the first night, when I had fifth row seats. It was the closest to the stage I had ever been up to that point. Mr Gilmour was right in front of us playing his lap steel. I was unaware of what was going on behind me, but he kept staring at something. I turned around to see the giant pig. The snout was hung up on the Cap Center scoreboard. He kept playing and looking up at the pig. I believe it was finally freed, to the roar of the crowd. Although it was a slight mishap, it will always be my best memory – him playing and watching that pig.

RUPP ARENA
7 & 8 NOVEMBER 1987, LEXINGTON, KENTUCKY

I WAS THERE: BRYAN BURGESS

I saw Pink Floyd while I was in college. It was the show they added after the first one sold out. It was also the first real concert I ever saw in an arena-type venue and it was amazing. Afterwards, my roommate and I sat in the car stunned by what we had just seen and my ears rang for two days afterwards. It is still the best concert I've ever seen. I also saw Roger Waters in 2017 in Louisville, Kentucky. I tell my friends that I've seen four-fifths of Pink Floyd!

I WAS THERE: BRAD CAGE

In the fall of my senior year of high school, Pink Floyd played back-to-back shows at Rupp Arena. My small group of friends had worshipped Floyd our whole lives. We went to both shows. Later that year, we were given the annual 'senior survey' – a summary of the pop culture superlatives from that year – as voted on by the high school's senior class. My friends got together and coordinated our answers so that Floyd swept the awards, all the way down to 'favourite colour' being voted as pink. The two-page spread in the yearbook that revealed the results mimicked art from The Wall and is a point of pride for all of us involved with the scheme to 'stuff the ballot box'. (The yearbook committee hated the results so much that they included the runners up in every category.)

COPPS COLISEUM
10 NOVEMBER 1987, HAMILTON, CANADA

I WAS THERE: DAVID CLAYTON, AGE 20

I've seen Floyd three times, David solo in 2016 and Roger solo in 2017. Floyd was my first real concert experience. I'd been fixated on them for a year or more and was deeply involved in collecting the back catalogue. My life *was* Pink Floyd. To read that they were getting back together – well, mostly – and touring was a dream come true. My life over the past year had not just been collecting the classic albums but rooting through bootlegs, books, posters and endless miles of oddities. Local record shops I visited had a basement of vintage wonders, spanning many bands and eras.

   Well, the day came. A friend and I rented a limo at great expense, filled the bar with beer, dropped some purple microdot and headed for the show. It was a day never to be forgotten – great floor seats, the screen, the crowd. 'Echoes' was the opening tune, later changing to 'Shine On...'. I was very happy with 'Echoes'. I had a great time. I was part of the Pink Floyd experience. We had a limo ride home, my ears still ringing from the crash of cash registers and clocks. My first concert was a blast and my Pink Floyd journey was complete.

HOOSIER DOME
12 NOVEMBER 1987, INDIANAPOLIS, INDIANA

I WAS THERE: DOUG DELANEY

The Hoosier Dome in Indianapolis was a huge venue and perfectly suited for a Floyd show. It was November and there was a slight chill in the air. I live an hour south of Indy, so for the trip up there we had eaten some magic mushrooms. We had ten people packed into a van that we had rented. We found our seats and I didn't move a muscle until the show was over. The burning bed made its appearance and crashed into the side of the stage. Awesome. 'Shine On' was the opener as usual. At this point, I noticed the group were sporting shorter haircuts, especially Gilmour, who had also added a few pounds. They played several tracks from the new album, mixed in with a couple of *Wish You Were Here* songs and most of *The Dark Side of the Moon*. 'Set Your Controls for the Heart of the Sun' was in there somewhere also. That was when the pig made its appearance. A huge flower appeared from the floor of the stadium also. I had noticed this huge black 'box' sitting on the floor but figured it was an electrical supply of some kind (I wasn't actually thinking real clear). I can't recall which song was playing at the time, but a gigantic flower arose from this black box and pretty well caught everyone by surprise. It was lit up in magnificent colour.

Halfway through the show, some overzealous fan fell, or leapt, from the high seats to about 30 feet down. The show wasn't affected by it, but I could see the stadium personnel taking care of it. The guy wasn't hurt too bad. He must have been drinking alcohol. It became a side story to the amazing show we saw that night. This was the best show I'd ever seen at this point in my life. I had decent seats and could see everything well. Oddly, there were no songs from *Animals*. The female singers were too awesome for words. It was beautiful. They also played a few songs from *The Wall*, and I believe they ended the show with 'Run Like Hell'. This was an unforgettable show and they outdid the *Animals* show. I had broken up with my girl about five months earlier, although we were still together when I bought the tickets and endured 14 hours of standing in line. So I ended up taking her to the show and we had an amazing night together. The stage setup was astounding. Lasers, bombs, the round screen… just way too awesome to perfectly put into words. Easily one of the most memorable nights of my 60-year-old life.

FRANK ERWIN CENTER
19 & 20 NOVEMBER 1987, AUSTIN, TEXAS

I WAS THERE: LANCE SAVAGE

I figure I've been to over 50 concerts and seeing Pink Floyd on the *Momentary Lapse of Reason* tour was the first time I was overwhelmed and sobbing. But it was just during one song and it's not even a personal thing. Everyone my age (I'm 51) can relate to this. Pink Floyd were a staple of AOR radio in the Seventies and early Eighties. Everybody knew all their songs and I think that's kind of unique to them. Everybody had all the records. They were mandatory purchases. Seeing them in Austin I had really high hopes, because you just didn't know when you were ever going to have this chance again.

I had decent seats, albeit not floor seats. The show did not disappoint. I was pretty pleased with all the stage elements – the flying pig, plane crash, flying bed, etc. They were a huge band and they had to have a dozen performers. It was a wonderful evening. The lights in front of the stage really weren't used much until the last encore, 'Run Like Hell'. In fact, a lot of the stage lighting made its debut during this song and it was literally breathtaking. Coming out of the middle interlude to the main melody that we are all so familiar with, in combination with seemingly a million lights going every which way and explosions every fourth beat, was overwhelming. I had walked down to the floor and I felt the heat from those blasts and my body felt the sped-up beat of the closing of the song, which grounded to a slow massive explosion. I was already in tears by then. Nothing has ever topped that experience. Go on YouTube and watch 'Run Like Hell' from *Pulse*. You'll see what I mean.

I WAS THERE: MARTIN BARROWS

I had started collecting and listening to music in the late Sixties and early Seventies. Being from a small town and with limited access to anything music related, I bought albums based on the artwork so if memory serves me, my first Pink Floyd album would have been *Wish You Were Here* or *Dark Side*. I can remember hearing tracks from *Dark Side* on WLS Radio out of Chicago. I would keep that radio station on all night – I couldn't pick it up in the day – and go to sleep and wake up to it. I drove 13 hours from Tennessee to Texas to see this show and U2 performing *The Joshua Tree* the very next night. In 1994, I camped out in the snow in February for 19 hours to be one of the first in line for tickets. I remember the *Pulse* tour was outside in a football stadium and complaints from surrounding neighbourhoods due to noise and traffic stopped any more concerts at that particular venue for several years, until the Stones came through on their *Bridges to Babylon* tour.

REUNION ARENA
21 NOVEMBER 1987, DALLAS, TEXAS

I WAS THERE: ANNA-MARIE A DIAZ, AGE 18

I saw Pink Floyd for the first time in 1987. I was 18, as were most of my friends. My 19th birthday was a few days later and the money for the ticket was a birthday gift. The concert was during Thanksgiving weekend. I remember that because we had a half gallon bottle of Wild Turkey. I went with my best friends Debbie and Anna and a couple of friends of theirs. Debbie was 16 and it was her first concert.

I spent between $25 and $30 on the ticket. We're from Fort Worth, about 40 minutes from Dallas, and going to Dallas was always a big deal. Half the fun was the ride getting there. Since we all got our tickets at separate times, we didn't have seats all together but we did end up sitting together in the nose bleed section, which turned out to be pretty cool. They opened up the show with 'Shine On You Crazy Diamond'. The flying bed flew right above our heads, which really tripped us out. The green laser lights were so cool and new. That was the first time I remember seeing a laser light show. The music sounded so perfect – songs from *Wish You Were Here* as well as *The Wall*, *Animals* and, of course, *Dark Side of the Moon*.

I wish I could remember more details but truth is there was a lot of pot smoking going on at the concert and it's been nearly 30 years. Overall it was a great show. We were not disappointed at all. It was well worth the $30.

K.A.O.S. On the Road *was Roger Water's tour to support his album* Radio K.A.O.S. *The 37-date tour started in North America on 14th August 1987 and concluded with two British shows in London that November. It just happened to overlap with the* Momentary Lapse of Reason *tour.*

WEMBLEY ARENA
21 & 22 NOVEMBER 1987, LONDON, UK

I WAS THERE: ALAN WINROW

I went to see Roger live when *Radio K.A.O.S* came out. That was a strange experience. He had a telephone box in the middle of the auditorium and you could go in and pick up the receiver and talk to him live on stage. He did one track from his new album and then a Pink Floyd track, then a track from his album and then another Pink Floyd track. It was amazing.

WISH YOU WERE HERE

REUNION ARENA
23 NOVEMBER 1987, DALLAS, TEXAS

I WAS THERE: KENNETH PATTISON

I worked for the local promoter setting up vendors and some sound and light equipment. But for this show I worked setting up the after party. There was a huge space with tables full of food, liquor, lights and sound. They hired about a dozen local stripers to host the event. I got to watch the concert and hung out at the party until things got going. It was quite late at this point. It was an awesome evening that I will never forget.

SPORTS ARENA
26 NOV – 1 DEC 1987, LOS ANGELES, CALIFORNIA

I WAS THERE: TIMOTHY ALEXANDER

My buddies and I went to see Floyd. We moved into vacant seats closer to the stage, thinking we'd get a better view. We should have taken a clue from the roped over section of seats adjacent to where we were now seated. A floodlight came on and illuminated a giant bedframe that descended from the rafters towards the stage. When the bedframe reached the stage, a giant fireball was released and all of us felt the flash of it!

OAKLAND COLISEUM
4 DECEMBER 1987, OAKLAND, CALIFORNIA

I WAS THERE: JOHN JOHNSTONE

I am from the UK but in 1987 I was living in Novato, California, working in IT for an insurance company. I'd always loved Pink Floyd since seeing them playing 'See Emily Play' on *Top of the Pops* in 1967, so it was a no-brainer when one of my English colleagues said that he had a couple of spare tickets for Pink Floyd's gig at the Oakland Coliseum and would I like them? Of course I would!

This was the first time that I had been to the Oakland Coliseum and I was impressed by the size of this indoor arena, which was full to the rafters with like-minded fans. The sense of anticipation leading up to the start of the show was palpable. There was a rather attractive scantily-clad blonde girl sitting at the back, opposite the stage, and she took many people's attention until the opening drone of 'Shine On' started. After that, no contest!

Once Pink Floyd started, it was amazing... the lights, the songs, the energy. I hadn't realised that the band had been augmented by additional musicians and a few songs from the latest album were new to me. No matter, they were all brilliant. The first half seemed to be over before it started but 'Shine On' and 'On The Turning Away' were quite memorable. 'Shine On' literally gave me shivers down my spine.

During the break, I managed to get a tour t-shirt, which I still have to this day (but it is a now a tad too small to wear). The second half started with a real favourite of mine, 'One of These Days', and the quadraphonic sound was unreal, with the bass notes swirling all around the arena. I could have listened to the song all night. Highlights for me were 'Wish You Were Here', 'Another Brick in the Wall (Part 2)', an amazing 'Comfortably Numb' and a rip-roaring 'Run Like Hell', with the drones going crazy on stage. I came away from the gig with my mind absolutely blown, and couldn't have been more grateful to my colleague for passing on the tickets.

I still have my ticket stub for my seat in section 202, row U, seat 7, and was lucky enough to get Nick Mason to sign it years later, at his book-signing tour in Norwich, long after I had returned to the UK. I never managed to see Pink Floyd again but have been fortunate to see David Gilmour, Roger Waters and Nick Mason on their solo tours at least twice each over the years. The songs and music of Pink Floyd are timeless, and my three sons have grown up to enjoy and appreciate the magic that they convey.

KINGDOME
8 DECEMBER 1987, SEATTLE, WASHINGTON

I WAS THERE: JEFF RHYNER

Pink Floyd were in top form all night. The show started with the lights going out and the opening notes of 'Shine On You Crazy Diamond' filling that huge building. When they got to the first chorus, we all went nuts! The entire show was one spectacular song after another. They played all their best songs from every album. I think everyone in attendance would agree that it was truly a concert to remember.

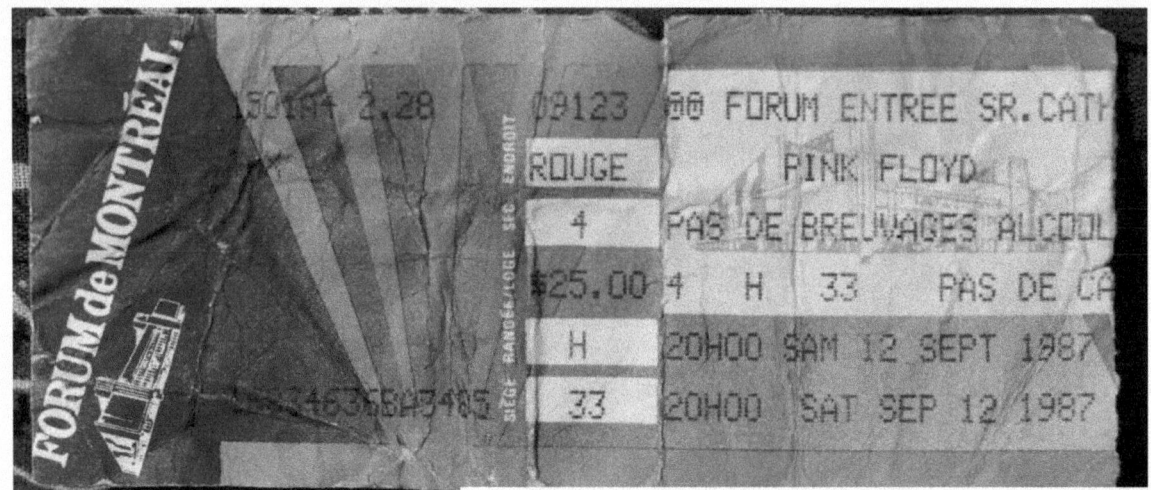

Clockwise from top left: Steve McGinley's ticket for one of the five *Momentary Lapse of Reason* shows he saw; Steve McGinley (right); Mario Lefebvre with David Gilmour, and with Nick Mason

Clockwise from top left: David Clayton rented a limo to take him to his first Floyd show; John Johnstone saw Pink Floyd at Oakland Coliseum; 880511 Jacques Delisle (right) and his buddies wore food vendors uniforms to get in for free; Mike Allen first saw Pink Floyd in 1988, but he also saw 'four in '94'

ASTORIA
23 DECEMBER 1987, HAMPTON, UK

1987 concludes for Pink Floyd with Roger and David meeting (along with David's accountant) aboard David's houseboat on the River Thames to hammer out a legal agreement. The agreement gives David and Nick Mason rights to use the Pink Floyd name in perpetuity. Roger's slice of the action includes control over The Wall.

1988 sees Pink Floyd embark upon a world tour, taking in New Zealand, Australia, Japan, the United States, Canada, Europe and the UK, playing 98 dates in total between January and August.

WESTERN SPRINGS
22 JANUARY 1988, AUCKLAND, NEW ZEALAND

I WAS THERE: GLEN THURSTON

As a child born in the mid-Seventies, I was brought up on the super sounds of the '70s. My parents discovered *The Dark Side of the Moon* from a stoner hippie living next to them in Mount Albert, Auckland so it was part of the soundtrack of my very early years. There it remained a curious part of their tape collection – the strange-looking album with the triangle and rainbows on it that sounded nothing like the others.

In 1987, Pink Floyd announced a single show in Auckland at Western Springs, which was (and is) perhaps New Zealand's premier outdoor venue. Mum and Dad obviously thought this was something worth doing and secured tickets, which were not cheap. $40.70 in New Zealand was a lot of money. The purchase must have been done prior to the impact of the 1987 stock market crash because, if the gig had been one year later, then there was no way we would've gone.

I started playing guitar at school when I was nine or so, and my parents nurtured that, and took me to my first gig, The Shadows, when I was ten years old. Because of this interest, they asked me if I wanted to go to see Pink Floyd. I said yes, not knowing what to expect. In the weeks leading up to the show, I'd got a Walkman for Christmas and was listening to heaps of U2's *The Joshua Tree* and Midnight Oil's *Diesel and Dust*. I gave very little thought to Pink Floyd.

On the day of the show, we left our home in Paraparaumu early in a secondhand brown Ford Cortina 2000E for the 600 kilometre journey north to Auckland. One of my parents' mates, Bill, came with us, so there were three adults and two kids, aged twelve and eight, in the car. The trip north was fast, hot and filled with lots of fun, games and stories of places and people. The aged *Dark Side of the Moon* tape finally crapped out. We arrived in Auckland and dropped my brother off at our family friends; they had a Commodore 64 computer and I felt jealous that I'd miss out on playing that.

From our motel in Mount Albert, we walked to The Springs, joined by an increasing stream of people of many backgrounds and ages, from kids to grandparents. Many cars had made the journey, decorated with Pink Floyd-related colours and images. It became clear that this was a big event and I kept close to my parents as there were so many people. We got searched by security at the gate, which we thought was weird, then walked into the stadium and saw a massive black stage with pictures on the scrim of the Pas, and speakers around the crowd. Again, the number of people struck me, as there were probably more people here than in my whole home town!

The stadium was already really full, but my parents found a spot roughly in the centre, on the top of the speedway seating area. Mum said it was a squeeze, but we were helped out by a gang member who picked me up and popped me into a spot. 'That young one needs a good view,' they apparently said. We were also sat next to a teenage girl who had a pair of binoculars that she shared with us throughout the night.

Although it was a hot evening, and there was a lot of booze and a thick cigarette haze (plus, I later found out, weed), the crowd was cheeky and friendly. Every vantage point was filled with people – on fences, trees, lighting towers, and even the toilet blocks! All up, it was estimated that approximately 60,000 people were there.

It felt like a long wait for it to get dark and the show to commence. We had a bunch of songs on the PA (I recognised 'Uncle Albert' by Paul McCartney) and there was a string quartet for the support act, that seemed to go down well at the start. But the longer it went on the less they were appreciated. This was followed by heaps of sound effects that buzzed around.

Finally, the band started and so it began. The songs were epic, the performances of the players, the power of the sound, the lighting and the props were incredible. Lasers, lighting droids, dry ice, a mesmerising circular 'Mr Screen', a pig on the wing, exploding flying beds, films and a mega-mirror ball. The stadium trees were lit up by the effects, so it must have looked great from the band's perspective too. For a just turned 12-year-old, it was a stimulation overload. Looking to my parents to help understand what we were experiencing was not much help as no one in New Zealand had seen anything like this before. It seemed to go on for a long time, yet not too long either. I recognised the songs from *The Dark Side of the Moon* and also 'Another Brick in the Wall (Part Two)', but none of the others. But when I did have all the band's tapes, I could recognise what had been played and what was not – the songs were seared into my brain. Everyone seemed happy and dazed afterwards as we inched our way out of the venue. We were approached by someone selling programmes and dearly wanted one, but the cost was too high.

The crowd was so big that they spilled onto the motorway and stopped the traffic as everyone dispersed. It was one of the latest times I had stayed up and my ears were ringing until the next day. The rest of the weekend was spent seeing friends and buying tapes at the record stores. My parents bought *Wish You Were Here*, *A Momentary Lapse of Reason* and a replacement copy of *The Dark Side of the Moon*. I'd been saving up for some other tape, but ended up getting *The Wall* instead. From there, it was Pink Floyd everything for many years, due in no small part to the diversity of their back catalogue. Interest in other artists grew, and I've seen many more live shows, always seeking some of that magic that I witnessed on that hot summer evening. That 1988 show was, in many ways, a fleeting glimpse into adulthood and its opportunities, and it created a shared connection with others that endures to this day.

I WAS THERE: GRAHAM HOOPER

I saw Pink Floyd at Western Springs in Auckland New Zealand. Dave Gilmour was the reason that I tried to get close to the front of the stage. I had a camera and managed to get past security checks and catch some great photos…

ENTERTAINMENT CENTER
27 – 30 JAN & 1 – 5 FEB 1988, SYDNEY, AUSTRALIA

I WAS THERE: KYLEE MARIE

They played a ten-night run. I had the ticket for years in my wallet until someone stole my wallet. I'm still gutted about that. It was the best concert. The lighting and display were phenomenal. We had seated tickets on the side where the pig with the laser eyes was on. He was zooming up and down above us and would swing, shining his eyes around. Because of the side seating, I didn't even realise there was a big screen display behind the guys on stage, until I bought the DVD. A fantastic night.

ENTERTAINMENT CENTRE
7 & 8 FEBRUARY 1988, BRISBANE, AUSTRALIA

I WAS THERE: PAUL MCMULLEN

I've been going to concerts and gigs (large and small) since 1972, including working for four years in the Nineties as a local crew roadie. For all the great acts and events I have seen, nothing quite matched that Pink Floyd concert. It is well known that Floyd present cutting edge technology across the board from stage sound, PA, staging and state of the art lighting and effects. This concert proved it and that's not even mentioning the quality of the song writing, the musicianship or even the emotional aspects of the music or the message.

We are familiar with the large circular screen, the flaming bed and the pig, which were dramatic enough, but the Dalek-like robotic thingies with their laser lights rising up from the stage floor along with an unbelievably intense lighting display was apocalyptic. And then there was the percussionist's 'cage', where he leapt up to hit percussion well above his head, the soaring quality of the female chorus, the glorious guitar work of David Gilmour. I've probably seen and/or worked on half a thousand concerts but this was the one. It was so far ahead of the pack, and set a whole new benchmark for the 'concert experience'.

NATIONAL TENNIS CENTER
13 – 20 FEBRUARY 1988, MELBOURNE, AUSTRALIA

I WAS THERE: KATHY IRVINE, AGE 19

I had been listening to Pink Floyd since I was very young thanks to my older siblings. We travelled about 30 minutes to get to the venue (Floyd were playing a run of eight nights here). Before the show they played random animal noises in the arena and it smelt of incense, maybe sandalwood. I also remember the laser lights and giant pig that floated out over the crowd. We were close enough that I could see how David Gilmour played 'Wish You Were Here' and the drummer jumping up to reach drums that were above him. It was a fantastic concert that I will never forget.

I WAS THERE: RONNIE FERRES

I attended the first of the Melbourne concerts with my girlfriend. We were given these crappy seats on the far right of the stage and were unable to see or hear anything from the left or the centre even, so everything came out in mono sound. I was peed right off so next morning I rang the organiser, the Paul Dainty Organisation, and was told by reception that Mr Dainty was a very busy man and I would have to wait for a very long time so I accepted. 90 minutes later he answered and I put my story, to which he politely replied that he had not received one complaint. I said, 'Well, you have one now.' In response he said, 'Well, if you show tomorrow night at the front entrance ticketing, there will be three tickets waiting for you and I hope you have a better time.' He was at all times extremely polite to me.

The following night, we rocked up along with a friend for the extra ticket and were given seats in the press section, dead in front and right behind the mixing box. This area contained about 40 seats and we had it to ourselves, as the press had attended on the first night. The concert was unbelievable, with the largest sound system I'd ever seen and I'd seen all the big groups perform over the years. The two main speakers alone were one million watts each.

They played their new album in the first half of the concert and their old stuff in the second half. We still got the flying pink pig and the bed on fire sliding on a wire from the rear top of the arena down onto the stage, where it exploded. The sliding roof was closed so the sound reproduction was fabulous. It was, to this day, the best concert I have ever attended and I've seen 'em all…

We kept the press passes we received and I thought 'hmmmm, perhaps I can use them again?'. As I was not told differently, I rocked up for the last three shows and sat in the 40-seat press area again all on my own. It was an unbelievable and completely surreal experience that I will never forget, like watching a movie five times over and noticing things I had missed previously. The only drawback was that Roger Waters had by then left the band, but the music sounded just the same as in the past.

The press gave them rave reviews. Unfortunately, they have never returned Down Under (to my knowledge). They are still my all-time favourite band and they are loved by all in Australia.

I WAS THERE: COL TURNER

It was 1988 or late 1987 when I heard the news I had been waiting around 16 years for: Pink Floyd to tour Australia. I hadn't seen them since 1971 and I was going to make the most of this tour. The day the tickets went on sale, I arrived at what I thought was a very early hour. It was about 5.30am and I expected to be one of the first in line. But when I arrived several hundred people were already in the queue in front of me. As one does when waiting in a queue for a long time, I turned around and started talking to the people who were just behind me. They asked if I had ever seen Floyd before and the second I mentioned I had seen them with both Roger and Syd up front, I had a crowd of around 30 people all wanting to hear about the early days! I think this was the first time I realised that I had witnessed something special in the early years of Floyd and that people wanted to know about it.

The tickets went on sale at 9am and the crowd in front of me were getting ever closer to the ticket booth. I was the next person in line to get my tickets when the attendant shouted out 'sorry, sold out'. I nearly died on the spot but figured that Floyd were going to do at least one other show, so I waited around… and so did everybody else! About 45 minutes later, the attendant shouted out the news that 'Pink Floyd have agreed to do another show'. A cheer went up from everybody.

I was now first in the queue for tickets to the second show and was expecting to get front row seats but the system was set up so that people phoning in got first pick. However, I did manage to get some very good seats just on the right of the stage and about 30 rows back. The first show was set for 13th February and the show I got tickets for was for 14 February (Valentine's Day). Later that week it was announced that Floyd were going to do a lot more shows in Melbourne (eight in all) and I managed to get tickets to the last show without too much of a problem. However, they were back row seats!

I waited in eager anticipation for what seemed like months. The day was getting closer and closer and I couldn't think of anything else. Floyd was getting flogged to death in my house and the neighbours were threatening to move out. The day before the show, I was working in my garden, dreaming about Floyd doing their first gig that night and dreaming that I was going to miss it!

However, I consoled myself knowing that I would be seeing them real soon. Boy, was I in for a surprise. At around 6.30pm, Sharon, a friend of my wife, phoned and asked to speak to me. 'Funny,' I thought to myself, 'I wonder what she wants?'. I then heard the sweetest words. 'Hi Col, a friend of mine can't come to the Floyd concert with me tonight. How would you like to go for free?' I couldn't believe my luck! I quickly jumped into the shower and raced around as fast as I could. The show was due to start at 8pm and I was over an hour's drive from the venue. I sped to Sharon's house, picked her up and put the foot down on the way into town.

As we got closer to the venue, the traffic really started to build up. We managed to get parked some way from where we had to go and sprinted the last mile or so. We got into the venue at exactly 8pm. As we were trying to locate which door to enter, I heard the first strains of 'Shine On You Crazy Diamond'. I must admit that I had tears in my eyes as we found our way to our seats.

We were seated to the left of the stage, about 25 rows away and almost directly opposite where I would be sitting the next night. The intro seemed to go on forever. The stage was still in darkness but the auditorium was lit by a fantastic array of lights. Then, as if by magic, Rick appeared in a cloud of smoke and ultra violet light. I was on my feet clapping and shouting but so were a lot of other people! The pulsating tones of the organ were being taken to new heights and then Dave's guitar reverberated at an astonishing volume that shook my very soul. The crowd were on their feet as the intro sadly finished all too quickly.

This was ultra Floyd. I had not heard anything so beautiful since Floyd performed 'Embryo' at Hyde Park in 1970. Floyd then deftly switched the pace by gliding into 'Signs of Life' and I got my first real look at how far the band had come in the 21 or so years since I had first seen them. A huge screen was now evident, where Floyd were showing this guy rowing a canoe as they performed a faultless version of the song live. I remembered the original light show from 1966 as being printer's ink between two slides in a projector!

If you watch the video, *The Delicate Sound Of Thunder*, you will get a really good appreciation of what this concert was like. I must admit to being impressed by the pig that hung overhead with its eyes glowing during 'One of These Days'. Likewise, the bed that crashed into the stage and exploded was also worthy of mention. And the light show? All I can say is it was the best I have ever seen. But when I really start to think about it, the heart of this Floyd extravaganza (or any Floyd show for that matter) was the incredible, sweet music.

They performed superlatively all night, with one heart stopping moment when they appeared to have gone off the rails, towards the end of 'Money'. It suddenly seemed as if for one brief second they had lost their way. But they had started a 'jam' and it took me by surprise. Up until then, they had almost followed what they had recorded down to the last note. Now here was something a bit different. The jam differed slightly on each of the three nights I saw them. I can't say it was a highlight, because some of it sounded a bit off key. But it took me back a few years to when Syd would go off and do his own thing. It seemed this little segment was included by Dave, Rick and Nick as a sort of 'throwback' to when they were an experimental band.

Scott Page fitted in really well playing his sax, and Guy Pratt seemed to have slipped into Roger's role without any detrimental effect on the overall sound. Tim Renwick also played a valuable part as did Gary Wallis, and I must not forget the three female singers – Margaret Taylor, Durga McBroom and Rachel Fury – who blew me away with their rendition of 'Great Gig in the Sky'. It was as good as the original. My ears were ringing as we left the Tennis Centre. What a night. What a concert. And I was getting to do it all again tomorrow night!

BUDOKAN GRAND HALL
2 & 3 MARCH, 1988, TOKYO, JAPAN

I WAS THERE: TOKYO MUSICUM STATION

More than 30 years ago, Pink Floyd came to Japan and more than 30 years later I still remember it. It was a two-and-a-half hour live show, opening with 'Shine On You Crazy Diamond'. A huge circular screen was installed in the middle of the stage and during the song the laser light reflected everywhere. They played *A Momentary Lapse Of Reason* in the first half. It was fantastic.

COLISEUM
15 APRIL 1988, LOS ANGELES, CALIFORNIA

I WAS THERE: MIKE ALLEN

The local station in Las Vegas was offering a complete package (bus ride and ticket) to see Floyd at the LA Coliseum. A bus filled with Pink Floyd fans, monitor and music left Vegas in a rain storm. It rained all the way there. Once we arrived, the seats were horrible, stage right and behind the stage. I told the friends that I met on the trip that I would catch up with them after the concert, and started making my way down to the infield, stopping every so often to act like an usher assisting people find their seats. I finally made it down to the ten feet high concert wall next to the infield and walked up to the engineering booth that was dead-centre on the 25-yard line. I positioned myself in front of it, pumped out my chest and started looking to the right and left slowly, pretending to be a security guard by occasionally touching my ear and acting like I was talking to someone.

A light fog and heavy moisture were in the stadium. The music was amazing. 'Comfortably Numb' started with multiple dark green lasers that created a series of five foot waves. They seemed to go the width of the infield, their roll fronts moving towards the engineering booth. These waves continued moving and engulfing me during the entire song. It was totally a religious experience, and one I have never forgotten.

In 1994, I saw Pink Floyd four times. I flew to Joe Robbie Stadium in Miami, Florida and picked up a buddy who had never seen Pink Floyd perform. It was the first date on the *Division Bell* world tour and there was heavy rain throughout. The gold and green lasers shooting up from the stage were full of the raindrops passing through them. A few weeks later, I had tickets for two nights at the Rose Bowl. The first night was amazing. The next morning, I was wondering whether to go again that evening. I had the ticket in my shirt pocket when I pulled into a 7-Eleven to get a coffee. As I came out, a police car pulled in next to me. I asked the cops if the night before had been too crazy for them. One guy answered 'no' and said that he'd love to see Pink Floyd. I asked him what time he got off shift that night. He said it would be after the concert started. I told him to ask his boss if he could get off earlier, pulled the ticket out of my pocket and handed it to him. I drove back to Las Vegas in my truck, smiling all the way as I remembered his reaction and the reaction of his partner!

A few months after that, I arrived in Washington DC to see Floyd at RFK with high school friends. I had already bought tickets, but a week before the concert, bought three more, dead centre in front of the stage and ten rows back. My friends and I showed up early and found three guys looking for tickets, so I sold them my spare tickets at cost and told them to go enjoy themselves.

I flew home a couple of nights later, and picked a window seat. As I sat there thinking about my trip to DC and catching the Pink Floyd concert. I looked out the window and looked down. Yep, there it was, another Floyd concert, taking place in Chicago. That's why I can say 'four in '94'.

OAKLAND COLISEUM STADIUM
22 & 23 APRIL 1988, OAKLAND, CALIFORNIA

I WAS THERE: MARK HOFFMEISTER

I skipped the *Animals* tour as it was outdoors at the football stadium. After seeing them in smaller venues, I wasn't up for the big outdoor event. I didn't see them again until the *Momentary Lapse of Reason* tour in San Francisco. Even without Roger Waters, it was an excellent show, with David's guitar playing and vocals top notch. I saw them again in Oakland, outdoors. It was pouring rain and I was surrounded by drunk or drugged out people who weren't hip enough to make it to the indoor show earlier on the tour. The blow-up pig looked particularly scary and I couldn't wait for the concert to end. That's why I skipped the *Division Bell* tour, although I did see Roger Waters' first tour at the indoor Oakland Coliseum, where I had a similar experience of a lot of obnoxiously drunk people around me. Roger performed 'If' and I could barely hear it. Most of the audience around me was unfamiliar with earlier Pink Floyd and seemed to come mainly to hear music from *The Wall*. I hope that David Gilmour tours again. I would like my son to see him.

MUNICIPAL STADIUM
25 & 26 APRIL 1988, PHOENIX, ARIZONA

I WAS THERE: DAMON JONES, AGE 19

It was an outdoor venue and, as they came on stage, the sun was going down, filling the sky with a pink pastel hue. It was surreal. I was going to tech school at the time. I never forgot the ticket price as I pawned a beautiful Ibanez acoustic guitar for a lousy $30 to buy that ticket. I went with three friends from school. We had decent seating. I remember the flying beds, pigs and a part of the laser show that made me feel as if I were under water looking up at the waves. Other than the occasional joint that came down the aisle, this was the first concert that I can remember not using drugs…

TEXAS STADIUM
28 APRIL 1988, IRVING, TEXAS

I WAS THERE: ANNA – MARIE A DIAZ

The next time I saw them was the following spring, at the old Dallas Cowboys Texas Stadium in Irving. The stadium had a hole in the roof and the weather was nice. The stadium seated more people. The show was just like the earlier one I'd seen in Dallas. One thing I vividly remember is that on the first two rows were a group of people who wore identical pale pink tuxedos with pink wigs. I thought that was pretty cool.

FOXBORO STADIUM
6 & 8 MAY 1988, FOXBORO, MASSACHUSETTS

I WAS THERE: TOM LEES

I was 13 years old when I first heard Pink Floyd, and 16 when I saw David Gilmour at the Orpheum Theater in Boston, Massachusetts in May 1984 on his *About Face* tour. What a great show that was. Then Pink Floyd came touring in 1988. General admission tickets were $100 back then. I went to both shows. On May 6th, it was rainy all day and the mist was rolling in. It was a beautiful night. Me and my friend Bill waited in line for a couple hours and ended up 40 feet from the stage, directly in the centre, where we stayed. I had a group of Russians to the left of me and a group of people from I know not where on my right. I recorded the show and have it on cassette tapes. (I need to get them transferred to CD because they're so old I'm afraid to put them in a cassette player now.)

Halfway through the show, a pig that was supposed to go all the way to the back of the stadium and then return to the stage got stuck on the pulley system halfway back and started to deflate. People began climbing on other people's shoulders with a crutch and poking at it. This pig was huge, and the cable on it had to be 50, 60 feet in the air. Then this guy shimmied out from the stage and along the cable, wrapped his legs around the pig and hauled it back to the stage. It was an incredible sight.

In those days, when you went to a concert you just had the speakers in front of you. But not Pink Floyd. They had speakers all around you. It was an intense show, and because of the pig mishap they actually played longer, almost two and a half hours in total. They split off from 'Money' mid-song and started playing an Elvis Presley song and then went into a Beatles song. It was just amazing. Bill and I couldn't believe it. I remember it like it was yesterday. Those Pink Floyd shows are the best I ever saw in my life and I've probably seen 200 bands. I've seen Australian Pink Floyd several times. They are really good too!

STADE DU PARC OLYMPIQUE
11 MAY 1988, MONTREAL, CANADA

I WAS THERE: JACQUES DELISLE

I actually slept at the old Forum back in 1987 to get tickets, but in 1988 I got in for free to a concert by pretending we were employees. My friends worked at the Olympic stadium (the Big O in Montréal, where Roger spat on a fan back in 1977!) during baseball games. They served hot dogs and drinks at a snack bar. So when Floyd came in 1988, we put on the snack bar uniforms and pretended we had to work. The security guards saw that we were not on the employee list but we lied to them by telling them that there were so many fans expected at the gig that night that they had to call in extras from downtown Montreal. We also did the same thing a few weeks later when Bruce Springsteen, Sting and others came for a benefit concert. My friends claimed they saw David and Nick racing golf carts inside the stadium.

I WAS THERE: MICHEL TOURNAY, AGE 26

There were speakers all around the perimeter of the stadium. I'd never seen so many. Once they start playing 'Time', the bass was so loud that you could feel the stadium shaking! I had visions of the ring-roof collapsing and it starting to rain concrete. I never thought any group would be able to fill that stadium with sound but Pink Floyd managed it.

UNIVERSITY OF NORTHERN IOWA DOME
18 MAY 1988, CEDAR FALLS, IOWA

I WAS THERE: JOHN HULLINGER

I was in a band in the early Eighties. During one of our practices, a neighbour who was a professional musician sat in with us. He started playing 'Another Brick in the Wall Part 2' and we all joined in. We enjoyed it so much we put it into our set list and this got my interest and I began investigating Pink Floyd's music. Some years later, my friend and co-worker Randy Pollpeter asked if I would like to go and see them in Cedar Falls, Iowa. I was surprised that they were touring and said 'absolutely'. Randy waited hours in line to get tickets. You had to get to the ticket outlet early, get a wristband and wait for your number to be called.

The concert was on a Thursday night. We waited until after work and drove about three hours to the UNI-Dome. Randy had made some mix tapes of Floyd songs and we got more and more excited as we drove along. We even talked to some road workers while we were stopped in roadworks to let them know that we were going to the concert. After parking the car, we noticed quite a few people gathered around watching a group of guys playing baseball outside the Dome. It was the members of Pink Floyd – playing baseball!

After watching the baseball for a while, we went inside to find that our seats were very high and off to the side, with a column in front of us. We went to the ticket booths to say that our view was obscured. They said, 'You can have a floor ticket.' Our new tickets were closer to the stage, so close that we felt immersed in the concert. We could see the light show above us. We were underneath the waves and we could feel the heat from the flames, hear the music and smell the smells. I kept saying to Randy, 'This concert is like the Disney of all concerts!'

Before we knew it, they were playing their last song. We waited until the floor started to clear. As we were leaving, several security guys were offering to sell their security shirts. We thought $25 and $30 was a little high but after leaving realised we should have bought the shirts. Stopping for a hamburger on the way, it must have been close to 3am when we got home. We were both working in the school the following morning and had to take a little cat nap at school. Now we get together once a year to celebrate that concert by watching a video of it.

 HUBERT H HUMPHREY METRODOME
24 MAY 1988, MINNEAPOLIS, MINNESOTA

I WAS THERE: JERRY POLNAU

From the flawless live concert with no audience in Pompeii to the sacred and raw *The Final Cut* (and it's super contentious as to whether it's them at the top of their game or at their worst; I am particularly infatuated with that album and remember shedding tears to it whilst laying in the dark on Minnesota winter nights), it didn't hurt that the guys were all so cool looking!

I went to see my favourite band with my best friend, David, and with mushrooms and hash (sorry, Elliot, that you have to find out this way that your dad, ah, 'experimented' some). There is no way that concert could deliver all of what I would want. But it still blew me away – the second the lights went out and Rick laid his hands on that haunting, wrenching first droned chord for 'Shine On', I surrendered and became super excited. And then that first crying note Dave played, which is so simple but which no other guitarist can quite do the same, just went through the whole sea of fans, who were all well aware of how lucky we were to actually see these guys!

The concert was fantastic, but I don't remember all of it. Not because of the mind 'alterants' as much as just the passing of time. I would have loved to see Roger with the others though, and enjoy that Lennon/McCartney-esque contrast of the smooth and rugged vocals and styles of Waters and Gilmour. I did see Waters do *The Wall* and I loved and adored it, but I felt some disconnect simply because he was a small expressionless figure from our far away seats. It's sad that I enjoy a concert from a DVD more in my older years.

GIANTS STADIUM
3 JUNE 1988, EAST RUTHERFORD, NEW JERSEY

I WAS THERE: MIKE ANDREACH

I saw them twice on the *A Momentary Lapse of Reason* tour. One show was during a horrendous rain storm. One of the fellahs I worked with had gotten tickets. We sat in the upper deck, just a little to the right of the stage, three or four rows from the very top of the stadium. It poured rain the whole night. Each of us had those old denim jackets, the ones that had like ten pockets, and we were able to smuggle in a lot of beer. I also had some herb with me and we managed to smoke it out of a soda can. By the time Pink Floyd came on, we were both pretty much ripped to the gills. We also managed to bogart some weed from the people in front of us. It must have been laced with something because after smoking it, I saw little green men carrying flags marching all around me. We were in the upper deck, just below where the pig came down to the stage. Not being exactly 100 per cent in my right mind, it made me freak out that we were being attacked by a massive farm animal. The music was incredible. They played the entire first side of *A Momentary Lapse of Reason*, including killer versions of 'One Slip' and 'On the Turning Away'. The encore of 'Run Like Hell' had a phenomenal light show to go with it. The band was spot on, jamming a bit on every song. Both of David Gilmour's solos on 'Comfortably Numb' gave me goose bumps. It was the best show I ever saw until I managed to score a ticket to the same venue to see them again. For this show I was 100 per cent sober – I was designated driver, voted to do so by an unfair election, but that's a story for another day. The effects were just as wild as the earlier night, only this time I was truly able to enjoy everything. To this day, it ranks up there as probably the best concert I ever saw, with the possible exception of The Who doing *Quadrophenia* at Madison Square Garden in the late Nineties. I had to get a third chance to see them somewhere else on that tour but had couldn't switch my nights off work. When they played at Yankee Stadium a few years later – again, the same thing.

I WAS THERE: DOUG GOUDSWARD

I saw Pink Floyd just once. This, of course, was the post-Roger Waters era, so they were already a little bit of a nostalgia act even though they were still producing new material. There were a lot of lasers and special effects, including a giant floating pig. Unfortunately, they were using surround sound. If you had good seats it probably sounded incredible. We, however, were positioned right near one set of the surround sound amplifiers and they overwhelmed the sound from the main set of speakers.

We only heard half of the sound and would have had a more enhanced experience if the sound system had been less sophisticated. On the other hand, it was the only opportunity I ever had to experience the band playing some of my favourite songs live, so I was glad to be in attendance.

 PLACE D'ARME, CHATEAU DE VERSAILLES
21 & 22 JUNE 1988, VERSAILLES, FRANCE

I WAS THERE: FINN NØRBY

The first time I heard about Pink Floyd was when they released their album *Dark Side of the Moon* in 1973. I was 16 years old. In 1988, I was working a night shift when I saw they were playing a concert in Paris. I called, bought two tickets and then called my girlfriend (now my wife) and asked her to go to Paris with me. We drove from Denmark on the Saturday in an old Ford Escort van, leaving at half time during the semi-finals of the European Championship football match between the Netherlands and Russia. We took a tent and spent a night camping just south of Hamburg. The next day, we continued towards France where, all of a sudden, the Château de Chantilly appeared. It's where the James Bond movie *A View to a Kill* was filmed, and we spent Sunday night there. The next day we drove to Versailles, arriving in the afternoon and grabbing the last available spot on the campsite.

On the Tuesday, we walked around Versailles and observed the sound check. On the day of the first show, we arrived early to be told that the concert had been pushed back half an hour because it was too bright to start the concert. The French government were there – there was a lot of security. After the second song, David Gilmour said 'bonjour Paris' and then they played for about three and a half hours without saying anything more. Following this, they announced that they had to take a break of 15 minutes to change their shirts. After ten minutes, the show started again with all of the extra numbers for full throttle for another 45 – 50 minutes. The first evening, there were around 70,000 people there. There were 90,000 the next evening. I have since been to Pink Floyd concerts in Germany and Denmark and I've seen Roger Waters four times, but Versailles was a very special event. It was my first real concert and I still have the tickets, t-shirts, catalogue and the French newspapers we bought, and which my girlfriend was able to translate for me.

I WAS THERE: BRETT DAMARELL

I went to see Pink Floyd in Versailles. It took 24 hours by coach and I missed the whole of the gig due to taking too much LSD. I fell asleep on a bench and woke up just in time for the last encores. Obviously I was gutted. But I then went back to the old Wembley Stadium in the August of the same year and saw them again – and didn't miss a note! They have been with me, it seems, all my life and although I stopped taking acid at least 20 years ago, I have had the odd flashback over the years, and always see the green lasers that were used at the Versailles gig.

PRATERSTADION
1 JULY 1988, VIENNA, AUSTRIA

I WAS THERE: BOB MANSFIELD

I set up my own local heating/plumbing business and my first apprentice had a brother who was part of the then separately controlled Pink Floyd lighting company. We met up with him during their first tour after the break up with Roger in Vienna. Trying to convince German Hell's Angels that we knew one of the road crew was interesting to say the least. The brother had control of the much disputed pig who the band retained by adding a pair of testicles, thus becoming a boar rather than a pig, to avoid prosecution by Roger. Thanks to our backstage connection, the boar turned mid-flight during the concert, shone two massive spotlights in our direction and nodded!

OLYMPIASTADION
3 JULY 1988, MUNICH, GERMANY

I WAS THERE: DIMITRIOS 'TAKI' BOGIATZOULES & SUSIE

My girlfriend Susie and I had planned our summer vacation for August. We thought we couldn't attend Pink Floyd's gig in Munich, because that was taking place in August. When we found out that we had mistaken the month, we were kicking our asses that we had missed the chance, but thought 'hey, that's life…'. But my best buddy and his girlfriend bought two tickets and then realised that they would be in France and therefore couldn't make it to the concert, the exact opposite of our error and – guess what? We got their tickets. We were in the arena, quite near the stage and it was a helluva gig with all the lasers, flying pigs and a crowd that celebrated a warm (and dry!) evening with one of the greatest bands ever.

WISH YOU WERE HERE

WEMBLEY STADIUM
5 & 6 AUGUST 1988, LONDON, UK

I WAS THERE: CHRISTOPHER MARCHANT

Although I had seen them on previous occasions, the 6th August concert was special for a number of reasons. Pink Floyd were playing again after a bitter legal battle over the use of the name with ex-Floyd bassist Rogers Waters. As a fan, it grieved me that there might never be another Floyd concert, so to be able to arrive at Wembley on a hot summer's day and watch and listen to a band I had been a fan of since I was 15 was quite an occasion.

The band had been resurrected with an extended line up and a new album. The tickets advertised 'An Evening with Pink Floyd' and in small print they mentioned their new album, *A Momentary Lapse of Reason*. Even this showed a change in the structure post-Waters. I had gone with my eldest daughter, who was 16, and a couple of friends. We sat near the Royal Box. My daughter wanted to go in front of the stage but past experience had told me that, at ten degrees hotter near the front on a hot day, this could be a recipe for disaster for the inexperienced.

I remember seeing people with t-shirts saying 'who the F**k is Roger Waters?' He had very few sympathisers at this event. The concert itself was extraordinary. As with all Floyd concerts, they pushed the boundaries. Here we had the Floyd droids. They were using the latest technology, optical fibre lasers that were very powerful and very manoeuvrable. In the opening sequence, they had sent a dummy on a hospital bed crashing into the stage from a crane at the back of the stadium. This was greeted with great cheers. It was a variation on the opening sequence of *The Wall* with the plane, but the profile of the dummy in the bed looked like Roger Waters!

This concert showcased Floyd's new album, which I confess I hadn't yet quite learned to love. We also had the classic songs from previous albums, all done with stunning lighting and the classic circular screen. This combination of old and new showed that Floyd had entered a new era and that they didn't need – or miss – their troublesome former bassist. For a fan like myself, who got his first album *The Piper at the Gates of Dawn* as a 15-year-old, to be able to sit and watch this with my 16-year-old daughter was a special moment. 'Money', 'Us and Them', 'Comfortably Numb' and 'Time' all brought back memories that I thought I would never be able to share with my own children in a live setting.

The end of this show was classic. They finished with a laser and firework display that seem to give Wembley Stadium a roof. It was a stunning finale to an extraordinary evening. I shall never forget looking up and seeing those lasers crisscrossing the stadium and the massive light explosion at the end. Pink Floyd had come back bigger and better. They were same, but different. Their music was new, but had the Floyd thread. As we made our way to the station, I saw that t-shirt again that said 'who the F**k is Roger Waters?'

I WAS THERE: PERRY RIDLEY

During the Eighties, and avoiding albums like *The Final Cut*, I thought my days of seeing Pink Floyd were long gone. Much to my surprise, the band released *A Momentary Lapse of Reason*, which considering everything was not a bad album. They toured that, and I saw them at Wembley Stadium in August 1988. Only Pink Floyd could master this venue, and with their effects, lighting and superb quad sound, they proved they still had the magic. We stood on the pitch and were thrilled to be there.

I WAS THERE: GARETH JONES

I have no great memories of the *Momentary Lapse of Reason* tour other than that I was there. Of course, it was moving on from Roger and I thought Dave, Nick and Rick more than acquitted themselves in terms of music and spectacle. The giant circular screen, the mirror ball and the wonderful climax of 'Comfortably Numb' all kept the Pink Floyd brand flying and I liked some of the new songs such as 'Momentary Lapse of Reason'. But it wasn't quite 'Pink Floyd'. A hard edge had gone.

There is no getting away from it that the Floyd line-up of Waters, Wright, Gilmour and Mason was the epitome of class rock music. The rhythms of Nick, the musicianship of Dave and Rick and the incredible concepts and lyrics of Roger together made an unbeatable combination whose music will resonate down the years for centuries. I was going to say that it is a shame they never wrote an opera, but I suppose that is what *The Wall* is?

Roger was an incredible songwriter at that time with *Dark Side of the Moon* being his pinnacle. I don't think either he or Dave has reached anywhere near those heights again in their solo work. Dave is a great guitarist but he is not a strong songwriter and he (or Polly maybe) lacks the edge and bite to their lyrics that Roger achieves. Roger though seems to have lost his song writing clarity and simplicity and become too absorbed by his politics. I know he has always been a challenging sort of guy and I know he feels passionately about the causes he supports, but watching him now is a bit like watching Bono. It is irritating that we have to tolerate the politics and the polemics to get to the great music and songs which we love him for. It is a shame that they can't separate out the concert from the political rally but – hey ho!

WISH YOU WERE HERE

I WAS THERE: NEIL PARROTT

I have been a Floyd fan since first hearing *Dark Side of the Moon* in 1973. My first time seeing them was at Earl's Court in London in 1980 for *The Wall* shows. I had never seen anything like it before in my life. All the props, and the grand scale of the event, was mind boggling. I was 18 and I had a good seat on the floor. It was totally amazing, from those opening moments when Master of Ceremonies Gary Yudman introduced the band, to the last part where the wall was demolished before our eyes, and with all Gerald Scarfe's work on screen and the blow up characters too. It is probably the best gig I have ever seen.

I also saw both Wembley Stadium gigs in London in August 1988. They were also bloody amazing. It was pretty much the same as a grand event, and all the special effects with the lasers and the plane and bed, and of course the pig in 'Run Like Hell'. The glitter ball used in 'Comfortably Numb' was dazzling. It was a great gig. I met a lot of great people. I also went the following year in 1989 to see them at Paris Bercy and the London Docklands Arena. They were bloody loud – and bloody amazing again!

I WAS THERE: ALAN WINROW

I went to see Pink Floyd live at Wembley Stadium without Roger and that was good. But I always felt that Pink Floyd weren't the same after Roger left. I always liked the Roger Waters era. I wasn't a great fan of *A Momentary Lapse of Reason*. *The Division Bell* was better, but I like Roger Waters' solo stuff. And I loved his 2017 album, *Is This The Life We Really Want?*. I love *Animals*. 'Dogs' is one of my favourite tracks. After I'd got *Dark Side*, *Wish You Were Here* and *Animals*, I then decided to go back and see what other stuff they'd done and I got *Meddle*. 'Echoes' is amazing. And then I got *Atom Heart Mother* but anything before that I'm not so keen on – the Syd Barrett era is all a bit too psychedelic and weird for me. Maybe they should have left it after Roger left but I can see why they didn't.

My dad listened to *Dark Side of the Moon* and he loved it. He was into classical music but he could tell what music it was and how good it was. And then he listened to *Wish You Were Here* with me and he loved it as well, especially 'Shine On You Crazy Diamond (Part One)'. I was so pleased that he liked the music that I liked.

In January 1977, he had a heart attack and went into hospital, and while he was in hospital, *Animals* came out. I went to the hospital and I said to him that I'd bought their new album and he said, 'Oh, when I come home I'll listen to it with you.' But then he had another heart attack and died in hospital so he never got the chance to listen to it with me. He was only 46. I was 16. Even to this day, every time I put that album on, as soon as it starts I think of my dad.

I WAS THERE: SUE WOOLLATT

Pink Floyd first attracted my attention when I was 17 in 1970 and at art college. I'm not sure whether I first heard them there or whether my Mum had started collecting their albums by then – possibly both. Anyway, I fell in love with *Dark Side of the Moon* and bought it, a huge purchase for a poor student on a grant of a fiver a week (plus a fiver from Dad to pay rent for my digs). It was so-ooo worth it though. The other albums followed over the years.

When I first met my husband in 1988 he was more into other bands, like U2, but became exposed to Pink Floyd as a result of making my acquaintance and came to enjoy their music too. Coincidentally, he was supposed to be going to a Pink Floyd concert with his mates. Tickets had been purchased and the due date was looming. We had only just started going out together and his mates realised I was dead keen, so one of them heroically donated his ticket to me so that I could go see them in the flesh. What a star! I shall forever be grateful to him for that. It was pretty much our second date.

The day dawned... Saturday 6th August 1988, the venue Wembley Stadium, London. It was the *Momentary Lapse of Reason* tour. I remember queuing outside with my now-hubby and his remaining pals and everyone in the dusk, and hearing the group doing the soundchecks. It created more than a frisson of excitement and I knew this was going to be something special. And it was. The atmosphere in the arena pulsated. The amazing light show that accompanied each song, the flying bedstead – oh, and wasn't there a floating pig too? Amazing. I was captivated and sang along, in a spell. My favourite track that night? 'Comfortably Numb'. Then it was over and we left in a daze of content.

Pink Floyd is a massive part of our iTunes library and we still have all my vinyl (although no record player – lol!) and although I'm now into my sixties, I still play Pink Floyd all the time and always shall. A tune of theirs will also feature at my funeral one day. Let's hope the vicar turns the sound right up!

I WAS THERE: NICHOL THOMPSON, AGE 17

I only took a chance on going down from Edinburgh to London to see them at Wembley because my friend Mikey had a ticket and I thought I'd go down on the off chance of being able to get a ticket outside. I was lucky enough to meet some Floyd fans on the bus and they had a spare ticket so it was all good. And Kev, Mikey's brother, gave me his ticket so me, and Mikey could go in together, because we thought all the stadium would be sectioned off. Then, as soon as we got in, we realised that we could meet him inside. It w as my first time in London and my first time at a big concert. First time on acid as well! That was like a whole adventure.

We were staying with some of our friends in West Ham. We got down early on the Saturday morning, and the gig was later that night. We went over to see a guy in Finsbury Park to get the magic stuff. And then we went from West Ham to Finsbury Park, and from Finsbury Park to Wembley. We took the stuff when we left Finsbury Park, and by the time we'd been on the Tube Pink for half an hour it all started kicking in. It was just like a big magical adventure.

We were just blown away by the scale of it. We couldn't believe we were actually at Wembley about to see Pink Floyd. Mikey had gelled his hair. He thought he looked fantastic. I thought it looked ridiculous. We were watching this guy pickpocketing people and we couldn't believe it was happening. We watched him for ages. It made us really paranoid every time somebody banged into us.

When the music started, we hadn't realised that Guy Pratt was on stage playing keyboards. We thought it was Jean Michel Jarre, because he was playing the Docklands round about the same time. It was just us that thought that. Nobody else did, and it took us about five minutes of jumping up and down like lunatics thinking we were getting two-for-one before we realised our mistake and someone said 'no, that's Guy Pratt'. And then the rest of the band came on.

We were blown away by the lasers. It was like a sea about a metre above our heads across the pitch area of the stadium. During 'Run Like Hell' we went as high up into the terracing as we could get and I'd never seen anything so powerful musically in my life. When the crowd settled down a bit during the interval, we decided to try and look for Kev. Me and Mikey were shouting 'Kev!' at the top of our voices from under the roof of the stadium and loads of people were shouting back 'what?'

It was just great, hearing these songs for real after growing up listening to their albums. I will always remember walking out of Wembley and everyone in the tunnels to the Tube station was making animal noises, like off the *Animals* album.

I WAS THERE: IAN CLEMENTSON, AGE 17

After buying *A Momentary Lapse of Reason* on a friend's recommendation in 1987, I was prompted to go out and buy Floyd's entire back catalogue using the money from my first ever pay packet in my first ever job (it was proper money in an actual envelope back then!). And so began my obsession with The Mighty Pink Floyd. The same friend also told me Pink Floyd would be playing live at Wembley the following summer and that we had to get tickets. I devoured everything Pink Floyd, in the way 16-year-olds do, and by the time August came around I was practically foaming at the mouth.

Two weeks before the concert, I had a motorcycle accident and ended up on crutches. I spent two weeks sweating over whether I'd be off them in time for the show. Fortunately, I was. We had tickets for the Saturday show but decided to go up on the

Friday to listen outside the stadium and take in the atmosphere – and it was brilliant! I remember walking up the long walkway to the famous Twin Towers in scorching hot sunshine and a guy selling knock off sunglasses saying, 'You'll need these to protect your eyes from those lasers mate!'. Hundreds of fans were partying outside, listening to stereos, selling dodgy posters and t-shirts, singing and just having a great time – and this was before the show even started!

When the show did start, the roar of the crowd inside was huge. I had never been to a football match or anything resembling a large gathering of people before (the old Wembley held about 80,000 people and the sound made my hair stand on end. You could hear the low rumble of 'Shine On' starting up, sounding like thunder echoing through Wembley. All the fans outside were going mental, like they were actually watching the band. The whole thing was just total excitement.

As the show went on and got darker, we could see the lasers coming out of the roof of the stadium and recognised each song in the set. It was a great teaser trailer for our Saturday show. After the Friday show ended, thousands of ecstatic fans came flooding out, which just lifted the atmosphere even higher. Along with hundreds of other fans, my friend and I ended up spending the hot summer night on the steps of Wembley just partying the night away and getting hardly any sleep.

Saturday morning came and already fans were arriving. The atmosphere was great. I remember buying a programme and reading it from cover to cover, looking over the pictures of the screen and the lasers, etc. and feeling the excitement building. The fans entertained themselves until the doors finally opened in the early afternoon.

I remember having to squeeze myself through Turnstile D. Entering the stadium was like entering another world... You could see the haze in the huge stadium, like it had its' own atmosphere. It is still the largest building I have ever stood in. I remember looking to the right and at the end of the pitch, there it was – the round screen – along with their massive stage set up. Seeing it all made me feel giddy. After a year of waiting, I was here and was really going to see Pink Floyd live!

As we were among the first in the queue after camping out all night, we had the choice of pretty much anywhere in the stadium, and we ran straight down to the pitch, getting a place centre stage and about 50 feet from the front barrier. Brilliant! The weather was again scorching, and I remember looking out of the roof and not seeing a cloud in sight.

The stadium slowly filled up. There were Pink Floyd t-shirts everywhere and the crowd entertained themselves all afternoon, doing Mexican waves, singing and drinking. I remember thinking how mixed the crowd was; ages, accents, nationalities, but how the one thing everyone had in common was total excitement, waiting for the start of the show. The crowd were getting louder and louder by the hour. At about 7.30pm, the sound effects started – the tape they used to play with birdsong, flowing water, footsteps walking along a gravel path. This was it. This was the beginning! I remember it going on for a really long time, maybe half an hour, and getting gradually louder until there was a sound effect of a plane flying over, and then at about 8pm...

Pink Floyd walked on stage! The 'real' three Pink Floyd members first, then the rest of the live band. The crowd noise was huge. You could hear it going round and round the huge oval stadium. The atmosphere was electric. I can remember looking at David Gilmour and having this really weird feeling of 'there he is!'. He was the first famous person I had ever seen, along with Nick and Rick. They were my idols. I remember noticing weird mundane things, like DG wearing a watch, RW having a bottle of water on the keyboards; just everyday stuff but, in my head, it had this weird new meaning – to associate these normal everyday objects with my total heroes. This feeling lasted for some time and I hadn't really noticed 'Shine On' was slowly building up, and up, and UP! It just got so loud! I can remember feeling the bass rumble in my stomach and just wondering how loud it would actually get. Then eventually, DG played those first few notes and the crowd roared. This is it! Pink Floyd are playing and I am here!

It was just magical, everything I hoped it would be and more. They finished 'Shine On' and then played pretty much all of *Momentary Lapse*. They had the Icarus figure fly out over the crowd during 'Learning to Fly'. As it got darker, they started using more lasers and the show just got bigger and bigger. I can remember feeling the heat of the flames on my face when they were bursting out of the stage to 'Dogs of War'. The first half of the show finished and then there was a 20-minute interval. All the fans, including my friend and I, were in total awe at what we had just seen and excited at knowing the second half of the show would bring all the classics.

At the time, 'One of These Days' was my favourite Floyd song, and after the interval, the wind sound effect started up. It was a feeling of, 'Yes! This is the real Pink Floyd and they're gonna play the 'real' Pink Floyd songs!'. I loved *Momentary Lapse*, but the second half of the show was really going to light up the crowd.

You could hear the famous bass line (wish it had been Roger...) booming out around the stadium, all the fans clapping along, and then it came to the last few bars (before the *Doctor Who* middle section) and two large bright lights appeared stage right behind the equipment and started to slowly rise up, and up, and up... and then... hold on a minute! It's a face! It's THE PIG! And then he was up and off, floating above the crowd (with his new rather large appendage for legal reasons...). He was rocking back and forth quite violently, with his searchlight eyes scanning the crowd. I remember being totally overwhelmed by the whole experience at this point; the atmosphere, my favourite band, my favourite song, the volume, the crowd noise, the weather, the night sky and the whole weekend. I remember crying and laughing at the same time (I've got a lump in my throat remembering it now). It was just the best moment in any show I've ever been to.

They then played all the classics including 'Time' (Nick's glowing drum sticks!), 'Money' (the cash register sound effects all in quad), 'Welcome to the Machine' (I was transfixed by Gerald Scarfe's scary metal dinosaur and sea of blood animation), 'On the Run' (the flying bed exploding on stage was brilliant), 'The Great Gig in the Sky' (the girls sounded great) and 'Another Brick (Part 2)' amongst others. 'Wish You Were Here' was another emotional moment, and also the biggest karaoke moment.

'Comfortably Numb' sounded epic (as was the mirrorball in front of the screen). For me it represents Roger and David's Last Great Moment. They finished with 'One Slip' and then encored with an everything-but-the-kitchen-sink effects-laden 'Run Like Hell'. The lights around the circumference of the screen exploded with the very last note and that was it. All the band took a bow at the front of the stage among the smoke and waved their goodbyes. I watched every one of them leave the stage, waving and watching them as long as I could see them. I remember frantically saying to my friend, 'Do you think we'll see them again?'…And we did, on the tours in 1989, the Knebworth show, Roger doing *The Wall* in Berlin, the 14 nights at Earl's Court in 1994 and all of Roger's tours since 2007.

I WAS THERE: PETER STUBBS

I first saw Pink Floyd in Coventry, when Syd Barrett was lead guitarist. Also on the bill were the Jimi Hendrix Experience and The Nice. I then saw them at Birmingham Town Hall after Dave Gilmour had joined them, when *Atom Heart Mother* was current. I was at Mothers night club in Erdington, Birmingham when *Ummagumma* was recorded, and I saw them at Knebworth in 1975. The last time I saw them was at the old Wembley Stadium on the most beautiful August evening in 1988. The weather conditions were superb, and they commenced their performance at about 8.45pm, terminating around midnight. It was truly an amazing concert.

MANCHESTER CITY FOOTBALL GROUND
8 AUGUST 1988, MAINE ROAD, MANCHESTER, UK

I WAS THERE: MICHAEL PLUMB

I saw Pink Floyd with my best friend, Andy, at Maine Road. We lived in Margate, Kent and chose Manchester to see them as my wife had family there and we stayed at their place. I had an old 750 Honda motorcycle at the time and Andy and I took turns at

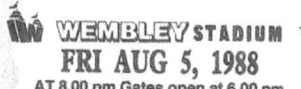

Clockwise from top left: Jerry Polnau regrets never seeing Roger Waters in the Pink Floyd line up; Taki and Susie still have their tickets; Sue Woollatt with husband Martin, who has clear instructions to play Pink Floyd at her funeral; Nigel Banks wasn't too impressed by *Atom Heart Mother*; Neil Parrott first saw the Floyd when he was 18 and in 1988 they were 'bloody amazing'

Clockwise from top left: Nick Brice was unaware of Pink Floyd until his dad took him to see them live; Laurent Pohu has Nick's autograph twice; Carol Corcoran's tickets; The 1989 Venice gig nearly didn't happen because of the city council; the second of Laurent's Nick autographs riding. We set off about 5am on what was a lovely hot day. We arrived at my in-laws around about lunch time on the day of the gig. We were both in our mid-20s then and really excited. After going to a local pub for a few beers, we bought a case of lager and headed off towards Maine Road. We arrived about 4pm and the place was buzzing.

We sat outside the ground drinking our lager and smoking weed, waiting for the gates to open and watching all the people. There were touts selling tickets. I don't know how much they were asking, but as soon as they saw a policeman they disappeared, only to return a few minutes later. We each bought an unofficial programme and t-shirt. By the time the gates opened we had drunk all but four cans of lager. Those that were left we gave to someone as we were told you could not take drinks into the stadium. As soon as we were inside, we asked a steward for the bar. He told us they only served soft drinks and non-alcoholic lager. We bought a bottle of Coke at a stupidly expensive price.

We headed out onto the turf and found a good place to sit. After a while, someone appeared on stage and the whole crowd, including us, surged forward. We were almost dead centre with the stage and not too far back. Andy then realised that, when we moved forward, he had left his fag packet with its contents of 'special' cigarettes on the ground. He went into the crowd to look for them. A few minutes later, he emerged with a triumphant grin on his face – he had found them!

We got talking to some guys who told us they were from *Brain Damage*, a Pink Floyd fan magazine. They took our photo and said they would publish it and I wrote to them sometime later. Unfortunately, the picture was too dark to publish but they did send us a copy.

When Pink Floyd came onto the stage, a girl next to us was trying to take photos but could not see over the crowd in front. Andy asked if she wanted to sit on his shoulders for a better view. She did. She must have taken a whole film's worth of pics, as she was up there for ages.

Due to the beer we had consumed and the weed, things started to get a bit hazy. I remember them playing 'Great Gig in the Sky' and being transfixed with the backing singers. My favourite track is 'Comfortably Numb'. When they played that, I was lying spreadeagled on the ground watching the lasers over everyone's heads. Andy started kicking me, saying, 'Mick, get up. It's 'Comfortably Numb'.' I answered that I was! I did get up and I watched the rest of the gig. To this day, it is the best gig I have been to.

I WAS THERE: NEIL DEANS, AGE 15

I went with my dad and I loved it. I remember seeing Pink Floyd on *Top of the Pops* with 'Another Brick in the Wall' and got into them in the Eighties through other lads in school talking about them. My dad had *Dark Side of the Moon* and *Wish You Were Here* so I started listening to those albums first and I loved them. After that, any spare money I got minding my cousins – Christmas money, birthday money and so on – I spent on buying of their albums and the solo albums. I have bought all the different versions that have been out since – the remasters, etc. I recently bought all the new vinyl editions and the *Early Years 1965 – 1972* box set, so I have been listening to a lot of Floyd recently and I really love the early stuff. If I had to pick a favourite album, it would be *Wish You Were Here and my* favourite song would be 'Echoes', but they do change from time to time.

I WAS THERE: MARTIN SANDFORD

Family life and bringing up children stymied our concert attendance in the years after first seeing Floyd but in the summer of 1988, we just had to see them appear at the Man City ground. With a very clingy boy of two who would create mayhem if separated from his mum's hug for more than three minutes, this proved to be a military exercise as we crawled past the side window and pushed the car into the street before driving off to the concert. Memories of the gig vary but apart from the obvious show that Floyd put on including Dalek-like bots floating around the stage lighting up the stage area, the overwhelming picture was of cables running from the audience end to stage end, upon which a big brass bed slid at a certain point in the proceedings. The inflatable pigs were de rigueur so it felt quite normal to see them floating above Maine Road. A great time was had by all and it the last time I saw them live.

Although the sight of Roger on stage with guys was something that pleased all the Floyd fans, it was clear to me and I guess many others that it was forced and that feelings and egos were still running strong and never again would the Floyd talent gel and creative juices flow!

ARENA CONCERTI, AUTODROMO
20 MAY 1989, MONZA, ITALY

I WAS THERE: NIGEL BANKS

I was aware of their existence via the hit singles, 'Arnold Layne' and 'See Emily Play', but knew nothing of Floyd's more experimental, progressive material until I was properly introduced to them at Oxford in 1970. A fellow student, who came from a well-off background, was in the habit of purchasing two or three new albums at a time. We duly sat round his small mono record player to listen to the recently-released *Atom Heart Mother*. I'm not sure I was bowled over, but my interest was piqued sufficiently for me to buy a much played, secondhand copy of *Ummagumma* from another fellow student. It was not a wise purchase, as both discs were very scratched and there was a lot of hiss. However, fast forward to the releases of *Echoes* and *Dark Side of the Moon* and I became a huge fan of the band's output.

In the '80s, I kept tabs on the band but less avidly than during my student days. In 1988, I moved to Italy to take up a teaching post at an international school in Milan. A colleague happened to mention that the band were playing a big concert at the Autodromo in Monza. The venue is situated in the middle of the famous Grand Prix motor racing circuit. A group of five or six us bought tickets and duly made our way to Monza. We made the mistake of stopping en route for refreshments and dallied longer than we intended. Consequently, by the time we arrived, the arena was packed and we found

When the band finally took to the stage, they were just tiny figures in the distance. There were two video screens which enlarged proceedings but one felt rather detached from the experience, although the sound quality was very good and the obligatory light show and visual effects were stunning. I picked out Tim Renwick as the support guitarist to Dave Gilmour in the much enlarged band line-up that the Floyd employed in those days – a far cry from the original four-piece when they started. I can't say that any particular song stands out in my memory from that gig over 30 years ago, but I do remember being swept up by the whole experience. The Italian audience was predictably ebullient and noisy, so one couldn't help being carried along by their enthusiasm!

OLYMPIC STADIUM
3, 4, 6 - 8 JUNE 1989, MOSCOW, RUSSIA

I INTERVIEWED NICK: ALEXANDER SPARINSKY

I'd been told 'no accreditation, no interviews' by the State Concert Committee (the organisation in charge of Pink Floyd's tour) and that 'after the first press conference, the musicians refused to meet with journalists and forbade photographs at the concerts. So, sorry…'. But I didn't want to return home to Ukraine with nothing. I'd been to see the band in Moscow with a friend, an Englishwoman of Ukrainian descent named Katherine Duliba, who had worked for the BBC for some time. She called the band's press officer direct and, being a native English speaker and referencing her work at the BBC, she secured me an interview with Nick Mason and guest guitarist Tim Renwick. Here's an extract of my interview, which was published in the *Moloda Hvardiya* newspaper in Kyiv, Ukraine on 25 June 1989.

AS: Mr Mason, have you met any Soviet musicians, do you know anything about our rock music?

NM: Unfortunately, almost nothing. I talked to a few musicians and heard about some events.

AS: What is your general impression?

NM: Your rock has to catch up: it's 15 years behind the state of European music. But now that there is an opportunity for contacts and access to Western musicians, this process will probably intensify. I don't mean that the West will stimulate Soviet rock. No! Intertwining, mutual enrichment will give your rock culture a corresponding boost... I know Brian Eno was here, and some others.

AS: You and David Gilmour have already visited the USSR?

NM: Dave and I were invited to the launch of Salyut 7 at Baikonur recently. One of the Soviet cosmonauts even took our album on board, into space. The atmosphere of the meeting and the warm welcome that was given to us were great incentives. At the end of last year, we seriously started talking about a series of concerts in Moscow: it's great to discover new countries!

AS: Is it hard to play nowadays, being so legendary?

NM: No, it's still easy and joyful for us to perform. If it wasn't fun anymore, we wouldn't go on stage. We'll continue as long as Pink Floyd keeps moving forward, not standing still.

AS: Tim, isn't it hard for you to work with such luminaries? How did you come to the famous band? Where did you come from?

TR: Oh, we've known each other for God knows how long. We studied with Waters at school. We've worked with David many times, though a long time ago, in the band Sutherland Brothers & Quiver. I'm a freelance musician but I've been working with Pink Floyd since August 1987.

AS: Nick, you and Richard and David all have solo albums. Isn't this a sign of disunity in the band?

NM: We're all individuals. Everyone is free to do their own thing. We think it's good for the ensemble, for its' individuality. Everyone brings to the group what they've learned outside of it. As long as the group remains interesting for its members, everything you learn outside of it is practical and important. For example, what I learnt from Michael Mantler and Carla Bley (trumpeter and pianist, leaders of avant-garde jazz) came in handy when we were recording our LPs.

AS: You started working in cinema in the mid-Sixties as musical performers for Michelangelo Antonioni with the film *Zabriskie Point*. Then there was *The Valley, More* (directed by Barbet Schroeder), and finally, your own work, the rock opera *The Wall*, which was later turned into a film. Is it a deliberate path?

NM: It was an accident. We started out as an ordinary band; we wanted to perform on

Top of the Pops, sell our albums and so on. It was only with time that we realised that there were many different paths in rock music that we could take. Film music is a discipline, even if it's not as creative. You are bound by the length of the play, the character, the imaginative emotionality. And even now, I do not make any serious plans for the future or think 'what are we going to do next?'. We just take on projects one by one. I am well aware of the importance and the unprecedented nature of our tour in the USSR. I doubt that this would have been possible five years ago. There was no serious talk of such things then. It's all the more interesting for us to be here today.

GLOBEN
12 JUNE 1989, STOCKHOLM, SWEDEN

I WAS THERE: PETER AHLANDER, AGE 26

I got the ticket from a person who had been sick. I went to the show with no expectations. The only song that I had really heard of was 'Another Brick in the Wall (Part 2)'. I sat for the whole show with my mouth open and just stared – it was a fantastic, an awesome show, and is still number one of all my favourite concerts. All the highlights – like the flying pig, the sound and the stage production – were just awesome. The highlight was 'Comfortably Numb', and my mouth was down to my knees when the mirror ball came down and opened up. After the concert, I just sat about for a long time – I was blown away.

LONDON DOCKLANDS ARENA
4 – 8 JULY 1989, LONDON, UK

I WAS THERE: NICK BRICE, AGE 14

I was basically unaware of Pink Floyd – incredible, I know! My dad, who I didn't live with as my parents were divorced, called me up and asked if I'd like to go to London to watch Pink Floyd as he had a spare ticket. I jumped at the opportunity, as it was a chance to spend time with my dad and also see a big band live. The day of the gig arrived and my dad came and picked me up early as we were about two hours' drive from the venue. In the car was my dad, his fiancée and her brother. They were all discussing the gig.

When we got to the docklands, we parked up and my dad and his fiancée had a joint on the walk to the Arena. The London Arena was just a big warehouse with poor acoustics – it's since been demolished! We sat at the back of the arena in an elevated position with a pretty good view. The atmosphere was electric and the noise immense. I was so impressed within the opening minute that it cemented my love of Floyd forever. I recognised obvious tracks like 'The Wall' and 'Great Gig in the Sky'. The light show was incredible, especially given this was nearly 30 years ago. I think the only comparison for special effects would be Jean-Michel Jarre.

On the way home after the gig, we drove into a KFC drive through on the Old Kent Road. My dad asked the server for a burger and was told 'we don't sell burgers – we sell fried chicken'. My dad said, 'I don't want chicken, I want a beef burger.' Maybe he was stoned but he certainly made us laugh. He conceded in the end and had chicken.

I got see them live again in 1993 at Earl's Court. I was now 18, so I could drink beer legally, and I was there with my dad, his wife, my brother and my best mate. This time it was better due to a better location and better acoustics. I went on to purchase all the Floyd's albums and the *Shine On* box set. I have a lot of good memories when I listen to Floyd now. It's a link to my father so it's bigger than music itself. Now Floyd are no more, my hope is that I can see David Gilmour before he hangs up his guitar.

I WAS THERE: ROBIN HADDEN, AGE 17

The friend who had turned me on to Floyd rang with exciting news: 'We can go see the Floyd!' At the time, I was quickly building my collection on vinyl (which I subsequently sold, and have since bought again) and learning everything. *Delicate Sound of Thunder* was already out and on constant rotation. Tickets were £33, which included return coach travel from Sunderland, in North East England, to London. I was so excited. This to be my first live gig and what a way to start nearly 30 years of concert going! The day came and we were armed with cash for merchandise and snacks. We raided the merch stall for t-shirts and programmes. I was totally mesmerised by the whole show and was blown away by how moving an experience it was, both sober and without drugs – just soaking up the music. I might add here that I'm a musician myself and a qualified music teacher. The show stays with me to this day and I still struggle to sometimes get across to other people the emotions that a live show generates in me. Music is an essential part of my life.

I WAS THERE: JACOB HOOD, AGE 16

My uncle and friends had travelled from Glasgow to see the *Momentary Lapse of Reason* tour at the London Arena, which has now gone. I lived in Bow in East London at the time.

We travelled by car to the arena without tickets, hoping to buy from a tout. Then it came over the public address system that there were tickets for that night's performance. As we were just outside the box office, we managed to buy four. On entering the arena, I was overwhelmed by the electric atmosphere that was created by the fans. It was like a volcano ready to erupt. The whole of the choreography throughout the show was awesome. My greatest memories of the night are of the flying bed and pig, the three lady vocalists, the drum cave, and the giant flames that came out of the stage which I could feel the heat of on my face (accompanied by the consumption of a Tangerine Dream). The performance from Dave Gilmour was simply amazing.

I WAS THERE: NICHOL THOMPSON

I saw them a year after seeing them at Wembley Stadium, at Docklands. By this time, I was living in the flat in West Ham that I'd stayed at the year before. We decided to chance it and just try and get some tickets off some touts when we got to the arena. We were in Stratford Tube station when I stopped a guy with two Pink Floyd tickets in his hand. I hadn't tried really hard to get tickets this time or when I went to Wembley – they just came to me.

A guy had a heart attack on the Docklands Tube about three stops from the Docklands Arena and to begin with it was 'poor guy'. But after half an hour it was 'get him off the train and get him to the hospital – we're going to miss the concert!' We got to the arena and we couldn't believe the queues. We knew it was a seated arena but we hadn't even thought that you have to go to the seat number that's on your ticket. We just went right down the front, as close to the stage as we could get, and then just as the band came on these people came and said 'oh, these are our seats' and we ended up being miles away, right up the back. But it was actually better, because you could dance where we were.

It was cosier than Wembley Stadium, a bit more intimate, being indoors. I'd never seen anything like the light show in my life. I just didn't know you could even do that with lights, never mind combine it with the music and get the whole effect it gave overall. It was just mind blowing.

I'd been a fan since I was a kid. I always remember *The Dark Side of the Moon*, which was getting played everywhere I went as a kid, either at my dad's friends or my dad's. And that was the first album I bought. When I really got into them under my own steam, I was probably 14. I've been to see the Australian Pink Floyd a few times as well in Edinburgh and, for a covers band, they're well worth the money.

PIAZZA SAN MARCO
15 JULY 1989, VENICE, ITALY

I WAS THERE: ANDREW DARDI

The concert was free, and people started to flood into Piazza San Marco only shortly before because Venice City Council only authorised the event at the last minute. Nevertheless, the estimated audience was more than 100,000 people. The stage was amazing, facing Piazza San Marco. The line-up was Gilmour, Mason and Wright plus Guy Pratt as bass player, Scott Page on saxophone and others. The town was under siege. All the shops closed and the city council had ruled that the volume should not go above 90 decibels. The band delivered an amazing performance. The first track was 'Learning to Fly' and the best executed song in my opinion was 'The Great Gig in the Sky', with the amazing voices of Rachel Fury and Durga McBroom.

The problem was that in the square there was no water and no WC. Many people started to feel sick and the following day the square was covered in junk. It was a sort of humanitarian disaster, and because of that the city council put a ban on concerts. No other event of this kind has ever taken place in Venice since. But for me it was a memorable experience!

STADE VELODROME DE MARSEILLE
18 JULY 1989, MARSEILLE, FRANCE

I WAS THERE: LAURENT POHU

I saw Floyd in Nantes in 1988 and in Strasbourg in 1994, but in 1989 I was a waiter in Saint Tropez when a friend told me he'd read an interview in which Bernard Tapie, president and owner of Olympique Marseille Football Club, said he would invite Pink Floyd to play in the Velodrome Stadium to thank all the OM fans for their support in winning Ligue 1. I said that Bernard Tapie might be very rich but that he couldn't just get Pink Floyd to play. They were ending their European tour with a huge concert in Venice. But three days later, I was indeed at OM's stadium. Bernard Tapie had done it… During 'Money', there was a moment when all the instruments stopped playing and only the singers and the bass guitar were keeping the rhythm, until David Gilmour started a duet with saxophonist Scott Page. The instruments slowed down, the musicians went behind the singers and just before they restarted the guitar/sax duet, Gilmour came out of the group and start playing 'La Marseillaise'. It was unbelievable.

I've also seen David solo three times. In January 2002, I went to Paris to see one of the five acoustic concerts David played in London and Paris, with Michael Kamen on piano and English horn, and special guests to sing Roger's part on 'Comfortably Numb'. Durga McBroom sang on the Paris shows, with Robert Wyatt, Kate Bush and Richard Wright doing London. I saw David again at L'Olympia during his 2006 world tour and we got an improvised 'The Great Gig in the Sky' and a great 'Echoes' that I'd never heard live before. And I last saw him at Chantilly Castle in 2016, on the *Rattle That Lock* tour. New security rules were in place as a result of the terrorist attack in Nice and, because the castle is surrounded by a moat and there are only two ways in and out, the concert started an hour late. David asked everyone to respect a minute's silence in memory of all the victims of the Nice atrocity. Everyone did.

In 2002 I met Nick Mason who was participating, along with his fabulous Ferrari 250 GTO, in the Le Mans Classic. He signed my Marseilles 1989 ticket.

I WAS THERE: ALEXIS MAINDRAULT

Pink Floyd were the soundtrack of my youth, to the point where I was that one oddball in middle and high school who didn't listen to New Wave or any type of '80s bands (I still am that oddball, to my wife's great dismay). I remember listening to 'Echoes' on my Walkman and scaring the crap out of myself before falling asleep. I was too young to know that they had broken up but I knew that the odds of me seeing them live were very slim. In the mind of a teenager, these guys were old.

So when Pink Floyd announced that they were not only touring but coming to a city an hour away from the small town I grew up in, my parents jumped at the opportunity and bought us tickets. I couldn't care less that it was sans Roger Waters. I had never been to a concert and never seen one on TV, so I had no idea what to expect. We were pretty far back, but I could see that big white circle on the stage. Shortly after the sun set, the show started. 'Shine On You Crazy Diamond' had always been one of my favourite tunes so it was a special treat to hear it live. The whole show almost felt like being at the opera, except with lasers, lasers everywhere and a wonderful light show! I remember thinking that I could have done without the songs from *A Momentary Lapse of Reason* and just listened to them play the classic Floyd tunes all night. It was the night 'The Great Gig in the Sky' became my favourite piece of music hands down. Hearing the three vocalists take turns to express so much emotion over a relatively simple musical background really spoke to my heart, and still does. This was also the last time I did something significant with both my parents together.

Fast forward five years and I was in college in Lyon. By then I had met other Pink Floyd fans, and one in particular who was still mad that he had missed them in

Marseille. We bought tickets for the September 11th show as soon as they went for sale. In hindsight, I wish I had also gotten tickets for the second show, because they ended up playing the whole *Dark Side of the Moon* album. It was a pretty dreary day but it didn't matter. As we drove in from outside of town with my friend, I knew that once the show started, it could pour and no one would care.

You know how, sometimes, you build up expectations that cannot be matched by the experience you're about to have? I had these types of expectations. And yet, when the show started, I was 16 again, staring at that masterfully illuminated stage, the lasers, the round screen (which seemed to have more content), the plane crashing at the end of 'On the Run', the flying pigs, the inflatable dogs, Gilmour's sharp and spacious guitar solos, the little bass improvisation in the middle of 'Money' and, of course, 'The Great Gig in the Sky'. I also remember distinctly getting chills when they hit the bell at the end of 'Breathe'. The show was as magical as the first time around.

KNEBWORTH PARK
30 JUNE 1990, STEVENAGE, UK

I WAS THERE: GUðBJÖRG ÖGMUNDSDÓTTIR

It was the *Silver Clef Award Winners Show*. It was a wonderful day, with eleven hours of great music, beginning at 12 noon and continuing into the night. Pink Floyd closed the show, but we enjoyed so many wonderful artists it was overwhelming. Tears for Fears, Status Quo, Cliff Richard with the Shadows, Robert Plant with Jimmy Page, Phil Collins, Genesis, Eric Clapton, Dire Straits, Elton John and Paul McCartney and Wings all performed fantastic sets. By the time Pink Floyd came on, it was raining heavily and we were quite exhausted. Due to the weather they only played a brief set which included 'Shine On You Crazy Diamond', 'Money', 'Comfortably Numb', 'The Great Gig in the Sky' and 'Run Like Hell'. The laser show was absolutely awesome.

After all this, we had the hard task of getting back to London. It was total darkness and first we had to walk for about half an hour, catch a bus to the train station and, once we got there, we had the utter chaos of thousands of people trying to get into the tiny station at once. It took two hours to catch a train and we didn't get to our hotel in London until about 5am! But it had all been worth it.

WISH YOU WERE HERE

I WAS THERE: ROBIN HADDEN

Pink Floyd were announced to headline the Nordoff Robbins Silver Clef concert at Knebworth in Hertfordshire – and what a line up; McCartney, Genesis, Robert Plant, Eric Clapton and others all on one day! Spending the £30 wasn't a difficult decision, as I was just about to start university. But there was a tough choice to be made, as Roger Waters announced he would be doing *The Wall* in Berlin which, even with travel and accommodation costs, was still a possibility. We decided to pass on it (thankfully, as I watched it on TV and thought it was dreadful!).

Memories of the Knebworth concert include the long coach journey overnight to arrive early Saturday morning in a coach park four miles from the venue. But it was a beautiful summer's day and an early walk got us in the mood. A huge crowd of 120,000 was (and still is) the largest I had ever experienced. It's amazing that the group of friends I'd travelled with managed not to lose each other what with all the toilet and refreshment breaks.

There was a great roar when the gates opened and we got a great position in the first few thousand (I'm even on the cover of the live album). The iconic circular screen hovered horizontally over the stage all day, but sadly it rained and got soaked and couldn't be used, though the lights still worked. It was an amazing set list, with guest sax Candy Dulfer and Clare Torry reprising 'The Great Gig in the Sky'. There was little banter from Gilmour apart from referring to the weather but his playing was flawless, although there was a little error in 'Run Like Hell', which was fixed for the release of the DVD.

I WAS THERE: PETER SMITH

I won a pair of free tickets in a competition – from *KitKat*! – and my wife Marie and I went down to London for the weekend. Because of the number of acts appearing, everyone played a short set. Floyd appeared last, after Paul McCartney, although he was officially the 'headliner'. This was the Waters-less line-up of Gilmour, Mason and Wright, augmented by Guy Pratt (bass), Jon Carin (keyboards), Tim Renwick (guitar), Gary Wallis (percussion), Candy Dulfer (saxophone) and backing singers Durga McBroom, Sam Brown (who had recently been in the charts with 'Stop!'), her mum Vicki Brown and original *Dark Side* vocalist Clare Torry. Their set was limited to 'Shine On You Crazy Diamond', 'The Great Gig in the Sky', 'Wish You Were Here', 'Sorrow' (the only track they performed from their most recent album), 'Money' and 'Comfortably Numb', with 'Run Like Hell' as an encore. We'd had a little wind and rain during the day, and by the time Floyd took to the stage it was raining again, and they weren't able to use their circular screen because of the wind. Floyd's appearance was a fitting end to a great concert and I particularly enjoyed 'Shine On You Crazy Diamond'. We left during the encore, and it took ages to find our car as there were no markings or lights in the car park.

A PEOPLE'S HISTORY OF PINK FLOYD

Pink Floyd are off the road again in 1991 and 1992, and play only one show in 1993 – a benefit gig for the King Edward VII Hospital. But 1994 sees Floyd on the road again, promoting new album The Division Bell *on a seven month long world tour.*

THE DIVISION BELL RELEASED

Reaching No.1 in the UK and US album charts and in the album charts of 18 other countries, The Division Bell *goes on to become Floyd's fourth-bestselling album after* The Dark Side of the Moon, The Wall *and* Wish You Were Here.

JOE ROBBIE STADIUM
30 MARCH 1994, MIAMI, FLORIDA

I WAS THERE: BRIAN FOWLER

I went to the *Division Bell* tour in Miami, without Waters, and it was a freakin' thunderstorm with lightning bolts all around. It was kind of cool but they ran off stage when it got too bad.

I WAS THERE: KEITH VITOVICH

I saw Pink Floyd twice, once in Pittsburgh in 1988, which was documented by a German film crew, I would guess for German TV. The second concert was in Miami, on the opening night of the *Division Bell* world tour. It was recorded and simulcasted across the USA and Canada. They had gold lasers and we got some rain that night, so with the lasers going through the raindrops it made it look like a million prisms. What a sight to see, made all the more special with the help of some mushrooms!

UNIVERSITY STADIUM
5 APRIL 1994, HOUSTON, TEXAS

I WAS THERE: DICK HEAD

Since the concert was at a conservative college stadium, there was no alcohol served. This kind of piqued the concert-goers a little. About two-thirds of the way through the show, it started first to sprinkle, then shower and then began an all-out downpour. David's guitar shorted out. He was handed a dry one and continued to play until there was about two inches of water on the stage floor. Not wanting to get electrocuted, once the PA system shut down, he yelled to the crowd that he was sorry but the rest of the show had to be cancelled. The crowd actually booed. We couldn't believe it – the band was standing in two inches of water, fearful for their lives, and idiots in the crowd booed.

Fast forward about six months. I was working a job in Dallas and I heard on the radio that Pink Floyd was playing Cowboy Stadium that night. After work and a bite to eat, I headed to the stadium box office. On the way I bought a half-pint of scotch, just in case. There were individual seats left and all I needed was one. I got to see the entire show this time. I drank all the scotch plus a couple of beers. It was a good thing the parking lot was a zoo after the show, as I had time to sort of sober up before heading back to my hotel.

Exiting the elevator on my floor, I saw a young lady in nothing but a long t-shirt. She looked distraught as she covered herself as best she could. I asked her if she needed help and she said she was putting her room service tray out and the door locked behind her. I opened my room door and grabbed my jacket and handed it to her and called the front desk. Someone came up immediately and opened her door. You couldn't make this stuff up.

I WAS THERE: CYNTHIA GONZALES

I was aware of Pink Floyd during *The Wall* but for 'Another Brick in the Wall'. It wasn't until the televised *Delicate Sound of Thunder* concert and tape came out, and a friend and his brother would play and sing along to 'Comfortably Numb' as they took me to school, that I became hooked. We got to the show late and, upon hearing them start playing 'Astronomy Domine' we, along with all the other late people, started running in and around the stadium to get to our seats. It was surreal to be running in to that song. The concert was supposed to be an all-weather event and it rained for most of the concert. During the encore, on 'Run Like Hell', a flooded portion of the overhang over the back up singers fell apart and drenched them. They stopped the concert at that point and said something like 'sorry, we can't continue, cheerio!' and ended the show. People were mad. We ran back to our cars, getting separated from our group. My group got to our car first and we stood there soaked to the bone and so cold we didn't dare move.

I was living in Austin and had the poster of the light bulb man from *Delicate Sound of Thunder* over my bed. When I went to college and took film classes, I put Pink Floyd songs from *The Division Bell* on the soundtrack to most of the projects I had to film. I wasn't good with the camera, but you could film something as simple as a tree swaying, use any Pink Floyd song as the soundtrack and the music would give it a more profound meaning. Their music takes you to a whole different place.

ROSE BOWL
16 & 17 APRIL 1994, PASADENA, CALIFORNIA

I WAS THERE: BILLY GALLEGOS
I saw their final Los Angeles County appearance at the Rose Bowl, when they played two nights. I was working in the South Pasadena area and, through the window of the building where I worked, saw the pig balloon flying over the city weeks before the show.

I WAS THERE: JOSHUA SILVA
My grandpa raised my mom on Pink Floyd. She used to tell me about being woken up for school by him blasting out *Animals* and *Dark Side of the Moon* on his record player. Once *The Division Bell* came out, my mom bought tickets to see them in Los Angeles and took me along. I was around 12 or 13, and it was the most amazing show I've ever seen, which says a lot because I've seen a whole lot of bands! The laser show was cosmic and the crowd smelled of burning marijuana. Everything was nicely put in place.

I WAS THERE: STEVE SHEPPARD
I have been listening to Pink Floyd since *Dark Side of the Moon* was released when I was a teenager. My best friend had a quadraphonic system and it was just the greatest music I had ever heard! I got my tickets to the Rose Bowl concert from a client in the business. I was centre stage, about 15 rows back, and it was one of the greatest shows I have ever seen. I went with my now ex-wife and I remember the huge projection screen, the giant inflated pigs on top of the speaker columns on each side of the stage rocking back and forth with the music, and Dave Gilmour's lead guitar riffs. It seemed as if everyone there was – how shall I say this? – comfortably numb.

COLISEUM STADIUM
20 – 22 APRIL 1994, OAKLAND, CALIFORNIA

I WAS THERE: SAM HERNANDEZ
I was fortunate enough to attend all three nights in Oakland. The most magical evening was the opening night. I went with my older brother Eddie and this was the first time either of

us had seen Pink Floyd live. I had won a pair of tickets and souvenir tour t-shirts from the local radio station. We took the train to the stadium. The train was at full capacity and many riders were standing. We managed to get seats for an estimated 25-minute ride and in front of us there stood a beauty. Make that a goddess. She was standing in front of her boyfriend, who was much taller than she was, and I could not take my eyes off her.

Her boyfriend noticed the shirts we were wearing and asked me where we had purchased them. I told him that I won them from the radio station with free tickets. He shouted out 'lucky fucker!' I said quietly to my brother, 'He is the lucky fucker.' She was just so beautiful that it was a strange feeling, like a dream that I just remembered having that had brought me to that moment. As we approached the stadium, they got off with us and then she disappeared.

Pink Floyd finally live – wow! My heart was pumping fast with excitement. We found our seats which faced the stage at a good angle and who should turn up five rows down from us but none other than the beauty and her boyfriend. Well, the concert itself was spectacular. They were about two weeks into the tour and sounded fresh. Gilmour is a guitar god. I mostly remember the awesome light show and songs from *The Division Bell* album. They hit it out of the park with 'What Do You Want From Me', 'Poles Apart', 'Take It Back' and 'High Hopes'. 'Shine On You Crazy Diamond' was flawless and, damn, there was that girl again, who kept passing up the aisle during the concert, a nice distraction. I can truly say that this was the best concert that I have ever attended, and I was glad that I got to experience it with my brother.

But I could not get that girl out of my head. She touched my soul that night in some strange way. Then, as luck would have it, I bumped into this same girl at a dance club in Modesto, California four and a half years later in 1998, not even knowing it was her until we both mentioned seeing Pink Floyd live in Oakland in 1994 and I talked about the conversation that I had on the train with that guy holding that beautiful girl. Fate, man! She remembered me and my brother and I remembered her. Three weeks later we started dating, three months later I moved in with her, and we were married in 2003. Thank you, Pink Floyd.

SUN DEVIL STADIUM
24 APRIL 1994, TEMPE, ARIZONA

I WAS THERE: MICHÄEL PERKINS

A friend won tickets on the radio so we skipped work and spent the day listening to Pink Floyd in our shared studio apartment living room. We took a cab to the show and filed in and down to our seats on the floor of the stadium, right next to the front of house. They were using the quadraphonic sound system and playing a really long audio collage/soundscape over the system before the show. It was the most amazing sound I had ever heard. There was a segment right before they started where it sounded like a lawnmower starting up and the ambient noises of a yard – flies, bees, a sprinkler, birds. The sound made me feel for a moment like my head was about to be chopped in the lawnmower blade!

It was a great show from my seat and, at the end, when the giant orb thing came up out of the thing right next to us – well, what an amazing finale!

I WAS THERE: CRYSTI DEUSTERMAN, AGE 22

My college girlfriends weren't into Floyd so I went with my friend Ben, who I'd known since third grade. The weather was perfect, sweet smells burned all around and David Gilmour wailed on guitar. It was mesmerising. I don't know much about music but I love the distinct sound of David Gilmour. I recall gazing out into the huge audience and fondly thinking of my parents, who were also there, and my brother too. It was surreal, my whole family all being out there, somewhere. My parents are not what springs to mind when you think of a Floyd concert-goer. I remember looking up from my seat and staring at an enormous inflatable pig, swaying in the breeze, red eyes aglow… But there was a lot of smoke wafting through the air, so who knows if they were actually lit? The concert was intense, almost spiritual. I am so glad I had the opportunity to see Pink Floyd live. I still love them. I am still friends with the guy I went to the show with, still close to my brother and my parents are still alive and well. There was an awesome box set released around that time... I still have that too. I listened to the song 'Eclipse' on repeat (yep, on my CD from the box set) while I watched the eclipse in my backyard in Arizona.

TEXAS STADIUM
28 & 29 APRIL 1994, IRVING, TEXAS

I WAS THERE: ROBERT SHAFER

I was a couple of months shy of my 40th birthday when the Floyd came to Dallas in 1994 for the *Division Bell* tour. I'd been a fan ever since *Dark Side of the Moon* came out. I was in college at the time, and it's still my all-time favourite album. I live in the Dallas area, so did not have to travel far for the show, but my then girlfriend came in from Memphis for it. It was at the old Texas Stadium that had the hole in the roof. There were thunderstorms in the area, and during the concert, it started pouring down with rain. We were sitting on what would be the sidelines of the football field, so when it started to rain, we were kept dry by the roof. However, the folks sitting just a few rows in front of us were getting soaked, as were the people on the floor. The laser light show was in full gear, and when the lights hit the raindrops, you could see little green lights everywhere. You could also see the lightning outside the stadium, and it matched the music and the lasers perfectly. It was probably the most visually spectacular concert I've ever been to, and a lot of it was from Mother Nature. It was surreal! The set list included most of the songs from *Dark Side of the Moon*, but I remember thinking after the show it would have been nice to hear them in order like on the album. The band did that later in the tour, and the result was *Pulse*, which I have on CD and DVD. It's one of my all-time favourite concerts.

I WAS THERE: GARTH ARMSTRONG

It was a nice warm day when we went inside but we knew the weather would be changing – at least, me and my significant other did, and we dressed accordingly. Along with my spouse were my two friends, Jerry and Greg. Jerry was in shorts and a t-shirt. Texas Stadium was famous for having a hole in its roof (so God could watch the Cowboys play) and we had floor seats smack dab in the middle. It was chaos from the moment we arrived at the stadium – a weather front was moving in and the winds had turned. It had already started raining. Floyd were unable to do their full light show due to the weather. It was still a spectacular show but by the end we were cold and miserable.

We proceeded to exit the stadium through a concrete tunnel that led up to street level. About 20 feet into the tunnel, we were suddenly knee-deep in cold water. The crowd was so packed in this part of the tunnel that we were moving in unison with the crowd. A few 'moo' calls were quickly replaced by looks of concern and fright in a very short order, and I saw true fear in people's eyes – one misstep and it would be disaster. Fortunately, this only lasted seconds. But Greg (RIP) was a big guy who carried some weight. That and the muddy slope coming off the freeway along the path we were walking did not serve him well. He lost his footing and slipped ten feet to level ground. We reached the car, got in, turned on the heat and just sat there – completely soaked, and Greg covered in mud.

I WAS THERE: JOE SANCHEZ, AGE 7

I was only seven! I've seen some great shows before and since, but this was the best live concert experience of my life. I went with seven other family and friends, including my mom and dad. Apart from the timeless music, the lasers, props and pyrotechnics made for a great show. My favourite moment of the show was when a giant mirror ball dropped in the middle of the stadium and illuminated the place in the middle of 'Comfortably Numb', during David Gilmour's second, elongated lead. There was a wicked rainstorm that night. Fortunately, we were towards the back, so we were sheltered from the elements. And the rain added to the visual flair of the show, especially during the mirror ball segment. I couldn't speak properly for the following three days, having screamed my fool head off the whole night, but boy, was it worth it. A huge thanks to my mom for getting us those tickets, and a giant shout out to David Gilmour and company for putting on a night I'll never forget!

BOBBIE DODD STADIUM
3 MAY 1994, ATLANTA, GEORGIA

I WAS THERE: DAVID MCCOY

The show opened with 'Astronomy Domine' and two young boys a couple of rows in front of me looked at each other. One said to the other 'must be on the new album'.

I WAS THERE: LESLIE LADD

My best friend, Becky, and I went to the *Division Bell* concert at the Bobby Dodd Stadium at Georgia Tech. Being an outside show, we had side view centre lower balcony section seats, so it was a great vantage point to see all the special effects. I remember they began with a song I didn't know well, 'Astronomy Domine'. We loved it as they had the most spectacular laser show I had ever seen. It was cutting edge at the time. During the show, a huge glitter ball dropped flower petals during 'Comfortably Numb'. I had never seen the floating pig before and I remember thinking it was scary and menacing looking. They did a two song encore, 'Hey You' and 'Run Like Hell', and we wanted more but that was it. It was pretty hot in the Southern heat and there were mosquitoes too, so I guess it was a good thing that it ended.

I have seen the tribute group Brit Floyd, which gives a great show, but I was also super excited to attend the Roger Waters *Us and Them* show in 2017. We took our son, who grew up listening to my music, and his girlfriend. He loves many of the newer bands, like Tool, but I told him these groups are amateurs compared to Pink Floyd. I wish I could have seen them during the Syd days.

TAMPA STADIUM
6 MAY 1994, TAMPA, FLORIDA

I WAS THERE: MICHAEL HOWARD, AGE 13

I went with my Dad and my two brothers, who had introduced me to Pink Floyd. The show was at the old Tampa stadium. This was the first major concert I ever saw and it remains in my top three out of hundreds of concerts I've seen since. I was sober because I was so young and it was still amazing. It was the first time I even smelled pot smoke. David Gilmour is one of my favourite guitar players. I remember there being many highlights during the show – the pigs in the speaker stacks, the mirror ball during 'Comfortably Numb', the video screens, the lasers, the massive stage set up. But the music is what stood out the most and what remains with me.

VANDERBILT STADIUM
8 MAY 1994, NASHVILLE, TENNESSEE

I WAS THERE: RICK PETTY

It was an amazing spectacle both visually and acoustically. My personal highlight was when David came out and sat on a bar stool to play 'Wish You Were Here'. To hear 45,000 people singing along in unison was enough to send chills down my spine, and well worth the three-hour drive to see what is still one of the best, if not the best, concert I have attended.

I WAS THERE: RANDY EARNEST

I had the gracious opportunity to see Pink Floyd in Nashville, Tennessee for the *Division Bell* tour in '94, the one and only time that Pink Floyd have ever played in Tennessee. I believe Floyd were to play in Memphis, although due to a scheduling conflict, The Rolling Stones played Memphis and Pink Floyd moved to Nashville. The show had two sets, with *The Division Bell* covering most of the first set, while the second set was *The Dark Side of the Moon*, ending with 'Run Like Hell'. The Vanderbilt Stadium is an outdoor stadium, and the show was so loud that the City of Nashville said it would be the last show in the stadium!

CARTER FINLEY STADIUM
10 MAY 1994, RALEIGH, NORTH CAROLINA

I WAS THERE: SEAN MARCUM

My friends and I purchased tickets from our local record store, Birdland Records. We were only able to get the cheap seats, in the back of the stadium on the grassy hill. We didn't care – we just wanted to go! The great thing about a Pink Floyd show is that you are always inside the event with sounds coming from everywhere. I remember a person standing at the gate saying we were all going to hell for going to this concert. I think we all threw coins at him because he had a hat on the ground or something, as if he was trying to raise some money.

There was a partial eclipse that night which gave off this weird light and made it that bit more magical. As we found our grassy hill to sit on, the stage went as dark as the night sky, and then all of a sudden we got this whooshing sound with all these planets appearing on the screen behind them. I was thinking, 'What the heck is this?'. Then the first sounds of 'Astronomy Domine' started and it took me a minute to realise what this song was. It absolutely blew my mind – and the show had only just begun and I was already in heaven!

Most of the set list is kind of hard to recall but I definitely remember 'One of These Days', with the pigs in the towers on either side of the stage. As the song ended, they came crashing down, looking as if they were writhing on the floor – freaking awesome! 'Wish You Were Here' was just a religious experience with everyone singing along and just an incredible sight to behold, with everyone holding up lights. 'Comfortably Numb', with the huge disco ball rising from the middle of the audience, was plain awesome while 'Hey You' was definitely a surprise and a great one at that. Another great memory is the sight of Richard Wright dancing his butt off the whole show. I wish I could remember more but it was quite a few years ago. But it was one of the greatest experiences of my life. It was a dream come true!

MEMORIAL STADIUM
12 MAY 1994, CLEMSON, SOUTH CAROLINA

I WAS THERE: MARTY KELLER

I was the reservations manager at the Greenville Hilton and had the privilege of arranging the rooms for the band and dealing with their requests. I got to sit with their families during the show. The gig was in Clemson, about 30 miles from Greenville, where I lived. I was in my mid-thirties and it was the concert of a lifetime. I was in awe.

I WAS THERE: ALICIA HILL, AGE 17

It was May 10th, 1994. I was sitting in my sixth period Spanish class and two of my classmates, Ashley and Tim, were talking about wishing they could go to the show. I joined in on the conversation and we decided we would try to get tickets! We got so lucky. We were able to find three seats together. They were in the nosebleed section, but we didn't care… We were going to see the legendary Pink Floyd!

We left straight from Boiling Springs High School as soon as the bell rang on Thursday May 12th. We all piled into Tim's car and headed to the Memorial Stadium. What should have been a 45-minute drive took almost three hours with all of the traffic pouring in for the concert. When we finally arrived and found our seats, it was the most exciting moment of our lives. It was my first concert without my parents and we were stoked! The stadium was very hazy and the amps were turned up. We jammed so hard to the set… the graphics and lasers had us mesmerised the whole show. It was more than a show… it was an experience. I still have my ticket stub in a scrapbook somewhere. To this day it is, hands down, the best concert ever!

FOXBORO STADIUM
18 – 20 MAY 1994, FOXBORO, MASSACHUSETTS

I WAS THERE: BRIAN PAONE

Pink Floyd have been my favourite band since I was six years old. My mother bought *Dark Side of the Moon* when it came out, four years before I was born, because of the song 'Money'. I don't believe she had heard a Pink Floyd song before that. When my parents bought me a Fisher-Price record player one Christmas, so I could listen to my *Sesame Street* and *Star Wars* records, *Dark Side of the Moon* had been out for ten years. My mother gave me the vinyl. And that was it. As a kid who loved sci-fi, when 'On the Run' started and the effect went from speaker to speaker, my mind was blown. I had heard the album played on the family stereo throughout my life, but something about now 'owning' it and being able to open the gatefold to read along to the lyrics meant that I became obsessed.

And not just with that album. I went backward and forward in their discography. I graduated to cassettes around ten years old, and with *The Final Cut* now being the 'new' album, I had a cassette holder in which I stored every album (chronologically, of course). I would bring this cassette holder to friends' houses, sleepover, visits to family members, car rides. My collection of Pink Floyd cassettes became my version of Linus's blanket from the *Peanuts* cartoons.

I was too young to attend the *A Momentary Lapse of Reason* tour in 1987 (my very first concert wouldn't be until my uncle Ray took me to see Yes in 1989). My brothers brought me home a tour sweatshirt from the *Delicate Sound of Thunder* show and I don't know if getting memorabilia from a concert by my favourite band that I couldn't attend made me feel better or worse. Just knowing Pink Floyd were a few dozen miles from my house, playing all the songs that had become the literal soundtrack to my life, killed me.

1994 rolled around. With a new album, *The Division Bell*, and with me being much older and already a concertgoing veteran, I knew it was only a matter of time before my favourite band announced shows in Boston. The only way one could learn about upcoming shows or ticket information back then was through the radio or local newspapers. *The Boston Phoenix* (New England's local music newspaper) came out every Thursday. I would get a copy each week just to keep abreast of upcoming shows. One fateful week, there was a full-page advert for Pink Floyd coming to MA… and for three days! Pre-internet, the only way to get tickets to shows was to stand for hours in line at any of the ticket counters spread across the state, or to try your luck with phone calls to Ticketmaster. The tickets for all three shows were going on sale while I would be in Florida on vacation with my family (what were the chances of that?) and so I only had the telephone to try to acquire tickets. And if any of you remember how much fun and easy it was trying to get an operator to answer the line before tickets sold out… I was only able to acquire tickets for the May 18th and 19th shows, but scoring tickets to two-thirds of Pink Floyd's stay in my home state was cause for celebration.

The shows were on weekdays, and the same week as of all my final exams in high school; exams one needed to pass to graduate. I figured I had this. I would certainly be able to go to school, take an exam, go see Pink Floyd, wake up and take another exam, see Pink Floyd again, wake up and take another exam. Easy, right? This had been my dream since I was six years old. There would be time for sleeping on the backend.

I took the first exam and went to see my favourite band for the very first time. It was a sensory and emotional overload, and I couldn't believe I was lucky enough to be able to do it again the next night (especially since I heard they were touring with two setlists, so the following night's show would be different songs). I woke up the next day pretty tired but took the next exam, and then went to see my favourite band for the second time.

They were even better than the first night, and being in the same space as them was breathtaking. The day after, I woke up exhausted but somehow stumbled into school. Why were the hallways empty? I kept trudging to the classroom where the exam

Clockwise from top left: Cynthia Gonzales with her brothers; Joe Sanchez went to see Floyd when he was just seven years old; Never mind the dark side of the moon, Sean Marcum remembers a partial eclipse of the sun at the Raleigh show; Leslie Ladd went with her friend Becky and a bunch of mosquitoes

Clockwise from top left: Alicia Hill was at the Memorial Stadium; the guitar on which Cory Ashe taught himself 'Wish You Were Here'; Brian Paone has been a Floyd fan since playing *Dark Side* on his Fisher-Price record player; Eric Jokinen with Roger Waters at the BOK Centre, Tulsa would be held. I was about three rooms from the door when the bell rang. Doors opened and students flooded into the hallway. I felt like a rock in the middle of a fast-moving stream.

I strode to the classroom and entered, only to see my English teacher look up at me and say, 'Well, nice of you to join us. But you're late. You missed the exam.' I frantically looked at the clock. He was right. I was an hour late. I had overslept. I realised I had two options: tell the truth or lie. I thought maybe he'd think it was cool that I had seen Pink Floyd the previous night. So that's what I told him. His wife was the creative writing teacher for the high school, and it was well known that I wanted to be an author, so she had a soft spot for me. I truly believe that it was because his wife liked me so much that he allowed me to make up the exam in the library after school ended that day.

My ears were still ringing from two consecutive nights of Pink Floyd tunes live while I muddled through my graduating English exam, but it was worth every second. To piggyback on how his wife was the creative writing teacher and how I wanted to be an author: not only am I published author and it is my main career (my first novel came out in 2007), but my novel based around and inspired by *The Final Cut* album, entitled *The Post-War Dream*, was published in 2022. My wife and I flew to England and interviewed ten veterans of the Falklands War as research for the novel. My love for Pink Floyd has transcended just listening to the songs and has made a huge impact on my own writing career. I think Mrs Patch, my creative writing teacher from Bishop Fenwick High School in Peabody, Massachusetts, would be proud of me after all these years. Although her husband might feel a tad different…

 STADE DU PARC OLYMPIQUE
23 & 24 MAY 1994, MONTREAL, CANADA

I WAS THERE: SÉBASTIEN SMITH
The moment the lights went out was the moment of my spiritual birth. 'Best show ever' doesn't even begin to describe the sheer transcendent experience I lived through that night. It's been nearly 30 years and it still gives me goosebumps.

I WAS THERE: CHARLES BUCKLAND SENIOR
We heard about the concert in Montreal at the Olympic Stadium and had to go. We bought our tickets through a deal that radio station WIZN from Burlington, Vermont was advertising. It included great floor tickets and a bus ride. Crossing the border was less of a

headache in those days. Being on a party bus was just an extra as far as we were concerned. There we were at the border, waiting our turn to pass through about ten buses back, when they came aboard to scan the bus for possible trouble (ie. drugs). I was chosen, along with maybe 20 others, to possibly be a problem. We were told to go inside and wait to be searched. What they didn't know (lucky me!) was that I was born in Canada and lived in the USA. When I produced my green card, they sent me back to the bus unsearched. Which was pure luck, because I had two eight balls of cocaine in my sock... Phew!

After departing the border crossing, it was party time. Pink Floyd put on a show for 80,000 fans. They were their own back up, so at intermission we could go smoke (numerous items – lol) and then enjoy a second set. I wouldn't have missed it. The laser show was so intense it even distracted the bouncers and security so that we were able to smoke right where we were as well.

I saw many concerts with my friends Bobby and Dave. I've probably been to 100 plus concerts, including outdoor jams that lasted for days. Each concert was unique and each holds memories of many different natures. Bands of the calibre of Pink Floyd are precious to have on the concert resume – I'm definitely glad to have grown up during my era… We had the Very Best Decade Ever.

CLEVELAND STADIUM
26 MAY 1994, CLEVELAND, OHIO

I WAS THERE: GREGOR DITTMAN

I saw them when they came back to Cleveland Stadium without Roger. My buddy, Pete, bought eight tickets and sold most of them to his buddies. He took some girl that nobody else knew. He had one ticket left so he gave it to one of his friends, who was hard on his luck. Pete got us all a limo to pick us up from our houses in Warren to go to the concert. We ran out of alcohol on the way there, so we stopped at a liquor store for more. Our seats were in three different sections but Pete and his 'date' and his broke buddy had the best seats out of the group. After the show, I found Pete walking around the parking lot, looking lost. I asked if he was okay. He said he had bought a t-shirt and a programme but somehow lost them both and had no money to buy anything else. I ended up buying him a bootleg shirt from someone in the parking lot, and then we made our way back to the limo and found the rest of our group. On the way home, Pete's 'date' and his broke buddy hooked up in the back of the limo, with Pete sitting right beside them. The rest of us laughed our arses off about it.

OHIO STATE UNIVERSITY STADIUM
29 MAY 1994, COLUMBUS, OHIO

I WAS THERE: JAMES HEINE

The laser beams are bright and more vivid in colour. Time just coasts along; each song seems to last longer than it is. A thick layer of smoke pervades the air and wafts down the ramps that lead up to the tiered seat rows. Mary Jane is everyone's date for the night. That girl is everywhere and her rich scent overwhelms all other odours, even the concessions. A giant round video screen shows various scenes related to the music. Soft lighting plays with the stage and on the audience. The psychedelic rock swirls with loud-soft dynamics and the whole concert is an experience like no other. Occasionally, balloons are launched and two spark-breathing pig balloons erupt on both the left and right sides of the stage after the distortedly spoken line in 'One of These Days'. 'Comfortably Numb' is highlighted by a mechanical light display projector and all the stops are pulled out when it is played – lasers, light shows, balloons, fireworks and smoke bombs! A wonderful time is had by all.

YANKEE STADIUM
10 & 11 JUNE 1994, NEW YORK, NEW YORK

I WAS THERE: CAROL CORCORAN

My husband and I went. We had seats at very top of bleachers. I don't like heights and I thought, 'I'm not going to be able to see anything,' but they were the best seats. When the inflatable pigs came out of the speakers, with the helicopters in the air and with the light show, it was just phenomenal. We saw a lot of concerts but this one blew us away and we loved every minute of it.

HOOSIER DOME
14 JUNE 1994, INDIANAPOLIS, INDIANA

I WAS THERE: DOUG DELANEY

My third time of seeing Floyd and the second time at the Hoosier Dome. We had difficulty in acquiring tickets this time but found three about two days before the show. I remember the weather was nice. Me and a couple of buddies were hanging around the steps outside the Dome when, lo and behold, who did we spot but my old girlfriend and her girl buddies. We didn't get together on this night but we talked and I tried to trade her out of her good tickets. Our seats were up and to the right of the stage, not ideal, but at least we made the show.

My buddies had never seen Floyd, so I felt like a guide. Little did they know what they were about to witness. This time the band had incorporated a new stage, around 75 feet high. At the top of it, and eye level for us, were two belfries or windows. I suspected these might come in to play later, as I was getting wise to how the Floyd would surprise you with things. They opened with 'Shine On', though I'd heard they were opening up with 'Echoes'. They played cuts from *The Division Bell, The Wall, Wish You Were Here* and *Meddle,* and *The Dark Side of the Moon* in its entirety.

They ended with 'Run Like Hell' once again. Two demonic-looking pigs floated out of the belfries during 'Set the Controls for the Heart of the Sun' and down to the ground. It was too awesome. The flower made its appearance and dazzled everyone. I'd heard that Dick Parry was playing sax. The women singers onstage were again mesmerising. They had put in some new film clips for the round screen but left in most of the old ones too. We were just smoking doobies at this show. Despite having to go through a slight search procedure at the gates and there being sniffer dogs present, I smuggled in about five joints of good stuff,

We were on our way home after the show when we spotted what looked like the Pink Floyd zeppelin hovering above the city. What a truly epic night. My buddies were floored – they didn't have proper words for what they had seen! I've seen a lot of shows in my lifetime, everyone from Zeppelin to Prince. Nothing compares to a Pink Floyd show.

WISH YOU WERE HERE

CYCLONE STADIUM
16 JUNE 1994, AMES, IOWA

I WAS THERE: ERIC JOKINEN

I became a fan in late 1989 just after the *Lapse* tour and figured I'd never see them live because they were 'old', in my mind at least. But in the winter of 1994, the local rock station announced they would carry live the announcement of an upcoming Pink Floyd album and tour. The first batch of cities were announced and the closest they were coming to me was Ames, Iowa. I secured my tickets and reserved a hotel room months in advance. I remember the clerk on the phone sounding a little confused as to why I was reserving a room on a weekday months in advance. Little did she know!

We got to Cyclone Stadium and had fun with the other lunatics before the show. It's a feeling that can't be described – thousands of people of all different walks gathered for one purpose. We got to our seats and waited. Soon the sound effects began; crickets, a lawn mower and other Floyd-like sounds. Leading up to this, the PA announced for a guy to report to take a phone call. The second announcement for him said it was an emergency. We laughed about this, saying, 'Leave the guy alone – he's at Pink Floyd!'

From our seats, we saw a large bus pull in behind and under the stage. Shortly after, the sound effects went down and the intro to 'Astronomy Domine' began. I had another feeling that can't be described – there were David, Richard and Nick on stage, something I thought I'd never see.

The stage was like it was alive. The *Pulse* video captures it, but it's not like seeing it. The pigs shooting fire for 'One of These Days', the lasers that went as far as you could see, the stage effects such as the reminiscent oil lighting for 'Astronomy Domine' and the video that accompanied 'Shine On…'. It was just amazing. I didn't known that the blimp had been damaged, so after the show many of us were looking for it and were slightly disappointed not to see it.

A week later, I saw them at the HHH Metrodome in Minneapolis, another great experience. Being indoors, the effects were louder and, during 'Run Like Hell', David popped a string on his guitar and apologised for technical difficulties and a few moments later started again. Being on the floor for this show, I could see the band much better than in Iowa. As this was pre-cellular, you couldn't easily get cameras in to a show but the images of them playing are something I will never forget. Shine on.

I WAS THERE: JEREMY POLLOCK

I had just graduated high school at Hempstead High School, Dubuque, Iowa. My girlfriend at the time was a year below me. She was a pretty good drummer. A farm girl, most of her music exposure was modern country – Garth Brooks, Tim McGraw, Brooks and Dunn, etc. Until she met me, she had never heard of Pink Floyd. I had been listening to Pink Floyd's music for most of my teenage years. Their music was introduced to me by my father and my brother-in-law, beginning with *Dark Side*, *The Wall* and then *Animals*, *Meddle* and *Wish You Were Here*. By my senior year, *The Division Bell* was released and I loved it

We knew they were planning a tour of the US and coming to our state. My cousin was attending college at University of Northern Iowa. A local radio station was doing a lottery of sorts to give away tickets. She lucked out and got tickets for herself, my sister, the brother-in-law who introduced me to the band and myself, plus two spare tickets. I decided that my girlfriend, being a musician, needed to attend this concert and experience the power of Pink Floyd!

The night was perfect. There wasn't a cloud in the sky and there was a full moon overhead. The sights and sounds of the performance were state of the art and unmatched by any show I have been to since. Hearing such an atmospheric-sounding album as *The Division Bell* live and outdoors on such a beautiful night was just incredible. To this day, when I listen to that album, I have to be outdoors, it has to be loud and I can't have interruptions!

At that point, I had only been to a few concerts myself, and mostly smaller local venues locally. This was my first ever stadium show and I was awestruck, as was my girlfriend. Her country boundaries broke down that night and she is still a huge Floyd fan now. I would love to see them again, but I would be afraid it wouldn't live up to my memories of that perfect night.

HUBERT H HUMPHREY METRODOME
22 JUNE 1994, MINNEAPOLIS, MINNESOTA

I WAS THERE: ROBIN EVANS

I got to watch Pink Floyd play the Metrodome just one month after I moved to North Dakota in May 1994. What a show! What made it so memorable was they said goodnight and left the stage, and the crowd went nuts for half an hour until they walked back out on stage and played *Dark Side of the Moon* in its entirety!

WISH YOU WERE HERE

COMMONWEALTH STADIUM
28 JUNE 1994, EDMONTON, CANADA

I WAS THERE: BJ HUSISTEIN, AGE 20

I had been a fan since I was 14. It was my first big concert and the best show ever. Me and two friends, Ian and Dean, travelled from Fort Saint John in British Columbia (population 18,000) to Edmonton, Alberta. It was a little mind blowing to see a crowd of 60,000, three times the size of the population of Fort Saint John, all in one building!

The show started with a sound of a frog going 'ribbit, ribbit, ribbit' and all 60,000 of us were looking for a frog, looking down and towards the stage. All of a sudden, the sound of thousands of birds came down from behind us, causing the whole crowd to be startled and quickly turn around and look over their shoulder. That's the exact moment the band appeared on stage and hit their first note. Once again, the whole crowd had to spin back around and there they were. The guitar solo for 'Comfortably Numb' went on for days. I loved every second of it.

I WAS THERE: KEN GIBBENS

I was busy with a crappy part-time job, working with a band trying to promote original music, when it was announced that the Stones were touring Canada... Well, that was a no-brainer. I had to finally see Mick 'n' Keef and the boys, when out of nowhere I saw a blurb on *MuchMusic* that Pink Floyd were playing Canadian dates for the *Division Bell* tour. All other plans were put on hold! There is only one decision, one plan... we will see Pink Floyd and all will be good with the universe.

After securing two tickets via my mother's credit card, the tickets arrived in the mail. I sat and stared at them in utter disbelief. Finally, I was to be in the same place and the same space, breathing the same air as Pink Floyd. A plan was put into motion to travel 500 miles to see the most epic band in the world. Having family and friends in Edmonton made our stay cheaper and a hell of a lot of fun. The weather upon our arrival in Edmonton was favourable and we visited family and old friends. We spent the night before the show with old friends, listening to music, catching up. It was a beautiful Canadian July evening.

We awoke the next day to rain. The sky had turned dark grey and it pissed down in depressing cold fat drops. I couldn't believe it, and scanned the radio stations for cancellation notices but they said 'the show must go on'. The hours passed and we jumped in our friend's car to head to Commonwealth Stadium. We parked near the university and took the train to the stadium to find many people with umbrellas and garbage bags trying to keep themselves dry. As we entered the venue, the stage hands were cleaning off the stage. Then it happened… The clouds seemed to disperse and the sun started to shine. There was a cheer from the crowds as the blue sky seemed to take over. Before we knew it, the sky was clear, some music came from the PA and the sound of a lawn mower came out of the PA in lovely quadraphonic sound and circled the crowd. Suddenly, 'Astronomy Domine' blasted through the crowd.

What an epic show. There was not a bad note, just an incredible explosion of sight and sound and every song a masterpiece, with the huge bends of Gilmour's guitar taking us higher and higher, the lights swirling in the clear sky and 55,000 people standing and cheering to the last note. When it was done, we headed for the exits with so many smiles, and as we left the stadium the sky clouded over and the rain came once again… But for a brief time, in that stadium, one only 2000 years newer than Pompeii, the Gods smiled down on us, and all was good.

I WAS THERE: JOE HANCOCK

I saw them at the Commonwealth Stadium in Edmonton on the *Division Bell* tour. We ate some mushrooms on the way. There were inflatable pigs and other thing floating around overhead, unless I was hallucinating... We sparked up some killer dope. A guy behind us got a sniff of it and asked if he could partake. He told us he had driven all the way from Regina in Saskatchewan, a seven-and-a-half hour, 490-mile drive. By this time, the reef was down to not much more than a roach. We told him that it was potent stuff. He said, 'Ohhh yaa, I smoke it all the time.' We said, 'Okay buddy, be careful!' He smoked the rest, passed out right away and missed the whole show. When it was over, the poor bastard woke up and started puking all over. We had to get the hell out of his way. Poor guy, but he was warned. I guess they had shitty weed in Saskatchewan…

WINNIPEG STADIUM
1 JULY 1994, WINNIPEG, CANADA

I WAS THERE: CORY ASHE

In the summer of 1978, I worked at a fishing resort when we had two 8-track tapes and just some crap player to play them on. The albums were *Foreigner* and *Dark Side of the Moon*. *Dark Side* got worn out first. The song 'Time' is so very true. I still have my hardly-played *Relics* record – my mom hated that record blasting on my stereo: 'I wish the boys would make nice music and save rock and roll!' *Animals* is my favourite album.

I had 73 humbuck pick ups on my 1973 Raven guitar. I learnt to play 'Wish You Were Here' on it as a kid. I got to see them in Winnipeg.

I WAS THERE: DONNY WAAGENAAR

This was my first big stadium show, and I was on the floor. I smoked an entire bag of weed during that show. The pigs were crazy, man.

CAMP RANDALL STADIUM
3 JULY 1994, MADISON, WISCONSIN

WE WERE THERE: JIM LOSBY & ADAM STANLEY

The Players: Jim, a big Rush fan who has hung around Adam too much in college and picked up far too much Floyd trivia and knowledge. Owns *Dark Side of the Moon*, *The Division Bell* and two boots. Couldn't recognise 'Echoes' if he heard it, but likes 'Crumbing Land' and 'Raving and Drooling'. Didn't 'Acute Perception' come out at about the same time 'Critical Mass' did? And Adam, co-winner *Dark Side of the Moon*-aholic contest 1994! Finally given up trying to have the US, UK, and Japanese versions of all the Pink Floyd CDs. Trying to decide if he wants to give up collecting radio shows (at Citibank's request). Has had 'ECHOES' on license plates since before *A Momentary Lapse of Reason*, has a cat named Cymbaline and tries to educate the Rush fan about everything Floydian.

J: Snuck in to stadium at 2 pm or so. Adam got pics of the stage. Unable to sneak in for soundcheck. All we needed was a concessions pass, and we'd have been in with cameras rolling for the soundcheck.
A: No problem getting past security. Made a big mistake not just staying in the stadium until the soundcheck, which was actually really, really short. They did the beginning of 'Keep Talking' and then the whole thing and then the last minute of 'Astronomy Domine'.

Set One

'Astronomy Domine'
J: Fantastic! Guilty confession: Not being the biggest Floyd fan, I couldn't remember what this sounded like until I picked up the 'Take it Back' single. In retrospect, I wish they had the wiggly oil projection for more songs. Nice to see Dave singing the high descending part.
A: Fabulous! The five of them sounded so nice and tight. I don't see why they think they

need more people on stage. I'm still not sure about that 'Astronomy Domine' to 'Learning to Fly' transition. The oils are great – much more psychedelic than the lasers! I don't understand how people could have thought that it was taped or at least lip-synced.

'Learning To Fly'

J: Got a decent response from the crowd. Perhaps it was the first song they recognised? Heck, most of the crowd, when hearing 'Astronomy Domine', thought, 'Hey, this isn't on the new album or *The Wall* or *Dark Side*! What gives?' Also, could someone please chain down Gary Wallis, the percussion monkey? Do we need two drummers? And why no 'Learning to Fly' film from the last tour?
A: Tim Renwick is slowly turning it into his song with his solo at the end. And I am surprised that they are still putting the 'Young Lust' riff in at the end.

'What Do You Want From Me'

J: The rain began – and didn't stop!
A: I wanted Dave to give me a raincoat!

'On The Turning Away'

A: Good response, but I think that it is time to retire it and add another *The Division Bell* song. Dave was just going through the motions. It's also neat to see how Dave goes to the Bruce Springsteen school of band control to tell everyone that he's finished soloing.

'Take It Back'

J: The hit single. Nice version, sounded like a different arrangement.
A: I really didn't notice a big difference, except that the beginning was a lot longer (like 'On The Turning Away' on the *A Momentary Lapse of Reason* tour).

'Great Day For Freedom'

J: Looks like no 'Poles Apart'. Damn.
A: Would have killed for 'Poles'. Out of three shows I get 'Great Day For Freedom' twice. Almost cleared the stadium as fast as 'Put It There' at McCartney in '89.

'Sorrow'

J: A real good showcase for Dave to go 'braaaww' with his guitar. Try counting how many songs have the 'brrraaawww' sound starting the guitar solo. It's fun!
A: I'm a big 'brrraaaawww' fan! 'Sorrow' just keeps getting better and better. Why does Guy have to jump during the end though? Definitely one of the highlights of the whole show ('Sorrow', not Guy jumping).

WISH YOU WERE HERE

'Keep Talking'
J: Second hit single of the night!
A: The quad sound was pretty cool where we were sitting, but it was funnier to hear Stephen Hawking before soundcheck with no other music.

'One of These Days'
J: Now I'm biased here. When I hear one member of a band play a really neat part, I expect the others to follow suit (is it obvious that Rush is my fave band?). It could have used a Les Claypool bass solo. Pretty good version, though I liked the one big pig version better. (Check out the *Here Comes The Pig* bootleg that Adam has for a good version.) Since it was Madison, shouldn't they have been cows or badgers?
A: I thought that the pigs were too evil-looking. I also would have liked it if they wandered around a bit. My big question is: Why does everyone who isn't playing anything (including Dave) have to leave the stage? Liability? Also, did the pigs get tossed out at all of the shows? At Ames they stayed in their pens. We saw a guy shooting the *Here Comes The Pig* boot on video at Cedar Falls in '88. During 'One of These Days', his friend says 'here comes the pig' and it really stood out! So naturally the shot shifts to the pig. What directing!

Set Two

J: I like the old stuff live. OK, so it's really the overplayed *Dark Side of the Moon / The Wall* stuff. So sue me!
A: Those intermissions keep getting shorter.

'Shine On You Crazy Diamond Parts I – V'
A: I still don't get the video. I thought I saw Anjelica Houston in one shot though.

'Breathe'/'Time'/'Breathe (Reprise)'
A: It's nice to get this instead of the 'On The Run'/'Time' duo of the last tour. For those of you left to see the show, here's something to watch for: when Nick is done hitting the toms with his neon sticks, Gary (always picking up the slack) starts playing the main part of the song while Nick gets back to his seat. Then Nick takes over and Gary goes back to being a monkey. Kind of interesting to watch; pretty well done.
J: OK, 'tolling of the iron bell' was nice, although it should have been only once. You didn't have to lead it into 'High Hopes' so obviously.
A: I agree! Too much bell too early and it was mixed too high.

'High Hopes'
J: Good. I think it fit in just fine here. Nice film.
A: I guessing that Dave thinks that 'High Hopes' is a keeper and thus put it into the second set. Now that Roger's gone, Nick has to play gong.

'The Great Gig in the Sky'
J: OK boys and girls, let's play the 'Great Gig' game. Who sang their part the best? Tonight's winner was contestant number two! Durga! Durga! Durga!
A: Durga McBroom is the hands down gig champion, but if Rachel Fury was on tour...

'Wish You Were Here'
A: I like the radio intro and Dave sitting down, but by this point of the show I feel sorry for him because he really can't wander around too much.

'Us and Them'
A: Nick shines on this one! I'm not sure why, but his drumming really stands out.

'Money'
J: This is my winner in the 'what old sing should we get rid of?' contest. We didn't really get any of the 'get up money children' reggae stuff. Bummer.
A: I used to really look forward to 'Money'. On the last tour, it just kept getting better and better and longer and longer, and this time it's not happening. However, at least we don't have to watch Scott Page sliming around Dave. No, instead we get the backup singers aerobicising around Dick Parry, who doesn't really play much. Yet another reason to do more new stuff in the first set. I still don't get this film either. Jim could explain to the UFO, then he got lost.

'Another Brick In The Wall (Part 2)'
J: Is the backup stuff rerecorded? The kids sounded different. I would have liked to hear the phone ringing and Roger ranting (or at least Jon ranting).
A: I thought so too. I also thought that the cash registers in 'Money' sounded off tempo. The 'hey teacher!' was neat to finally see. At Ames and MPLS, I was on the floor and couldn't see it. The intro is a definite keeper, but they should jam a bit more at the end.

'Comfortably Numb'
J: Three keyboard players? Hey, don't they trust Rick or something? He's no Tony Kaye, but just who the hell is?
A: I think Dave cut the solo short due to the rain. The mirror ball was really cool in the rain (and at this point it was coming down in droves). I liked the 'aaahhh' part with the lights blinding us again.

Clockwise from top left: Cory Ashe and the guitar on which he taught himself 'Wish You Were Here'; Pete Chios gave his son his Floyd baptism at the age of five; Stéphanie Decoutre's heart races at the mention of the Chantilly concert; Pete Lush (right) and his brother Brian drove up from deepest Somerset

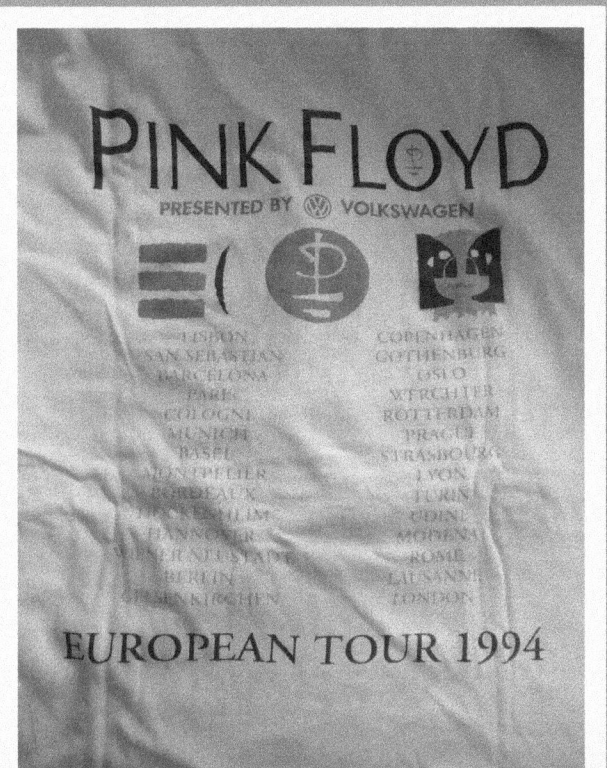

Clockwise from top left: Steve Lonergan in his Floyd t-shirt plus close ups – it didn't get him into the after show party with Kate Bush; Margaret Bills still has the signed photo she was given

Encore

'Hey You'
J: Nice to see that Jon Carin can do a reasonable Roger rant, but why was he limited to only one song? Have him sing all the Roger stuff! It's just not right to me to hear the lines in 'Run Like Hell' passed around from person to person like a hot potato.
A: I thought that he screamed too much. If they wanted to do a lot of *Wall* stuff they should have put in 'Young Lust', which is actually co-written by Dave. Interesting choice.

'Run Like Hell'
J: Yes, we got 'send you back to Madison in a cardboard box!'
A: Guy should not be allowed to sing, I mean yell. We ran like hell back to the car to get out of the rain and didn't wait to see if Dave mentioned anything about coming back next year. I started worrying on the way back that perhaps they'd do a second encore of 'Rain in the Country', but then I figured not.
J: Overall, there were too many people on stage. Toss the percussion monkey and let Jon Carin sing all the Roger stuff. Perhaps the backup singers should sing something else besides 'ooohhh' and 'aaahhh'.
A: Always a good show. If I sound negative it's just because I'm bitter that I didn't see them in '71, or at least see Echoes in '87. The rain was kind of a neat effect. The sound was perfect throughout. I feel sorry for the guy on alt.music.pink-floyd who was far away from the stage because the stadium was huge! Sadly, no more shows for me on this leg. I guess I'll just wait and see if they come back next year! Tapes, anyone?

 CANADIAN NATIONAL EXHIBITION STADIUM
5 – 7 JULY 1994, TORONTO, ONTARIO

I WAS THERE: GORDON PHINN
The tour to celebrate *The Division Bell* was a complete and convincing return to form, from the Satie-influenced 'Cluster One' to the elegiac 'High Hopes', waltzing its way into our hearts as it reached for the cosmos beyond and with everyone's favourite saxophonist, Dick Parry, back in the saddle after too long an absence. The tour, memorialised in the *Pulse* DVD, including – to my taste – the absolute pinnacle performance of David's brilliant showpiece 'Sorrow', with its haunting 'one world, one

soul' chorus, chanted to huge audiences around the planet. And, lest I forget, possibly the most polished and passionate rendition of *Dark Side* in its full video and audio glory, preserved for the seemingly endless generations of younger fans.

I satisfied myself by again joining the population of the ticketless outside the low CNE gates, absorbing the almost perfect sound balance as it spilled over into the endless night. You would not suppose one could enact that Grateful Dead frug and wiggle to Floyd's trademark 'slow majestic four', but I and others somehow managed it, such was our Floydhead frenzy. On the third night, I was approached at intermission by two drunken fans from Buffalo, New York. They'd arrived at the stadium ticketless, gone back to their hotel to retrieve their tickets and lost their pal along the way. They offered me a ticket. Not being a complete fool, as David once said of Nick's offer to join the band in January 1968, I said 'sure'. And what a blessing that was, the last half of the last night with overwhelming blasts of perfectly balanced instruments and voices surrounding us. It was ridiculously good, awesomely awesome, ecstasy beyond words. I didn't leave my body, but holy shit it was close. A transcendence equalled only by Gilmour's partial resuscitation of the Floyd ethos, with Richard Wright, in his Millenial touring band, as evidenced on the *Live at the Albert Hall* DVD.

I WAS THERE: JUSTIN VAUGHAN

I get overwhelmed with emotion by some Pink Floyd songs. I don't know what it is – maybe just the tone and the playing style of David Gilmour – but there is something outstanding about their music, old and new. The live show was over the top and one of the ultimate best experiences of my life. I have never seen a show that has ever compared. The sound just flows right through you. It rattles your insides. One thing that was pretty cool was the number of third generation fans, ie. grandfather, son, grandson – kids as young as 13 or 14 in the crowd. The kids may not have had the same connection as their fathers and grandfathers at that moment, but will one day, when they grow up a bit and look and listen back.

I WAS THERE: PETER CHIOS

I camped out – the good old days – for four days with my brother to get my *Momentary Lapse of Reason* tour tickets in Toronto and got front row seats for both shows. It was just incredible, even without Roger Waters. I sneaked in my Sony recorder with separate left and right mics clipped to my shirt and made recordings for my personal use; I never made copies or sold a copy.) In 1994, I took my five-year-old son Constantine to the *Division Bell* tour as he needed to be baptised. I remember him looking at me during the show. The boy had tears in his eyes and didn't say much on the way home. The next day, he asked if I was taking him again for the second show. I told him I wasn't and he didn't talk to me all day. I got home after the show that night and he was still up waiting for me. We stayed up all night listening to Pink Floyd and he didn't go to school the next day. He still says he'll never forgive me for not taking him to that second show.

 SOLDIER FIELD
12 JULY 1994, CHICAGO, ILLINOIS

I WAS THERE: ANGEL LEDEZMA

By the time I became a fan, Waters was gone and the Floyd were back with *A Momentary Lapse of Reason*. When I saw them it was at Soldier Field in Chicago, the site of their last show with Roger in 1977, a fact not lost on me. I went with my brother and our high school social studies teacher. We had the cheap seats, all the way in back, which wasn't a big deal since we could get a great view of that massive stage that was supposed to look like the Hollywood Bowl. I have a great memory of walking to our seats while the band kicked off the set with 'Astronomy Domine'.

I remember being knocked out by the quadraphonic sound system, the pigs, the lasers (rumour was that the band weren't allowed to shoot lasers over the roof), the giant mirror ball that came out from the centre of the stadium and the fireworks, which freaked our teacher out because it reminded him of Vietnam. I was bummed when I heard that they performed *Dark Side* a few days later in Michigan.

I WAS THERE: TIM WINTER, AGE 21

Seeing Floyd was a dream come true. I had eighth row seats. They opened with 'Astronomy Domine' which totally blew me away, as I'm a huge fan of the Barrett era. I remember a girl behind me smoking the longest fattest joint I'd ever seen! It started to rain just as they kicked into 'One of These Days', and the rain falling through the lasers looked amazing. Another highlight was the *Division Bell* track 'High Hopes', which climaxed with Gilmour's lap-performance. One of my all-time best concerts!

PONTIAC SILVERDOME
14 & 15 JULY 1994, PONTIAC, MICHIGAN

I WAS THERE: DAVID PALKO

I was fresh out of high school, working with my dad in a steel factory doing a mandatory 52 hour work week and no time off. The concert was sold out within an hour of tickets getting released and were 'pricey' to say the least. The day of the show arrived, and I was sitting at my lamicoid tag-engraving machine, half asleep, when the classic rock station announced that Pink Floyd would be releasing tickets for another section of seats at 10am at a regular cost of $25 a seat. I probably had a half hour. I had no time to call any of my high school friends that coincidentally I was in a cover band with, and which even covered Pink Floyd's 'Time'. The only other 18-year-old at the shop was my (smoking) buddy, Doug. I ran through the shop probably a good 200 yards, looking for him, and for my dad. My pops said he'd put two tickets on his credit card for us.

We left at noon. On the way there we stopped at a gas station for a soda, and to ask directions for the Silverdome. As a line formed behind me at the register, I couldn't for the life of me, count to $1. The directions we got were to 'look behind you'.

We got to the parking lot, which goes completely around the arena like a doughnut, parked the car, ran up to the doors, and forgot to look and see what section we parked in. We only found the car after the show in some divine stoner miracle. During the song 'Sorrow', I felt the hair on my legs resonating at a different frequency than the pants I was wearing. During 'One of These Days', I was not expecting the giant inflatable pigs to be eye level with my section, and maybe 50 yards to my left.

As an aspiring guitarist, I was completely fixated on David Gilmour's playing. During his solo in 'Comfortably Numb' (my personal favourite guitar solo of all time), the giant disco ball illuminated from the centre floor, directly in front of me, and reflected beams of light on everyone. I could see everyone's face from across the stadium. As if my mind could not be blown any more, the ball then stopped spinning and opened up, blossoming into the most magnificent silver illuminated flower I have ever seen. I swear God himself tapped me on the shoulder and said 'pretty cool, huh?'. The best concert ever. The *Pulse* DVD is this very concert, and of course I own that as well.

I WAS THERE: CURT SPEERSCHNEIDER, AGE 17

I had three brothers who were all Led Zeppelin fanatics but I became a Pink Floyd fan when, aged 12, I heard *The Wall* from my older brother's collection. I was instantly hooked. There was just so much more to that album than anything that I was listening to at the time. I got into the Waters-era Floyd first, listening to *The Wall* and then *The Final Cut* over and over. Then I ventured into the Gilmour-era *Momentary Lapse* and discovering live Pink Floyd by listening to and watching *Delicate Sound of Thunder*. I began reading anything about Pink Floyd I could get my hands on, learning about Syd Barrett and their history, David and Roger's fall out and lawsuits, how much they changed over the years, etc. I literally became a Pink Floyd expert. I take great pride in being able to ramble off random trivia about the band, album covers, lyrics, etc. I've met many Pink Floyd fans and I've always given them some info that they didn't know. I'm sure there are bigger fans who saw them back in the days of the underground in London. I'd love to talk to them.

I saw Pink Floyd the *Division Bell* tour. I went with a few high school buddies. It was the talk of the town and almost like prom for us high schoolers. Tickets went on sale a few months prior to the show, selling out in less than an hour. I was lucky enough to get tickets on the twentieth row for the first show and on the sixth row for the second, for the modest prices of $32.50 and $60 respectively. Most decent shows seem to be well over $100 now. The first night blew our minds but we were ready for more and we were geared up for the second night's show.

The first half was about as expected – some Pink Floyd classics mixed in with the new *Division Bell* stuff – and all great. Cool movies on Mr. Screen, laser lights, explosions, inflatable pigs, etc. Then the relatively normal opening up the second half with 'Speak To Me' and 'Breathe'… sweet. Then they kept going into 'On The Run' and 'Time'. I thought, 'Wow, they're playing a good chunk of *Dark Side*.'

Gilmour's guitar on 'Time' just soared. It sent chills down my spine. When they went into 'Great Gig', I turned to my buddy and we both said the same thing in disbelief: 'They're playing the entire *Dark Side*.' Once the cash registers and movie came on for 'Money', it was confirmed. Unbelievable. I went into some dream state, not believing what I was seeing and hearing. I felt like we were a part of rock 'n' roll history. We sort of were. I thoroughly enjoyed the rest of one of the greatest albums ever made being performed live in front of me. It all ended with the movie of the moon eclipsing the sun on the screen as Gilmour sang '…but the sun eclipsed by the mooooooon'. After that set, we all just sat there in amazement at what we had just witnessed. Then the sound effects for 'Wish You Were Here' started up and off they went again. 'Comfortably Numb' was probably my favourite. The world's largest mirror ball created an awesome effect in an 80,000 person stadium, and Gilmour's guitar was unbelievable and at his absolute best. Then the show stopper, 'Run Like Hell'. What a finish of energy, lights and sounds, everything concentrated on the domed stage area and then the whole freakin' screen blew up with sparks flying out everywhere.

What was great about that effect was that seeing it live imprinted an image of an eclipse on your eyes if you closed them afterwards – the circle screen with a huge bright explosion behind it. I have no idea if that was an intentional special effect, but it was pretty cool. I had read that Pink Floyd were one of the loudest bands back in the Sixties, the rumour being that they played so loud they once killed fish in a nearby pond. My ears were ringing for days after. The funny thing is, I didn't want that ringing to go away. That was the lasting effect of live Pink Floyd. I saw Roger Waters numerous times, including *The Wall*, but no concert experience compares to those two nights of my life. I'll cherish it forever.

My favourite track? There are so many. 'Echoes' has to be up there. 'Echoes' at Pompeii is even better. *The Final Cut* is great too. Gilmour turns out a great solo and Water's lyrics are so powerful. It's amazing to think they weren't talking to each other at that time.

I WAS THERE: RICHARD E KELLEY

The band had sold out football stadiums throughout North America for one, two or three nights. Playing so many multiple night stands, the band were mixing up the set lists to give fans attending more than one show more value. The Pontiac Silverdome, 30 miles north of Detroit, welcomed two such evenings at the tail-end of the American leg of the tour and I attended with my brother-in-law, a friend – and 80,000 of our closest pals. The first set presentation was dazzling, full of bright lights, special effects and note-perfect musicianship as David Gilmour led the small orchestra of ten musicians on stage through a career-spanning array of Floyd favourites. But nothing had yet had been performed from *Dark Side of the Moon*, which was now over two decades old and still lolling about on the *Billboard* Top 200. I was still oblivious when the lights went down for the second set and the familiar heartbeat and voice effects that begin *Dark Side* began to permeate the semi-darkness. We enjoyed faithful and colourful renditions of 'Speak to Me' and 'Breathe', and only when a special effects airplane flew the length of the stadium and crashed into the stage at the climax of 'On the Run' did I stop to ponder…could this really be it? Indeed, 'Time' followed as did 'Great Gig in the Sky', which employed three marvellous female vocalists to recreate Clare Torry's original part. 'Money' came next, lasting nearly ten minutes, and by then we knew we were witnessing something special. 'Us and Them' was similarly elongated while 'Any Colour You Like', 'Brain Damage' and 'Eclipse' followed the original versions pretty closely. As the heartbeat in tandem with the disembodied voice of the old man returned to close out the performance and inform us 'there is no dark side of the moon… as a matter of fact it's all dark', the Detroit audience was on their feet, howling in ecstasy. Through the din, Gilmour managed to impart, 'For the first time in over twenty years. Thank you very much, Detroit, and goodnight.'

WISH YOU WERE HERE

CHATEAU DE CHANTILLY
30 JULY 1994, CHANTILLY, FRANCE

I WAS THERE: PAUL J LOVE, AGE 29

I can remember the exact moment that I heard about the 'new' Pink Floyd album. I was in the lounge of my girlfriend's house when I heard screaming from the bathroom followed by feet running down the stairs and was then confronted by my girlfriend Tracy (aka Russ), still damp from the bath, shouting, 'I just heard on the radio that Pink Floyd are releasing a new album and it's called *The Division Bell*'. What a strange title, I thought.

It was for this reason that, only a few months later, we found ourselves in a 'foreign field' about 50 kilometres from Paris on a summer evening in the grounds of the Chateau De Chantilly. I had seen the reconstituted Floyd many times in previous years and had my mind blow each time. This was the perfect setting and, as soon as we caught sight of the enormous stage, I just knew we were in for a night to remember. There was a strict 'no camera/video camera' rule as usual on this tour so no one had any idea what the set list would be or, critically, what amazing visual effects would accompany each song.

Looking back through the blur of time, the gig itself still has moments that I will never forget, from the typically French crowd chanting 'asseyez-vous' in the more chilled parts of the concert so that everyone could see, to the bombastic spectacle of two huge inflatable pigs appearing on top of massive towers either side of the stage during 'One of These Days'. It was a perfect night filled with seas of lasers populated by clouds of dry ice, spectacular guitar solos, over excited crazy fan antics, moments of bliss and many breathtaking surprises. I have a dim memory of 'Hey You' being played as an encore, but I could be wrong. Towards the end of the gig, real forked lightning slashed the night sky to the sounds of screams and cheers. I have no idea if there was any accompanying thunder as the band were far too loud.

When the performance had finished and we stumbled exhausted but still high on adrenaline, along with the over 100,000 other fans, back to our various modes of transport, my beautiful girlfriend (now wife) looked up at me and asked 'One question, how did they ever manage to do that thing with the lightning?'

They blew our minds again later in the year at Earl's Court but that's another story…

I WAS THERE: STÉPHANIE DECOUTURE

It was my first concert. It was huge, magnificent, magical. The members of the group arrived by helicopter and, from the first notes played by Richard Wright, I had the feeling of no longer touching the ground. Everything was so impressive that I no longer knew where to turn my head and ears; between the quadraphonic sound, the play of light, the circular screen, Gilmour's guitar playing and the giant disco ball, it was totally amazing. And the icing on the cake? I'm on the sleeve of *Pulse*!

VALLE HOVIN
29 AUGUST 1994, OSLO, NORWAY

I WAS THERE: JØRN GRENI, AGE 22

I wasn't a huge fan but who doesn't like Pink Floyd? Valle Hovin was packed with people and the air was equally packed with the smell of ganja. It never gets really dark at night in Norway in summer, so their laser show didn't really stand out as it probably does in other countries. I enjoyed the inflatable pig though – I should have taken it home with me. The highlight for me was *The Division Bell.* When that piano intro hit the summer skies with its lonely and sad sounding notes, I was in a trance.

STADION FEYENOORD
3 – 5 SEPTEMBER 1994, ROTTERDAM, NETHERLANDS

I WAS THERE: GRAHAM MAHON

I got into the Floyd in the early Eighties. As they didn't tour that often, when the chance came in '94 I had to go. I took my sister, who is in a wheelchair, to Rotterdam stadium. When we got off the bus, there was a long flight of stairs down to the entrance of the stadium. I had to ask some guys to help me carry her and her chair down, and she's not the thinnest of people. There was a small stage on the field for wheelchairs so we had a great view. As soon as Gilmour struck the chords to 'Delicate Sound of Thunder', it started getting dark. Perfect timing. After the gig, the same guys who helped my sister downstairs took her back up. I went to London a week or so later by myself to see them again at Earl's Court. They are the best live band and it was the best light show ever and an experience I'll never forget. RIP Rick Wright.

WISH YOU WERE HERE

I WAS THERE: NICHOL THOMPSON

My mates had bought tickets months in advance but I wasn't really interested. I caught a train from Scotland to the overnight ferry and then to the station to say 'cheerio' to them as they were off to the 'sold out for months' concert. A guy on the station platform offered me a face value ticket and so I went long for the ride. The first half was full of songs that I sort of knew and then there was a half hour break to fill up on beers. This was timed to perfection as it got dark in this half hour. The second set started with two planes flying over the crowd and it all just went ballistic from there. They played the whole of *Dark Side of the Moon*. 'The Great Gig in the Sky' had me in tears. I'd never heard it before. The ground literally opened up at the end and this ten metre wide glitter ball rose up to the top of the dome of the stadium roof and started spinning. Lights flashed onto it, illuminating 80,000 people. It was like Mecca. Absolutely un-fucking-believable.

STADE DE GERLAND
11 SEPTEMBER 1994, LYON, FRANCE

I WAS THERE: JONATHAN PICKLES

Driving up and down France is easy. Driving across isn't. This didn't deter me. Two tickets in hand for the *Division Bell* tour concert at Lyon's football stadium, my girlfriend and I set off from Poitiers that sunny morning in a battered old VW Golf, not knowing if we would make the destination. Seven hours later we arrived at our hotel, a few minutes from the stadium. We had a beer and walked in. There was no seat numbering or VIP status – your ticket gave you access to almost everywhere. We went for a comfortable position directly in front of the mixing desk, not far from the stage. And waited a while with another couple of beers…

Jazzy-type music was playing over the PA. I love that, when you go to a gig and you've never heard the background music before yet it seems so right, so fluid and calming. People were chatting around us, almost whispering (in French), 'I can't believe we're here.' I was secretly proud to be English and in awe of what we were all about to experience. Some of these people had waited a lifetime for this moment. As had I!

The lights went down, there was a huge roar from 40,000 people and we got the opening sequence of 'Shine On You Crazy Diamond'. The quality of the sound was incredible. I have seen dozens of bands before and since, both in smaller venues and in large stadiums. None of them have ever been on a par with what I experienced that night. At the half-time break, we wandered to the back of the stadium and climbed up into the terraces. The band came back on stage and set into *Dark Side of the Moon*. It was at this point that I noticed the quadraphonic sound and the small sets of speakers strategically positioned around the stadium. I was blown away. It was like listening to the studio album but better! Sam Brown's vocals on 'The Great Gig in the Sky' were flawless and perhaps my favourite part of the evening. That said, I'm a keyboard player and seeing Richard play live was a great honour. He has been my mentor and has shaped my musical influences for over 40 years. It was a monumental experience.

 EARL'S COURT ARENA
12 – 17, 19 – 23 & 26 – 29 OCTOBER 1994, LONDON, UK

I WAS THERE: PHIL DAVIES

I was back at Earl's Court in 1994 for my final Pink Floyd show. I was very lucky to have been given a VIP ticket by a journalist friend. I arrived early and surveyed the empty arena, looking up at my seat from 21 years before, excited this time to be situated in the 27th row floor seat, directly in front of where David Gilmour would be standing on stage. In the hospitality tent, I drank plenty of very nice (and free) wine, watched the new promotional videos and prepared for another wonderful night of music from my favourite band. As the house lights were brought down, I relaxed in my seat and Richard Wright's keyboard sounded the first chord of 'Shine On You Crazy Diamond'. Then... nothing happened!

The house lights were brought up and soon someone appeared on stage to say there would be a delay while some technical issues were dealt with. I headed straight back to the hospitality tent for more wine, and after a while was informed that there had been a serious collapse of some scaffolded seating and the show was cancelled for the night. I was devastated. We were all allowed to stay on for a while and then told the show would be rescheduled. While leaving the venue, I saw people crying and I spoke to one couple from Norway who had spent a fortune to see the band and would not be able to come back for the rescheduled show. So sad.

I made it back for the rescheduled show and repeated the hospitality stuff, which was somewhat less glamorous than the first time, and sat in the same great seat and was blown away when they opened with a track from their first album, 'Astronomy Domine'. It was a fantastic night.

Each of the three concerts I saw was special for me in its own way. The first was the most impactful just because I was 15 years old and attending my first ever concert. The second was a huge event, but suffered somewhat because of that. The last one was definitely the best sound and production and, for me, the best songs. I would have loved to see them more but never got the chance.

I WASN'T THERE: STEVE HOWES
On the first night, a friend of mine was there and one of the side grandstands collapsed. The Floyd played one extra night to make up for it.

I WAS THERE: GARETH JONES
The *Division Bell* tour was the last proper Floyd concert I went to and it was notable to me for a few things. One of the stands collapsed on the first night and there was some concern about whether the gig I had tickets for, on the third night, was going to go ahead. Fortunately, it did. It was the only Pink Floyd concert I ever went to where I bought the t-shirt. I hardly wear it though because the design of giant heads across the front lacks subtlety. The band used certain concerts to support charities (which they've done throughout their career) and on this night they were raising funds to tackle motor neurone disease. This was ironic because, only a few days before, my mother had died of motor neurone disease and we had delayed her funeral so that I could still go to the gig. It would have been what she wanted. The things I did for the Pink Floyd!

I WAS THERE: PERRY RIDLEY
The next opportunity to see them was at Earl's Court in 1994. I managed to secure seats on the arena floor, 20 rows from the front, and considering the demand for tickets I felt extremely lucky to have got them. I'd read that they had performed *Dark Side of the Moon* in its full form for the first time since 1975 on some shows. (They had played parts of the album over the years, including 'Money', 'Us and Them' and 'Time', but not the full album since 1975.) When I saw them on this tour, I avoided reading any concert reviews, so I would have no idea what the set list would contain. When they started the second half of the set with the heartbeats from 'Breathe', I thought to myself, 'Wow – they don't do this very often.' As they went on they did the album in its original order, and when they finished 'Us and Them' I thought to myself 'they could well do the whole album', and they did. When they finished it and the heartbeats closed the piece, the arena rose to give them a rousing standing ovation, and a tear came to my eyes. The performance, effects, sound, and lights were just stunning and it remains the best gig of the several hundred that I have seen since my first one in 1972. This would also be the last time I would see Pink Floyd.

A PEOPLE'S HISTORY OF PINK FLOYD

I WAS THERE: DAVID LARGE

I had waited years to see them after just missing out on free Knebworth tickets. My wife Sue was a little apprehensive, looking up and seeing the speakers hanging from the ceiling all pointing in various directions. There was also what appeared to be a giant disco ball. The crowd was chattering, but there was also a subtle noise which sounded as though it was moving up and down the room. This became a little louder and people started to look where the sound appeared to be at that point. The sound became more like a crowd and louder again, and then everyone in the stalls stood up and started cheering as if the band had come on stage. It was just someone testing the sound system, but what a sound system!

During the concert, we were treated to everything from giant pigs on top of speakers and an aeroplane flying into the side of the room and exploding through to lasers and the central video screen, which was a giant circle behind the band. They played new songs from *The Division Bell* and some of the greats, including 'The Great Gig in the Sky' with Sam Brown on the vocal solo.

The finale was spectacular, 'Shine On You Crazy Diamond' with the sound moving around the room. At one point, the sound appeared to be coming from that giant disco ball, by which time everyone was looking at it. The ball opened, sending light streaming in all directions from the mirrored interior, one of the brightest white lights I have ever seen. The ball then became a giant diamond-shaped object, beaming out brilliant white light with everyone staring at it.

Sue said she had really enjoyed the show, knowing more songs (which she put down to me playing them in the evening at home after a couple of glasses of vino) than she'd expected. Floyd are one of the greatest bands I have ever seen and such a shame they will never play again.

I WAS THERE: NIGEL MOLDEN

It was to be 26 years before I next saw the band, at Earl's Court as part of the *Division Bell* tour. It was towards the end of the year-long set of dates, and one of the last full length performances that the band would give. By this time, Roger Waters had left and the remaining three members were augmented by a notable array of session musicians and vocalists. It was another outstanding performance over two full sets. I particularly remember the wave of heat generated when the huge bank of lights along the front of the stage flashed on and off during 'Another Brick in the Wall'. Newspaper reports for the concerts stated that the nightly capacity was 15,000. However we might look at it, it was a long way from the thousand people in the gymnasium at the Regent Street Polytechnic.

WISH YOU WERE HERE

I WAS THERE: CHRISTOPHER CARR

The last time I saw them was when my mum bought me tickets for my birthday, which was two days earlier. It's what most fans call the *Pulse* tour. I never imagined a three hour concert nor was I expecting *Dark Side of the Moon*, so I had tears in my eyes the moment the first riff was played. It was definitely the best night of my life. But don't tell the missus!

I WAS THERE: ALEXANDER G MITLEHNER

Having seen Roger in 1984, I saw the other three band members in 1994 at Earl's Court. A friend had got some really good downstairs tickets with a superb view, not up in the gods as in 1984. This time there was an incredible sound system and it truly delivered! It was great to see Dave Gilmour, Rick Wright and Nick Mason walking onstage and they started with the whole of 'Shine On You Crazy Diamond' which really set the scene, and got my spine tingling. Next to us were a couple of cheerful Scousers who handed us a strange-smelling cigarette (smoking was allowed in venues in those days) and this definitely heightened the experience! The rest of the concert was something of a haze but I remember them playing the whole of *Dark Side of the Moon*, plus several numbers from *The Wall* including a blistering Gilmour guitar solo on 'Comfortably Numb', during which the glitter ball opened up and laser light bounced off it around the auditorium. Truly memorable, and the spitfire and the pig came out, so the real McCoy this time!

I WAS THERE: MARK GUEST

From the moment I booked the tickets for myself, my brother and my two mates I was in countdown mode and couldn't wait. We drove up to Earl's Court from Southend-on-Sea and, as we reached the venue, someone pulled out of a parking space and we pulled in, a two-minute walk away. Result! I'd wager there wasn't another parking space for about five miles.

Touts were coming up to us and offering us a fortune for our tickets, but they weren't for sale at any price. We made our way into the venue where big silver men on stilts and all sorts of other freaky people were wandering around – this was Pink Floyd, after all. We had a few beers and made our way to our seats, upstairs front on the left hand side of the stage. When the music started for 'Shine On', the loudest cheer I've ever heard rang out. I was mesmerised for the rest of the show. One of my overriding memories is of a guy sat opposite me being totally wasted and asleep for the whole show. I would have given myself a black eye for that – what a numpty!

They finished the show and said goodbye without my three favourite songs. I remember thinking 'they'd better come back for the encore'. Which they did. 'Wish You Were Here' was amazing with the lasers and my absolute favourite, 'Comfortably Numb', smashed it with the giant glitter ball, the whole of Earl's Court full of millions of little white rings of light. I still get goosebumps thinking about it now. It was the best night of my life, even though my throat was hoarse through singing and shouting and the car broke down in the Limehouse Link tunnel on the way home. None of us could care less; it was a fantastic night in the presence of a fantastic band. RIP Rick Wright, and thanks for the music boys!

I WAS THERE: STEVE LONERGAN

What can I say? 'Amazing' doesn't really do it justice. I felt I was part of something really special. The high point for me was 'Comfortably Numb', the disco ball opening as a flower, and – well, I just adore that song anyway. After the show, we got lost trying to get to the coach and actually ended up at the entrance to the after show party. I'm pretty sure that Kate Bush walked past me. Was she even there? I don't know. I have also seen Roger Waters at the O2. We were right at the back – miles away! Again, the Pink Floyd music he played was stunning.

I WAS THERE: SHANE OCKENDEN

I was there for the night that they did the video recording of *Pulse* live. Despite my being fairly high, the *Dark Side of the Moon* set in the second half of the concert was just bliss, and better than the studio album! And the encore was just brilliant. I can remember 'Run Like Hell' and having a massive inflatable pig blow up very close to where we were seated. It kind of freaked me a little, looking into its red eyes and with smoke streaming from its nostrils. It was a totally brilliant experience and one to remember for a lifetime.

I WAS THERE: PETE LUSH

I'm the youngest of eight children. My three much older brothers all had their favourite bands and albums and I heard *Dark Side of the Moon* on my brother Derek's quadraphonic stereo. My girlfriend wanted see the *Division Bell* tour but suffered badly from epilepsy – even carnival lights set her off. If she'd had a fit and ended up in hospital, it would have ruined the night for everyone else! In the end, I went with my brother Brian, friends Jon and Nikki, and Nikki's mum Ruth. I was straight on the phone when tickets were released. I wanted Saturday night tickets and was slightly disappointed when the box office said the only row of five they had left was right at the back of the hall. But at least we were going! The six months wait for the concert seemed to drag on and on. Then came the terrible news of the first night seating collapse. Thinking the tour might be cancelled, I (and probably thousands of others) rang up to be told to ring back the following day, when I was relieved to hear that the concert was still going ahead.

The day came and we all piled into my brother's Ford Sierra and set off from deepest

WISH YOU WERE HERE

Somerset. We parked at Richmond and caught the Tube to Earl's Court. My only previous experience of seeing a major artist was Chris Rea on his *God's Great Banana Skin* tour the previous year at the Bath & West Showground. He was good, but it didn't prepare me for what I was about to see. I was gutted when I found out that we couldn't take cameras in; we entered the hall camera-less, grabbed some refreshments and the programme and t-shirt – or, in my case, three t-shirts, one of which I immediately put on. Reaching our seats, I said to my brother, 'Bloody hell, we are miles away from the stage.' But they turned out to be the best seats in the house, at the back but also right at the top and bang in the centre. We could see everything in front of us, whereas if you were at the front, you would need an extra pair of eyes in the back of your head.

After waiting what seemed an age, the lights dimmed and the long intro to 'Shine On You Crazy Diamond' grew louder, accompanied by the most amazing visuals and a massive circular screen, which went from vertical to horizontal, changing into a giant lighting rig. Then a spotlight came on, highlighting Dave whilst he played the haunting opening guitar solo to 'Shine On', before Nick came in with heart-stopping pounding on the drums. My bottle of Carlsberg was vibrating with the beat; we may have been at the back of the hall but the power of the world's largest quadraphonic sound system was just astonishing. After 'Shine On', Floyd went through some of their greatest tracks and a selection from *Division Bell*, with the most amazing visuals for every track. They ended part one of the show with 'One of These Days', with giant pigs perched on top of the speaker stands and spotlights used for their eyes.

After a 15-minute break, the house lights dimmed again and we could hear the unmistakable sound of a heart beating. What followed was what I can only describe as the best hour of my life (apart from my wedding ceremony, of course!). It was mind-blowing, especially as I was breathing in the fumes exhaled by the chap in front who had somehow managed to smoke some weed without getting caught. The visuals to accompany *Dark Side* made the experience even more powerful. *Dark Side* got the longest standing ovation I have ever seen, followed by 20,000 people chanting 'more, more, more'. The band returned and played the most amazing encore. When it got to Dave's legendary guitar solo in 'Comfortably Numb', out popped the biggest glitter ball I have ever seen. It opened up like a giant glittery chocolate orange, submerging the whole hall in millions of white dots. Seeing 'Wish You Were Here' brought a tear to my eye and ended with the brightest lasers I had ever seen, static but effective. To finish we had the unmistakable guitar riff of 'Run Like Hell', the lasers now shooting around the hall in all directions, and then explosions followed by the brightest lighting I have ever seen, rotating vertically and horizontally, and then more massive explosions.

On the way home, we spent the whole time recalling the many highlights. I still have the ticket and programme but my tour t-shirts sadly succumbed to the Persil Power washing powder scandal and disintegrated after a few washes. As a DJ, and inspired by Pink Floyd's live show, I now spend as much time on the projections, lasers and psychedelic lighting I use as I do the music I play.

I WAS THERE: TREVOR DAVIES

When the *Division Bell* tour was announced, I got very excited as my mum was coming too. Their UK stop was multiple evenings at the world famous Earl's Court. The album had been a birthday present from my mum and come the concert we were both well versed in the songs. We went by coach from Oldham, which was full of eager Floyd fans like ourselves. On arrival, the outside of the venue looked fabulous, with the two heads from the album sleeve on the front of the building. The gig was phenomenal, including all the usual bells and whistles – the circular screen, the lasers, the floating pig, etc. The band were on blistering form with plenty from the archives and the latest album too. After a short interval, the second half was outstanding and a surprise – all of *Dark Side of the Moon*. It was absolutely stunning. How could they follow that? Only with 'Comfortably Numb', complete with a mirror ball that opened into a lantern, sending spots of light all over the auditorium. Both myself and my mum came out lost for words. What a night!

I WAS THERE: MARGARET BILLS

I saw Floyd twice in the Eighties, once at Maine Road, where they had a flying bed as well as a giant pig. The second time was at Earl's Court. One of the stands collapsed and the show was abandoned. I wrote to Steve O'Rourke, Floyd's manager at the time, and told him I was at that concert. I got a nice reply inviting me back as a VIP. I watched the concert from a box and was given a signed t-shirt and programme plus a signed black and white photo. I gave the programme and t-shirt to my brother-in-law but kept the photo.

The Earl's Court shows represent the last live performances by Pink Floyd for more than 20 years.

MONTAGE MOUNTAIN PERFORMING ARTS
13 AUGUST 1999, MOOSIC, SCRANTON, PENNSYLVANIA

I WAS THERE: CAROL CORCORAN

My husband and I saw Roger Waters at Montage Mountain. It was lightning and thundering and their plane was circling, waiting to land. It was such a storm that everybody was leaving, including security guards. My husband asked if I wanted to go. I said, 'Hell, no, I will get pneumonia for them…'. We looked like drowned rats. There were maybe 40 people left. We moved to the third row. They came on stage and Roger Waters said, 'I can't believe you guys stayed. We're going to give you one hell of a concert.' And they did! They played for about two and a half hours. It was phenomenal. When Roger Waters announced the 'Us and Them' 2017 tour in Philadelphia, we were straight in there – no 'ifs' and no 'buts' – and I pre-ordered our t-shirts!

AMERICA WEST ARENA
16 JUNE 2000, PHOENIX, ARIZONA

I WAS THERE: MICHÄEL PERKINS

I have worked a few of Roger Waters' solo concerts as a stage hand. The first was the 2000 Phoenix show. I was part of the truck loading in crew, starting at around 5am. We unloaded eight or so tractor trailers-worth of equipment and rolled the cases to handlers who pushed them into the arena for the correct area, lighting, sound and so on. This lasted until 7am, after which I assisted the travelling road crew in assembly and hoisting some screens and other visual elements of the show into place, as they were using multiple layers of visuals including vintage oil and water colour psychedelic lights. I was asked to come back for the show as a stage hand and basically stand off stage at stage right, put dry ice into a machine and press a button three times during the show with another stagehand who did the same thing with a second machine. The rest of the time, I was free to watch, out of sight lines. I got to hear the raw band onstage from behind the speakers and they were simply stunning.

Between 1995 and 1998, there is minimal concert activity by members of Pink Floyd, together or solo. Then, in 1999, Roger returns to the road after a 12-year hiatus. The In The Flesh *tour takes in 105 shows between July 1999 and June 2002.*

WEMBLEY ARENA
26 & 27 JUNE 2002, LONDON, UK

I WAS THERE: SIMON PEARCE

I used to know Roger Waters' mother, Mary, in Cambridge as she taught me maths when I was a teenager. I met Syd Barrett many times in Cambridge when he was alive. He would never sign autographs. The first time I saw him, in Sainsbury's Coldhams Lane superstore, he did indeed have 'black holes in the skies' for eyes. My mum and I went backstage with Roger's mum when Roger played Wembley in 2002 and I met Nick Mason. That was an occasion. Sitting opposite me was the army captain, James Hewitt, who had an affair with Princess Diana. I will never forget it.

2003 and 2004 sees a hiatus in live appearances by band members past and present. On 2 July 2005, Pink Floyd reform – with Roger Waters in the line-up – for the very last time at Live8 *in London, one of a string of benefit concerts timed to mark the twentieth anniversary of* Live Aid *and highlight the lack of progress by the world's largest economic powers in tackling global poverty. The appearance of Waters and Gilmour on the same stage is engineered by Bob Geldof, the Boomtown Rats lead singer and one of the architects of* Live Aid, *20 years before. Gilmour resisted Geldof's initial advances, but Waters rings Bob direct and then, apparently at Nick Mason's suggestion, Waters rings Gilmour. It is their first contact in two years.*

I said I'd call him back the next day when I'd thought about it. I thought about it, and thought that I'd probably always regret it if I didn't do it. **David Gilmour**

LIVE 8, HYDE PARK
2 JULY 2005, LONDON, UK

I WAS THERE: JANSSY LARIVIÈRE

My father would leave my grandmother's store and visit the store next door to listen to the music. It was there in October 1970, aged eleven years old, that he fell in love with Pink Floyd. I followed that voice from birth because I was born with *The Dark Side of the Moon*.

In 2002, I was ten years old and saw David Gilmour for the first time, with Richard Wright. I was happy. But in July 2005, I was even happier. I was in the UK and I knew that *Live 8* was taking place. Friends went to the same event at Versailles, at home in France. But I didn't know that I was going to experience it, and when I heard the first notes being played by Pink Floyd, I screamed. A couple looked at me and said, 'It's great to see a young man who loves Pink Floyd.' It was crazy, and of course I cried with joy. We were far from the stage but it didn't matter: there they were – David, Nick, Richard and Roger – together on stage.

Looking at the screens, I could see people around me singing, and others screaming when Gilmour started the solo on 'Money' and the second solo on 'Comfortably Numb'. I remember the discussion with my father on the way back to France: 'Enjoy these moments my son. In 20 years, there will be nothing left.' And I answered, 'I saw Pink Floyd, I saw Pink Floyd!'

It was and will remain the most beautiful concert of my life. I'm 31 years old and lucky enough to be able to say 'I saw Pink Floyd live'. Pink Floyd is also a family story. One of my kids likes them too. The third generation of Floyd fans in my family.

I WAS THERE: MARK REED

The day before my birthday and, somehow, I was seeing Pink Floyd. Yes, there was *Live 8*. There was REM and U2 and Madonna and… um, UB40. But everything else faded in importance because I was fulfilling a long-held dream. I was going to see Pink Floyd. And 224,999 other people were going to as well. Pink Floyd hadn't existed for over a decade. And this time, for the first time since 1981, and for the last time – David Gilmour, Nick Mason, Roger Waters and Rick Wright – were Pink Floyd again. Most of them hadn't performed these songs in public for over ten years, and some of the songs had last been performed by this line up of Pink Floyd in 1975, when I was two years and two days old. By the time the band took the stage, 11.00pm, the show should have finished hours ago.

It was a short 24 minutes. Yes, they were hesitant occasionally. And there were some first night nerves. It was, after all, the first time in 28 years that Mason had been the only drummer on stage at a Pink Floyd concert. But it was a Pink Floyd concert.

What you didn't see on TV was the mystery of the moment. The mass hush and whispers of 'fuck yes, it's the Floyd!' when the heartbeat pulsed out of the speakers discreetly, the videoscreens slowly fading to a green beeping line. On the live broadcast, there was an inexplicably loud cheer about two minutes into 'Breathe'. The roar of the crowd was when Roger finally got a close-up on the huge screens. Even though, for many of us, even those of us who were relatively near to the stage, Pink Floyd were tiny dots about one centimetre tall in the far distance. The sense within most of us that… Yes. We. Were. Seeing. Pink. Floyd. That was history in the making.

But it was beautiful to see Pink Floyd together again. When I first encountered Pink Floyd, as a 15-year-old in suburban Birmingham in 1989, the idea of my ever seeing

Pink Floyd seemed impossible. And, as time progressed, as David faded from public life for twelve years, as Pink Floyd quietly floated apart, the idea of *anyone* ever seeing Pink Floyd – let alone with Roger on bass – seemed increasing impossible.

Grown men cry when they see things they never thought they'd see, and hear songs they never thought they'd hear: to hear songs I lived with for decades live again; to see Roger and David and Nick and Rick singing songs that they last shared with us 30 years ago; to see the pig floating over Battersea, and know that Battersea was only a handful of stops away on the train. The screens faded to a wall. The guitar solos for 'Comfortably Numb' flew over us. I. Am. Seeing. Pink. Floyd. Perform. Comfortably. Numb.

And in case we forgot why we were all supposed to be here, red handwriting stated clearly: 'MAKE POVERTY HISTORY'.

It was the greatest show on Earth. And then it was over. On one hand, Roger waved cheerily to us all – acting as if 'I'm back!'. At the same time, David waved a final goodbye. A chance, as he once said, to show his children who he once was. There was an awkward, unexpected group hug that was all over the newspapers. And that was the last time Roger, David, Nick and Rick performed together as Pink Floyd.

I WAS THERE: GUðBJÖRG ÖGMUNDSDÓTTIR

I attended with my 15-year-old grandson. As with the Silver Clef Awards at Knebworth back in 1990, it was 12 hours of fantastic music by the greatest artists including U2, Coldplay, Madonna, Elton John and The Who. Pink Floyd with Roger Waters was the last act to perform before Paul McCartney led an all-star finale to the show. As at Knebworth the show ran late, but this time Pink Floyd played their whole set without having to shorten it. It was the highlight of the day. They played 'Breathe', 'Breathe (Reprise)', 'Money', 'Wish You Were Here' and 'Comfortably Numb'. This was an incredibly moving experience to finally enjoy seeing Pink Floyd together again and playing fantastically in such wonderful weather. I really cherish the memory of this day and it was wonderful to have my grandson there.

I WAS THERE: PETER SMITH

Gilmour announced the reunion less than a month before the gig: 'If reforming for this concert will help focus attention, then it's got to be worthwhile.' I went with my wife Marie and two of my children, David and Laura. I scored tickets in the enclosed area near the stage so we were close to the front with a great view. Pink Floyd were sandwiched between sets by The Who and show closer Paul McCartney. Their set consisted of 'Speak to Me', 'Breathe', 'Money', 'Wish You Were Here' and 'Comfortably Numb', a good choice of songs for their short appearance. Waters said on stage, 'It's actually quite emotional standing up here with these three guys after all these years. Standing to be counted with the rest of you. Anyway, we're doing this for everyone who's not here, but particularly, of course, for Syd.' 'Wish You Were Here' was particularly powerful; you felt they were singing the song for Syd which, of course, they were.

I WAS THERE: DAVID BELL

I actually cried when they reformed for the *Live8* concert, especially after all the bad blood!

David Gilmour releases his third solo album, On An Island, *on 6th March 2006 in the UK, the occasion of his 60th birthday. The accompanying tour encompasses 33 shows, starting in London on 7th March 2006 and finishing in Poland with a show at the Gdańsk Shipyard to celebrate the founding of the Solidarity trade union, in front of 50,000 people. The show is released in 2008 on DVD as* Live in Gdańsk.

MERMAID THEATRE
7 MARCH 2006, LONDON, UK

I WAS THERE: MARK REED

I've seen it a hundred times or more. Reprinted in magazines. Webpages. DVDs remastered from grainy VHS tapes. Documentaries and books. And now, I'm seeing it with my own eyes. Though this time he isn't on a gantry at the top of an 80-foot polystyrene wall or on my television. Stood in front of me, no further from my eyes than my kitchen, David Gilmour is silhouetted in light, a clear-cut shape of man at one with his guitar. The notes pealing out. Playing what was once voted The Best Guitar Solo In The History Of Mankind.

I entered a competition to attend the public premiere of David Gilmour's upcoming tour at the Mermaid in London, capacity 610 people. A far cry from his last public appearance to 225,000 people at *Live8*. Knowing my luck, I never win. But as my mum taught me, 'if you don't ask, you don't get'. So I chance my arm. And win.

Cometh the hour, and we queue in bitter wind and British rain outside a theatre in Blackfriars, London. Being 28th in the queue is worth it. They open our doors – on the right – first. Barely able to maintain my repressed British façade, we descend to the stairs. Somewhat oddly, the few in front of us choose to sit in the second row. And the first row is so inviting…

So we sit there. Roughly equidistant from David and Rick, we sit. And about then, it starts to seem real. I am sat about 14 feet from David Gilmour, 20 feet from Rick

Wright, and not much further from Pink Floyd's touring support of Jon Carin, Guy Pratt and Dick Parry.

So how does it feel? Unreal. Surreal. Superreal. Like I don't know where to look or what to do or how to act. There is too much to see, too much detail. Kurzweil organs that I last saw in Hyde Park from the distance of a hundred metres or more, guitars I remember from old television programmes. Lap steel guitars last seen on the insert to million-selling live albums.

Under a shroud of darkness, Jon Carin sits at his keyboard, and the opening notes of 'Castellorizon' begin. A man who looks like Rick Wright – but happier – sits at the keyboard next to him. And then, from the left, the shapes of the backing band filter on. Barely has the applause subsided when a 60-year-old comes to the stage. To thunderous applause.

Gently and discreetly, he picks up a trusty black guitar, fiddles with a couple of dials. And then from nowhere, the familiar tones. The whalesong of guitar. The elegant, unfussy notes of emotion. Tapping into some long-hidden feeling that other bands can often only scratch at the surface of.

And then, as darkness turns to light, the band open with 'On an Island'. And first and foremost, these songs uncurl in concert. If there were any reservations about the discreet and almost understated feel to the intimate album of the same name, they are silenced. In the flesh, these songs tower about their studio incarnations.

As I said, from the front row, there is too much to see. Too much detail. The way David seems to scratch his nose at the end of every number. The way that Rick Wright glances at his bandmates and smiles to himself. The way that Jon Carin sometimes looks up and glance surreptitiously at the crowd. The way Guy stalks the stage and catches David's eye as they share a moment of humour that turns into a wink and a smile. The way Phil Manzanera stands stock still stage left, eyes closed, transported away as he duets notes with David during 'Shine On You Crazy Diamond'.

Ah. I'm only two songs in. I haven't even mentioned 'The Blue'. The songs are too new, too fresh, for me to do anything but passively accept. I don't know them. Unlike the other songs, burrowed into my subconscious like words through a stick of rock, an integral part of me, those songs are just getting settled. The newer songs are smaller, more personal. Very obviously bearing the hallmarks of his former band, but also more intimate. Closer. Dealing with the personal and the individual, with emotions and with feeling, instead of the perhaps more universal, more sweeping nature of Pink Floyd's music.

Eyes closed, lost in the moment, bathed in red and white and blue light, David Gilmour sings the songs from his heart and the rest of the world can slip away. As if nothing else existed. And then, as he speaks through his guitar – and there really is no other way to describe it than that (the guitar speaking in the language beyond words) – his head turns, tilts, his mouth makes that look of intense concentration and... Sometimes there are no words. If words were enough, we wouldn't need or want music.

'Take a Breath' is a monster. An insistent, pounding beat – magnified under the capable hands of Steve on drums – the song rolls forth like Panzers. Rick and Jon lose themselves in the moment. Live, these songs breath and unfold their wings. Grow from acorns to big oak trees. And it all makes sense. It clicks. David stood in front of me, and the PA hypnotises me.

As I said, too much to see.

RADIO CITY MUSIC HALL
4 APRIL 2006, NEW YORK, NEW YORK

I WAS THERE: ROGER CHARRON

Becoming a fan all started when I was very young, listening to my dad's old records and cassettes. I remember being listening to 'In The Flesh' on *The Wall* and being frightened when I heard Roger Waters screaming along with the roaring engine of the airplane at the end of the song. I can remember reading every word on the sleeves of both records of *The Wall* while listening to the music. I noticed that some words didn't match the recorded lyrics. I had picked up on the differences between the movie soundtrack and the album. That created an obsession and so the journey began!

I have always had a thirst for Pink Floyd's music and knowing more about them. I think the most unique thing I've learned was that the word 'ummagumma' was Cambridge slang for fucking! I wanted to go and see Pink Floyd on the *Delicate Sound of Thunder* tour in 1988 but I was too young (my dad went). But I got to see Pink Floyd in May 1994 in Foxborough, Massachusetts. My most magical moment has to be seeing David Gilmour at Radio City Music Hall on the night of my birthday and hearing 'Echoes' played live for the first time.

KODAK THEATRE
19 APRIL 2006, HOLLYWOOD, CALIFORNIA

I WAS THERE: MARTY YAWNICK

My story of seeing Pink Floyd live is one of more regrets than of magnets and miracles. I was living in Los Angeles in 1980 when the first of the original *The Wall* live shows were performed. A friend had an extra ticket and asked me at the last minute if I wanted to go. I declined. I had class that night, or a date, or plans to hang out drinking with my friends. I don't remember why I said no. Years later, all I remember is how much I regret that decision.

I have seen Roger Waters and David Gilmour on every tour they've launched since 1999. In 2006, a buddy and I flew to Los Angeles to see David Gilmour's *On An Island* tour at the Dolby Theatre in Hollywood, California, specifically choosing one of the smaller stops on the tour. Richard Wright was sharing the stage with Gilmour, and the show was incredible. I remember being gobsmacked and weeping tears of joy when the opening piano notes for 'Echoes' started to play. This was a track that we never expected to hear live again. It was long, incredible and perfect. Hearing Richard Wright and David Gilmour play live together, you could hear their friendship in the music and how their solos and flourishes played off each other. We did not know at the time that Richard was ill. It was one of his last performances.

BRIDGEWATER HALL
26 MAY 2006, MANCHESTER, UK

I WAS THERE: PHIL CHAPMAN

I had no idea what to expect. I'd bought *On An Island* and liked it but hadn't tried to find out what the supporting tour was like; I hadn't even read any reviews. This meant I was in for some very pleasant surprises. The first half got under way with *Dark Side of the Moon*'s unmistakeable 'Speak To Me' played over the PA as the band took to the stage, leading straight into 'Breathe'; a good start. I was sorry to see Jon Carin rather than Richard Wright taking the harmony vocal, but it sounded right. 'Breathe' blended straight into a second *Dark Side* track, 'Time', again sounding good and this time with Wright singing the second vocal line. 'Time' was played in its entirety, including the 'Breathe' reprise.

WISH YOU WERE HERE

After this David Gilmour addressed the audience for the first time and told us they'd be playing the whole of *On An Island* in the first half of the concert, which went down well; the opening numbers appeared to have satisfied anyone who might have been impatient for a bit of Floyd. The arrival of David Crosby and a typically barefoot Graham Nash for the title track from the album was great to see; I'd enjoyed their vocals on the album but hadn't expected to witness them performing the live version. *On An Island* in concert definitely added something to the studio version. It had more soul and depth and I enjoyed it.

The light show was good throughout this concert and really enhanced the music, particularly the more dramatic passages. The acoustics aren't always great at the Bridgewater Hall and the vocals lacked a bit of clarity at times in the first half, but the guys on the desk seemed to get that sorted as I didn't notice it after the interval; or perhaps I was just too carried away with the music. It didn't take an Einstein to work out that the second half was going to involve some more classic Pink Floyd, but just how classic I would never have guessed. Gilmour opened with a refreshingly light and bluesy rendition of 'Shine On You Crazy Diamond', with Crosby and Nash adding their distinctive harmonies to the main refrain. The Floyd set included three post-Waters *Division Bell* tracks, starting with 'Wearing the Inside Out'. However, before hearing 'Coming Back To Life' and 'High Hopes, we were treated to 'Fat Old Sun' from *Atom Heart Mother* and the Barrett-penned debut single 'Arnold Layne', sung by Richard Wright; these were real unexpected gems. They'd saved the best until last of course; as the applause for 'High Hopes' died down, there was a single 'ping' from Richard Wright's keyboard and a shiver went down my spine. I never expected to witness the mighty 'Echoes', *Meddle*'s side two, performed live. We got all 22 minutes, with Gilmour's and Wright's vocals sounding as good as they had back in 1971. What a brilliant way to finish the main set; if that had been the end of the concert, I wouldn't have felt at all cheated.

Two of the three encore pieces were predictable, though that didn't diminish them at all. As at the start of the first half, the encore commenced with a bit of pre-recorded and familiar Floyd: the 'radio tuner' introduction to 'Wish You Were Here', leading into the live version of that song, with Phil Manzanera performing twelve-string duties. The second number was another surprise: David Crosby and Graham Nash returned to the stage to perform the short Crosby, Stills and Nash song 'Find the Cost of Freedom' acappella, with David Gilmour singing Steven Stills' line. There was only one song this concert was going to end with and 'Comfortably Numb' didn't disappoint, with Wright singing the verses and Gilmour the choruses. Nearly two and three quarter hours after first taking to the stage, a backlit, smoke-engulfed David Gilmour brought the track and the concert to a suitably dramatic and satisfying conclusion.

Courtesy of a friend, I was on Phil Manzanera's guest list and we popped backstage after the show. Our host and David Gilmour had already left to catch their *Later with*

Jools Holland performance on TV, but Richard Wright was there, standing quietly to one side, the antithesis of a rock star. I couldn't think of anything to say so I just nodded and smiled and he reciprocated. Less than two-and-a-half years after the concert I'd just watched he succumbed to lung cancer. 'Echoes' was without doubt the highlight of the night for me and it was a privilege to see him perform it.

I WAS THERE: NEIL COSSAR

I was 13 when I was introduced to Pink Floyd after my best friend's brother returned from university with a whole new batch of albums, which included a copy of *Meddle*. 'One of These Days' blew me away as did the rest of the album, and three years later the same happened with *The Dark Side of the Moon*. I never had the opportunity to see Floyd play live but in 2006, after playing David Gilmour's *On An Island* album constantly for a few months, I was lucky enough to blag a pair of tickets to see him in Manchester.

I've never been to a concert before where the artist plays an album in its entirety from start to finish as Gilmour did on this tour, but it really worked! And the standard of musicianship from everyone on stage was amazing. It was played note for note as you knew it from the album.

Along with the tickets I'd blagged from the record company came two back stage passes so myself and my partner Liz made our way backstage with the hope of meeting David and his band. Once backstage, we discovered that they had all returned to their hotel except for Richard Wright. I was chatting to some other fans when he walked into the room and joined in the conversation. He was in fine spirits as we all chatted about the night's performance. It was a privilege to meet you Richard – wish you were still here.

CLYDE AUDITORIUM
27 MAY 2006, GLASGOW, UK

I WAS THERE: BRIAN MCATEER

I have a short bootleg of this and can be heard on it shouting 'gawn yirsel David!' at the start of 'Wot's… Uh The Deal'. The guest that night was David Crosby, as Graham Nash was attending a family emergency, as Gilmour went on to explain. The gig was nothing short of brilliant and the second half definitely raised the roof with regards to the classics as well as making a very rare play on Scottish turf. At the start of the second half, David introduced all of the band in his usual punctual and polite way, addressing each member with attributes that he felt relevant, including Phil Manzanera as a true lifelong friend. He ignored Rick Wright completely. The crowd even started shouting about Rick and the fact he was not mentioned – this was obviously deliberate as he went on to chant 'Rich-ard, Rich-ard, Rich-ard!' and all was well.

At the end of the show, I decided to exit quickly and run round the back of the Armadillo to try and catch any of the band members as they exited. This is something I never normally do, but as I would have Gilmour's kids (if at all possible) I thought what the hell! It was probably my only chance (however slim) to meet him. We stood at the short fence outside the stage exit and witnessed Jon Carin, drummer Steve DiStanislao, Guy Pratt, Phil Manzanera and the backup singers all leave, but no Gilmour and no Rick Wright.

There were a short couple of minutes of silence and then David Crosby appeared with his minder. The lady next to me was carrying a Crosby Stills album and was baying like a mad dog to have David sign it for her. After much shouting, David turned round and said 'sorry darling – I don't do that stuff anymore' and flicked his hand with a dismissive sweep. In true Glasgow fashion, she reacted beautifully without respect for her hero and with dignity for herself: 'Get yersel' tae fuck, ya wee fat prick. Selfish wee bastard so yi are. It's folk like me that made you what you are.' I could not stop laughing, as did the few round about who heard it. However, I quickly sobered up and realised that, if Gilmour should now appear, what would I say? What would I shout? If he was to dismiss me in any way like that, I would have been completely and absolutely devastated. So I backed off and remembered the fantastic experience for what it was.

ROYAL ALBERT HALL
29 – 31 MAY 2006, LONDON, UK

I WAS THERE: PERRY RIDLEY

In July 2005, the news came that stunned the music business – the classic line up of Gilmour, Waters, Wright and Mason would re-form for one show, at *Live8* in Hyde Park. But I couldn't get a ticket. Since then, I have had to draw satisfaction from Roger Waters and David Gilmour still touring. I saw Gilmour twice at London's Royal Albert Hall in May 2006 on his *On An Island* tour. Rick Wright played keyboards, and they did a stunning version of 'Echoes'. The band included the fabulous backing vocals of David Crosby and Graham Nash. I was privileged to be there the night David Bowie came on and did 'Arnold Layne', and the co-vocal on 'Comfortably Numb'. I also witnessed Mica Paris absolutely destroy 'The Great Gig in the Sky'.

A PEOPLE'S HISTORY OF PINK FLOYD

I WAS THERE: MARK REED

It's been a long time since David appeared at the Royal Albert Hall. But close your eyes and it could be 1971 again. Flying pigs, flaming beds, crashing airplanes, rotating mirror balls and massive video screens are merely window dressing; the opening trio of songs taken from *Dark Side of the Moon*, performed merely as a band and some lights, are as compelling as any stadium rock moment.

Whilst on record the songs sometimes appear detached, in the flesh they have been liberated, set free, and the concert versions improve dramatically upon the album. 'Take a Breath', a fluid and open rocker that recalls the Floyd's rockiest, unravels to its full potential in a concert setting, as indeed does almost all of the new material.

Touched with themes of mortality and love, the mournful playing of Gilmour's tasteful solos – where it's as much what you don't say as what you do that matters – casts an air of mastery. Gilmour doesn't need to show off with his ability, and combined with the minimal presentation he proves that often less is more.

It's only in the last half hour of the entire evening when the gloves are taken off. As 'Echoes' builds to a crescendo, the hall is bathed in a glorious cacophony of tribal drumming, people all around me are lost in their own silent reverie and, all of a sudden, like a revelation, lasers are everywhere and it's an instant timewarp back to the Pink Floyd live album of 1988.

The long, improvisational takes upon 'Fat Old Sun' (equal to any of the band's legendary jams of the Seventies) and the aforementioned 'Echoes' leave me in no doubt that this is as good as it gets. Steve DiStanislao pounds the drums as if he's lived the song. There are really no words to describe this; music that transports, explores and yet never, never, loses you.

And the performance is by no means perfect; the acoustics for the opening handful of songs are fairly poor, and Gilmour's voice is showing signs of three nights of three hour shows in a row. Mica Paris, guest vocalist on 'The Great Gig in the Sky' seems to have forgotten the melody to the original and improvises her own, less effective tune on the spot. But these are mere technicalities. No matter what they are playing, be it the first Pink Floyd single ('Arnold Layne'), the last ('High Hopes') or a cover of Syd Barrett's 'Dominoes', the band are fluid, tight and as much a joy to watch as it seems it is to be in it.

At times, the band seemed to achieve that rarest of things – the state of levitation and telepathy that can see a song turn and change character purely at a shared glance – and also bristling with a kind of enthusiasm and ability that is not befitting 60-year-old elder statesmen of rock.

In an evening of highlights, it's difficult to pinpoint a crowning glory. Perhaps then, the most obvious would be the encore where the band are joined by drummer Nick Mason, reuniting the final Pink Floyd line-up on stage for the first time in twelve years. Grown men have tears in their eyes in some form of stunned rapture as this band live and breath

Clockwise from top left: Phil Chapman's Bridgewater Hall ticket and backstage pass; Robert Owen in pre-gig preparation mode; Janssy Lariviere, pictured with David Gilmour, inherited his love of Pink Floyd from his father

Clockwise from top left: It's just another brick in the wall for Michäel Perkins; Ali Gilbert's husband likes the champagne lifestyle; Amy Jeppesen's son meets David Gilmour; Marty Yawnick checks out Roger's chair again for a few brief minutes. In front of the smallest public audience Pink Floyd have officially performed in front of since 1973, they give us 'Wish You Were Here' and a final, beautiful 'Comfortably Numb'.

And with that, maybe they were gone for ever. What no amount of money can buy and no American promoter's blank cheque book can tempt, 5,220 people from across the world packed into a room in West London to witness.

2006 also sees Roger Waters on the road with his The Dark Side of the Moon Live *tour, beginning at the* Rock in Rio *festival in June 2006 and concluding two years and 119 shows later. The shows features a mix of Waters solo material and Floyd classics in the first half and the entire* The Dark Side of the Moon *post-interval.*

THE SHOWGROUNDS
29 JUNE 2006, MARQUEE FESTIVAL, CORK, IRELAND

I WAS THERE: ROBERT OWEN

A friend and I went to the venue early in the day to spec out the entrances, etc. As it was a big top, it was not a problem. When we arrived for the concert, we found ourselves in a group of people ready to be let into the arena. We were then let forward and we aimed straight for the central mic stand, as we knew this would be Roger's. Move on a couple of hours and we were in the middle of 'Perfect Sense' and all was going well. There was a second drum kit set up, so we had a good idea Nick was going to turn up for *Dark Side of the Moon*. All of a sudden, the explosion following the commentary occured and – bang – out went the power with the exception of one microphone and a spot on Roger. This is when PP Arnold came over to the mic and joined Roger to look down at the people immediately at the front to finish the song a cappella. This incident became known as *Tripped Out in Cork*, but to me it was an accident that led to one of the greatest minutes of my life, singing along to the end of 'Perfect Sense Part 2' with just Roger and few others around me. Thanks be to iffy Irish generators.

SYD BARRETT DIES
7 JULY 2006, CAMBRIDGE, UK

Syd Barrett dies at home of pancreatic cancer, aged 60. He had stepped away from the music industry and been retired from public life for more than 30 years at the time of his death.

PIAZZA SAN MARCO
11 & 12 AUGUST 2006, VENICE, ITALY

WE WERE THERE: CHRIS AND SHARON HALL

It all began back in 2006 with David's *On An Island* tour. We were living in Crete at the time and had always said that the next time David toured we would go, wherever it might take us. Imagine how chuffed we were to learn he was performing live for two nights in Venice in August – what a venue! We duly booked ferries from Crete to Venice and a hotel, thinking we would make a weekend break out of it. Tickets and hotel confirmed, off we went. The ferry to Venice takes around 30 hours so we slept on the floor as there were no cabins or seats left but no matter – we were chomping at the bit.

We arrived in Venice and took the vaporato to our hotel. As we were checking in, the desk clerk asked if we were here to see David Gilmour and, hopping from one foot to the other, we said we were. The clerk told us it had been cancelled. Horrified, we said 'no, it must be a mistake'. But it wasn't, as the clerk read from the morning's paper to say that the stage had not been erected correctly and was sagging to one side and therefore for safety reasons the show had been cancelled. However, David was talking to the council with a view to doing the concerts the following weekend and would honour concert-goers' tickets. Our hearts sank at this point and, not sure what we would do next, we unpacked and decided to take a look in St Mark's Square for ourselves. Sure enough, we saw that the staging was listing to the left and buckling. We bumped into a couple of American guys who were also looking forward to the show but who didn't know it had been cancelled, so we were the harbinger of bad news. One of them said, 'Look David is just over there. Why don't we talk to him to get the low down?' But as he sings in 'Comfortably Numb', 'we turned to look but he was gone'. Damn.

We went back to Crete and straight to the booking office to book flights back for the following weekend. That Friday, we flew back and stayed at the same hotel. Our ticket was for Saturday so we decided to go to St Mark's Square on Friday evening to listen to the whole concert. As we were walking to the concert, which had just started, so our hearts lifted and we start to immerse ourselves in the music on this wonderful balmy summer evening. Casually walking around people watching, Sharon suddenly said, 'I think I've walked in something liquid as my foot feels wet.' We looked down and blood was pouring from her big toe. She had stepped on a broken bottle. We stemmed the flow as best we could and found somewhere to rest while the blood stopped flowing and the music continued.

Saturday, and the day of the concert, the weather was lovely and sunny but nicely cooled down a bit. As we left the hotel we noticed that clouds had started to appear.

We took our seats and, just as David was about to arrive on stage, the heavens opened and the downpour began. We were soaked to the skin in minutes but, to give David his due, he ordered the roadies to give everyone a poncho to wear and a couple of free posters to take home. He did his level best to sing and play above the deluge but people were abandoning their seats to take shelter under the cloisters along the length of the shops. The mood of the music was lost, and there was more rain and people on their damn phones drowning out the music. At half time, the rain stopped and we returned to our wet seats. Part two began and, thank heavens, there were no more problems. Our two weekends away and the concert cost a cool £2,000. But what else could we do?

SHORELINE AMPHITHEATRE
10 OCTOBER 2006, MOUNTAIN VIEW, CALIFORNIA

I WAS THERE: DAVID HUGHES

When they went on sale in May, I bought tickets for me, my girl, my concert buddy and his girl for Roger Waters' rendition of *The Dark Side of the Moon*. But my concert buddy moved to Boston so his tickets went on the resale market. My girl and I got to the show. Just before it started, the couple who'd bought the resold tickets arrived at their seats and handed me a note. It read, 'Hey Dave, enjoy the show. Your friend, Graham.' It's truly cool that the folks that bought the tickets did this.

ESTADIO UNIVERSITARIO, DE NUEVO LEON
2 MARCH 2007, MONTERREY, MEXICO

I WAS THERE: KELLEY STICKSEL

What we were doing for Roger had never really been done and was technically not legal in the US. So we had to figure out how to make it legal in a very short period of time. Casey Stack is probably the leading expert in the US on laser safety and I always joke that he had the hot line to the laser police in Washington. I received a call from Casey years and years ago saying that one of the things on his bucket list was to have worked for Pink Floyd or one of the guys doing lasers. And he said to me, 'Kelley, I have an idea that out of all my colleagues in the industry, you're probably the one guy that can deliver that to me on my bucket list before anybody else can.' He put that in the back of my head.

And not two years later I get a call from Marc Brickman wanting to do something crazy. He gave me a couple of days to think it through; something to do with lasers and the famous prism. I assembled the team of people that I knew had the only lasers in the world that were capable of doing this correctly, did some very quick engineering and came up with the concept – and they liked it. What we were doing was sending beams into the crowd and that's what Roger wanted to bring the effect full circle. But when you want to send beams into the crowd you have to prove that the human eye will not be damaged by that. There are set standards in the law based on lots and lots of tests that have been done on lots of past subjects, like from the US Navy, that show just how much laser power can go into the human eye during a certain period of time.

When you look at the prism that we made, one end appears to be a white beam going in and the other appears to be a fan of colour going out the other side. Since this thing had to rotate, that was half the battle. This thing weighed well over a thousand pounds in its smallest format. And when it starts rotating, it doesn't stop on a dime. There was our safety mechanism. Even if this thing all failed, it would keep rotating. So we put a very high powered laser inside the prism and we drew the rainbow by scanning very, very fast on a very wide pattern.

We had to prove it was safe to each local jurisdiction. Casey was one of those guys who had to sit down with the local 'laser police', as we jokingly called them, and walk them through the calculations at almost every location.

It really made for an immersive experience if you were in the crowd. And invariably, as we sat in the different crowds as they toured, people anticipated that rainbow swinging around and painting them. They anticipated the lasers swinging by, you'd get a Mexican wave as you would at a soccer crowd, and the crowd just got noisier and noisier. To me, it signalled an incredible success. We created a really immersive effect. I know Roger was thrilled as he'd see it, because he'd look out into the crowd and get a big old grin on his face every

It had never been done before. It set our industry on fire because everybody wanted to copy it. We figured out what we called the 'secret sauce' to making it happen. And just a few years later, Casey and me did it on a full scale for Justin Timberlake on his *20/20 Experience*, where we had 26 lasers scanning into the audience, legally, for the first time in the United States. I still believe that Roger's was the most artistic and jaw dropping effect, because it was absolutely iconic. It got the crowd going wherever it went.

The prism could scale up in size or down in size. It was really a marvel of engineering. There were so many things on that that were difficult engineering tasks that the audience never knew of. And that's really our job – to make it look easy and have people not think about what went into it.

WISH YOU WERE HERE

Light looks much brighter coming at you. It can almost be invisible going away from you, and so when we did the legs of the tetrahedron we knew that, as the thing rotated around, the legs would pretty much disappear. Roger wanted this thing to totally disappear and be invisible to the audience until the lasers turned on for the finale. So this thing would either be docked backstage or pushed forward out into the audience, who'd be totally oblivious to it as it did not look like a prism. It looked like nothing, because the walls of the prism didn't exist until the lasers came on.

What we had to do was bounce the laser back on itself. We ran the initial laser beams down pipes so you couldn't see where they were coming from until we got into the position of one of the boundaries of the prism and then the laser beam came out, hit a mirror, bounced across, hit another mirror and bounced up to the top to make two legs of the tetrahedron. Then it bounced back on itself so that it was bright in both directions as it rotated around towards people. And then the beam went back up inside and terminated.

Three lasers formed the walls of the prism, all hidden in an air conditioned box, and then two massive lasers formed the beam that went in and the fan that came out the other side. We built two solid state lasers for this tour, the largest entertainment lasers ever built. There were several innovations, several firsts that happened, things that have never been duplicated.

Roger's touring right now and one of our competitors did another prism. It's very, very large over the crowd and forms a massive prism overhead. It's a different take on it and I'm glad that the gag wasn't repeated on another tour, but the prism still lives in laser light. It's fun to see that reincarnated with other people's designs.

I would probably say it's the high point of my career. I will always be honoured that Roger and Marc Brickman had faith in me to pull this off. And then it was all about the team. I couldn't have done it on my own. I'm getting goose bumps now just talking about it. It was that emotional. It was cathartic for me, All of us were in tears the first time we saw it, in the studio out in LA.

We knew when we turned it on the first time that we had something that was going to be historic. And we immediately snapped pictures and sent them to Marc and to Roger and we got the go ahead at that point. But It was nothing compared to seeing it out there in Mexico, over the soccer stadium the first time. When it came at full scale, we all looked up and saw it in rehearsal, even without an audience there, it was pretty incredible. And the first night, with the crowd, it was an emotional experience for all of us to hear that crowd go nuts in Monterey. It was the same place we rehearsed. Then we took it to Mexico City, to a massive crowd in the stadium there. That was really amazing. That's where the wave-type thing started developing.

I only went to the first few shows and then we had technicians handling it. But no matter where it was in the world I was getting calls every night because we had challenges at different venues, due to the wind or whatever. There were a few times when we were performing in really high wind locations where Roger would look up from the stage and the stadium haze would go away for a minute and the prism would be looking wispy. I loved that effect, as the clouds blew through it, because it became almost psychedelic, but Roger wanted to see it full all the time. It's his icon. So we went through different iterations of adding clear tubes, putting gas in the tubes and other modifications.

Roger has some of the highest standards I've worked with. He's a perfectionist extraordinaire. Not only in his music. He's aware of everything that's going on on his stage, no matter how complicated the stage is. You'd get notes at the end of the show. And those are the guys we really want to work for because we really want to make them look good. And we use those notes on a nightly basis to improve what we do. And there were frequent notes on things – it was an expensive gag, especially for one or two songs at the end of the show.

He's always analysing. When we'd sit with him out at front of house during rehearsal he's a quiet man. He would think and then, when he spoke, everybody listened. A man of few words. Sometimes it can be nerve wracking, waiting to see what he's going to comment on as he's sitting there staring. And there were other times he couldn't fight the grin because it's just such a cool gag. It's one of those things I will never forget in my entire career. As a laser guy, a rock 'n' roll guy, it's just kind of synonymous. The opportunity to work for Pink Floyd is one of those things you just never forget.

I WAS THERE: CASEY STACK

George Lucas was once quoted as saying that his core demographic was eleven-year old boys. And I was eleven years old in 1977 when *Star Wars* came out. A couple of years after that, there was a concert put on in my home town of Portland, Oregon with the State Philharmonic, with William Shatner and with the orchestra playing a whole bunch of space-related music. My mother happened to be given two tickets so my father and I went along, and the thing that absolutely captured the imagination of this eleven-year-old boy was that they started doing laser effects and filling the Coliseum in Portland with laser beams in every direction, using effects in that actually you can't do today because of regulations put in place since.

By the age of 14, I had procured for Christmas – following a year of constant badgering of my parents – a very, very low power introductory laser and I started building laser light show effects in my parents' basement. I went to college but after a couple of terms I discovered that there was nothing I could learn at college about producing laser design technology or laser light shows, because the technology had not yet moved from industry to the university, I landed a job at OMSI, and there started my formal and commercial career in laser light shows.

WISH YOU WERE HERE

After a year there, I moved to Seattle where the parent company, Laser Fantasy, was based. And within a year I became the technical director for the company, so I got an early start in lasers. In 2004, I called Kelley Sticksel and said, 'Before I get completely out of this business, the one thing left on my bucket list is I've never worked with Pink Floyd on a touring live basis. I'd love to do this.' Kelley said to me 'I hear you' and three years later Kelley calls up and says, 'Roger Waters is touring and is looking for an interesting new effect and let's do something.'

After weeks and months of crazy, crazy running around, this laser effect was fabricated in Los Angeles and was the first of its kind using the first real large deployment of solid-state lasers – you couldn't have done the big laser prism gag previously with the older style technology. It just wasn't feasible.

And there was a hard deadline – there's a tour, there's tickets sold – and all this stuff's gotta happen. So people were up all night for weeks, pulling it all together before the tour so that the laser prism gag could be deployed on the first tour stop of Roger's 2007/08 *Dark Side of the Moon* tour.

The first show was Monterrey. We had all flown down there, and the equipment was set up that day. This was the night before the show, so the stage is all there, everything's rigged and in place. Roger showed up as the sun was going down. There were four or five of us sitting front of house, and Roger comes and sits down and says, 'Okay, let's look at this. Show me what you got.' And the lighting designer and our team start playing with stuff, and showing this and that. I did some technical work on this project and some of the actual fabrication, but most of my contribution was the legal aspects of how do we do this legally and safely, since when this thing rotates it's going to scan the people in the upper seats with laser light. When it came to the actual operation of it, I was just standing in the background.

So it gets to 1am and it's kinda cool and it's dark, and we're on the grass in the middle of this giant soccer stadium, and Roger looks around and says 'can I get a cup of tea?' And what you had was basically a bunch of Yanks that were just focused on the laser thing, and guys that maybe didn't drink tea. And after another minute or two Roger looks around and he says again, 'could I get a cup of tea?' And I thought, 'This is my chance to step up and be a contributor.' So I stepped up to him and I said, 'What can you tell me about your cup of tea? Is there anything special? Sugar? Cream? Anything?' I don't remember exactly what his response was but I thought, 'Okay, I will go and do my best.' So I walk across the field and behind the stage and find the craft services, the catering area, and there's nobody there. It's been shut down for hours. There are a few things sitting out but all I find is a teabag for making Lipton's iced tea. I knew a couple of things. One, I knew that Brits are very, very serious about their tea. And two, no Yankee knows how to make a good cup of tea that will make a Brit happy.

And so here I was trying to figure out a way, at 1am under unusual circumstances in the almost dark, how I'm going to make a good cup of tea, not just for a British subject, but for someone who I had the utmost respect for, someone you might almost call an idol. So I delivered a hot cup of tea with packets of sugar and cream, knowing that probably a serious British cup of tea would be made with fresh cream if you liked cream, and not a little American 'tear it open' packet. With greatest apologies, I handed Mr Waters his tea. He was appreciative nonetheless and I explained I didn't really know how to make a good cup of tea and how I wished I could have delivered him a perfect cup.

Besides the wonderful laser effect and the effect it had on the crowd when it comes, when Roger looks up and draws attention to it and says something like 'wonderful' or 'glorious', other than the effect itself and its presentation in the show, I will always remember trying to make this man who I revere so greatly a good cup of tea under terrible circumstances in the middle of a soccer field, in the middle of the night in Mexico.

O2 ARENA
18 & 19 MAY 2008, LONDON, UK

I WAS THERE: ALEXANDER G MITLEHNER

I saw Roger Waters again in 2008, on his *Dark Side* tour. As well as playing the whole of that album, he played many more from the Floyd back catalogue. This was my first gig at the O2 Arena and was far bigger even than Earl's Court. However, the sound was far better Roger's set came across much more clearly. If anything, he'd improved with age and the older numbers were reproduced with crystal-clear clarity. The video backdrops were great too. Especially poignant were the songs played with footage of Syd Barrett who had recently died, so this was very emotional. Thank you, Pink Floyd members past and present for some truly memorable experiences, one of the greatest live acts ever.

I WAS THERE: PERRY RIDLEY

Roger Waters toured with his *Dark Side of the Moon Live* tour. I saw him at London's O2 in May 2008, and he did a brilliant show, backed by the fabulous PP Arnold. She did the backing vocal on one of my all-time favourite songs – 'Tin Soldier' by The Small Faces.

CADOGAN HALL
15 JUNE 2008, LONDON, UK

I WAS THERE: ROBIN ATKINSON

This was the second of two nights of a performance of *Atom Heart Mother* given as part of the Chelsea Festival by Ron Geesin and an Italian Pink Floyd tribute band called Mun Floyd, with Caroline Dale on cello with the Canticum Choir and the Royal College of Music on brass. David Gilmour performed on the second night only, and I managed to get a ticket on eBay in the front row. It was just sublime. David treated the band with respect and the performance was well rehearsed and completely professional. I had seen Pink Floyd perform it at the Bath Blues Festival and then in Hyde Park, both in 1970, but never believed I would see this performed again. David played the slide on a separate guitar while seated but with his prototype black Strat attached. He then effortlessly stood up and started playing his Strat. Filming was strictly forbidden but there are some video snippets on YouTube.

RICHARD WRIGHT DIES
15 SEPTEMBER 2008, LONDON, UK

Richard Wright dies at home of lung cancer, aged 65. David Gilmour calls him 'my musical partner and my friend. In the welter of arguments about who or what was Pink Floyd, Rick's enormous input was frequently forgotten.'

In December 2009, on the 30th anniversary of its release, Roger Waters announces plans to tour a new production of The Wall. *Waters defends his decision to perform the Pink Floyd work without any other members of the band: 'It stands on its own as a piece.' The 219-date tour lasts three years, from September 2010 to September 2013, and grosses $458 million, breaking the existing record for a solo musician.*

KIDDINGTON HALL
10 JULY 2010, OXFORDSHIRE, UK

Despite lingering tension between the two, Waters accepts an invitation from Gilmour to take part in a charity fundraiser. The terms of the deal are simple: Gilmour will play 'Comfortably Numb' at one of Waters' Wall *shows if Roger will duet with David on The Teddy Bears' 'To Know Him Is To Love*

Him' at the charity event. Waters duly obliges, and the pair also perform 'Wish You Were Here' and 'Comfortably Numb'. Pink Floyd fans wonder when Gilmour will fulfil his part of the bargain. The event raises £350,000 for a charity to aid Palestinian refugee children.

MADISON SQUARE GARDEN
5 & 6 OCT & 6 NOV 2010, NEW YORK, NEW YORK

I WAS THERE: DAVID BALDWIN

I have seen Pink Floyd and Roger Waters a few times, back in the late Eighties with the *Momentary Lapse of Reason* and the *Radio K.A.O.S.* tours in, respectively, Washington DC and Laurel, Maryland. I then went with my son to see Roger Waters perform *The Wall* at Madison Square Garden. When this older lady sitting next to us handed him joint, my son didn't know whether to hit it or pass it on.

VALUE CITY ARENA
22 OCTOBER 2010, COLUMBUS, OHIO

I WAS THERE: JAMES HEINE

Roger Waters was giving a theatrical performance of the rock opera, *The Wall*. Everyone there pretty much knew the story but there would be many new twists and surprises. First Roger came out to a standing ovation and he told us to hold on as it would start in about 15 minutes. His hair was longish but he still had a full head of hair. It was grey – steely grey, not mousy – and his eyes were liquid azure in hue. His face, etched with the crags of age, was adorned with one or two days' stubble. He looked calm and wizened, with his experiences and past conflicts settled for good. Other former Pink Floyd members appeared at certain shows on this tour, but this night wasn't one of them. Of all the ex-Floydians, Roger looked really good for his age.

The show began with dimmed lights and audio recordings of his early life: Churchill's 'finest hour' speech, the climactic scene from the movie *Spartacus* (the gladiators will all die together), George Carlin's 'Seven Words You Can Never Say on Television' (it was so fast, I could only make out the words 'cocksucker' and 'motherfucker') and other stuff. The first song, 'In the Flesh?', erupted in full glory and Roger sang the words wearing shades and a trenchcoat. A toy Messerschmitt plane roared across and exploded when it hit a wire. Standby firefighters doused the fire. The album continued.

During 'Another Brick in the Wall (Part 2)' a giant teacher balloon was displayed, a children's drama class group danced on stage and the song was 'lightened up' by a musical extension consisting of a funky soul groove with an electric organ played in a dry sawdust sound with a 'spoon on a can' rhythm pumping it – call it a New York groove. 'Empty Spaces' played, featuring no backwards message, which proved that the crack band was playing the songs and not using tapes.

The first disc finished with a wall up and projections on it of 'disappeared' people from authoritarian and totalitarian nations ranging from Chile and Argentina to El Salvador and Iran. After a 30-minute break, the second disc commenced. A giant pig balloon hovered over the crowd, festooned with slogans like 'FUCK HATE', 'FUCK WAR' and 'STRIVE FOR PEACE'. 'Bring The Boys Back Home' featured homecoming American soldiers arriving in schools to greet their children. That song was extended up to eight minutes and it was very heartfelt. The audience applauded this one.

A fuse blew up on a synthesiser and Roger told us to 'hang on tight, it'll be fixed in 15 minutes'. It was done in ten and Roger said, 'Let's give these guys a hand.' We did. On one song, a guitarist was suspended on the wall, playing. More projections were put on the wall. Roger had a great band of skilled players, and background vocals were courtesy of an a cappella group, Venice, who competed in *Star Search '83*. In 'The Trial', there were additional scenes different from the *Pink Floyd: The Wall* movie of 1982, as well as additional dialogue to throw you off. There was 'go on, Judge, shit on him!' and 'tear down the fucking wall!' – there's no 'fucking' in the original song lyrics. Everybody screamed and cheered in delight when the wall came down. For 'Outside the Wall', Roger tooted a trumpet and cheerfully declared that he was happy. So were we. After that song, the whole crew did their big bow and the show was over.

Me and others lived out in our minds various scenes and emotions of our lives in this tale of alienation. We laughed, we cried, we screamed, we cheered, and, after the show at a bus stop in the bright moonlight, I conversed with some other concertgoers about the 'bricks' in our lives. Are we going to build walls to shut ourselves off from everyone? Or are we going to strive to make things better?

A statement projected on the fake wall near the end of the show quoted Dwight 'Ike' Eisenhower about how a nation makes itself great by taking care of its people, neglecting no one and striving for peace, unity and freedom – not war. Jesus Christ and others implied that too. This wasn't just a concert, it was theatre and an incredible experience, running the gamut of life's ups and downs. I felt completely chilled and relaxed after the show. It was a unique and special evening.

US AIRWAYS CENTER
27 NOVEMBER 2010, PHOENIX, ARIZONA

I WAS THERE: MICHÄEL PERKINS

Having worked Roger's 2000 Phoenix solo show, I also worked the 2010 and 2011 solo concerts as a stage hand and have a brick from 'The Wall'! I arrived at 5am and began assisting ground rigging with the organisation of components of the quad audio system, and also helping with the set-up of a staggering number of subwoofers, trussing, rigging, cabling and speaker cabinets all day long.

After soundcheck, the local crew were dismissed for two hours and, when we came back, my essential function was to begin breaking down some parts of the sound system underneath the stage as the show was concluding above. I was under stage left. After the noise above stopped, I looked up from my task to see Roger, GE Smith, Graham Broad et al walking slowly down the rampway toward me, singing and performing 'Outside The Wall'. Roger went back up onstage and said a long 'thank you' as the rest of the band left and handed off their instruments.

I was barely over that when Roger walked off, pulled his in-ear monitors out and took a breath. I was not supposed to say anything to him (my employer's stipulation) but I did say 'thank you' loud enough to get a thumbs up gesture from Roger before he walked off with three or four others.

A moment later, a black Fender bass and an Ampeg amp, some picks and such were wheeled up by me on a dolly to be packed by another stagehand. I helped him lift the flight case for the bass and he went about his task as I went about mine. I plucked the lowest string on the bass.

After the three hours of load out was complete, there were numerous pieces of brick left over, but only two or three were whole. I asked the stage manager if I might take a souvenir and was told 'if I don't see it, I don't care'. He went off down the hallway. I managed to get a brick into my car and home. When I unfolded and reshaped it, I noticed a large splotch of green-grey paint on an upper corner, from the plane during 'In The Flesh'!

O2 ARENA
12 MAY 2011, LONDON, UK

I WAS THERE: JENNY SPIRES

I didn't see the Floyd play again for 45 years, but I am really happy to say I saw them at the O2, as if by magic exactly 45 years to the day after *Games for May*! It was Roger Waters' show, *The Wall*. I didn't know David was also playing, although I knew he was going to join Rog's show for one gig. The chances of it being this day seemed unlikely, but it turned out to be the one. I was in a corporate box as a guest, left of the stage, almost on a level with the top of the stage set of The Wall. Rog was in the spotlight singing 'can you show me where it hurts?'. Seconds before, I saw a figure standing on top of the wall, and as soon he moved his arm I knew it was David. I nudged the person next to me. 'It's Gilmour!' I said, just as Dave cut in: 'there is no pain…' and, as other people in the box realised, they burst into tears. It was very moving. And I think for them, massively so, and probably very cathartic after the years of despair, hope and wonder the Floyd had generated.

As David's sound percolated, it resounded, bouncing off the walls, and came crashing into perception. It was exciting. Like a tsunami, a huge roar travelled up from the floor as David Gilmour's guitar tone tumbled, cascading and scything its way over and into the light drenched audience. As the lights came up, it was astonishing seeing him up there on the wall.

I have now seen both *The Wall* and David Gilmour's shows… They are fitting tributes to the early Syd Barrett we knew, back then in the underground… Syd Barrett, who touched so many with his experiment into sound which was carried by Pink Floyd evermore.

I WAS THERE: ALI GILBERT

I've seen Pink Floyd a few times but the best was when Roger and Dave appeared together at the O2 Arena and performed 'Comfortably Numb'. Many years ago, my husband helped his friend get the big inflatable pig to Manchester for the Chinese new year. A whole crew turned up and set it all up. Another good memory is Hamburg in 2018. Roger threw a champagne glass into the crowd and my husband is now the proud owner of that glass!

I WAS THERE: ROBIN ATKINSON

I saw them doing *Atom Heart Mother* a couple of times. I saw the 14 April 1969 show at the Royal Festival Hall, entitled *More Furious Madness From The Massed Gadgets Of Auximenes*, and we were amazed by the sound of bird singing moving around the auditorium by the Azimuth Co-ordinator. I also saw them that year at the Rex Ballroom in Cambridge, the Bath Festival in 1970, Crystal Palace in 1971 and on the *Animals* tour at Wembley in 1977.

Finally, I saw David Gilmour join Roger Waters at the O2 to play 'Comfortably Numb' in May 2011. They never engaged with the audience as much as I felt they could have done. Certainly, when I went to see them on the *Animals* tour, you felt at times that really there was a little bit missing. They were never great showmen. Roger Waters is more than David Gilmour is. But I appreciate, from playing the guitar myself, how much they had to concentrate, because some of that music is quite complex and requires a huge amount of concentration to pull it off right, especially things like 'Shine On You Crazy Diamond'. There's a phenomenal amount going on in there, and when you realise that you can give them a bit more credit for what they're doing and what they did. It's fantastic.

There'll be something that'll bring David and Roger back together. Some songs, like 'Wish You Were Here' and 'Comfortably Numb', are classics where there are two verses and where it needs the two of them.

MEMORIAL COLISEUM
19 MAY 2012, LOS ANGELES, CALIFORNIA

I WAS THERE: MARTY YAWNICK

We saw Roger Waters' *The Wall* tour in 2010 and again in 2012. Spectacle, pure spectacle and larger than life! It was huge and amazing, and everything was over-the-top. I truly understood 'that warm space cadet glow' from the sense of anticipation I felt as the show began. Faithful in spirit to the original *Wall* shows, technically the shows were so much better than what I imagine the original 1980 performances must have been. As my buddy and I were leaving the arena, we saw an area curtained off in the concourse. Behind it, we could see where the crew were moving many of the cardboard wall bricks that had just come down minutes before. 'You wanna have a look?' 'I don't think we should be back there, but sure…'. We took a look behind the curtain and among the props that were stowed there was 'The Chair' from the 'Nobody Home' set. In front of us was a focal point of greatness. My buddy and I each took turns sitting in The Chair, quickly exchanging cameras and poses. It was actually touching part of The Wall. It was the same feeling I got the first time I stepped onto the crossing at Abbey Road.

KEY ARENA
24 MAY 2012, SEATTLE, WASHINGTON

I WAS THERE: JOHN RIVERA

It was announced that Roger Waters would be performing *The Wall* with interactive media. I hesitated before buying tickets because of his political outbursts, but how many people can say they've seen *The Wall* performed in two different centuries? I purchased tickets for my wife, my son and myself through Roger's web site. The seats turned out to be perfect. The stage was the same as I remembered from LA in 1980, with the iconic round screen, but the speaker system was now surroundsound rather than quadraphonic. The show started and was just as awesome as the previous version. Roger had an excellent band, including Snowy White from the earlier days of Pink Floyd. The concert was very similar to the 1980 show I had witnessed, but both Roger and the band appeared more relaxed. The plane made its descent onto the wall as before, with fireworks, flags and people marching to the music. The Teacher puppet appeared and when Roger sang, 'Mother, should I build the wall?' the bricks started floating into place, lighting up like a screen and showing a picture. A puppet of Mother appeared, as she had 32 years before, complementing one of my favourite Floyd tunes.

The show continued with 'Comfortably Numb', with Robbie Wyckoff and Dave Kilminster taking Gilmour's place atop the wall for the solo parts. It was good, but Gilmour was better. The hammers appeared again for 'In the Flesh' and Roger donned a long black leather coat to act as the fascist Pink. He repeated his voices for 'The Trial', and when the wall crumbled to the stage, the crowd went wild as they had in LA 32 years previously. The strings started for 'Outside the Wall' and the band marched out from the side of the stage where Roger was playing a trumpet. As he sang the final lines of the song, the band began to march back offstage. The crowd went crazy, and when the band appeared for the final bows the crowd went wild again, Roger actually smiled.

MANCHESTER ARENA
16 SEPTEMBER 2013, MANCHESTER, UK

I WAS THERE: DAVID MILLINGTON

I got tickets to see Roger Waters off a friend free of charge. I had just started a new job from which I had to ask for an early finish to attend said gig. When we arrived and asked for my name at the ticket booth, we got four tickets but there were only two of us. I waited to find someone looking to buy tickets off a tout and gave my two spare tickets away. The tickets were backstage and we proceeded to go backstage where there were free beers and many people chatting. Halfway through the show, we went backstage again. Harry Waters (Roger's son, who was playing in the band) came in and started talking to everyone. It was a mind-blowing experience and more than just a gig. It was a movie, art, a play and an album all in one.

THE ENDLESS RIVER RELEASED
7 NOVEMBER 2014

Released as a tribute to Richard Wright, The Endless River *is a collection of unused material exhumed from the Pink Floyd vaults and consists almost entirely of instrumental and ambient music recorded during sessions for* The Division Bell. *Despite its origins, it becomes the most pre-ordered album of all time on Amazon UK and the vinyl edition is the fastest-selling UK vinyl release since 1997. It reaches No.1 in the UK charts, No.3 on the* Billboard *200 and tops the charts in 19 other countries.*

In 2015, David Gilmour undertakes his Rattle That Lock *tour, encompassing 50 shows between September 2015 and September 2016, grossing $78 million and culminating in five nights at the Royal Albert Hall in London.*

HOLLYWOOD BOWL
24 MARCH 2016, LOS ANGELES, CALIFORNIA

I WAS THERE: AMY JEPPESEN

I wish I were lucky enough to see Pink Floyd. I did see David Gilmour at the Hollywood Bowl in 2016, and met and spoke with him. I told him my children thought I named my iPod David because whenever I felt stressed I would get it and say, 'I need to listen to David.' His voice and guitar relax me better than anything else, as it does for many people. He shook my son's hand (imagine the kindness to bother) and said, 'Hi, I'm the guy your mom named her iPod after.' I was shocked at how humble he was. He has been famous for 50 plus years and still seems so down-to-earth.

My son asked for *The Division Bell* when he was 13. He had it on his devices so I asked if I could borrow it for my car and it has never left in seven years, although I did move it from one car's CD player to another when I changed cars. I never get tired of it.

Seeing David is like a drug and makes you want more. I spent the rest of the tour trying to figure out if we could go see him at any of his European dates, looking up flights and different options. I couldn't get other family members schedules to match up. I should have gone alone. I saw Roger in 2017 in Sacramento. I admire his writing brilliance and he does some songs that David doesn't. Like most Pink Floyd fans, I believe they are best together but I don't take sides or chose one over the other. I value each of them and the incredible talents they both possess. I appreciate anything they care to share with us.

UNITED CENTER
4 & 8 APRIL 2016, CHICAGO, ILLINOIS

I WAS THERE: TOM SNIDER

David Gilmour is a musical hero of mine, and getting to see him live was a dream come true. My wife Sarah and I try to take the week of our wedding anniversary off every year. When David announced a North American leg to his *Rattle That Lock* tour, with a Chicago date that happened to be that week, I went back and forth for three days whether to pull the trigger before I eventually got two tickets for the April 4th show. I can't tell you how excited I was.

Arriving at the venue, we found our seats and sat there watching the stage hands set up the instruments and lighting. When the lights finally went out, excitement filled the air as the small hum of music built up with opener, '5AM'. Stood there was the man I had idolised since my childhood. I could only sit there in awe as some of my favourite songs were played, and I heard David's playing through a new emotion and very different from the albums. The song list was a good variety of new material, classic Floyd and even one song, 'Blue', from his previous solo album, *On An Island*. I've seen many Pink Floyd videos and how the light show coincided with the music, but seeing it first hand was an experience in itself. However, a few people tried to take it a few steps further by lighting up and security kicked out at least five people from our section. The worst was during the opening solo to 'Shine On You Crazy Diamond', when a man sitting at the balcony had started dancing erratically. He kicked and screamed as they dragged him out and security then found hits of acid on him.

During the solo to 'Money', David Gilmour had broken out into the whitest of white guy hand shuffles, dancing to the music. On 'Us and Them', one of the lights around the screen was out of sync with the rest – as they shone inwards it would shine outwards and vice versa. 'In Any Tongue' isn't one of my favourite songs from *Rattle That Lock* but I have to listen to it now because, when the ending solo had started, it startled a woman sitting next to me and she spilled her cocktail on me. And, fittingly for Chicago, during 'Run Like Hell' the band wore Blues Brothers style-sunglasses (they wore these throughout the tour to keep the strobe lights out of their eyes). Then the lights came on, David thanked us for coming, the band waved and walked off the stage and – no one moved.

They hadn't played 'Comfortably Numb' and we knew there would be an encore. The lights went out again, the alarm clocks for 'Time' started going off at an almost deafening volume and the crowd exploded. During 'Breathe (Reprise)' we all sang in unison 'home, home again, I like to be here when I can'. That moment was probably the most magical. 'Comfortably Numb' was next, and last. Lasers went off with different colours for each chorus, David played a thunderous ending solo, the lights and lasers were changing, the crowd erupted and just like that the show was over and the band gave a final bow.

Richard Wright was sorely missed and I wasn't around to see Pink Floyd back in the day, but the band was fantastic nonetheless and I couldn't have asked for a better show. I picked up a guitar because of David Gilmour, and watching him play was one of the great honours and one of the greatest nights of my life.

AMPHITHEATRE
7 & 8 JULY 2016, POMPEII, ITALY

I WAS THERE: BILL CHOW

I first became a Pink Floyd fan in the mid-Eighties when I was a teenager and I first saw them in concert in September 1987 in Toronto and then again in 1994. I also saw Roger Waters perform *The Wall* in 2010 and David Gilmour in Toronto in April 2016. Seeing the Pompeii concert cemented my love.

I went to the first night. I was able to get a Pompeii concert ticket at face value (400 euros) three weeks after they went on sale. I was sceptical about going all that way to Italy for a three-hour show but I am a big tennis fan, so when I found out I could go to Wimbledon for the tennis as well, I bought my ticket! There was a lot of planning to co-ordinate this trip since I had never travelled anywhere alone, or ever been to Europe, but everything worked better than I thought.

WISH YOU WERE HERE

The Pompeii Amphitheatre is a rock 'n' roll shrine everyone should visit. I was so fortunate to have seen an original member of Pink Floyd perform there on the tenth anniversary of his band mate Syd Barrett's death. It must have been very close to David Gilmour's heart. Everyone there was so into it and to see the amphitheatre lit up was incredible.

I WAS THERE: MICHAEL CONNELLY

I couldn't believe that David had arranged to play a gig in Pompeii. This was going to be a hard ask, trying to secure a ticket for this one! I had to register with ticketone.it, an Italian ticket agency. I logged into the website just as the tickets were going on sale and tried to purchase two but it would only allow me to place one in the basket. I finished the transaction and logged back in and completed a second transaction for another ticket – result! Anytime there is a tour or gig by the members of the band, my best friend Mark and I have always tried to get tickets and to get there by hook or by crook. This has been the case since *The Division Bell/Pulse* tour of 1994. To say that we were both excited to be going to this momentous gig was an understatement.

Mark had been to Pompeii previously with his wife but this was going to be my first visit, and what a visit it turned out to be. We drove from Glasgow to Liverpool, took a flight into Naples and then taxied through to our B&B in Pompeii. We got our luggage settled in and then walked through to the centre of Pompeii and found an outside bar. Later in the evening, we were joined by a couple from the Czech Republic who had come over for the gig. They told us both that it was a great spectacle and that they didn't want to spoil it for us, but that we would be amazed.

The following day, we queued up at the venue to collect our tickets. In this area there were plaster casts of the bodies in glass cases from the destruction of Pompeii in 79 AD. We then queued for access into the venue and saw the sign at the gates stating that the concerts were being filmed. The amphitheatre looked absolutely stunning from outside and we couldn't wait to get inside. It was a long walk down through the tunnel that led us into the amphitheatre. We turned the corner and walked upwards slightly and saw 'Mr Screen' at the end of the arena.

It was a truly magical feeling to be stood in a place where Roman gladiators fought epic battles to the death. It was a beautiful night and we had to wait until it started to get dark before the concert started. To the left-hand side of the arena, we could see the Gilmour family atop a scaffold platform. David's wife Polly was moving around, taking numerous photos throughout the gig.

A beautiful opening piece with '5 A.M.' got things underway. It was also fantastic to hear 'One of These Days' being played, as it was one of the songs from the *Pink Floyd Live at Pompeii* 1971 documentary film. It sounded absolutely amazing, and got a fantastic reception from the crowd. At one point the crowd was chanting for 'Echoes' to be played, but David told them that, "Echoes' is a musical conversation between two people, Rick (Wright) and me. Sadly Rick is dead, and that's a conversation I can no longer have.' I too would have loved to have heard 'Echoes' played, but I totally understand David's decision and that's why I welcomed 'One of These Days'. 'Run Like Hell' was amazing, with a fantastic firework display that totally lit up the arena and the night sky in various colours. The lasers in 'Comfortably Numb' were also amazing, with the smoke from the machines drifting through them.

The fire pits that were lit around the top of the arena for the second half was how it would have been back in Roman times, however the drone that was flying around the arena from just outside was certainly not from those times! But I am sure those gladiators would have approved of the music, the songs, the light show and the sublime talent of the band and of David Gilmour. As David himself said, 'It's lovely to be back here in this beautiful place after all these years, amongst all you people and all these ghosts, ancient and recent.' This was definitely a nod to Rick Wright and to Syd Barrett, who had died ten years before.

ROYAL ALBERT HALL
23, 25, 28-30 SEPTEMBER 2016, LONDON, UK

I WAS THERE: PERRY RIDLEY

I continue to follow David Gilmour, and saw seven shows on his *Rattle That Lock* tour. I went to the preview show in his home town of Brighton in September 2015. I saw two shows at the Royal Albert Hall on the first leg of the tour in September 2015, the Teenage Cancer Trust show in April 2016, and three more, including the last night of the world tour, in September 2016. I had the luck of securing arena floor tickets for all of the Royal Albert Hall shows. I did consider going to what would be the highlight of the tour, when David did two shows at the Roman Amphitheatre where they shot the *Live in Pompeii* film in 1972, but unfortunately the ticket prices were so expensive I could not afford it. I will probably live to regret this decision…

Dark Side of the Moon remains my favourite LP ever released, and is the greatest album in the history of modern music. It is a sonic masterpiece, with one of the most iconic record sleeves ever designed. It is the screensaver on my phone, my desktop PC, my laptop, and my iPad. I am unashamedly obsessed with *The Dark Side of the Moon*. My all-time favourite song is 'Comfortably Numb', which I have requested be played when I am on my final journey to the great gig in the sky.

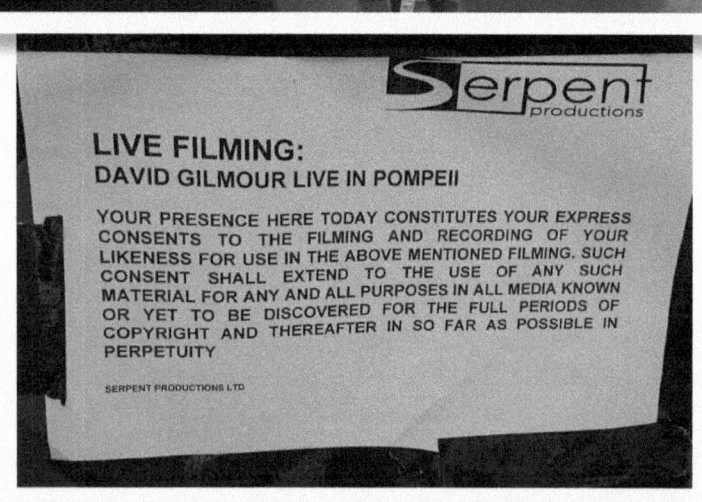
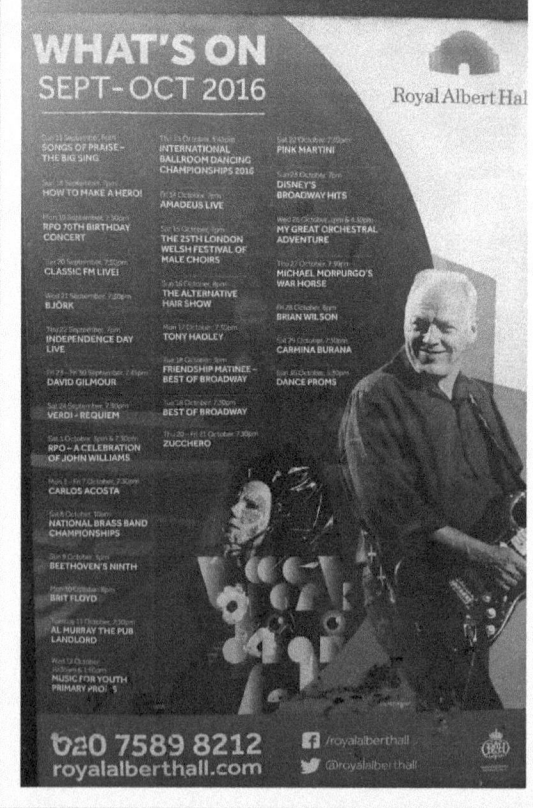

Clockwise from top left: Bill Chow was at Pompeii in 2016; Gabrielle Cornett hung around outside the venue the night after the gig hoping to get an autograph; Michael Connelly was at what might be David's last ever gig

Clockwise from top left: Guadalupe Villalta had been waiting to see Roger Waters for years; Gabrielle Cornett's swag; David and Roger embrace (Mark Reed); Michael Connelly was at Pompeii for David's return after 45 years

WISH YOU WERE HERE

I WAS THERE: MICHAEL CONNELLY

This was the last night of David's *Rattle That Lock* tour and the last gig he has played (thus far). I met Damian, a guy that my friend Mark and I had met in Pompeii (we had shared a taxi in Pompeii to our respective abodes, and a flight back to Liverpool Airport). A lot of fans who'd met via David's website blog had arranged to meet in the Queens Arms pub in Kensington. It was a great atmosphere but there was a bit of trepidation that it was the final gig of the tour and possibly one of David's final gigs ever. For many of the people there had seen several gigs on that tour; it was my third, after the preview show at the Brighton Centre in September 2015 and then Pompeii. David and the band were on fine form for this final night. I had seen all the songs on the setlist throughout the tour but witnessing them in the Royal Albert Hall was great. It is a truly magical venue and, with an artist as sublime as Gilmour, it is truly fantastic. The only thing that made me unhappy was having my ticket taken from me on the night by the door stewards. But I contacted the venue after a few weeks and provided my details and they sent me a duplicate. A great finish to a great set of concerts.

In May 2017, Roger Waters embarks on his Us + Them *tour, performing a total 157 dates and grossing $261 million before the tour wraps in Monterey, Mexico in December 2018. Focusing on his most recent album,* Is This The Life We Really Want?, *and Pink Floyd material pre-1980, the tour attracts headlines not least for the extended verbal assaults on US President Donald Trump, drawing a mixture of reactions from fans.*

I WAS THERE: MARK GREGA

I worked for Laser Media, a company working out of Los Angeles, California, and Laser Media was hired for the *Momentary Lapse of Reason* tour. I was on the Deep Purple tour when Ritchie Blackmore broke his finger in Albuquerque, so when I woke up the next morning in Phoenix, we all got sent home which made me available for the Floyd tour. If Ritchie hadn't broken his finger, I probably never would have been connected with the Floyd!

We started with the droids which were like a laser simulator. There were four of them on the stage and I was the operator of that and also part of the laser crew. Our responsibilities were to set up the lasers and set up the droids and, during the show, I would operate the colour ray. I went everywhere that tour went. I missed one show in Cleveland, because my mother was in the hospital and I had to go home. We didn't do the *Division Bell* tour because they'd hired a different company, and then I started my own company in 1996 and that's when Marc Brickman, the lighting designer, called me for David's On An Island tour. That was only supposed to be one night, for the show at

Radio City Music Hall, and it turned into the rest of that tour. We did the Gdansk show for the 25th anniversary of Solidarity, and we did that DVD shoot. And then we flew right from there to Long Island for the beginning of Roger Waters' *Dark Side of the Moon* tour. That was 2006, and that led into Roger's *The Wall* tour and we've just completed David's tour for *Rattle That Lock*. We did all of the pyro for the shows in Pompeii, the pyro on the top part of the amphitheatre, and the lasers for that whole tour.

I remember seeing the original *Pink Floyd: Live at Pompeii* movie and going 'wow, what a great show', and then years later I get an opportunity to do it. There's no way I'm not going to do that. And then we started Roger's *Us + Them* tour. So I've worked with them from 1987 to 2017. I wasn't fortunate enough to work with both of them together, but you take what pieces you can get.

We work with a variety of different artists, but the Floyd – the music, the lyrics, the experience – is what it's about in the end. If you have to listen to the music every night, which we do as a crew member, there isn't anything better to listen to every night than the Floyd.

David's take and Roger's take are very, very different. Roger is about every moment of the show. David wants to get on the stage and play the music. He allows Mr Brickman to do pretty much whatever he wants, because he knows it'll look great. Roger's a little more concerned about every moment.

It's a very unique band and they have had an impact on the fans and on the people who have worked for them. There's not many of us that have worked for Floyd, for David and for Roger, but people who have been connected with them – it goes with you forever, like a badge of honour. Floyd care about their audience. They could get on the stage and just play and I think everyone would be happy, but it's always that doing something extra for the audience.

We were in Greece and we were all outside playing softball – the band, the crew – and 80,000 people were walking into the venue to see Pink Floyd but not one of them recognised Dave or Rick or anyone in the band, because Floyd isn't about those little people on stage with instruments. It's always about bigger than life, and if you are in a nosebleed seat the show's designed for you. It's designed to be as majestic and as epic as it possibly can be. If you're in the front row, you actually have the worst seat in the house. You want to be in the cheap seats.

The show we did in Venice was a once in a lifetime. It will never happen again. Putting a stage up in the middle of the Grand Canal, those are the kind of things most bands wouldn't even be able to comprehend, never mind imagine what it could be and have the resources to make it happen. And then the entire government of Venice got fired because of it! Because of the 300,000 people that were there, it was a memorable event. I'll never forget it.

The *Rattle That Lock* tour was about how we always played truly unique venues. It wasn't about the biggest venue that you could squish the most people into. It was 'what's the most unique place that you could play?' and then that's where we played. It wasn't easy.

None of those venues were easy from a production values point of view. But it was about the event and making those shows something that people will never forget. And I think if you ask anyone that went to a Floyd show, no one will ever forget it.

 STAPLES CENTER
20 & 21 JUNE 2017, LOS ANGELES, CALIFORNIA

I WAS THERE: GUADALUPE VILLALTA

It was late summer or early fall 2016 when Roger announced a 2017 tour. It was right after his two weekend shows at *Desert Trip* 2016. I was so excited. I've always been a fan of Pink Floyd, but mostly a fan of Roger Waters. His solo career has been great. The music and lyrics he creates are so powerful. My favourite album by him is definitely *Amused to Death* with the song 'Watching TV' being my favourite from that album. People don't seem to appreciate his solo career. I think it's because he didn't take the same path as David Gilmour and continue as a psychedelic/progressive musician. Roger has always been very political and his lyrics are always contemporary, but many don't give them a listen.

I remember deciding not to attend my 10am lecture just so that I could get my ticket before they possibly sold out. I was so anxious – I just wanted to buy it! And after the timer counted down '3, 2, 1', I entered the site. My heart was pounding as I bought the ticket and then realised I was going to see the man I've been wanting to see for years!

I counted the days until the concert, every day being one day closer to seeing Roger Waters. When the day came, I was over excited. I didn't know what to expect from the show, except that it was going to be a good one. I arrived at the Staples Center two hours before. We we were allowed in an hour and a half before show time. I arrived at my section, my heart pounding loudly. The concert hadn't even started but I was ready to see him!

Then it was 8pm, and time. He came out with the rest of the band and began playing. Everything was great. The light show, the effects, the images. Everything, and it being tied up with his music was simply amazing. I remember befriending the people in my section and all of us singing along in unison with Roger. Everyone had huge smiles. Some, like myself, had a few tears too. I couldn't hold them back. The show was everything I had ever wanted. The long wait from buying tickets in the fall to the following summer was worth it. Roger Waters is, and has always been, an amazing musician. To see him live was a privilege. I only wish that I could have been the same age around the time Pink Floyd were around as a complete band. 21st June 2017 was the best night of my life.

NILTON SANTOS STADIUM
12 JULY 2017, RIO DE JANEIRO, BRAZIL

I WAS THERE: ARISTIDES LOBÃO NETO, AGE 36

I had an unforgettable experience seeing Roger Waters in Rio de Janeiro, where he performed *The Wall* with an excellent band on a big stage. I went to the concert with a friend called Cláudio, another Pink Floyd fan. The concert was one month after the carnival, which my wife and I had been to, but she didn't understand why I was coming back to Rio to see Roger Waters. She was very annoyed with the 'trouble' this caused, but I couldn't miss this opportunity. Roger sang all the music off *The Wall* and one of the most incredible moments was when he sang 'Another Brick in the Wall', accompanied by a group of children from Rocinha, a famous local slum. The crowd loved it. Another special moment was when the concert finished. While Roger was singing, a group of people were building a big wall and exactly the moment when he finished the last song, the wall was there – perfect! This concert will stay in my mind forever.

VERIZON CENTER
4 AUGUST 2017, WASHINGTON DC

I WAS THERE: GABRIELLE CORNETT

I waited 20 years to see Roger Waters live in person and it was worth the wait. This was the best show I've ever been to in my entire fucking life. I wish I had brought some psychedelics with me but I was unable to find any before the show (I found some after!). However, the lights and the wall in the music and everything were awesome and amazing even though I wasn't tripping. The next night, I hung out outside the Verizon Center after the show, trying to get my limited-edition *Rolling Stone* Pink Floyd magazine signed by Roger. As he was leaving, he passed right by me. I had my ticket in my hand from the night before and a piece of the 'Resist' papers that fell from the floor. He rolled the window down and smiled. I was ten feet away from Roger Waters. OMG! My fiancé was too far behind me to get a picture of his actual face. Had he been standing right next to me, I would have a picture of Roger Waters very up-close-and-personal. I laughed my ass off when he made fun of Donald Trump. It was just completely awesome – the best thing ever.

In 2018, Nick Mason forms 'Nick Mason's Saucerful of Secrets' to perform the early music of Pink Floyd. After a sold-out test show at the 500-capacity Dingwalls in London in May 2018, the band play European and North American tours. On 18 April 2019, Roger joins the band on stage at New York's Beacon Theatre to sing 'Set the Controls for the Heart of the Sun'.

ROUNDHOUSE
4 MAY 2019, LONDON, UK

I WAS THERE: MARK REED

Starting your solo career at 74 is a strange place to be, but so be it. Nick Mason – the only member of Pink Floyd to play on every album – occupies the enviable status of being both the last man standing for this great band, and perhaps its' most fervent cheerleader. But Pink Floyd have never been the most conventional of bands. One can hardly accuse Mason of hurriedly exploiting the band's name for glory; starting his first solo tour in his seventies, in theatres about 50 times smaller than the final Floyd tour, and with ticket prices being at least half what you might expect from an original member of the band. Having waited a diplomatic quarter century to do so, it feels like a faithful and proud reclaiming of the band's often overlooked early material. There's a sense that this tour is the sole result of his phone never ringing, and Mason wanting to simply go and play drums on songs he loves with his friends. No song in tonight's set is less than 47 years old. Frighteningly, none of these songs were recorded whilst I was alive. And I am in my lateish forties.

The early Pink Floyd – with Syd Barrett – is a band that ceased to exist 51 years ago; if you saw them then, there's a slim chance you aren't in your seventies. And an even slimmer chance you remember any of it. It feels like a fleeting glimpse of what may have happened then: every song is dispatched with a sonically pure, precise but faithful sound, with Mason pounding the drums in the way that demonstrates how, whilst he always played to the benefit of the song and not his ego, his strength came in knowing when not to overplay the song. Material such as 'Interstellar Overdrive' sounds muscular and powerful – the way the records never quite captured thanks to limited technology and rushed studio budgets.

The choice of songs is astute; a clear selection of strong material cherry-picked from the first six studio albums – including three songs from the much overlooked *Obscured By Clouds*, including the brilliant, and pounding title track which slips effortlessly into 'When You're In'. There's a medley of 'If' and 'Atom Heart Mother' which – if you close your eyes – could be any one of a million early Seventies live recordings. And alongside them are songs which, if you'd told me five years ago I'd be watching a founder member of Pink Floyd perform 'Vegetable Man' or 'The Nile Song', I'd've told you to stop lying to me. The early Floyd material is – was – fiercely inventive and fun, but sporadically brilliant and sometimes rubbish. Such was the life of a young, hardworking band who made an album every year whether they had written enough songs to justify it. By the time the set comes to a close, 'See Emily Play', 'Bike' and 'One of These Days' reaches a thunderous ending, it feels like an authentic recreation of what Pink Floyd might have been like. The pensioner in a tie-dye shirt headbanging on the front row seems to agree.

Huge chunks of this are Mason fronting a tribute band to himself, but if anyone has the right to play the early Floyd material live, it's Nick Mason. Nobody else is doing it – as both other living members rarely, if ever, play anything recorded earlier than 1973. And this band's material ends at 1972. Overall, it was an unexpected, revelatory treat that showed just how wrong anyone who writes off their early years is.

Tonight felt like a glimpse into what these songs might once have been like and a vital restatement of the band's early work – making these songs live and breathe again on stage in a way almost all of us have not seen in our lifetimes. It's better than I hoped, and more than I expected. And, as happens every time I see a member of Pink Floyd, I have no idea if this is the last time I will ever see any of these songs performed live. But when I was younger, I spent over a decade thinking I'd never see any member of Pink Floyd ever. How glad I am to have been wrong so many times.

July 2022 sees Roger touring again, on his tongue-in-cheek 'first farewell tour', entitled This Is Not A Drill. *Dates are planned to the end of 2023, although two planned dates in Krakow, Poland after cancelled following comments by Roger about Russia's 2022 invasion of Ukraine. Fuel is added to the flames by Polly Samson, David's wife, who tweets in February 2023 that Roger is 'antisemitic' and a 'Putin apologist'. David retweets Polly's tweet.*

A live reunion of the three remaining Pink Floyd members appears further away than ever…

PLACE D'ARME, CHATEAU DE VERSAILLES
21 & 22 JUNE 1988, VERSAILLES, FRANCE

I WAS THERE: AJAY MANKOTIA

We were here to watch Pink Floyd, our abiding companion through college and beyond, the one which told money to go away, and that if we got a good job with more pay it would be okay. It made us wonder which of the buggers to blame and to watch the pigs on the wing. It asked us whether we thought we could tell heaven from hell, blue skies from pain. It solicitously enquired of us when we were out there in the cold, getting lonely, getting old, whether we could feel it.

We had thought arriving three hours prior to the concert start time would give us an advantageous position in the forecourt of the Palais but the massive arena was already packed and people kept streaming in. We had paid through our nose for our prized tickets and felt we deserved a ringside view of the proceedings. We weren't there to watch the stage from a mile away or look at the goings-on on the giant screens sprinkled all around the vast grounds. We wanted to see the action up close, see the expressions of the musicians and have an intimate connection with the band. Something clearly needed to be done.

We came out and walked along the road to the rear service entrance meant for the musicians, crew, security and other personnel. To our immense good fortune, we met the film director who was going to shoot the concert and asked him to help us get in. He was shocked to see two Indians attending a Pink Floyd concert, and even more shocked at our bizarre request.

He agreed to help us get in provided we could pass the Pink Floyd music test he would conduct. He cycled back to his hotel while we jogged along beside him. He went up to his room to change while we waited in the lobby. He then conducted a half-hour test (which we aced) and he ceremoniously handed over a pair of film crew badges to us. On reaching the venue, he led us in through the rear entrance and planted us in the front row, bang in the middle. This was a view that no amount of money could buy.

The stage went dark. Rick Wright started playing the keyboards, creating the dense, ethereal effect. The crowd recognised the introduction instantly and went into raptures. David Gilmour then waded in with his distinctive guitar, Nick Mason followed on the drums and, after the most mind-blowing prelude, the vocals by Gilmour began:

Remember when you were young
You shone like the sun
Shine on you crazy diamond

We screamed our approval. The show was underway…

We were coming to the end of the concert. As the opening strains of 'Comfortably Numb' were heard, the crowd went delirious. No concert was complete without this song.

I can't explain
You would not understand
This is not how I am
I have become
Comfortably numb

The two guitar solos – one in the middle and one at the end – have been rated as the best guitar solos ever. Gilmour didn't disappoint and his guitar work cut through the evening like a laser through fog. The crowd was ecstatic. After the show, as 'film crew' members, we went to the hospitality tent for drinks and dinner. And after dinner, we met the man himself – David Gilmour. What an end to a glorious evening!

I saw 75 per cent of Pink Floyd – Dave Gilmour, Nick Mason and Richard Wright – that night. But if you consider Roger Waters' contribution to the band, then I saw much less than half the band. Many songs sung that day were his. The band just could not do without his songs. I would finally see the missing piece at a Waters solo concert in 2007, reconfirming that the man was indeed the embodiment of the band.

I watched Waters' *The Dark Side of the Moon* concert in Mumbai on February 18, 2007. It was a delightful and emotionally charged show. The crowd knew the words to most of the songs. That clearly moved Waters and he made a mention of it at the end of the show. There were many Pink Floyd songs interspersed with his solo repertoire, including the full *The Dark Side of the Moon* album. The show ended with the eternal crowd-pleaser, 'Comfortably Numb'. The theatrics were all there – including the prism colours of *Dark Side*. For good measure, the incorrigible Waters also had a floating pig sporting the legend 'Kafka Rules', 'Get Rid of the Caste System' and 'Sab Jaati Ek Hain'. When the pig was let loose to float away, 'Free at Last' could be read emblazoned on its belly.

Roger Waters is yet to hang up his boots. He is sometimes aggravating and occasionally troublemaking. 'Hanging on in quiet desperation is the English way' is a line from the Pink Floyd classic 'Time'. It is not Roger Waters' way.

POSTSCRIPT

Pink Floyd Syd Barrett died in Cambridge on 7 July 2006, aged 60. The occupation given on his death certificate was 'retired musician'. A tribute to Syd, which received the blessing of Gilmour, Mason and Wright, was arranged for the following May, marking 40 years since Pink Floyd had exploded onto the scene. Although the four other members of Pink Floyd didn't appear together at the Barbican, Roger and then David, Nick and Richard all took part. Roger chose to perform one of his own songs rather than a Syd or Floyd song, telling the audience 'without Syd, I don't know what I'd be doing'.

MADCAP'S LAST LAUGH, BARBICAN THEATRE
10 MAY 2007, LONDON, UK

I WAS THERE: PHIL CARTER

When Syd Barrett died they did a tribute to his music at the Barbican. My friend Paddy and I popped down to see it. Roger Waters appeared and then, much to my amazement, later on the Floyd came on and performed 'Arnold Layne'. Oh, joy of joys.

I WAS THERE: STEFANO BARONE

In 2006 David Gilmour was touring *On an Island* with Richard Wright in his band and I saw them at the Royal Albert Hall in May, on the night David Bowie guested on 'Arnold Layne' and 'Comfortably Numb'. Meanwhile, Roger Waters was touring *The Dark Side of the Moon* with Nick Mason playing in a few shows, and I saw them together in Hyde Park in July. The Pink Floyd line up was split in two, even playing some of the same songs. There was a sense of everything coming back together, and fans began to hope that 2006's reunion could spark a new Floyd era. But nobody knew that in a short period of time Pink Floyd would lose Syd Barrett and Richard Wright forever and that, with the loss of the latter, Pink Floyd were gone forever too.

Syd hadn't contributed to the band's music since his departure in 1968, but his spirit was in every Floyd record until the most recent. He wasn't just the founder and the man who initiated and inspired everything; he was some sort of holy ghost in the Floyd creativity, in Waters' lyrics dealing with life, perspective and the struggle for sanity in contemporary society.

I was in shock when I heard of his passing. Floyd fans knew it was extremely unlikely we'd see him perform on stage or join the band, but it was still a shock, a sense of void, a sense of great loss. His death took him from the world of colours and imagination we were thinking he belonged to and back to the world of mortals, though he will always live in his legend. Artists from all over the world paid tribute to his genius and his priceless contribution to the history of music.

When the Barbican Centre announced the official tribute concert, which involved the Barrett family, my best friend (also a huge Floyd fan) and I wanted to be there to pay our respect to Syd's music and memory. Many guests were announced, from Damon Albarn (Blur and Gorillaz) to Robyn Hitchcock, from Captain Sensible to early Floyd producer Joe Boyd and Syd's family members. There were performances of Syd Barrett songs and some were beautiful, some poetical, some clever and ironic – like 'The Word Song', introduced by Damon Albarn as some form of early rap (that's how far ahead of his time Syd was) – and performed with unusual instruments like a saw.

The official programme didn't mention any Pink Floyd presence or any of their members. But it was the official tribute, endorsed by the family and in support of a mental health charity (SANE); it was unlikely none of his former bandmates would say anything or fail to pay tribute. And indeed they did. At the end of the first part of the show, Roger Waters came on stage with Jon Carin. He described his emotions, explaining also how frightening these intimate venues were compared to big arenas, and how fearless was Syd, ready to jump on stage with no sense of shame whatsoever, ready to take all risks. Roger expressed his gratitude, saying he wouldn't be the Roger Waters we know without him. When some 'Floyd! Floyd!' shouts arose from the audience, he replied 'later, later…' suggesting there could be more to come. He performed a very touching 'Flickering Flame'.

After a second part that included a beautiful version of 'Chapter 24' with a choir, a powerful 'Astronomy Domine' by Captain Sensible and Jon Carin, John Paul Jones of Led Zeppelin joining Robyn Hitchcock for 'Gigolo Aunt' and some other great performances, Joe Boyd came on stage. He talked about organising the show and gave his own account of working with Syd before calling on stage 'a suitable band to close the show: Rick Wright, David Gilmour, Nick Mason'. Interestingly, he announced them by their individual names, not as 'Pink Floyd'. They gave a wonderful performance of 'Arnold Layne', the single that started Pink Floyd's career as music stars. There was incredible excitement, as four classic Floyd members were in the same building, more shouts of 'Floyd! Pink Floyd!' came from the audience. To those calling out 'Roger!', David Gilmour responded, 'Yes, he was here too.'

It was a wonderful night, but most of all a wonderful way to say goodbye to the genius that started Pink Floyd, who had the vision, who created the immortal legend of one of the greatest and most inspiring bands the ever exist. It was great to see the

WISH YOU WERE HERE

four members of Pink Floyd say their goodbye to Syd and be part of it. Goodbye Syd, and thank you again for starting what inspired and transformed my life; thank you for adding colour to the music, for adding vision to talent and inspiration, for being an explorer, a pioneer, an adventurer of imagination. Shine on Syd!